# PASSAGES:

## STUDIES *in* TRADITIONALISM *and* TRADITIONS

## Volume II

**Edited by**
Jafe Arnold
Evgeny Nechkasov
Luca Siniscalco
Lucas Griffin

2025

**PRAV Publishing**
www.pravpublishing.com
prav@pravpublishing.com

Copyright © 2025 PRAV Publishing

All rights reserved. No part of this book may be reproduced or distributed in any form or by any means, electronic or mechanical, including photocopying, recording, or by any information storage and retrieval, without permission in writing from the publisher.

*Cover images:*
"The Kiss of the Light" (2012), *Speaking Stones by Light* series;
"Persona" (2018), *Nykvist and Bergman Tribute* series,
by Aima Lichtblau (Luisa Papa)

ISBN 978-1-952671-24-1 (Paperback)
ISBN 978-1-952671-25-8 (Ebook)

# PASSAGES:
## STUDIES *in* TRADITIONALISM *and* TRADITIONS

Volume II

# TABLE OF CONTENTS

| | |
|---|---|
| From the Editors: Speaking of Traditionalism | 9 |
| Tradition as Language<br>*Askr Svarte (Evgeny Nechkasov)* | 17 |
| The Language of Tradition<br>and the Paradigms of the Modern Sciences:<br>Rectifying Names and Measuring Distances<br>*Alexander Dugin* | 45 |
| The Ontology of Language in the Light<br>of Integral Traditionalism<br>*Maxim Medovarov* | 87 |
| Telling the Origin:<br>Language, Myth, and the Sacred<br>*Andrea Scarabelli* | 113 |
| A Few Remarks on the Spiritual Importance<br>of Languages<br>*Tamás Bencze* | 127 |
| The Four Levels of Meaning:<br>Polysemic Hermeneutics of Traditional Texts<br>*Sebastiano Fusco* | 145 |

Cosmogony and Anthropogony:
Symbols, Language, and Sacred Music
in the Vedic Tradition     165
   *Nuccio D'Anna*

Giorgio Colli, Julius Evola,
and Hellenic Mysteriosophy:
Can Language and Writing be Truth-Makers?     197
   *Giovanni Sessa*

Truth and Language:
Attilio Mordini's Sapiential Hermeneutics
of Language     221
   *Adolfo Morganti*

Neo-Archaic Terms in the Theology
of Contemporary Slavic Native Faith     251
   *Veleslav Cherkasov*

The Traditional Understanding
of the Non-Traditional     285
   *Maxim Makovchik*

*Mouseion, Kunstkammer,* and the Classical Museum
as Models of Reality:
The Transformation of Museum Practices
and Our Image of the World
from Premodernity to Modernity     293
   *Alisa Zagryadskaya*

The Existential Dimension of Traditionalism
in the Works of Julius Evola:
Towards the Fundamental Principles
of the Being of the Differentiated Man     309
  *Dmitry Moiseev*

András László's Fundamental Contribution
to Metaphysical Tradition     329
  *László Virág*

The Idea of Tradition, Its Precedents,
and Signs of Decline     345
  *Róbert Horváth*

About the Authors     377

# FROM THE EDITORS:
# SPEAKING OF TRADITIONALISM

In Stefan George's 1919 poem "The Word" (*Das Wort*), we hear of a traveler on a mission to bring an unnamed "wonder" (*Wunder*) or "dream" (*Traum*), later called a "treasure" (*Schatz*), back to his native land. Upon reaching the border, he must wait for a being called a "*norn*" to search the depths for this mysterious valuable's name. When the *norn* returns to tell the traveler that nothing has been found, it vanishes from his hands, never to enter and bless his land, and the poem comes to an end with the words "*Kein ding sei wo das wort gebricht*" — "Where word breaks off no thing may be."[1]

To Traditionalist eyes and ears, the traditional inspirations and allusions of this poetic work are obvious. The *norn* (George intentionally eschewed the standard German capitalization of nouns) is one of the three fate-carving Norns of Germanic mythology, known in Old Norse as Urðr, Verðandi, and Skuld (cf. the Greek "Fates," the Moirai). The *born*, the watery depths in which the Norn seeks the wonder-dream-treasure's name, alludes to *Urðarbrunnr*, the Wellspring of Urðr located at the roots of the World-Tree, Yggdrasil[2] (cf. Odin's self-sacrifice on the tree, whence he descends into the depths and acquires the runes[3]). This, combined with the fact that George describes the Norn as "gray," suggests that the Norn in question is Urðr. Thus, the word for George's mystery is sought in the depths of, and by the Norn of, that which we would vulgarly call the "past," but which is, ontologically and metaphysically speaking, the origin, the beginning of

---

1 See the translation and reading in Martin Heidegger, *On the Way to Language*. trans. Peter D. Hertz and Joan Stambaugh (New York: HarperCollins, 1971).

2 Elder [Poetic] Edda, *Völuspá* 19-20.

3 Elder [Poetic] Edda, *Hávamál* 138-139.

fate, that which "has been coming to be," unfolding as the world and history we can recollect, i.e., something that is "coming over" rather than "having been overcome." Speaking of wells and recollection, Germanic myth knows another special well located at one of the roots of the World-Tree, *Mímisbrunnr*, the Wellspring of Mímir, the "Rememberer," one of the primordial beings killed during the war between the Aesir and the Vanir that established the present cosmic order. Mímir's wisdom-sharing severed head is carried by Odin, who sacrificed one of his eyes at the well in exchange for knowledge of the cosmic fate.[4] Given the associations with Urðr and Mímir, we intuit that the right name for the poet's treasure is meant to be "recollected" from the primordial origin. After all, as Askr Svarte reminds us, "Where else to look for names for wonders and dreams if not the world where *mythos* ruled and rules?"[5] But, alas, not even the Norn plumbing the primordial depths could offer a single word...

What shows itself to us in "The Word" is a poetic reflection of the situation that René Guénon beheld and which Traditionalist thought still faces. In the world of Modernity, we are at a loss for the original, proper words for "wonders," "dreams," and "treasures," those known to spiritual traditions and those which might still have revealed themselves on distant travels not too long ago. In other words, the cosmic decline into Modernity is characterized by a problematization of language, by a need for sacred words, and by a halt at different borders and dimensions that were once open. A similar situation to that of the traveler of "The Word" confronts the journey

---

4   *Elder [Poetic] Edda*, *Völuspá* 28; Snorri Sturluson, *Younger [Prose] Edda*, *Gylfaginning* XV. Along this symbolic chain, a correspondence could also be drawn with *Óðrerir*, the vessel of the mead of poetry containing the blood of Kvasir, the wisest of all beings who was generated out of the spit deposited by the Aesir and Vanir as part of the truce to the primordial war. See Snorri Sturluson, *Younger [Prose] Edda*, *Skáldskaparmál* V-VI.

5   See Askr Svarte, *Towards Another Myth: A Tale of Heidegger and Traditionalism*, trans. Jafe Arnold (PRAV Publishing, 2024), 157-170.

*From the Editors: Speaking of Traditionalism*

undertaken by Traditionalist thought. Seeking to retrieve the "wonders," "dreams," and "treasures" from the world's spiritual traditions, Traditionalism finds itself confronted with the wonder-less, dream-less, spirit-less world-paradigm of Modernity, where the words known from traditions have been distorted and suffused with quite different meanings and conceptualizations over the history of ideas (for example, *par excellence*, "myth"). Approaching the borders entrenched around the conceptual frameworks and "terminologies" constructed by Modernity, Traditionalist thought searches for its paradigmatic presentation and representations in terms: is it a matter of "philosophy," "metaphysics," "[sacred] science," "method," "exoteric" or "esoteric," "traditional" or "Traditionalist," etc.? Endeavoring, seemingly against all odds, to re-inspirit profaned realms and beings, even if only a few, the Traditionalist struggles with discerning the right names and measures, invoking the right words, and translating between different languages and discourses. Even "Tradition" as such, worded in so many ways in so many texts and traditions, is by no means simply "translatable" as a "signification" of one order or another. Seemingly like the traveler in George's poem, Traditionalism is on a mission in the likes of the ancient Greek *theoria*, that is, a sacred travel, but now only to be at a loss for words, for the words themselves to be missing, unintelligible, or subject to doubt as if they were theorems. Just as the modern term and concept of "theory" has little left to do with its Greek ancestor, so is the Traditionalist situation no matter of mere "terms" or "terminology," as if what is at stake was merely tweaking (pre-)concepts; rather, it is the challenge of living up to and conveying the power of words, rediscovering the ontology of language, and unearthing the correspondence of "symbols" that unveil a reality quite different from the one in which our homelands have found (or rather lost) themselves. Traditionalism finds itself faced with the need to reflect upon — and to reflect — the deepest experience and meaning of words in a world that, having already made them mechanical, is increasingly handing them altogether over to machines.[6]

As "The Word" shows, now perhaps not even a Norn is here to help carry this along. Beholding the modern hellscape and discerning the qualitative difference between the profane modern paradigm and the sacred paradigm that was all too recently still at large — and seemingly still in charge elsewhere, in the East — Guénon himself searched the depths for a name and word: "Tradition," or more precisely, "Primordial Tradition." Within a few decades, "Traditionalism" became a name for this endeavor at a "rectification of names." As the writings published in *Passages: Studies in Traditionalism and Traditions* attest, this name, as well as the paradigm bound up with such a naming, is still a matter of lively discussion, seeking, recollecting, and even renaming. We are all the traveler in George's poem.

What does it mean that not even Urðr, the Norn of Primordial Fate, could help the poet-traveler carry his wonderful treasure along? In line with the general cosmic trajectory and "state of affairs," is Traditionalism itself doomed to an inability to express and convey the treasures it retrieves, even if only to a few? Or, in other words, as some Traditionalist thinkers have dared to ask, what does it mean to be a Traditionalist, and what does Traditionalist thinking mean to say, "in the absence of Tradition," or when even the word "tradition" is dispersed and diluted? What is the difference between the thoughtful language we hear in traditional texts and the language in which Traditionalism thinks upon them? In the face of the event of the Norn's silence, we hear that Traditionalism is something and somehow "different" from Tradition itself,

---

6   See Askr Svarte, *Tradition and Future Shock: Visions of a Future that Isn't Ours* (PRAV Publishing, 2022).

like George's poem in relation to the original Eddic myths, and the word for the inner connection between them is a matter of deep seeking.

Thus, the depths and heights of Traditionalist thinking, discourse, and traveling beckon us back to the very beginning, to the Word, to Language, which Heidegger famously (yet, by his own admission, "clumsily") called the "house of Being."[7] Of the limitations of this house's expression, Guénon wrote in *Man and His Becoming According to the Vedānta* (1925), speaking of approaching the unconditioned state of *ātmā*:

> in language, every direct affirmation is necessarily particular and determinate, the affirmation of something which excludes something else, and which thereby limits the object so affirmed. Every determination is a limitation, that is to say, a negation: consequently, it is the negation of a determination which is a true affirmation, and the apparently negative terms which we find here are, in their real sense, pre-eminently affirmative.[8]

And in *The Multiple States of Being*[9] (1932), speaking of "certain states of non-manifestation that lie beyond the degree of pure Being," Guénon reiterated:

> the very constitution of human language obliges us to retain this same term [(pure) Being] in such a case for want of a more

---

7   Heidegger, *On the Way to Language*, 5; Martin Heidegger, "Letter on Humanism," trans. Frank A. Capuzzi in Martin Heidegger, *Pathmarks*, ed. William McNeill (Cambridge: Cambridge University Press, 1998), 239.

8   René Guénon, *Man and His Becoming According to the Vedānta*, trans. Richard C. Nicholson (Hillsdale: Sophia Perennis, 2004), 103.

9   After many years of apparent silence, we must raise our voice on the crucial mistake of translation (and not only translation) in this title as well as throughout the text: in question is not "a being" or "the being," but "Being" as such. On the ontological difference between "being(s)" (*das Seiende*) and "Being" (*das Sein*), between "the being of being(s)" (*das Sein des Seienden*) and "Being" (*das Sein*), and even between "Being" (*das Sein*) and "Beyng" or "Be-ing" (*das Seyn*), we refer our readers to the works of Martin Heidegger – not in the sense of deferring to an authority, but in order to encourage the confrontation and dialogue between Traditionalist metaphysics and Heideggerian fundamental ontology which, as contributions to the first volume of *Passages* already suggested, entails far-ranging implications for understandings of metaphysics and the history of Western thought in which Guénon's voice emerged with certain words.

adequate one, but we attribute to it only the purely analogical and symbolic meaning... In language, any direct affirmation is in fact necessarily a particular and determined affirmation — the affirmation of something particular — whereas total and absolute affirmation is no particular affirmation to the exclusion of others since it implies them all equally; and from this it should be easy to grasp the very close relation this presents with universal Possibility, which in the same way comprehends all particular possibilities.[10]

The wonder-bearer and word-awaiter of George's "The Word" would, without a doubt, raise the same questions as we shall in Guénon's wake: How can any word ever be rightfully "found" to determine some "actuality" out of the divinely-fathomed depths of universal possibility? Or otherwise, how does language both restrict and reveal the manifestation of "what there is," or of Being as such, or even of that which is "beyond Being"? Furthermore, to refer back to Heidegger: What has hitherto remained "unsaid" in what Traditionalists have "said"? Between the intense rigor of philosophical deliberation and the solemn quietude of meditation, the Traditionalist journey leads us to pose for thought not only the matters of which we speak, and not only the ways in which we speak, but also the ways in which we are spoken to, from the ancient revelations of traditions to contemporary Traditionalists' wordings.

Questions of this order, which already emerged in the first volume of *Passages*, inspired the motivation and open-ended invitation for this second volume. We are pleased to confirm that, as the present volume demonstrates, the vast theme of "language" inspires much to be said on diverse fronts and in diverse ways by those who hear in the history and present of Traditionalist thought so much to be said. In response to our Call for Papers thematizing "language," 15 authors from four countries, writing in three different languages, were moved to submit contributions

---

10 René Guénon, *The Multiple States of the Being*, trans. Henry D. Fohr, ed. Samuel D. Fohr (Hillsdale: Sophia Perennis, 2004), 4, 9.

treating a wide range of topics pertaining to the sources, history, thought, and future of what "Traditionalism" actually and possibly has to (re)iterate. In this respect, we can agree with a recent review of *Passages* by Mark Sedgwick, who wrote that *Passages* represents a "new generation of Traditionalists"[11] – but on the condition of the following qualification: *Passages* is a "new generation" not in terms of one or another chronology, age, perceived tendencies, or any other "categorizations," but precisely in that it presents itself as a re-generating and re-enlivening of primordial, perennial, and urgent questions which the question-worthy matter of Traditionalism leads us to pose with newfound sensitivity and attunement.

*Jafe Arnold,*
*Evgeny Nechkasov,*
*Luca Siniscalco,*
*Lucas Griffin*

---

11 Mark Sedgwick, "A new journal and a new generation," *Traditionalists* (10 November 2024) [https://traditionalistblog.blogspot.com/2024/11/PRAV.html].

# TRADITION AS LANGUAGE

## *Askr Svarte (Evgeny Nechkasov)*

It is not so much the case that tradition, understood as the unfolding of culture initiated by the sacred, is reducible to language, as it is the case that the very notion of language is extendable to all of culture as the foundational metaphor and structure.[12] Everything is language: specific speech practices, gestures, rules, laws, taboos, everyday affairs, the material culture of crafts, hunting, plowing, and harvesting, the structures of kinship, marriages[13], estates, and hierarchy, styles of speech, notions of space and time, systems of numbering and accounting, the events and life course of surrounding nature[14], etc. All of these are semiotic spaces, and therefore lingual. Outside of language and semiotics, which can be brought together as a whole, there is no world.

Tradition acts as a language, as a grammatical and poetic (in the sense of bringing beings-into-Being) system which ensures the coherence and correctness of the most diverse expressions and discourses. Language does not pronounce judgments on the truth of one or another expression; it only gives them the space, structure, meaning, and time for being told. An expression or utterance within a tradition can be any individual theological or philosophical school, a series of jewelry-like ritual objects, a *Männerbund* warrior campaign, a dynastic union, the architecture of a cult site,

---

12  The present text is excerpted from Askr Svarte, *Towards Another Myth: A Tale of Heidegger and Traditionalism*, trans. Jafe Arnold (PRAV Publishing, 2024).

13  See Lévi-Strauss, *Structural Anthropology*, trans. Claire Jacobson and Brooke Grundfest Schoepf (New York: Basic Books, 1963).

14  See Eduardo Kohn, *How Forests Think: Toward an Anthropology Beyond the Human* (Berkeley: University of California Press, 2013).

ritual laments and songs, etc. The song form reigns supreme among sacred texts and addresses to Deities because songs and poetry are essentially the language of the Divinities, the ones who sing and dance. There are as many traditions, as many manifestations of the sacred, as there are languages and divine songs.

Language gives the space for different discourses to be and to affirm themselves in the world. Rising up to a broader vantage point, we can see the plurality of languages as structured by different grammars (metaphysics) and yielding the infinite diversity of noetic, discursive universes. In other words, we are dealing with the open possibility of inexhaustible mythopoiesis. Like a wanderer between lands, moving between language-traditions demands of us the subtlest and most sensitive art of translation, if it is possible at all, as well as a handy meta-language with which we might correctly correlate different and distant tradition-cultures and, no less importantly, formulate the question of the ultimate sources of lingual diversity in the manifest world. Such a meta-language must inevitably be philosophical and Traditionalist.

Earlier, we drew a fundamental distinction between the Deities (*Götter*) and the Divine (*Gottheit*) that is the apophatic ground of the former: the Deity concealed in self-revelation is the ground (*Grund*) of the world, and it itself rests on a groundless ground (*Abgrund, Nichts*). The situation with languages is analogous: every language is the ground and all-pervading structure of culture and thinking, but languages themselves have their roots in the *Abgrund*. The path of the emanation of language can be mediated by a Deity that gives the gift of a tale about itself, about man himself, or about language itself (the turning of language towards itself). The ensuing branching out into languages and their respective discursive, social, political, cultural, and material manifestations resembles a single tree.

## Tradition as Language

In mythopoetics, the tree is a symbol and metaphor not only of the human being, but of tradition as a whole. Its roots run into the earth and its crown reaches up into the heavens. Earth is the mystical soil, the topogenesis and surrounding landscape, climate, and nature in whose bosom a people lives and which is reflected in a people's culture and imprinted in their thinking. This is Mother Earth. The heavens are the patrimony of the Heavenly Father, the vertical spiritual principle of a people, its sacred myths and traditions, the upper world of the Deities, spirits, and ancestors. It is sometimes said that the Tree has its roots in the sky and its leaves spread across the earth. This emphasizes that the single root of tradition is up above, growing toward the earth and branching out into numerous spiritual paths, the cults of different Deities, and the traditions and legends of various estates and families, etc. The leaves are the immense abundance of manifestations of one or another path (the Slavic *vervi*) within a specific culture, of all its music, songs, spiritual poetry, architecture, crafts, smithing, decor, styles of embroidery and drawing, typical gestures, postures, corporeal plasticity, etc. Each particular people lives in the middle world between its earth and its heaven, sprouting out of one root with the generous sweep of a branching crown. All peoples together form the forest of traditions. The totality of the forest, its forestness as such, corresponds to language as the common element that unites the manifold within its oneness. The branches and leaves subject to the winds of history and seasonal fall in the lead up to winter best reflect the temporariness and mutability of the forms of the manifestation of the sacred in the world and in particular things. But the deep foundation that draws and transmits the fluids that nourish the entire tree, the roots that run into the impenetrable darkness of the *Abgrund*, are authentic thinking in its innermost bond with language.

Bearing in mind the plurality of language-traditions, it bears examining in detail the connection between language and thinking, how language affects the thought process itself as well as, consequently, culture. The very affirmation of such a connection and of the influence upon thinking exerted by language, with its grammar, syntax, semantics, morphology, etc., seems to be well-established, but this was not always the case. The tight bond between language, speech, and thought was pointed out by many ancient thinkers and traditional, often mystical schools, ranging from the Indian subcontinent to Mediterranean and European antiquity. In addition to what has been expounded in the preceding chapters, it is worth mentioning the caste-specific sociolects know in the Indo-European languages with their intrinsic phonetics. Differences in the "professional" occupations, rituals, and social status of various groups within society — the source of which, in sacrocentric thinking, is in the will of the Divine as recorded in a given set of myths — are reinforced by linguistic differences, ranging from knowledge of certain words to literacy and writing systems which exist among the twice-born but remain unknown to the lower varnas. To this should also be added the feminine sociolects that exist among different peoples as well as the special linguistic constructions and discursive forms associated with the structure and hierarchy of the traditional family.

Drawing on the problem of expressing mystical experience in language in the case of Meister Eckhart, the linguist Johann Leo Weisgerber argued that language is "the process of recreating the world in the word," or "wording the world" (*Worten der Welt*).[15] Special attention has been paid to the influence of language on thinking by German philosophers and linguists, although their basic formulations and approaches have undergone significant changes since

---
15 Sergei Borodai, *Iazyk i poznanie. Vvedenie v postreliativizm* (Moscow: Sadra, 2020).

the first perspectives were offered. This line runs from the founder of linguistic philosophy, Justus Georg Schottelius, to the anti-Enlightenment philosophers, such as Johann Georg Hamann, who was the first to substantiate on the basis of faith in God the thesis that thinking is linguistically relative, and Johann Gottfried Herder, the author of the beautiful maxim "peoples are thoughts of God." Herder insisted on the leading role of language in the human being's formation in becoming human. This line was later continued by Wilhelm Humboldt and the Humboldtians, such as the Russian linguist Alexander Potebnya and the German linguist Leo Weisgerber. Nor can we refrain from mentioning the German philologist and scholar of religion Friedrich Max Müller, the founder of the discipline of comparative religious studies. Müller proposed examining the development of religious ideas by analogy with the development of language and thinking, and he demonstrated the influence that the form of a word and naive etymology play on the development of religious representations.[16]

This line also includes the German-educated ethnographer Franz Boas, who studied the indigenous population of Canada. Boas was one of the first to insist on the equivalence of all languages and cultures, and thus rejected the division of languages into primitive vs. developed in terms of a singular evolutionary path of mankind. For Boas, "civilization" is a particular case, a relative value, that is not at all necessary for different cultures around the world. The evolutionary criteria of one "high civilization" cannot be applied to evaluate other cultures and people — such would be gnoseological racism and chauvinism. This is partly consonant with the even earlier argumentation put forth by Potebnya, who defended the plurality of languages as a diverse, complex palette of conceptual styles as opposed to universal projections of a single synthetic language or the establishment of linguistic hegemony, which,

---
16 Ibid.

in Potebnya's opinion, would lead to the degradation of thinking in general. Boas also drew on the works of Müller and Humboldt. Moreover, he proposed that the imperative nature of a grammatical system presupposes a special way of schematizing experience in verbal activity. Hence the thesis that different languages' classification models are unique. Boas also established the now commonplace practice of comparing and contrasting the Indo-European languages with the modern European languages as well as more exotic ones, such as the Amerindian languages. One of Boas' foremost students was Edward Sapir, who went on to become the founder of the entire field of linguistic anthropology, an active defender of the American Indian population, a prolific author and visionary of linguistic science.

As soon as Sapir's name has been mentioned, we already know what theses we are approaching. Appropriating and mastering Boas' main theses, Sapir developed them in his own vein. His absolute maxims include the argument that it is impossible to think and reason without language. Language is present in cognitive processes even where and when it cannot be identified introspectively. Language is no mere isolated and cold instrument for cognition and the expression of thought, as Immanuel Kant insisted, but is an active co-participant in the formation of thought in the very form and content that thought itself manifests. In his book *Language: An Introduction to the Study of Speech*, Sapir cited a number of examples to illustrate the thesis that grammar compels one to express certain meanings and organize thoughts in a specific way. What for European language is necessarily grammatically encoded, i.e., what can be expressed in the language only by sticking to the important accents of thought (the obligatory use of the verb "to be," for instance), might be simply absent in the grammars of non-Indo-European languages, or expressed on the lexical level, or not expressed at all. The converse is also true: the grammatical and lexical structures of the language of North American tribes encode and accentuate as of primary importance certain modes and details which in European languages pertain to supplemental or secondary clarifications of a situation.

Sapir draws a close connection between language and the notion of "meaning." An element of element is a "house" or "symbol" that brings together thousands of different phenomena of experience and is capable of uniting thousands more. The perception of external reality, the "stream of experience," happens through the deep lingual distribution of meanings. A phonetic system plays an important role as the "foundation." Let us cite one of the classic comparative examples:

> In reality, symbolization involves shaping a thought or impression in accordance with the structure of a native language. To substantiate this claim, Sapir refers to a variety of conventional modes of expression. For instance, observing an object called a "stone" flying towards the ground, a native English speaker analyzes this event using the notions of "stone" and "falling"; combining these two representations into English expression, he says: "The stone falls." Speakers of German, French, and Russian would add to this an idea of gender, while the Chippewa Indians would add the idea of inanimateness. A Russian would be puzzled why a definite reference to the stone, coded by the article "the," is needed in English. Meanwhile, a Kwakiutl Indian would consider all of the preceding statements incomplete, since they do not convey information about the visibility of the stone and its spatial relationship to the participants in the situation. To a Chinese speaker, on the contrary, these expressions would seem redundant, since for him there is enough information about the presence of an object that is in a state of falling (without indicating the gender, time, direction, etc.). The most exotic form of expression is to be found in the Amerindian language of Nootka, in which this situation is described with the use of a verb form consisting of two main elements: the first denotes the general movement or position of the stone-like object, and the second the downward movement. This expression might be conveyed by the artificial phrase "It stones down."[17]

---

17 Borodai, *Iazyk i poznanie*.

Here, it becomes obvious how the language system of any given people within its culture gives the one and the same phenomenon a unique shape and accentuation. On this basis, Sapir proceeded to proclaim the principle of linguistic relativity, which holds that a given language influences certain formal domains of thinking. As in the case of Boas and Sapir, an important role in the development of this line of ideas would be played by Sapir's talented student, Benjamin Whorf. Mastering the basic principles of his teachers and continuing to study the Amerindian languages, especially Hopi, in comparison to the so-called "Standard Average European" (SAE[18]), Whorf reinforced the argument for linguistic relativity and the influence of linguistic structure on thinking. In particular, Whorf argued that identical physical phenomena do not necessarily lead to a uniform conceptual system for constructing experience out of represented information. This argument entered scholarship and mass culture under the collective name of the "Sapir-Whorf hypothesis." The most widespread version of this thesis has both strong and soft formulations:

> Strong version: Language determines thinking, and linguistic categories accordingly limit and determine cognitive categories.
>
> Soft version: Language only influences thinking. Alongside linguistic categories, thinking is also formed under the influence of traditions and certain types of non-linguistic behavior.[19]

Neither of these, however, has anything to do with the real state of affairs. Whorf was in many respects an independent and original thinker (who was even influenced by Eastern metaphysics and esotericism). He was never Sapir's co-author, and, moreover, he did not formulate any "hypothesis" on his own or jointly with his teacher. Whorf greatly developed

---

[18] "Standard Average European" (SAE) refers to the European languages that possess common grammatical properties. The group includes the Romance, Germanic, Balkan, and Balto-Slavic languages.

[19] Sergei Borodai, "Sovremennoe ponimanie problemy lingvisticheskoi otnositel'nosti: raboty po prostranstvennoi kontseptualizatsii", *Voprosy iazykoznaniia* 4 (2013), 17-54.

what Boas had already foreseen as the influence of language on the categorization of experience and the formation of thought (the relationship between form and meaning) up to the point of linguistic and cultural pluralism. He insisted on the need for further research to verify such theses.

The problem with the "Sapir-Whorf hypothesis" is rooted in subsequent linguists' completely erroneous understanding of their ideas. It is to later linguists, following the Chicago conference of 1953, that the "invention" of this "hypothesis" is owed, including its strong and weak versions which are nowhere to be found in the original works authored by Sapir and Whorf. Whorf simply followed his teachers and did not put forth any hypothesis, instead preferring to discuss empirically observed patterns and facts. The completely balanced generalizations he drew on the basis of the material available to him did not need verification due to the obviousness of the very difference between languages. Only later, by dint of a combination of misunderstandings of Whorf's ideas and critiques arrayed against a "hypothesis" falsely attributed to him, were the ideas of linguistic relativity and linguistic determinism "rejected," giving way to the prevalence of linguistic theories that were hostile to "Whorfianism."[20]

Nevertheless, the further development of Whorf's ideas, along with later investigations of the erroneous trajectory of understandings of his project and the essence of the "Sapir-Whorf hypothesis," have exerted a colossal influence not only on linguistics, but also on many related and separate sciences, including ethnolinguistics, psycholinguistics, ethnopsychology, philosophy, cognitive science, etc.

The discovery of the linguistic specificity of thinking exerted particular influence on the theory of "conceptual

---

20 In his fundamental monograph *Iazyk i poznanie. Vvedenie v postreliativizm* [Language and Cognition: An Introduction to Post-Relativism], Sergei Borodai traces in detail the trajectory of the maturation, formulation, perception, and large-scale influence of the ideas of the Boas-Sapir-Whorf line.

metaphor" developed by George Lakoff and Mark Johnson.[21] Proceeding from comparisons of how time is conceptualized differently in SAE languages and some Amerindian languages, Whorf often remarked that Europeans understand time through the metaphor of space, e.g., approaching/coming, passing by, ahead of/behind oneself, etc. Lakoff picked up and developed this idea and discovered that speech and thinking generally, all the way down to everyday, routine speech practices, are thoroughly permeated and structured by metaphors and systems of combinations, insertions, and transferences of metaphors. A metaphor is no mere decoration, trope, or established linguistic construct like an idiom. The conceptual metaphors which have become established and fixed in a culture integrally constitute the organized cognitive models of a given society. Metaphors are not simply descriptions of the surrounding world; they participate in forming the cognitive style, the very thinking and key notions that define the world. From these deep notions grow styles of behavior, actions, evaluations and ideas about the world. Lakoff says that the whole of "social reality" and culture, which is necessary for any society within which systems of hierarchies and relationships to the environment function, is built on an established, corresponding structure of conceptual metaphors.

Also of interest is Lakoff's reference to Quine's idea that there is an "ontological relativity" built into every language. According to this approach, the conditions and very notion of truth cannot be given objectively in universal terms, as part of a universal and common logic, but rather will always be expressed in a specific way within a language and, by extension, a culture. Different languages divide the world into different categories of perception in a unique way, thereby

---

21  George Lakoff and Mark Johnson, *Metaphors We Live By* (Chicago: Chicago University Press, 1980); George Lakoff, *Women, Fire, and Dangerous Things: What Categories Reveal about the Mind* (Chicago: Chicago University Press, 1987).

creating the unique and diverse structures of metaphorical thinking. For example, there are peoples who completely lack any spatial metaphor for "right" and "left" in their language and thinking; for another people, the expression "the stone falls" is impossible if the speaker does not guarantee that that such an event happens; for others, the expression would be meaningless without clarifying whether the event is in the line of sight of the speakers or in relation to a specific landmark, etc. This thesis has enjoyed development in the new anthropology, which recognizes the plurality and uniqueness of different peoples' ontologies and rejects the uniform, Eurocentric, evolutionary, and progressist projects.[22] Thus, not only is there a plurality of different structures and modes of being-in-the-world (*in-der-Welt-sein*), but also the possibility of various intra-lingual and intra-cultural truths.

The role of metaphor is key to thinking and to the capacity of higher abstractions, as going further up requires a greater number of complex, interconnected metaphors. Here, the mythopoetics of language, never fully displaced, still makes itself manifest. In principle, it is impossible to speak of something higher "dryly" or "straightforwardly," without the use of allegories, figures of speech, transference, and systems of references to phenomena of the same or another kind. Conversely, as Lakoff notes, metaphors are less needed, or not needed at all, to describe physical laws and the material slice of being. The rich saturation of ordinary language with metaphors and their leading role in shaping the language-specific styles of thinking constitutes one of the most important matters when it comes to defending and upholding mythopoetic being-in-the-world.

Closely related to the topic of lingual and ontological relativity is the classic problem of the possibility of translating statements and meaning from one language

---

22  We treated cultural, ontological, and natural pluralism in detail in *Tradition and Future Shock: Visions of a Future that Isn't Ours* (PRAV Publishing, 2023).

into another, especially if these languages are not related and are even exotic to each other. From the standpoint of universalism, all natural languages are mutually translatable, i.e., a complete semantic translation is possible and can transmit the objective truth of an expression. This is an altogether naive delusion proper to Modernity in the spirit of objectivism and materialism. Several arguments can be raised against it:

(1) Most modal significations (if not all of them) cannot be divorced from their sociocultural and pragmatic context. In order to convey something said, it is also necessary to convey a person's understanding of what they have said and the circumstances in which something is said.

(2) Meaning is expressed within the framework of a language's grammatical system and bears the stamps of this system.

(3) Every language possesses a unique rhetorical style, including a unique means of reference.

(4) The formation of a semantic field in one language substantially differs from the analogous process in another language.

(5) The cognitive and neural processing of every language is unique.[23]

These quite obvious theses are most glaringly manifest when it comes to that most complex task of translating poetry and its tropes, and especially we're dealing with the words of unrelated and exotic languages. The lexemes that are intelligible and evoke corresponding associative series in their native culture might require several paragraphs or pages of meticulous explanations and examples in the language into which they are being translated. This gives rise to the inescapable dilemma of translation method, i.e., whether to render a translation word-for-word or interlinear, or completely change the structure and words of the original verse in order to convey not the words

---

23  Borodai, *Iazyk i poznanie*.

themselves, but the spirit of the author's expression.[24] Borodai emphasizes that for a more or less successful translation it is sufficient to evoke in the reader's consciousness a similar mental model within which the translated statement, text, or verse can function. Yet, it is impossible in principle to evoke a completely identical mental model with all the corresponding nuances, cultural references, implications, emotions, jargon, polysemy, contexts, idioms, dictums, etc. More often than not, translating requires significant changes or updating, expanding expressive means of the recipient language often at the cost of transferring (calquing or borrowing) grammatical and lexical structures and constructs from the donor language. Thus, the conclusion may be drawn that any word that sounds and functions in its native language with its polysemantic links and contexts cannot be fully translated or have complete analogues in another language.[25]

Finally, we can raise the more radical question of the fundamental possibility of translating that which the Indian grammarians, poets, and after them the philosophers of Kashmir Advaita called *dhvani*, that is the hidden voice of Shabdabrahman that is always present in any speech. Ritual and sacred mythopoetics are the space where the subtle play of decorations is a constant indication and gentle transmission, the maieutics of that state in which the mind slips into understanding the fact that in poetic speech it is the the Divine itself telling its tale. This require on the poet-translator's part the highest mastery of their own language so as to transplant the seed of this state into the soil of their native language. The *dhvani* will

---

24  See, for example, the history of the translation of German poetry into Russian in the 19th century: G.I. Ratgauz, "Nemetskaia poeziia v Rossii" in idem (ed.), *Zolotoe pero. Nemetskaia, avstriiskaia i shveitsarskaia poeziia v russkikh perevodakh 1812-1970 gg.* (Moscow: Progress, 1974).

25  Hans-Georg Gadamer remarked that when two thinkers do not know each other's languages, their conversation is ultimately no more than a dialogue between their translators. See Hans-Georg Gadamer, *Truth and Method*, trans. Joel Weinsheimer and Donald G. Marshall (London: Bloomsbury, 2020).

then resound in this language as well, or more precisely: upon inspiration by another model, a poetry will have been created which gives the Divine a place for its subtle voice craving an interlocutor.

The further development of the theses inspired by Sapir and Whorf, reinforced by a number of field studies and experiments, has led to the paradigm of post-relativism on the question of the mutual influence between language and thinking. The resulting contours of this cognitive architecture and the role of language (in all its manifestations) therein can be briefly summarized as follows. Language occupies the central and connecting place in the cognitive architecture. It facilitates the formation of an original cognitive style and is the main means of accessing higher mental processes. Language can be understood as the organization and categorization of conceptual representations of significant elements from external experience. The formal system of language is in a state of dependency upon its content. Any natural language represents a unique system of distributions, references, and distinctions among various categories and definitions. Explaining any given category requires referring to other categories which in turn also require a system of explanations and references within one and the same language and culture.

Linguistic specificity begins whenever language interacts with information from a given external experience, construes the semantic sphere, and distributes this experience into categories. Linguistic specificity is manifest at all levels: grammar, morphology, syntax, classification in terms of parts of speech, discourse, and reference. Post-relativism concludes that, in essence, every natural language bears traits that are unique to it in all spheres.

> The main way in which language influences cognitive processes is by implicit verbalizations. Insofar as these verbalizations are genetically bound up with the language of a particular community, they inherit a particular semantic organization. It is for this reason

that, in order to clarify the role of language in cognition, it is important to study the particular rhetorical style or conventional manner of speaking, and not abstract grammatical structure. The impact of a certain semantic or formal component will be higher the more often it is found in real speech, which means in inner speech. Conversely, the presence of some exotic grammeme which is almost never used in real speech entails a low relevance for cognition... Behind the linguo-specific structure of a language there must be a linguo-specific semantic map.[26]

As a child grows up, their assimilating of a language means not only their immersion into a culture, but also the formation of a new cognitive architecture that is filled by language and permeates the work of other systems. Thus, a linguo-specific style of thinking is assimilated on the deep cognitive level as a fundamental system. Borodai writes:

> It bears highlighting at least three complex factors that heavily contribute to this process: sensorimotor constitution, cultural practices, and language system. These factors are interconnected. Sensorimotor constitution is partly innate and partly discloses itself over the course of the ontogenesis that occurs in socio-cultural conditions. A language system constitutes and transmits the current cultural knowledge as well as previously conventional practices that have undergone crystallization in linguistic form. Cultural practices form the broad field for ontogenesis, but they are partially transmitted through language and are unthinkable outside of language. The combination of these factors gives rise to a unique style of categorization which is in turn reflected in a unique cognitive style.[27]

It follows that language "specifies" memory, visual perception, auditory modality, motor system, gestures, imagination, spatial representations, and the emotional sphere. Moreover, the use of language, even in inner speech and thinking, leads to specific bodily reactions and the activation of the body's sensorimotor systems. In other words, whenever we speak to ourselves in our mind, our speech organs, tongue, jaw, larynx, as well as other parts of the body and individual

---

26 Borodai, *Iazyk i poznanie*.
27 Ibid.

muscles experience tensions and tones that are recordable by instruments. In some cases, general fatigue of the lips and cheekbones can be observed after intensive thinking just as if a person had been speaking out a whole array of information.

Taken together, the deep penetration of the body by language, the linguistic specification of sensory perception, and the theory of conceptual metaphors led John Lakoff to argue that the mind as a whole is embodied. In other words, the mind is not simply the superstructure, but is rooted in or "mixed in" with corporeality. Therefore, speakers of different languages not only interpret corporeality differently, but literally have different bodily and sensorimotor responses and behaviors, and these differences are conditioned by language. These variations are fully accountable, noticeable, and play a role within their culture.

Furthermore, Borodai concludes that native speakers "should be studied primarily in authentic conditions, that is, within the boundaries of their native settlement, since the grounding of cognition is manifest not only in involvement in 'cultural knowledge,' but also in the bodily, experiential, motor attachment to a specific landscape, 'groundedness' in the literal sense of the word."[28] The rootedness of language in the body correlates with its external rootedness in the specific landscape in which its speaker, the tribe or people, dwells. This is connected to, among other things, how some peoples might not have a relative system of orientation (relative to themselves), but instead an absolute orientation centered around unique features of the area (for example, a mountain as the central point of orientation and indication of the position of things and people relative to it). All of this lucidly reinforces those theses and theories which posit the unavoidable and obvious influence of the surrounding landscape, space, climate, flora, and fauna — topogenesis in

---

28  Borodai, *Iazyk i poznanie*.

general — upon the culture of the people that dwells in their midst. The surrounding manifest world is reflected in culture and is linguistically specified in a complex way — all the way to the corporeality of a given person and their cognitive architecture.

This situation leads us to argue that it is impossible for the intertwinement of language, thinking, and environment to be unraveled and disintegrated into autonomous domains. One leading component cannot be singled out between them, because all three factors mutually condition one another in a particular here-being and being-in-the-world. If we prioritize one component out of the triad, then we can speculatively rank and rebuild the whole structure in a certain subordination to this leading component. This is what universalists, materialists, idealists, and cognitivists do in accordance with the principle that their systems hold to be primary. Language is etched into thinking like a complex ornamental pattern is etched into wood or metal.

Proceeding from the linguistic specificity of thinking, we can speak of perspectivism from the standpoint of sacred tradition as language. In turn, we can raise the question of the need to study the role and integral meaning of sacred words, metaphors, theonyms, and taboo systems within the system of the linguistic specificity of thinking. In full accordance with the fact that the elements and styles of speaking play a large role in this specification, it is necessary to devote attention to the dialects of estates, to sacred vocabulary, to the peculiarities of using special sacred names for the Divinities and even avoidances of directly naming them, and to their rendering in poetic tropes and decorations, etc. Their role in the specification of mythopoetic thinking must be clarified. Impetus to this course of study is also imparted by the fact that when Boas, Sapir, and Whorf drew parallels between the Amerindian, Central and South American languages on the one hand and the Standard Average European (SAE) on the other, they virtually ignored the huge, fundamental difference in cultural-epistemological paradigms between still archaic tribes (traditional, sacrocentric, albeit in some cases already severely crippled by colonization and genocide) and the already deeply modernized Europeans, and how such is reflected in their discourses and everyday language.

Despite the absolutely correct rejection of the progressive scale of "primitive vs. developed peoples," sacrocentrism on the one hand and aggressive secularism on the other have not been treated as significant. Thus, it would be more interesting and logical to compare, for example, the Proto-Germanic or Old Norse language before the Christianization of Scandinavia with the language of the Hopi or another archaic tribe, rather than with modern German. Despite the direct kinship between German and Proto-Germanic, in the former there are reflected and at work secular and anti-sacred discourses, scientific and cognitive strategies, classifications of experiences in terms of different values, morphosyntactic and semantic shifts in terminology and lexemes, etc. Taking this problem into account requires close study at the intersection of linguistics and Traditionalism.

Once again, this time proceeding from yet another scientific paradigm and trajectory of argumentation, we have confirmation of the thesis that there is a plurality of truths as variations of tales within the singular space of language. Concepts dealing with the truthfulness of a statement and truth in general are also linguo-specific in culture, in the sphere of being of a particular people.

Based on the actual linguistic specificity of thinking, we can draw the fully concrete conclusion that there is a need to protect not only linguistic diversity, but also the regional dialectisms of one language within a large culture. Dialects show variations of speech styles and discursive forms, word usages, and whole reserves of archaisms, etc., all of which belong to the larger and unified cognitive style of the language and the colloquial koine. This diversity provides greater material for the scholar and generates the regional map of a particular language's variations. Linguistic specificity is a powerful tool for upholding mythopoetics and cultural autonomies, for affirming the plurality of thinking styles and truths, and for overthrowing modernist universalism.

Another close conclusion that follows from such a position is defending a linguistic pluralism that pays close attention to the semantic fields and connections that are formed when a new lexeme is incorporated into a recipient language. For example, all the words needed in modern society as they pertain to scientific-technological progress, technology, and the IT sector come mainly from English and Latin with modern semantics. Such words should be translated and positioned in a recipient language in semantic domains with negative, dangerous, anguishing, demonic connotations. We can find a textbook example of this in the highly purist Icelandic language. In modern society, a computer is a technology, an instrument which is treated strictly positively. A computer is a source of entertainment, a tool for work, a sign of wealth and social status, and in general a long-established element of a normal, even good life. In the Icelandic language, which doesn't tolerate borrowings, the lexeme *tölva*, consisting of the two words *tala* (number) and *völva* (seeress), was created to denote "computer." The nuance is that, in Old Icelandic, as well as in other Germanic (and not only Germanic) societies, a seeress is far from always a pleasant female character. Most often, a seeress is a witch or an isolated women endowed with the negative sacred, her status closely associated with danger and the expectation of deceit. In the *Elder Edda*, Odin even appeals to a dead seeress by raising her out of her grave and forcing her to speak. This motif of necromancy is widely known, as is the general gender distribution of such magic. Feminine forms of divination and magic were either outright taboo or were not welcomed in patriarchal, male society. Thus, translating the notion of computer as *tölva* functions in Icelandic with reference to the witch-like, the feminine, the necromantic, and partially taboo semantic field. Such rigor of interpretation is not always observed in translations, and it does not always function properly within modern society precisely because of the difference in paradigms of thinking that we pointed out above. In the modern society of Iceland, a different episteme and system of values is in operation, one in which the traditional and the religious are regarded as a stage in the development of society long ago overcome and abandoned as the "childhood of humanity," hence references to "digital seeresses" do not invoke the due caution and practices warranted by operating with such a device. They are merely a tribute to established customs, an extravagant translation, and a safe reference to cultural remnants, like "folk comics" (cf. Russian *lubok*).

Borodai speaks of the threat of losing linguistic diversity thusly: "When faced with more 'prestigious' languages, the languages of small peoples are subjected to their influence and are often subjected to their reductions." This is indeed the case, hence the thesis that "language does not degrade, but is constantly changing" should be discarded as naive, narrow-minded, and even ideologically biased. It bears recognizing the obvious degeneration of many languages, including the leading European ones, not to mention the extinction of languages that were and are peripheral to Eurocentric civilization.

The abundance of borrowed words, whole expressions, and styles of speaking and writing is often dictated by altogether mundane considerations for fashion, the imitation of social status within a political or cultural colony (the aboriginal who imitates the language and style of speech of the metropolis thinks that his status is increased), marketing strategies (Anglicism sells better than the usual native word), and general cultural-political hegemony on the global

## Tradition as Language

or regional scale. This directly leads to the degeneration of a language and culture. While recognizing that the world at large is moving along a downward trajectory of decay entailing the diminishment of the good and its eschatological source, it also bears recognizing that language within the world is subject to the same decline.

Ferdinand de Saussure argued that "there is nothing in language but differences." Following Carl Schmitt's definition of "the Political" as a matter of differentiating between friend and enemy, we can affirm the immanently political nature of language. In this light, the preservation of dialects takes on a political dimension in contrast to the state center and literary norm of a given language. For centuries, the numerous rebellious peoples of Zomia in Southeast Asia have practiced actively, consciously changing their language so as to prevent themselves from speaking the language of the Chinese Empire or local rulers.[29]

A significant contribution to the formation of linguistic standards, even at the intersection with purism, has been made by translations of the Bible into local languages. In the genesis of the English nation, for instance, one of the most significant events in the formation of the English language, as well as in the resolution of confessional problems, was the King James Bible. In the Russian Orthodox tradition, it is believed that distortions in the text of the Bible are introduced by demons who interfere with and misguide the hand of the monk-scribe. Misprints made under the influence of demons or frivolous word choices distort the true meaning of the Gospel, leading people to heresies, erroneous interpretations, and the death of their soul. Hence the sacrally motivated struggle for the purity and uniformity of translations and canons. An analogous example exists in Islam, in the story surrounding the "Satanic verses"

---

29  See James S. Scott, *The Art of Not Being Governed: An Anarchist History of Upland Southeast Asia* (New Haven: Yale University Press, 2009).

allegedly crossed out of the Koran by Muhammad for being inspired by Ibis.

On the flat plane of secular, Western-centric globalization, the uniformization of language is possible only in step with an ever lowering bar. Languages must be replaced or simplified to meet the common version of the hegemonic language (Simple English) or degrade under the influence of global Internet slang and texting methods (1337 speak, Emojis). This facilitates the onset of uniformity and globalization over cultures, whereby all local civilizational-cultural features, including language, are turned into exotic-cosmetic frame for one and the same content.

Recognizing the influence of the environment on the formation and preservation of a language, we can conclude that the global urban monotony of megacities and even more so the virtual environment contribute only to fundamental, existential alienation, degradation, the molding of defective and limited forms of language and speech styles, instilling in natural languages pronounced tendencies and elements from synthetic languages, such as programming languages and the subcultures surrounding them. Ultimately, all three elements in the dynamic interrelationship of language, environment, and thinking are subject to decline, dissolution, and involution.

The counter-thesis from the side of mythopoetic thinking is the affirmation of the strict need to immerse children into the linguistic environment of tradition from the perinatal period, such as songs and lullabies sung to the fetus by the mother and midwives (ποίησις), and over the whole course of their ontogenesis, upbringing, and education. The child ought to assimilate from their surrounding environment and family the local dialect, speech style, vocabulary (including sacred and taboo), etc., which will cultivate a a direct embedding of the linguistic specification into their cognitive structures, and thus render high metaphysics and mythopoiesis even more open and easier to assimilate. This, of course, is a rather big problem that inevitably raises the issue of opposition to the surrounding environment of the dominant culture and separation from society as the bearer of a hostile culture. These problems, which are beyond the scope of our present examination, must be solved at the intersection of philosophy, linguistics, folklore, and pedagogy.

Another conclusion of obvious importance is the urgent need to preserve and study the isolated and archaic languages and cultures that still survive.

Another interesting case study is posed by philosophical language, which is distinguished by a high degree of syncretism: it operates with the most complex spatial, historical-temporal, cross-cultural, and interdisciplinary constellations of terms, metaphors, and images, which are often elevated to the level of highly abstract categories. Philosophical language also has the tendency to generate independent discourses that refer to and operate with respect to other philosophical concepts and narratives rather than donor cultures. In other words, the field of philosophical thought and language within the scope of classical metaphysics has the tendency of becoming detached from the soil and forming a field of "pure thought." However, as studies by linguists have shown, the grammar of language and folk etymologies have exerted a strong influence on the development of philosophical categories of thinking and theological constructs. This played a definite role in the (onto-)linguistic turn in philosophy in the 20th century. We can speak of a dialectical or hermeneutic approach to the development and disclosure of the philosophical foundations of folk language with excursions into high philosophical metalanguage, and translations made from the latter in the spirit of a thinker's descent from the mountain peak down into the valleys. Discoveries by linguists and the post-relativist project of grounding the linguistic specification of thinking can have a powerful impact on philosophy and the plurality of *logoi*, i.e., paradigms of thought which do not have to be reduced to a universal cognitive model, culture, or fate.

Whorf wrote that metaphysics is implicit in language. It is well known that the grammar of the Greek language decisively influenced the structure of Greek and, consequently, all of Western metaphysics. Émile Benveniste drew parallels between the structure of the Greek language and Aristotle's categories:

> The category of substance corresponds to the noun, the category of quantity and quality to the adjective, the category of relation to the comparative adjective, the category of place and time to adverbs of place and time, the category of position to the middle voice, the category of state to the perfect voice, the category of action to the active voice, and the category of undergoing to the passive voice.[30]

In the SAE languages, "time," "space," "cause," "effect," "progress," "past," "future," "substance," and "matter" are essential segments. According to Whorf, the metaphysics of the culture of SAE languages can be generally outlined in the following way:

> Thus the implicit metaphysics of SAE culture presup poses a uniformly flowing 1-dimensional time-order, a 3-dimensional space- order distinct from it, a universe consisting of a void or 'holes' b substance or matter which has 'properties' and forms island-like 'bodies', an absolute un bridgeable difference between the matter and the 'holes', events 'caused' by 'preceding' events, things happening to matter, nothing happening in the void.[31]

Furthermore, citing his favorite example of the Hopi language, Whorf shows the contrast between the different structure of metaphysics implicit in the latter and the modern European languages:

---

30 Borodai, *Iazyk i poznanie*.

31 B.L. Whorf, "Yale Report" (1938), in Penny Lee, *The Whorf Theory Complex: A Critical Reconstruction* (Amsterdam: John Benjamins, 1996), 264.

The Hopian metaphysics has no time and space orders like ours has a contrast of two realms; a the causal, or unmanifested which includes the future and the mental-psychic and is dynamic and in a process the end of which is manifestation, and b the manifested, which includes the present, past, and physical or apparent, and does not act causally per se, but contributes to causality by helping as it were to maintain a general well-being that aids the cycle of events. Within realm b there is a contrast of two modes of existence and/or extension; punctual (outlined around a point-center) and tensive (extending more or less indefinitely), which contrast takes over much of the work of the SAE matter-void contrast and is worked out throughout grammar and vocabulary in literally thousands of ways...[32]

Borodai also cites the research project of V.G. Lysenko, whose main thesis says that "the development of atomism in Greek and Indian philosophy was conditioned by reflection on the phonological structure of these Indo-European languages, while the specific phonological structure of the Chinese language and its method of fixing the written word prevented the formation of an atomistic natural philosophy."[33]

Charles Kahn developed Benveniste's ideas to show that an important condition for the development of Greek metaphysics was the specificity of the Greek verb εἰμί, which combines the semantics of existence, vitality, truth, and the matrix of stativity, durativity, and locativity. Greek philosophers used all these shades of the word without specifying its nuances, since such were implicitly clear to them. Kahn thus concludes: "We can say that Parmenides created the meta- physical concept of Being by bringing together all of the aspects and nuances of the Greek verb into a single concept of the immutable Fact or Entity: *to eon*, 'that which is.'"[34] In this example, we encounter yet another striking feature of the difference between the archaic state of metaphysically, sacredly saturated languages, and

---

[32] Ibid., 265.

[33] Borodai, *Iazyk i poznanie*.

[34] Charles H. Kahn, *The Verb 'Be' in Ancient Greek* (Indianapolis: Hackett Publishing Company, 2003), xxviii.

the average modern SAE and its culture. This difference lies in fundamental polysemy, semantic richness, and symbolism, all of which are characteristic not only of key ritual and mythopoetic terms, but also everyday verbs and nouns. For instance, the ancient Indian notion of *Rta* (from Indo-European *$*h_2R\text{-}to$*, "right") is generally untranslatable into other languages, as it is simultaneously and literally means "truth," "order," "cosmos," "being," "law," "way," "sacred word," "prayer," "hymn," etc., and in other texts its meanings encompass associations with the sun, light, fire, movement, cart, axle, sacrifice, fat, etc.

In deeply sacred, mythopoetic cultures, such words and notions are manifold — ποίησις, τέχνη, οὐσία, το ὄν, λόγος, *runa*, *oðr*, *Sein*. They are irreducible to any single meaning that would be familiar and comfortable for instrumental use and translation by modern man. Such words and their status cannot be algorithmized. In this lies the fundamental difference with the modern paradigm which strives to truncate the polysemy of words and reduce symbol to one strict sign or formula. Key here is the early Wittgenstein's "atomic fact," his project of cleansing language of allegory, and the complimentary project of analytical philosophy, which hedges all stakes on logical-mathematical accounting, analysis, and propositioning about philosophy and the world. In turn, this lays the specific instrumental foundations for creating a basic mathematical language to account for, digitally calculate, and completely digitize the manifest world. Heidegger spoke of this prevailing closing of all access to Beyng as the domination of the *Gestell*, the reduction of all Being to "calculating and calculable beings." In other words, the trajectory of man's alienation from his being has as its horizon a virtual culture in which the only that exists is that which can be accounted for in mathematical language and ultimately reduced to binary technological calculation. Drawing on Lakoff's thought, it could be said that this is a conscious movement away from highly abstract metaphors, philosophy, metaphysics, symbolic culture, complex natural languages and the authentic here-being of man within the world, within his unique language culture and cosmos.

At this point, we cannot ignore the special case of the philosophy of Martin Heidegger, who accomplished a fundamental linguistic turn in ontology with his maxim that "language is the house of Being." Following the event of the "turn" (*Kehre*) in his philosophy, Heidegger turned to the primal matrix of language in which we constantly pronounce and utter Being in the regular verb "to be" — in German *ist, bist, war, waren, wessen, west*, etc. In the Russian language, this verb linkage has practically disappeared, as we can speak without the obligatory indication of "is" without losing the meaning. To Heidegger belongs the important indication that "*die Sprache spricht*" — "language speaks," or "telling tells [itself]" — expressed in his classic manner of forming a verb out of a noun. Heidegger thus called for paying close attention to what language itself constantly says in itself, in its discourse (*Rede*) and talking (*Gerede*) that are existentials of Dasein's dwelling in the world.

The necessity of the turn towards language in Heidegger's philosophizing proceeded from different premises and grounds than those underlying the project of linguistic relativity for Sapir, Whorf, and later post-relativism, but they have a rather close and altogether specific horizon of convergence and mutual enrichment in the sphere of philosophy.

At the center of Heidegger's later project stood the leap of thinking about Another Beginning of philosophy as the Event (*Ereignis*), the eventing of the truth of here-being beyond classical metaphysics, whose decisions and solutions Heidegger held to be erroneous and irrelevant. Such a posing of the question in the light of ontolinguistics demanded that Heidegger create and develop an entirely different style of speaking and expressing philosophy. This language is grounded in a hermeneutic circling, in immersion into words, in rejecting the ready-made concept-words of metaphysics. Heidegger developed a special, non-conceptual language for speaking and clearly embodying his program, at the heart of which lies an interlinking: "another beginning of philosophy requires another thinking, and that means another language." Language as the historical word is the "hail of the gods" of earth and world. For the German "prince of philosophers" and "Black Forest shaman," attuned and rooted in the mountainous provincial landscape, there can be no question of creating some kind of artificial language like Esperanto. Rather, Heidegger developed the language of Another Beginning out of the very same Swabian dialect of the German language, which he began to structure and pronounce in a special way and with sensitivity to archaisms that mark the important distinctions made over the course of his thinking (*Sein* → *Seyn*, *ist* → *west*, etc.).

As we can see, the field of intersections between linguistics, philosophy, metaphysics, the sacred, politics, ethnography, thinking, and education is so enormous and full of examples, projects, tasks, and problems, that even an approximate map of such a continent cannot possibly be described and composed in brief.

To return to the metaphor of tradition as language and as a tree, we can firmly conclude that there is the fundamental possibility, like an open path with no hindrances, of speaking forth another myth, or other myths, and engaging in the mythopoetic and philosophical (philo-mythical) maieutics of planting and cultivating a new tree in the soil of the heavens and the soil of earth.

# THE LANGUAGE OF TRADITION AND THE PARADIGMS OF THE MODERN SCIENCES: RECTIFYING NAMES AND MEASURING DISTANCES

*Alexander Dugin*

### Disciplinary Languages and Participation

There are disciplinary discourses that present themselves as utterances, and there are disciplinary languages. The latter study and investigate the field, the environment from which expressive utterances come. Traditionalism (if we consider it as a discipline) is a language.

In Orphic cosmology, there is one being: Phanes. It represents the primordial condensation of transcendental darkness and occupies an intermediate position between the manifest world and the divine Nothing. A certain fog of obscurity precedes the cosmological phenomenon (manifestation). It is no longer Nothing, but not yet something. In principle, the reality of language is in some ways analogous to the ancient Greek ideas about Phanes. In studying language, we are studying precisely the basic, primary program, the set of primordial elements whose various combinations yield all possible spectra of discourse-utterances. Fully-fledged Orphic mythology began with the description of Phanes — the first condensation of the primordial haze.

I ask you to actively participate in the intellectual process. Participation is one of the key terms of our spiritual position and worldview. It is important not only to listen, remember, and record information, but to move together along the terrain of utterances, to master thought, to turn an expounded thought into our own content, our own filling. Dostoevsky wrote about his character Kirillov: "the idea ate him." The task is to have the idea swallow each of you. In fact, there is nothing frightening about an idea eating a person. After all, any given person as an individual, in and of himself, is not particularly interesting. I think this will gradually become clear to everyone. The idea, on the contrary, is very interesting! Moreover, it does not matter whether the idea is right or wrong. The idea itself, and the very existence of the sphere of ideas, of the ideal, the eidetic, is much richer and more interesting from all points of view. It is more worthy than the aggregated existence of a person as such (in which there is too much that is superfluous, unnecessary, that could well be dispensed with). Thus, by participating in the mastering, understanding, and assimilation of what has been said, we "feed" our individualities to predatory ideas, to the vultures of the eidetic plane. This is an extremely positive, invaluable experience.

## Holism (Polar Cognition)

In the world of Tradition, science did not have an independent status. When we call alchemy, magic, the art of building cathedrals, and other forms of activity within Tradition "sciences," we are, of course, making a certain *a posteriori* assumption. Of course, there were no sciences as such, but there was something analogous to them. These were elements, sectors of an essentially single, organic ensemble. There is a remarkable Greek word: *holos* — "whole," "integral," "indivisible." There is a special system of views based on the concept of *holos*: holism. Holism is the notion that in any phenomenon, thing, or sum of things or phenomena, there is a unity, a whole that precedes the constituent parts. Anything can be considered as a sum of parts – this notion is mechanistic, not holistic. But there is the notion that the unity of a thing, its organic integrity, precedes its division into constituent components. Any problem, thing, or phenomenon can be considered either as a sum of separate independent elements or as some organic unity, that is, as *holos*. At the core of the holistic approach lies this formula: the whole is something more than the mathematical sum of its constituent parts. It is the whole that is endowed with its own being, while its parts (individual elements) are only endowed with being indirectly; they draw and borrow being from the whole. Consequently, being is a property of the whole, while the parts are only indirectly ontological.

It is this holistic approach that is the axis of the traditional world, the basis of the sacred experience of being. The very idea of sacrality, of Tradition, is identical to the idea of holism. There is no Tradition outside of holism, and there is no sacrality outside the idea of a single and integral world that precedes its parts and immeasurably exceeds their mathematical totality.

A few more words about the term *holos*: the Greek word *holos* etymologically goes back to the same Indo-European root as the English "whole," Russian *tsel'nyi* and *tselyi*, German *Heil* ("good," "health," "greeting"; hence *heilig* - "sacred," "holy"). Thus, the term *holos* means "health," "fullness," "perfection," "integrity." Note that the Russian word for "kissing," *tselovanie*, or "kiss," *potselui*, originally indicated only a greeting (not an actual kiss), the same way the ancient German greeting *Heil* is preserved in the English "Hail." This is a blessing, a wish for salvation, for goodness, holiness, unity, integrity, perfection, inseparability, and indivisibility into constituent parts, i.e., a wish for "holism."

The holistic approach is typified by yet another trait: a certain continuity (sequence), or the absence of breaks. The holistic approach assumes the simultaneous grasp of the entire phenomenon, thing, object, or insight into the essence of what is common to a chain of beings, things, phenomena. This style of cognition denies the need (and even the possibility) of a special scientific language, of categorical thinking. Categoricality assumes a strict definition of terms, in which each term describing a thing or phenomenon is clearly designated. In Tradition, in its inherent holistic approach, no such categorical division exists.

Tradition does not know a "thing" as such at all. One of the axioms of formal logic on which categorical thinking is based, the axiom that underlies the very definition of what is "scientific," states that $A = A$. This, it would seem, is indisputable. But such a statement is radically opposed to the holistic view of the world. The holistic, sacred worldview does not know of a single thing that would be identical to itself. In the world of tradition, A is never equal to A! Any A is always equal to A plus something else. This something, a certain special ontological remainder, signifies the incompleteness of each separate part, the incompleteness of some specific, separate constituent element of which the whole is supposedly composed. No thing is identical to itself, since in being it only replaces something else, it is only a symbol, an indication of what is absent at the moment and expresses its being through the otherness of itself in this specific thing. The world of Tradition (the holistic method, the holistic paradigm) leaves open the possibility of metamorphosis of any thing (phenomenon, essence, object) under study, the possibility of taking a step to the side, of discovering something that was not grasped, seen, or recorded at first. The holistic method, which assumes multidimensional continuity (the continuous interconnection of various phenomena), always preserves the possibility of discovering a second side, an additional dimension, a new, emerging system of connections behind a thing (a phenomenon).

Holism presupposes the precedence of the one, the general, in relation to the particular. This one essence, the essence of a thing or phenomenon under consideration, is not some simple abstract category, not a postulate of abstract, rational, rational thinking, not the result of comprehension, secondary in relation to the things themselves, not a conclusion from observations. In the world of Tradition, each phenomenon, each thing, set of things, or set of phenomena has some really existing *holos* – that space, that dimension, that point in which all being is present simultaneously and taken together, which is the innermost, deepest, and existential dimension of the visible ensemble of things. The concepts of "pole" and *holos* in traditional, sacred gnoseology almost coincide.

How is a thing (a set of things or phenomena) cognized in the world of Tradition? Let us suppose that we are investigating two objects within the framework of the language of Tradition (holistic methodology). These two objects are compared, connected, and coupled with each other, but their relations are not clarified in isolation, as though one after the other, but rather through the mediation of a certain third point, which is the *holos* or pole of both of these objects. A is not equal to A. There is a pole (*holos*) of A, in relation to which A acts as its substitute, as its "icon." We perform the same operations on B. Thus, the study of the relationship between A and B in the "polar" (holistic) methodology is carried out through the study of a pole, "C," of each of these things and, at the same time, a common pole for the entire set of things or phenomena. As Evgeny Vsevolodovich Golovin said, quoting an alchemical text: "Only at the North Pole does the heart of Mercury sleep." This heart is the *holos*.

A and B lose their fixed boundaries (as fundamentally indefinable quantities) and seem to flicker. They are only links in a chain of ontological metamorphoses and are related to each other through their common pole, C. But this is not enough. The very relationship between A and B gains an additional essence; hence, an additional instance arises: the pole of connection. Thus, in the world of Tradition, cognition occurs along a very complex spiral of metamorphoses. Let me remind you that within the framework of formal logic, in this case, the process of cognition is exhausted by a head-on comparison of A and B, after which the tired researcher simply washes his hands of it. Where the competence of modern science ends, sacred science is just getting started.

## The Debate over Universals and the Ontological Double

In medieval Europe, there was a dispute between the advocates of nominalism and realism. Some, such as the realists and idealists, claimed that each thing has objectivity and essence, to which the nominalists responded: "Why do we need such duality? The thing itself is enough for us."

This was a conflict between the sacred method of cognition and an emerging purely profane gnoseology. After several centuries, the profane nomalists won. But what does this change entail? Things still need to be doubled and, contrary to the opinion of the nominalists, they constantly are. Jean Parvulesco states that "everything that approaches its essence splits." In holistic methodology, every thing, every being (a person, for example) is, at a minimum, a dual phenomenon. On the one hand, there is something that declares (directly or indirectly) of itself "I am." For instance, "I am Fedya, I have such-and-such hair color, I am such-and-such, I have such-and-such a social background, so-and-so are my parents, I earn such an amount, I can do this, I can't do that, I have been arrested this many times, etc." In a word, he tells us about his current status (biography, general anthropological characteristics, psychology, external parameters, etc.). Fedya's reality, which encompasses everything, is A. This is nominal Fedya, Fedya as an actual individual, the undivided, self-identical Fedya as he is or as he is commonly perceived.

In the sacred gnoseological model, there is always someone else behind Fedya, someone who lives through Fedya, someone whose icon, proxy, or substitute is Fedya. Fedya, like all of us, from the perspective of Tradition and sacred gnoseology, is nothing more than a bill of exchange for the sum of deposits in the "bank of the pole." We may not recognize this bill of exchange, or perhaps we recognize it but do not "present it for payment" – we may ignore its presence or even vehemently deny it. Nevertheless, sacred (holistic) gnoseology insists that every thing, every being, every situation has an ontological double (*ontologische Doppelgänger*), called essence or being. This ontological double is the pole (*holos*). Every person has such a pole; however, the paradox is that, being inside and next to us ("closer than our jugular vein"), it is as far from us as we are far from the Golden Age. Our entire environment (the language of the modern world) is arranged in an anti-holistic spirit, where the paradigms of nominalism are triumphant, creating an insurmountable distance between us and our true "I".

When we talk about holism, we encounter a clearly expressed polar system of coordinates. In the world of Tradition, everything — from everyday trifles to religious cults, from a system of knowledge to civil laws, arts, professions, crafts — belongs to a single, holistic ensemble. In this world, if a person says "I am a carpenter," this statement means much more than just an indication of his profession. After all, God is also, in a way, a carpenter! In Greek, "the matter from which the world is molded" and "wood" are one word, "ὕλη". Hence the idea that any carpenter is to some degree a "demiurge," a creator, a minor deity. The same can be said about a potter, a builder, a sculptor, a plowman, a designer, an inventor. Therefore, a simple carpenter, a simple man with a jointer, did not exist in the world of Tradition. Every carpenter was something else, because his activity, in addition to the economic, material, and business aspects, was endowed with symbolic meaning.

Many, if not all, people have a tradition of sacred hospitality. Of course, the point is not that the bearers of this tradition are just kind and sociable people. There is a serious holistic model behind it. Let us recall Abraham, who received three men, treated them and hosted them together with his wife. The three strangers turned out to be angels, but Abraham did not know! He greeted all guests with equal cordiality. Meyrink's book *The Green Face* illustrates the initiatic teaching that a random guest can turn out to be a hidden angel. Every person who comes our way, or every object appearing in the sphere of traditional gnoseological consciousness, can turn out to be a substitute for the highest angelic entities. As the Kabbalists say: "Every guest, even a familiar person, can turn out to be Elijah." We cannot know when he will come, and therefore we must be ready to see some other entity in any being who comes to us. The arrival of a guest is a serious symbolic and psychological drama: something else comes into our dwelling place, something whose ultimate meaning, in the sacred aspect, we might never be able to determine. Behind this lies the holistic teaching that every being is potentially (or in some special spiritual dimension) not itself, but someone else. It can be said that the entire method of cognition within the framework of sacred civilization is based on this principle of hospitality. We encounter a thing, for example, a branch, a pipe, a cat. Rational thinking says: "A pipe is a pipe, A is A, a cat is a cat, a branch is a branch, a tree is a tree." Sacred thinking never agrees with such an unambiguous qualification. It is possible, of course, that this particular cat is not a messenger of the lunar spirits, that this particular tree is not a secret object of worship, and that this pipe has no meaning beyond the forgetfulness of a plumber. But at the same time, all of these objects, even in the most dense, objective, pragmatic and non-sacred contexts, can turn out to be carriers of additional, non-obvious, elusive forces and entities. Even the most ordinary, gray, shabby cat potentially always represents something else. There is no world, no reality, where a thing would mean itself alone, where a cat would be only a cat. In every cat sleeps a higher aspiration...

## The Spherical System of Onto-Gnoseological Coordinates

Tradition's understanding of the structure of the world can be described using the sphere or circle. This is a very convenient geometric figure. Plato began with it, claiming that the first person (androgyne) was round and spherical before being split into two parts, creating the two sexes. The circle itself is the fundamental, original symbol of Tradition, the matrix of its entire language.[35]

In a sphere (or circle) there is a periphery and a center. Everything presented to us in concrete sensations, every object of contemplation that is comprehended, every phenomenon that we encounter is, from the point of view of Tradition, always only a periphery. We ourselves are the periphery. But somewhere, perpendicular to everything, in a radically inward direction, there is a certain vector pointing toward the pole.[36] This is the polar axis of ourselves and the things that we encounter. The entire sphere is in continuous

---

35 On this symbol, see René Guénon, *Le Symbolisme de la Croix* (Paris, 1996) [René Guénon, *The Symbolism of the Cross*, trans. Angus Macnab (Hillsdale: Sophia Perennis, 2004)].

36 Evgeny Golovin once illustrated this thesis by quoting the German poet Gottfried Benn: "*Alles ist Ufer. Ewig ruft das Meer.*" The whole strophe reads:
Die weiche Bucht, die dunkle Wälderträume,
Die Sterne, schneeballblütengross und schwer.
Die Panther springen lautlos durch die Bäume.
Alles ist Ufer. Ewig ruft das Meer.

motion, guaranteeing the life of the world in its true fullness and complexity. Islamic esotericism differentiates in this movement, which precedes any concrete physical activity, two opposite directions: *mabda* and *ma'ad* — "manifestation" and "return."[37]

In Hinduism, in the yogic teaching of Patanjali, there is also the concept of the inhalation and exhalation of the universe, the inhalation and exhalation of the gods. The essence of these similar gnoseo-ontological concepts from different traditions is as follows: in the sphere of being, there is a certain special pulsation: moving away from the pole and approaching it. This pulsation is sacred being. The pole itself is motionless, independent, unchangeable. However, between the center and the periphery, existential, vital, spiritual, gnoseological flows are continuously moving. All of them, in their paradigm, in their internal scheme, skeleton, in their gnoseological, spiritual basis, represent two movements in opposite directions: outward exhalation (manifestation), and inward inhalation (return), exit from the Center and return to the Center. All knowledge in the world of Tradition is characterized by this cyclical rhythm. Everything here is a combination of two paradigmatic movements. All practices of spiritual transformation associated with breathing (yogis), ritual dance (Sufis), etc., are the application of a metaphysical model that represents the world as a constant rhythmic inhalation and exhalation of the pole to the subtle physiology of man. The pole expels light from itself and absorbs it back, goes to the periphery and returns to the center. Buddhist and Lamaist mandalas are illustrations of this principle.

As one moves away from the center (the ontological pole), multiple peripheral circles push away, leading a thing, a situation, a person away from returning to the center,

---

37 *Mabda* literally means "manifestation," "appearance," from the Arabic verb *bada'a*, "to manifest itself," "to show itself." *Ma'ad* means "return" from the verb *'auada*, "to return."

drawing them into a swastika-like rotation on the periphery. After a thing leaves the center, forces that prevent its return immediately begin to act on it. This is the inertia of exhalation (*mabda*). Typically, they manage to disrupt the movements of return, prevent it, involve the being either in a circular motion or in a radial removal even further from the center. The serene logic of "departing and returning" exists only in pure theory. This tragic circumstance is the guarantee of the adventurism and riskiness of being. This is the metaphysical root of the heroic myth, the drama of the initiation and spiritual realization of beings.

This is precisely what the fabric of real life consists of, the meaning of which, from the point of view of Tradition, is to transfer a thing from the periphery to the pole and to bring down from the pole an ennobling, uplifting, transforming effect upon a specific point of the periphery.

The metaphysical meaning of the hesychastic practice (the repetition of the Jesus Prayer: "Lord Jesus Christ, Son of God, have mercy on me, a sinner") has the same meaning. The first phrase, "Lord Jesus Christ," is repeated with an inhalation, and "have mercy on me, a sinner" with an exhalation. Inhalation is the absorption of the Divine Name, the invocation of the polar point, the ontological pole of the Orthodoxly understood world. When we say "Lord Jesus Christ," we absorb this transcendent source, this unity. When we say "have mercy on me, a sinner," we expel concreteness and peripherality from ourselves and, elastically, like a spring, we cast aside our immanent, categorical, fixed being as "sinners." Together with "have mercy on me, a sinner," we literally release the spirit, we die as individualities. We cast aside our immanent individuality to dissolve in the pole. We do this many, many times, until this prayer, this rhythm, becomes the inner content of the one praying. Thus, the repetition of the Jesus Prayer is an act of the highest knowledge and the ultimate form of the gnoseological cycle, the shortest path of spiritual realization.

## The Blossoming Methodology of the Sacred Sciences

But let us return to what we started with: is there an analogue to modern science in the world of Tradition?

We can say that, up to a certain point, the sacred sciences are such an analogue. Sacred science occupies an intermediate position between the ontological pole of the sphere of being, where everything is present simultaneously in a single holistic synthesis, and the area of the periphery, where things and creatures are represented as separate and individual. Sacred sciences presuppose a certain specialization, a restriction of the subject of research, a certain structuralization of methodology, and the development of conceptual tools. This resembles the modern sciences, and one can indeed trace a historical connection: the modern sciences developed out of sacred sciences. But at the same time, the sacred sciences never lost their connection with the onto-gnoseological pole — they were called to serve it, and consequently, their praxis was connected with the theurgic, soteriological side, i.e., not merely an act of cognition of the real, but an act of transforming the real, bringing the real to holistic completeness. This aspect of sacred sciences, on the contrary, contrasts sharply with modern science, which has never set such goals, as such are considered in the modern world to be the exclusive prerogative of religion, magic, etc.

The sacred sciences belong to the domain of incomplete detailing; therefore, they have special features that are unique to each particular sacred science, as well as general, universal aspects that elevate each discipline to the singular "polar" source. The sacred sciences are connected with the development of the rational features in man, but this sacred-scientific rationality differs significantly and qualitatively from pure rationality, which has become the gnoseological criterion of scientificity in the modern era.

Of course, humans as a species possess rational thinking. The man of Tradition has it to no lesser degree than modern people. Man cannot help but single out some specific fragment, a sector of being, a certain set of phenomena, into a separate abstract category torn away from others. The rational handling of reality is inscribed in the program of man. No matter how holistically and integrally the man of Tradition is oriented, when he sees Vasya, he says "Hello, Vasya," and not "Hello, Masha." An ascetic immersed in spiritual contemplation, in comprehending the polar principle, may not notice where he is and what is around him; it is no wonder that he might confuse Vasya, Masha, and Fedya, since he fundamentally does not care about them. But an ordinary person, even in the world of Tradition, is forced to deal with details that are fixed, singled out into something independent, obeying the mechanisms of rationality. The sacred sciences describe reality with rational methods that are partly reminiscent of modern scientific models. But in them, the selection of a specific element, the snatching of it from the general environment, is never final.

A person fixates on some thing, begins to describe it in detail, but then at some point steps back. He says, "Yes, of course, I see that this is, indeed, a tree, I looked closely at this tree, and not something else." But then sacred attention, like a video camera, moves away: "But a tree is a sign, a symbol of the axis of the world, an illustration of how the spiritual soil from which we are created, a certain pre-worldly principle, releases our own souls, feeding on the juices of meaning, like green leaves." Thus, cognition of the tree as a fixed "botanical" reality does occur, but only for there to be a "rollback" to symbolic reality. Therefore, within Tradition there is no science that is strictly separated from the others and has an unambiguously defined subject and clear-cut methodology.

Alchemists themselves, for example, usually do not know what they are writing about. They write about the transformation of elements, but it is absurd to think that all the developed mythology incorporated by the

Hermeticists is just an artificial encryption of specific chemical processes. Take lead for example. Alchemists take it and touch it with their fingers, but their attention immediately moves away from it; the concreteness of lead disappears, dissolves in the knowledge that lead is Saturn, Saturn devouring his children, Saturn-time. The concrete lead immediately dissolves amidst a complex array of ideas about time, about primordial matter, about "work in black", and who knows what else... *Plumbum nostrum*... A mysterious, multidimensional reality, explained by an even more mysterious reality... Not a crossword puzzle, not a charade, but a risky, operative mystery. Lead is a descent into hell, inferno, death, decay. Chemically, existentially, aesthetically, ethically, ontologically... Sacred chemistry, the luxury of elusive meanings...

The structure of sacred science is such that it is never ultimately categorical. It operates with a certain system of terms, but these terms (questions about the Latin etymology of the word *terminus*, "final," "strictly defined," "limited") are never final. They "flicker": now they mean one thing, in a moment they mean something completely different. Therefore, the idea that alchemy, like any other traditional science, including magic, can be deciphered by purely rational means is doomed to failure.

What does this or that magician mean by the "spirit of Venus"? Maybe one thing, maybe another, or perhaps still something else. A subtle influence, a set of physical and spiritual properties, voice modulations, a combination of colors, the misty appearance of a creature summoned from beyond...

In alchemy, the transmutation of metals (for example, lead into gold) sometimes works, and sometimes doesn't. What this means is never quite clear. There are physical gold bars obtained through transmutation just as well as there is testimony of the spiritual achievements of historical alchemical practitioners.

Let's turn, for example, to botany. This discipline emerged from vegetal (floral and arboreal) magic, witchcraft. Who used to collect herbs? Witches, sorcerers, healers. They knew the qualitative, causal aspects of plants. When profane German scientists burst into this field and began to pierce butterflies and dry herbariums, full-fledged sacred botany rooted in healing and witchcraft was finished. Here again, we see violence against the polar model, a rupture, a denial, a rejection of the holistic worldview in favor of the nominalist belief in the priority of the individual over the universal.

There is a "polar" uncertainty in the way traditional consciousness views objects, in how it qualifies and catalogs them. This peculiarity can easily be traced throughout the treatises of medieval authors. Albertus Magnus, for example, writes about botany, metals, and the properties of stones. You can learn from him how to properly smelt copper and how to make poultices when you've been bitten by a snake. There are also interesting passages about the angelic ranks, about prayer practices, about sacred history, etc. There is no concept claiming the incomparability of the high and the low, and there is no divide between the technical and the moral: everything represents one holistic space. The pole is visible behind everything, the pole is predicted behind everything, and this pole is the main goal, the task for a person who cognizes the world, himself, and the surrounding environment within the framework of Tradition.

Such a method of cognition can be called "spherical." It is like a blossoming flower. The flower opens up in all directions at once. This is the complete opposite of rational discourse. If we learn botany in Tradition, then we are also learning demonology, theology, medicine, music, the art of building cathedrals, etc. That is why there is a certain slowness to sacred consciousness. If a flower opened only in one direction, it would do so instantly. But it must open in all directions, so it waits for the first rays of the sun, it waits for the pre-dawn dew. It slowly opens its bud and discovers its pole, and then, with the same tedious slowness, it goes through the opposite procedure on the eve of lunar midnight. The opening and closing of a flower is a favored symbol in Tradition for describing the process of knowledge. Fairies and elves are believed to feed on the scent of roses, as subtle beings apprehend reality in a "spherical" manner.

## The Paradoxes of Wisdom

The completeness and perfection of knowledge in spherical, holistic coordinates lead the person of Tradition to a state of wisdom. It is worth noting that, in our contemporary [Russian] language, the term "wise one" [*mudrets*] is often used mockingly, almost as an insult. A "wise one" is typically either a complete fool or someone who has uttered some remarkable absurdity. Hence the expression "nice one, wise guy" [*nu, ty namudril*], meaning that someone has committed a senseless and unproductive folly. When people wish to praise someone, they often say: "This is a learned [*uchennyi*] (knowledgeable, competent) person." This distinction is not incidental. In Tradition, the completed, positive process of knowledge is the attainment of the state of wisdom. However, the "wise one" does not know anything specific, nor does he wish to know such things.[38] He knows everything as a whole. If you ask him a specific question, you are likely to receive an answer that seems foolish at first glance. The rightness of the wise one, as a rule, is only revealed after a period of time — sometimes a long one. The wise one transcends any professional in any field. He knows everything as a whole. The wise one is the guru of the spherical coordinate system: a being who

---

38   Nicholas of Cusa, an outstanding representative of holistic thinking, introduced the term *docta ignorantia*, "learned ignorance," to designate the paradoxical character of polar wisdom.

imitates the pole, is fixated on the pole, and is immersed in the pulsation of the One. The more he knows the All (that is, the pole), the more he attains polar wisdom, the less he knows anything concrete. The concrete interests him little, if at all... Ultimately, the concrete does not concern him. The sages of the "second category," who write verbose treatises on subjects such as botany, angelology, or strategy, often revere such silent, concentrated sages. They say, "If the silent guru were to speak, we would all be shamed by our meager knowledge; the distance between the whole and the many is far greater than the distance between the many and the few." Wisdom is not merely the arrogant claim of a charlatan; it is the genuine revelation of the transcendental pole, which simultaneously represents the pole of all things. "Atman is Brahman," says Advaita Vedanta. He who has come to know his own pole (Atman) has come to know the pole of all other things and has thus become the pole of these things.

## The Sacred-Scientific Definition of Love

Now, let us sharply pivot from the topic at hand and attempt to formulate how Tradition understands love.

This concept is often "polluted" by human emotions. Everyone has encountered it in various forms: in classical literature, modern pop music, bourgeois novels, and moralistic sermons. Few things provoke such predictable reactions in people as appeals to love. People respond to the topic of love in much the same way Pavlov's dogs responded to light bulbs and electric shocks.

Typically, love is associated with some form of sentimental, excited, nervous spasm, a surging wave, a subcutaneous itch. However, in addition to the emotional, purely psychological, and sentimental understanding of love, there exists an almost mathematical definition of it. This definition is easy to articulate. The great Orthodox ascetic

Abba Dorotheus expressed it as follows: "Love is the coming together of the spokes of a wheel as they approach the hub. Therefore, love for God as the hub (this is the first Christian commandment) and love for one's neighbor as a spoke (this is the second Christian commandment) are inseparable from each other; they are analogous. In striving to draw closer to one another, we approach the third—the hub, God; and in striving toward God, we draw closer to one another." In this patristic explanation of love, we find the original, universal exposition of the Traditional worldview, which is effective in all aspects. This demystification and desentimentalization of love, which reveals its essence, allows us to evaluate it with almost mathematical precision. What could be closer than the union between the knower and the known? This represents the highest degree of love. In knowing, we identify ourselves with what we know. When this happens at the polar level, it constitutes perfect love. Thus, the processes of knowledge and the path of love in Tradition, devoid of sentimental adornments, are strictly identical. It is highly significant that this quote from Abba Dorotheus appears on the first page of the Pustozersky collection of *The Life of Archpriest Avvakum*.

## Sacred Language Operates with Synthetic Concepts

The basic paradigm of sacred science, the holistic method, the spherical model of cognition, and the gnoseology of love all coincide with what we previously referred to as the language of Tradition. The language of Tradition is nothing other than the constant, multidimensional, and diverse reproduction of the polar circle and the movement within it. Initially, the language of Tradition coincided with the language that preceded the Tower of Babel. In the pre-Babylonian era, language in the paradigmatic, structuralist sense coincided with what we understand by language in the ordinary sense. When Tradition was one and perfect, everyone spoke the same language. This language was built on an ideally sacred principle, as close as possible to the clarity of the mathematical-geometric spherical model.

We can find traces of this primordial holistic language in various etymological patterns. This original language did not recognize strict categories. For example, it did not have clear distinctions such as gender. There are two Russian words: *tyotya* (aunt) and *tyatya* (father, man). However, initially, these were one word, which meant neither a man nor a woman, but simply a "big person" from the perspective of a small one. This is how children referred to all adults, regardless of gender (hence the classification of this word as "children's speech").

Another example of the preservation of elements from the proto-language is the presence in the Russian language of the neuter gender (a deep layer of the linguistic level, where words or concepts precede sexual differentiation). The same can be said about color differentiation. There is the Russian word *chernyi* and the Slavic *chermnyi*. One means "black" and the other "red." Of course, initially, it was one word. It is said: "The richer the people, the more shades of color there are in their language." This is, in fact, a fallacy. The more "primitive" a people, the more they "mix" colors and use one word to describe whole groups of objects and concepts. In this sense, such a people is closer to the sacred paradigm, and thus, they are more sacred.

But let us return to *chernyi-chermnyi*. How can we explain this linguistic minimalism? This word contains the idea of a certain color load. The degree of this load can differ, including the maximum (the color black), but it can also be simply strong, distinguishing deep red from pale and faded red (in this case, *chermnyi* means *krasnyi* [red]).

An even more interesting example is the word *light* [*svet*]. Light has always been associated with something luminous and white. This is a very ancient root *su*, but then the "u" hardens (a common phenomenon in linguistics: *u* becomes *v*), and we get the German *schwarz* (black), *Schwan* (swan), and even *Schwein* (pig). The word *svet* ("light"), *svetovoi* ("illuminated"), *belyi* ("white") can, upon developing into a certain categorical, fixed world, mean the exact opposite. Originally, *svet* ("light") and *tsvet* ("color") (cf. *su*) meant some kind of radiance. Radiance can be perceived both as light (something bright on dark) and as color (saturation on light). This is still a typical holistic method. It is no coincidence that Zen Buddhist koans (for example, "if you meet the Buddha, kill the Buddha") are considered the most direct path to knowing reality.

Orthodox theology, for its part, is entirely built on supra-rational dogmas (the Trinity of God, the two natures of Christ, etc.), on things that are fundamentally opposed to categorical thinking. It is no accident that the apostle said, "Christianity is a stumbling block to the Jews, and foolishness to the Greeks." This is a sure sign of sacred language, where paradox and mutually exclusive statements do not disqualify a statement, but rather, to the contrary, confirm its authenticity.

### The All-Word [*Vseslovo*]

All sacred symbols are intended to open up the polar space that lies on the other side of the rational veil of the external world. In the primordial language, every word signified not only two opposite concepts but also everything — absolutely everything! Such words still exist today. They have been preserved in liturgical practices and sacred arrays, which remain an effective tool for spiritual realization in various traditions. One example is *dhikr* in Islamic esotericism. The Sufi constantly repeats "Allah, Allah, Allah," and thus this word becomes an all-encompassing word for him. Its meaning begins to absorb, take in, and ultimately transcend all other words. No matter what one tries to express, his lips utter only "Allah."

Similarly, the Jesus Prayer among the Hesychasts plays the same role. The Christian tradition contains another word that seeks to fulfill the role of such an "all-word." This is the human analogue of the angelic voice: "Hallelujah." The conventional etymology of the word "hallelujah" is literally "glory to Thee, O God" in Hebrew. There is no mystery here. However, the situation was greatly complicated by the Russian Old Believers. They realized that this word is much more significant than its literal translation from Hebrew. In essence, it means "all together." In the Russian liturgical tradition, it was customary to pronounce "hallelujah" [*alilluia*] twice, followed by "Glory to Thee, O God," which is a Slavic translation of the formal content of this formula. When Nikon decided to introduce an additional, fourth "hallelujah" (in the Greek manner contemporary to him), the best representatives of the Russian spiritual tradition rebelled, believing that such a quadrupling of "hallelujah" symbolically introduced an "additional person" into the Holy Trinity.

The most intriguing aspect of this controversy is the Old Believer polemicists' interpretation of the symbolic meaning of the word "*alilluia*" itself: "*al*" symbolizes God the Father, "*ill*" the Son, and "*uia*" the Holy Spirit. This claim was not supported by any distinct "scientific" argumentation. All of this could be dismissed as mere curiosity, if not for the research of Herman Wirth.[39] In the 20th century, during the reconstruction of the proto-language of humankind, it was discovered that in the Nostratic and even pre-Nostratic layers of this proto-language, the most ancient sacred formula for addressing God was a combination of three vowel sounds: "a," "i," and "u." It turns out that the Old Believers, in some unknown way, preserved the most

---

39 See Alexander Dugin, *Giperboreiskaia teoriia* [The Hyperborean Theory] (Moscow: Arktogeia, 1993); idem, *Absoliutnaia Rodina* [Absolute Homeland] (Moscow: Arktogeia, 1999), and the lecture "*Mify Novogo Goda, Veilikii Iul*" [Myths of the New Year, Great Yule] in *Filosofiia traditsionalizma* [Philosophy of Traditionalism] (Moscow: Arktogeia, 2002).

ancient, millennia-old (and possibly even older) forms of sacred invocation of the Divine as late as the 17th century.

Let us now place these vowels on the runic or calendrical circle. "A" is at the bottom; it represents spring. "I" is at the top; it marks the summer solstice. "U" is again at the bottom; it signifies the solstice. If we superimpose this calendrical-primordial model of sacred linguistics, as studied by Wirth, onto Christian doctrine and dogma, we obtain a worldview that is shocking in its depth, integrity, and harmony. Thus, we uncover a genuine, sacred Christianity, rather than the surrogate with which we are usually confronted.

## The "Progress of the Sciences" and the Trick of the Language of Modernity

The question may arise: "If the people of Tradition were so wise and knowledgeable, and if they were constantly immersed in polar contemplation and truly embodied wisdom, then why didn't they, for example, know that the Earth orbits the Sun, or invent the cellphone?" Behind such questions lies a very interesting model: the language of modernity announces itself. The question is posed in us, but not by us. The notion of the "progress of the material sciences," the supposed unscientific nature of the Primordial Tradition, and the imperfection and technical ignorance of ancient societies — all of these are products of an illusion, a hypnosis, instilled in us, behind which stands the language of modernity. It is worth focusing on this moment, opening René Guénon's *Crisis of the Modern World*, carefully examining the first and second lectures of this series, and reflecting on these ideas thoroughly.

This is not a simple matter, but it is essential for the paradigm of the language of modernity to become evident in your consciousness, so that you understand how it operates. The task of the New University is to seriously and deeply explore such detailed matters as the language of Tradition and the language of modernity — not once, not twice, but numerous times, in order to conduct an intellectual experiment on ourselves. This requires constant reflexivity regarding the language of modernity, whose influence within us must be continually tracked. Such reflexivity needs to become a permanent intellectual practice.

## The Ontological Catastrophe

We now come to the heart of the origin of modern sciences. Where lies the boundary between sacred science in the world of Tradition — the gnoseological, spherical, holistic array I have attempted to describe — and modern science? What is the source of our illusory conviction that we know more than the ancients?

The first point to understand is that between modern and sacred sciences stands one of the most important, pivotal events: a colossal and irreversible intellectual catastrophe. In the polar array, where everything lives and moves within the complex, adventurous, and heroic reality of the unveiling and concealing of the polar principle, a sudden fracture occurs. Something departs and has not returned. There is no way back. There was an exit, and now the entryway is blocked. Someone was thrown out of the restaurant, and the doorman slammed the door shut with the boldness of a henchman. Now you are outside, at night, unable to re-enter, and the metro is closed. A catastrophe has occurred. The things on the periphery can no longer find their way back to the pole. The pole can no longer extend itself and ennoble things with its pure influence – the radiant beams that once transformed the things on the periphery.

There is a cosmogonic theory in the Safed Kabbalah of Isaac Luria, the concept of the *tzimtzum*, which considers the creation of the world to have resulted from a catastrophe. This theory stands in opposition to the usual cosmogenic myth of divine emanations. In the doctrine of emanations,

God overflows from His own abundance, giving rise to the world. In Lurianic doctrine of the *tzimtzum*, however, God contracts and withdraws into His inner core. The "nothing" from which God hides and conceals Himself is a vacuous, empty space — an ultra-thickened void — which, in tragic bewilderment, is cast out to the periphery, away from the divine and now outside of it. As the Lurianic Kabbalists say, "All things are no longer where they should be." Everything is altered: what was once at the bottom is now at the top, and vice versa. This traumatic world, full of tragedy, wanders confusedly and deliriously through the labyrinths of alienation.

A similar view of the ontological catastrophe is found among the extreme Bespopovtsy Old Believers, who view our world through an eschatological, apocalyptic lens. Holy Rus', the world of love, salvation, true Faith, and the polar breath whose radiant beams transform people, the elements, and all things by drawing them into the process of unification — gathering them into the fold of the Church and making them one — is violated by an anti-force, a demon or spirit of the outer twilight. Some other power temporarily gains control over the periphery. It is the spiritual Antichrist. The holos, integrality, oneness, and organic nature of the polar links are shattered, and the periphery falls under the dark domination of an external being operating from an instance opposed to the pole. The golden threads that once connected things to their polar, ontological archetypes are now severed by a malicious hand, the spiritual gardens are laid waste, and villages are uprooted from their foundations.[40]

Here emerges the landscape of the post-sacred world — a cityscape after a bombardment. Like Picasso's *Guernica*. This road once led somewhere, but now it leads nowhere. Strange, disparate objects lie scattered everywhere. Household

---

40  See *"Iskusstvo razbivat' sady"* ["The Art of Planting Gardens"] in Alexander Dugin, *Russkaia Veshch'* [The Russian Thing] (Moscow: Arktogeia, 2001).

utensils are thrown about in chaos. Nothing here can be understood unless one is familiar with the picture that preceded this devastation. This post-catastrophic relief of an ontology whose essence has been drained is what so-called "modern science" attempts to cognize, conceptualize, and restructure.

## The Anti-Holism of Modern Science

Modern science originates from an anti-holistic principle. Everything that is labeled "modern science" and belongs to its sphere is founded on the unspoken law of rejecting holism and the holistic worldview as unscientific, unnecessary, incorrect, or non-existent. Modern science studies a post-holistic, post-sacred world in which everything is strictly equivalent only to itself, where $A=A$, and where the relationships between things must be understood by proceeding from the things themselves, without appealing to any common denominator.

The proclamation of such a catastrophic approach can be traced back to the position of the nominalists, who rejected the idea of "doubling" things. However, the full extent of these monstrous, aggressive, eschatological overtones was realized only much later, during the Enlightenment. As Heidegger said, "The time of birth of the world picture is the birthday of the modern sciences."[41] This period marked the emergence of the idea that science is something special — self-sufficient and autonomous.

Before, nothing besides craftsmanship, skilled workmanship, and the possession of certain artisan skills was ever designated by the Russian word for "science," *nauka*. If you could skillfully forge a horseshoe or craft kites, you were "learned." The Russian word *nauka* does

---

41 Martin Heidegger, quoted in P.S. Gurevich (ed.), *Novaia tekhnokraticheskaia volna na Zapade* (Moscow: Progress, 1986). [See Martin Heidegger, "The Age of the World Picture" in idem, *Off the Beaten Track*, trans. Julian Young and Kenneth Haynes (Cambridge: Cambridge University Press, 2002)].

not carry the fundamental meaning inlaid in the Latin *sapientia*, the English "science," and the French *la science*. In the European languages, the term "science" means the way the world is cognized after the catastrophe that beset the holistic array and an attempt (a rather successful one) at constructing a particular gnoseological model that denies the spherical, polar, holistic model of cognition on which Tradition is based.

Imagine that the globe became a circle, and a circle became a circumference, i.e., a dimension — what constituted the ontological essence, the invisible but most interesting aspect of things and connections, has been lost. If previously the rhythmic, onto-gnoseological center went back-and-forth to the periphery (and in this consisted the essence of sacred science), then now the periphery is sharply fixed as such; henceforth, even the thought that there is some kind of path running inwards has come to be perceived as an absurdity.

Many years ago, I was drinking a beer with a young "cadre." I was saying to him: "You understand, the inner world..." And he asked: "What is this 'inner world'? I have a liver and guts. Generally, everything is in order." This is the case with the representatives of modern science: whenever you talk with them about the "ontological pole" of a thing, they'll say "What other 'ontological pole?' Molecules and atoms I understand. What else could there be inside?"

In this catastrophe, in this fundamental, gnoseological, spiritual bombardment of humanity, the very content of reality was taken out and evacuated. An excavator scraped out the space of the sacred gnoseology of the process and replaced it with a very unstable model with horrific consequences, one that united the periphery by proceeding from the periphery alone. A thing started to be seen as A=A, and only A. The laws of formal logic "came into force" (henceforth in a totalitarian regime) — laws that are non-ontological and which ignore the very phenomenon of being.

I once wrote a programmatic text entitled "Literature as Evil."[42] We could just as successfully advance the thesis "science as evil." One could offer varying assessments as to whether modern science is the cause of evil or, conversely, its victim (and the same question goes for literature). In that text of mine as well as now, I cannot answer this question.

However, it is completely obvious that modern science fixates on a horrifying, post-sacred picture of the world. By the very fact that it does so smugly and with satisfaction, and not tragically, undoubtedly exacerbates this situation.

Let's go back to *The Life of Archpriest Avvakum*. On the second page, an interesting symbol is depicted: an anti-pentagram which the author saw as the mark of the Antichrist. It looks like this: a five-pointed star outside a circle and inside a triangle. Inside are the "rays of love" (as per Abba Dorotheus) that bring together all the bearers of the real church. "God" is written in the center. To this center there lead five rays ("paths") which form the five-pointed star with a vertical orientation. Inside the circle are five human heads with five Orthodox eight-pointed crosses and five inscriptions reading "holy" or "saint." Outside of the circle, at either end of the inverted five-pointed star are five heads with the names of the main hierarch persecutors of the Old Faith. At the bottom is Patriarch Nikon. Christ unites everyone with the inner star of love and leads them to the pole. The Antichrist divides them, drawing them with the morning star away from the holy circle into the outer twilight.

*The Life of Archpriest Avvakum* was written in the very moment (and this can be precisely established

---
42  See Alexander Dugin, "Literatura kak zlo" in *Russkaia Veshch'*.

mathematically) when Russia witnessed a rejection of the holistic worldview of the Russian Middle Ages, of normal, fully-fledged Orthodoxy, in favor of the profane, post-sacred, un-holy modern system. Avvakum and other Old Believer authors are of colossal significance for understanding the metaphysics of Russian history. Their feat takes on special meaning in this context.

## The Sciences of Causes and the Sciences of *Qlippoth*-Effects

There is a widespread opinion that modern sciences are continuations of more ancient sacred disciplines. For example, modern mathematics is said to be the continuation of Pythagorean mathematics, algebra an element of Islamic culture's use of ciphers, chemistry a product of alchemy, physics of natural magic, and astronomy of astrology, etc. Insofar as reality is viewed within the framework of modernity as a process of progressive development, the precedence of the sacred sciences is interpreted as a sign of their inferiority, defectiveness, insufficiency, and embryonic character. It should be noted that in this respect, the modern approach is the opposite of Tradition. In the world of Tradition, it is said, "Thus it was before, as the ancient fathers said," which is an ontological confirmation of the thesis that referring to the sources is both positive and qualitative in nature.[43]

In the modern world, however, the view is reversed: "Ah, well, that was before, in the time of Tsar Gorokh; the people then were ignorant." Anything can be discredited with this argument. The language of modernity contains the idea that the modern sciences developed out of some kind of archaic, defective embryo. They had to develop to

---

[43] On qualitative time, see the first lecture [Alexander Dugin, "René Guénon: Traditionalism as a Language," *Passages: Studies in Traditionalism and Traditions*, vol. I (PRAV Publishing, 2023)].

the point where they transformed into the majestic edifice of modern science, resplendent with perfection.

But what is actually new in modern science? What is purely modern in it? The issue is not the time they emerged but the quality of their gnoseological approach. The more emphatic the rift with ancient holism, the more modern a text, scholar, or scientific method appears. If a modern person even slightly appeals to the holistic approach, they will immediately be considered hopelessly outdated, old-fashioned, or politically incorrect. It can be said that the idea of de-ontologization as an active process — the increasing removal of the polar, holistic center from the field of world cognition — has been clearly recognized by representatives of modern science (especially within its positivist trend) as an overall positive phenomenon. The course of "eliminating (annihilating) metaphysics" has been set. In the 19th century, a range of serious scholars (serious from the perspective of modern science) embarked on a crusade against the vestiges of the holistic worldview. This tendency became known as "positivism," followed in the 20th century by neo-positivism[44] and post-positivism.[45] (Post-positivism should not be seen as having overcome the main premises of positivism; rather, it was an attempt to preserve the basic principles of the positivist approach by adapting them to the complex, critical situation that arose due to the discovery of numerous errors and absurdities in the classical positivist approach.)

The periphery of the ontological sphere was intended to become the sole domain of study for modern sciences. It began with a precise fixation of disciplines: "This is only chemistry, that is only physics, this is only botany, that is only zoology, this is only sociology." The sharp division

---

44 Rudolf Carnap, Friedrich Waismann, Otto Neurath, Hans Reichenbach, Hans Hahn, Ludwig Wittgenstein, etc.

45 Karl Popper, Imre Lakatos, Alan Musgrave, etc.

between the humanities and the natural sciences is one of the most important elements in the dissolution of holism.

In the holistic, sacred method, there is no such thing as "only chemistry" or angelology strictly demarcated from it. Angelology sooner or later merges with ritual, eschatology, history, and eventually with botany and chemistry. Conversely, starting with the practical domain, the fundamental logic of symbolism sooner or later leads to the study of metaphysical questions.

The modern sciences took shape through the total demarcation of the objects of study.[46] Whereas before, the ontological pole influenced the periphery, creating an atmosphere of living interaction around a particular discipline and blurring its boundaries, in the language of modernity, this polar influence has been abolished. In the language of Tradition, the pole does not cancel but dissolves the fixation of determinate sciences, objects, phenomena, and beings, making their borders transparent. In the positivist approach, metaphysics is subject to total elimination. In turn, things, particular methods, and disciplines dissolve the pole, which is "ridiculed" and "humiliated" (and equated to prejudice) by the apologists of modern science. This is the process Nietzsche captured in his horrific formula: "God is dead. You have killed him. You and I." Nietzsche was perhaps the only one to fully grasp the deep meaning of what is happening in the modern world; he was one of the most honest, correct, and profound thinkers of our

---

46 The specialization of the sciences is inherent in Modernity's orientation towards studying local situations and the prevailing use of inductive methodology, which became the leitmotif of English empiricism and the slogan of the English Royal Society ("Not from words!" is the slogan of radical nominalism). Heidegger wrote: "This focusing (specialization) is, however, by no means merely the dire side effect of the increasing unsurveyability of the results of research. It is not a necessary evil, but rather the essential necessity of science as research. Specialization is not the consequence, but rather the ground of the progress of all research" (Heidegger, quoted in *Novaia tekhnokraticheskaia volna na Zapade* [Heidegger, "Age of the World Picture", 63]).

*The Language of Tradition and the Paradigms of the Modern Sciences*

era — probably the best. Unlike the progress optimists, he was a tragic and honest thinker.

The fundamental difference between a traditional science and its modern counterpart was beautifully formulated by Fulcanelli in the case of alchemy: "Alchemy is the science of causes, chemistry is the science of effects."[47] The alchemist can exchange places of things in the sphere of causes and achieve a result that would seem absurd to the chemist. For the alchemist, everything is in motion, and hence there is no such thing as simple copper, for example. Copper is immature silver. With certain skills, copper can be artificially transformed into silver. Copper is not equivalent to copper, and silver is not equivalent to silver — behind all lies the causal, polar, holistic array (which in alchemy is called "Mercury" or the "philosophical sea"). The domain of causes is the sphere of closeness to the pole (recall that "the heart of Mercury sleeps at the North Pole"). Operations in this realm change the structure of the periphery synchronically (non-locally).

Fulcanelli's definition can be successfully applied to designate the distance between any traditional science and its modern analogue. One could say that modern physics has the same relationship to natural magic as chemistry does to alchemy. Physics is post-magic. When magic ended, the causal aspects of reality were bracketed, and people began to study the exterior shells of things and phenomena. Thus, modern physics quickly discovered (on the basis of the second law of thermodynamics) the inevitability of the world dying by heat. This is supposed to follow naturally from the very entropy of the world of things that have been separated from their invisible causes. The primal impulse that started reality, having been placed in time (the "Big Bang"), inevitably faces only one prospect: fading away under friction until it is extinguished. Since the language

---
47  Fulcanelli, *Le Mystère des cathédrales* (Paris, 1979).

of modernity posits the cause of things on the same level as effects, the cause becomes completely diachronized and immanentized, losing its soteriological qualities and the capacity to intervene at any moment to fix the phenomena of crisis that are growing within the domain of what is actual and left to its own devices. Isaac Newton, one of the foremost architects of the language of modernity, encountered this problem in natural science. Absolutizing the inductive method (Newton's iconic sayings *"Hypotheses non fingo"* and "Physicists, less metaphysics!"), Newton saw the hopeless, tragic prospects of the God-forsaken world, and in the second half of his life, he turned to extravagant theories from the arsenal of the sacred sciences (Kabbalah, alchemy, magic, etc.) in an attempt to save what he perceived as a dead universe awaiting catastrophe. Newton was compelled to acknowledge the periodical intervention of a transcendent cause in immanent reality. According to his doctrine, for instance, the Divine voluntarily corrects the orbits of the planets, or else the planets would wreck under the impact of gravity. This compensatory side of Newton's doctrine is completely ignored by the language of modernity.

In the world of shells and peripheral objects, only one tendency can exist: downward and outward. The polar and anti-entropic tendency of inward and upward is absent. Within Tradition, we deal with a magical, living, vital universe, where behind every particular physical object and process stands some kind of joyful (or not very joyful) essence. The World Soul rotates, turns, moves, and enlivens the entire construction of the universe. This World Soul is not a speculative abstraction. Theoretically, one can commune with it through certain spiritual practices. But there is nothing of the sort in modern science. The World Soul has been removed, leaving only a dry shell. The world of shells and membranes (*qlippoth*) is the only object of study in modern sciences.

*The Language of Tradition and the Paradigms of the Modern Sciences*

## The Metaphysics of Infinitesimals and the "Polar Double"

Why did I title this lecture "Measuring Distances and Rectifying Names"? It's clear when it comes to "rectifying names": it is necessary to delve into what the modern sciences actually are, identify the language of modernity at work within them, understand how it functions, and so on. But why "measuring distances"?

To understand this, let's examine modern mathematics attentively. René Guénon's The Metaphysical Principles of the Infinitesimal Calculus once made a very strong impression on me.[48] In my opinion, it is one of the best books of the 20th century, comparable to *The Crisis of the Modern World*.[49] Every self-respecting intellectual should read it. It is rather dry and difficult, but it is so important and so fundamental that without it, we wouldn't know how to continue living.

In this book, Guénon describes the scientific theories of Leibniz and Newton, who were Rosicrucians, Kabbalists, and Hermeticists, and who also happened to lay the foundations of modern scientific methodology. These prominent thinkers had one foot in the sacred world of the holistic worldview and the other in the language of modernity. They were transitional figures, borderline personalities, and, of course, it is no coincidence that Guénon chose them.

In *The Metaphysical Principles of the Infinitesimal Calculus*, Guénon works out several fundamental concepts, including the mechanism of counterfeit substitution that

---

48 René Guénon, *Les Principes du calcul infinitésimal* (Paris, 1995) [René Guénon, *The Metaphysical Principles of the Infinitesimal Calculus*, trans. Michael Allen and Henry D. Fohr (Hillsdale: Sophia Perennis, 2004)].

49 René Guénon, *Krizis sovremennogo mira*, trans. Natalia Melentyeva, ed. Alexander Dugin (Moscow: Arktogeia, 1991) [René Guénon, *The Crisis of the Modern World*, trans. Marco Pallis, Arthur Osborne, Richard C. Nicholson (Hillsdale: Sophia Perennis, 2004)].

modern mathematics has introduced at the very core of the legacy it inherits from one of the supreme sacred sciences. We all went through the following formula in school: lim x / x→1 = 1. This may seem banal, but it means that x, or any other indeterminate value, in tending towards a determinate limit, ultimately reaches this point to which it tends, to the extent that it coincides with it. It is crucial that mathematical equality is at work here. If we tend towards some point and continually move in this direction, then sooner or later, our tendency will become the fact of reaching this point. This axiom of equality is the foundation of the model of differentials and integral calculus, and indeed of modern mathematics itself. It is like the law of universal gravitation — something that is supposedly self-evident and taken for granted.

However, Guénon argues that this formula contains a fundamental stretch and a violation of ontology and gnoseology that carries unimaginable consequences. Why? Leibniz and Newton were the first to use the limits formula in calculating geometric distances. Let's imagine a very close distance, say, up to 10 meters. The maximal closeness is not exactly 10 meters, but almost 10 meters. The original 10 meters is the length of a fence we need to build. In the case of the fence, we can disregard a minor error as negligible and agree that it is 10 meters. The small difference — the least of any significance — does not alter the outcome. Even the most meticulous architect would not protest. "Indeed," he might say, "you've convinced me that this is equal to 10 meters." But this approximate, pragmatic principle of the "fence" was embedded at the very foundations of modern mathematics — supposedly a "precise" science.

Guénon argues in his book: "Very little does not mean nothing." Between "very, very little" and actual "nothing" there exists a colossal ontological difference. Of course, we can neglect some errors for the sake of convenience in solving a specific task. But we must recognize that our conclusions will therefore be ontologically invalid. Consequently, any of modern mathematics' conclusions about the structure of being, based on the limits formula, are not true. Let us recall Zeno of Elea's paradox:[50] "Swift Achilles is chasing a tortoise." But in the meantime, the tortoise has already covered a certain distance, albeit modest. No matter how close Achilles may be, the tortoise is still ahead, as he is reaching the point where it just was. Guénon concludes: $\lim x / x \to 1 = 1$ is only valid given a rift in continuous movement — the gradual diminution of any value can never yield pure nothingness. The limit can only be reached by grasping the entire space at once. The tendency, remaining an immanent process, will never reach the goal, as the accomplishment is transcendent to the tendency.

This principle is universal. For example, a person practicing yoga may feel that they are changing, becoming someone other than they were before. This is not self-deceit — they truly are "becoming." But "becoming" and "to become" are not synonymous. Tending in itself is not the reaching of a limit. The limit is a transcendent boundary in relation to the tendency.

---

[50] It is worth recalling that Zeno was a student of Parmenides, a representative of the Eleatic school, which was distinguished by its emphatically holistic, ontological orientation. "Parmenides likened Pure Being, as a global paradigm, to the symbol of a sphere. 'Once it is seen that Being is complete from every point like the mass of a well-rounded sphere, the motive for such a comparison becomes clear. The point is that the mass of a sphere in equilibrium around the middle is in all parts of equal strength' (Leonardo Taran, *Parmenides: A Text with Translation, Commentary, and Critical Essays* [Princeton: Princeton University Press, 1965], 158-159). Naturally, the phrase about 'mass' here should be understood symbolically: Pure Being, for Parmenides, is not a material substance. An important element of Parmenides' teaching (he defined his own views as a mystical revelation dictated to him by a luminous being, a 'goddess') is the absence of a void (non-being) and the doctrine that a part does not have autonomous being. Only the Whole exists, and the part exists only insofar as it belongs to the Whole" (Alexander Dugin, *Evoliutsiia paradigmal'nykh osnovanii nauki* [The Evolution of the Paradigmatic Foundations of Science] [Moscow: Arktogeia, 2002]).

The person of old, with the pole — who we are — finds themselves in this kind of relationship. Our pole is not what we can become; it is what we are not. As Paracelsus said, "When a thing is, the quintessence isn't; where the quintessence is, the thing isn't."

Another important point that highlights the non-ontological nature of the modern mathematical model is the idea of mathematical infinity. René Guénon is absolutely right when he observes in the same book that it is impossible to reason about any genuine infinity of the material or the infinity of any manifest thing. Any manifest thing is determinately finite, as it is surrounded both externally and internally by the domain of the unmanifest. Genuine infinity does not have a particular, peripheral expression. Time, space, and numerical series may be indefinitely large; we may not see their imminent limits, as we are inside the same peripheral reality, but there is a limit. All things in the domain of the actual carry this limit within themselves. The world — and everything in it — has both a beginning and an end. The beginning is not somewhere very far in the past, nor is the end somewhere very far ahead. In fact, the beginning and the end are points that coincide. They are here and now, alongside each other — they are the constant pole that is co-present with being, always and everywhere on its inner side. For this reason, Guénon proposed replacing the expression "mathematical infinity" with "indefinitely large" or "indefinitely small." This is entirely correct, because within the scope of the qualitative world, we can never actually find the ultimately largest number. Something bigger will always be found ($N=1$), but it will never be infinity, because everything ends when the quantitative plane itself is fundamentally exhausted. It is important to remember that this exhaustion is not diachronic but synchronic. Reality demonstrates ontological limits at any point — one only needs to move forward along the luminous ontological perpendicular toward the northern pole of the spirit.

Real infinity is transcendent and vertical in relation to everything determinate. A practical conclusion can be drawn from this: there is no "spiritual progress," no matter what neo-spiritualist or Christian neophytes claim. There is us, and there is the pole. As long as there is us, there is no pole, only an illusion. We cannot leave ourselves to go anywhere. The new, true, polar man lives here and now, but he lives outside of us, besides us. He is our "polar double." Immanent development along the horizontal plane does not bring us closer to the end at all. The "polar double," the cover of the soul, is discovered instantaneously and irreversibly, and in the very act of its fulfillment, it integrates all possible directions of one's life path.

## The Ambiguity of the "End of Science" and the Exhaustion of the Anti-Christ Fantasy

Measuring distance is not a declaration; it is a process. It requires our active participation. The fundamental rejection of Tradition that underpins all modern sciences is not something that immediately stands out. Generally speaking, scholars and authors of scientific works carefully avoid questions concerning the foundational principles of the scientific disciplines in which they are engaged. They focus on particulars. In general, many individuals who enter the field of science are simply seeking to escape physical labor. This is their genuine scientific "credo." You will rarely hear an average scientist discuss the meaning of physics. Only geniuses attempt to engage with such questions. They are the ones truly interested in these matters.

It is necessary to dispel the hypnotic fog of modernity's language that has so tightly enwrapped the sciences in the modern world. We are constantly, everywhere, victims of banal illusions. And not only in science — but in everything. However, it is this domain, connected as it is with rational thought, that seems to me the most suitable for beginning to uncover the deceit and unravel (or cut through) this tightly wound knot. Doing so is becoming increasingly difficult. As the negation of Tradition, modern science now finds itself in a state of profound crisis. It is ending.[51] A strange situation of a negation upon negation is gradually taking shape.

Modern science began with the rejection of ontology, excising and rejecting the pole. It destroyed the sacred worldview and eliminated metaphysics. However, by the mid-20th century, it came to the conclusion that, by destroying the pole, it had destroyed everything. It turned out that the periphery has no self-sufficient being and that the atomic fact does not exist. As a result, honest scholars, representing various natural sciences (and the humanities), could not avoid discovering the impossibility of answering the most fundamental question of being within the framework of modern scientific mythology. A series of "little revolutions" followed. The term "holism" gradually became one of the most popular among representatives of modern physics.

For instance, Fritjof Capra attempted to apply an interdisciplinary approach, integrating several scientific disciplines, and proposed the use of a "new paradigm." He spoke of a kind of "Tao-matter."[52] Chaos theory (as articulated by Kolmogorov and Prigozhin) also became increasingly popular as a post-scientific (postmodern) attempt to rethink the paradoxes that classical science could not solve in a new vein.

---

51 John Horgan, *The End of Science: Facing the Limits of Knowledge in the Twilight of the Scientific Age* (New York: Broadway Books, 1997).

52 "New concepts in physics have generated a deep modification of our view of the world: from the mechanistic concept of Descartes and Newton we have come to a holistic and ecological view in full accordance with the theories of the mystics of all times and all traditions." Fritjof Capra, *Le temps du changement* (Paris, 1983). See also idem, "*Dao fiziki*" (Saint Petersburg, 1994) and *Smena paradigm i sdvig v shkale tsennostei*" in *Odin mir dlia vsekh* (Moscow, 1990).

This is a very difficult and complex process. On the one hand, we could say, "Well, great, the people of modern science, 'science as evil,' have acknowledged the incompetence of their approach and have finally understood and recognized that, by annihilating the heart, by cutting out the polar content, the periphery fell apart and ended up as pure non-being. The nihilistic essence of scientific mythology has been discovered. They've given up and started studying depth psychology, the history of religions, structural linguistics, and the anthropology of archaic peoples." (Yet, Jung and Eliade were not classical modern scholars, but were closer to the paradigms of Premodernity and the sacred sciences). "The modern, scientific, correct, classical, academic world has gradually been penetrated by 'politically incorrect' thinkers who reflect holistic, Premodern, sacred models." (For modern science, this is the same as the Russian Orthodox Church recognizing the correctness of the Old Believers.) Victory, it seems... But...

Séverin Batfroi,[53] a student of Eugène Canseliet (who popularized and continued Fulcanelli's work), and an alchemist and Traditionalist who was not exactly a genius, but still a loyal "guardian" of classical, "museum" Hermeticism, once expressed an interesting thought that resonated with me: "Yes," Batfroi says, "there are now journals on alchemy, and our science has been rehabilitated. Just a few decades ago, everyone spoke of alchemy as some kind of pre-scientific pseudo-knowledge. Now they are slowly, bit by bit, albeit arrogantly, acknowledging its historical validity..." How many battles have we, advocates of the traditional, holistic worldview, waged and lost in the modern world! And now they suddenly tell us: "Well, fine, you've endured, you've

---

53 See Séverin Batfroi, *Du chaos à la lumière: contribution à une prospective d'ésotérisme traditionnel* (Paris, 1978); idem, *Alchimie et révélation chrétienne* (Paris, 1976); idem, *Alchimiques métamorphoses du Mercure Universel* (Paris, 1977); Séverin Batfroi and Guy Béatrice, *Terre du Dauphin et Grand Oeuvre Solaire* (Paris, 1976).

held out, and now we'll no longer protest." Yet there is no remorse or repentance from them.

In the end, the question arises: have we won? I suspect (in fact, I insist) that this is a very cunning and dangerous "Postmodernist" move on the part of our opponent, the enemy of the pole. I do not suffer from the manic paranoia of being surveilled, but I still have the unpleasant feeling and suspicion that this pseudo-rehabilitation of Traditionalism and holism is the final move of our eternal "scientific opponent," the "clever wolf." There is no point in falling into depression and believing that everything around us is counterfeit, that we are surrounded by enemies, spies, double agents, and secret "scientists." It is necessary to simply measure the distance, thoroughly study the genesis of modern science, its evolution, and identify the particular points of rupture with the holistic worldview.[54] It is necessary to concentrate our undivided attention on the places where these ruptures are found. If the connection is restored, we can consider the statements of post-science to be credible. If these ruptures remain, however, the conclusions of post-science should be treated with distrust, despite their exterior attributes. Guénon performed something analogous in "rectifying the names" and "measuring the distance" between genuine Tradition and neo-spiritualism.

## The Soteriological Functions of Traditionalism Applied to the Sphere of the Sciences

No matter what, we must begin a global revision of modern science – we must not merely repeat what Guénon and other Traditionalists have said on this topic, but rather, be fully conscious of the issues at hand, and take concrete steps within individual disciplines.

---

54 This is partially carried out in Dugin, *Evoliutsiia paradigmal'nykh osnovanii nauki*.

*The Language of Tradition and the Paradigms of the Modern Sciences*

Without fixating on the maneuvers of the opposing side — the maneuvers of the spirit of the modern world, the prince of the modern world — but still considering their movements, our task is to correct the sciences in line with our own Traditionalist initiative. We must take the dead-end disciplines and elevate them to the holistic paradigm from which they catastrophically fell.

This requires colossal intellectual labor and the tension of scholarly will. We should not wait for holism to emerge from the current scientific community. Its path was originally directed into the darkness. We must affirm and soteriologically extract from under the burden of the spiritual Antichrist everything in these sciences that has been preserved from the pre-modern, sacred order.

More precisely, we must revive the sacred sciences against the profanation to which they are subjected today.

Only this will be the New University's adequate response to the fresh and, as far as we can see, final strategy of our ontological enemy.[55]

*Translated by Jafe Arnold and John Stachelski*

---

[55] The present text was originally a lecture delivered at the New University in Moscow in 1998, subsequently edited and published in Alexander Dugin, *Filosofiia traditsionalizma* [Philosophy of Traditionalism] (Moscow: Arktogeia, 2002).

# THE ONTOLOGY OF LANGUAGE IN THE LIGHT OF INTEGRAL TRADITIONALISM

*Maxim Medovarov*

Many of the fundamental figures of integral Traditionalism, as well as other prominent authors close to their views, have paid exceptionally great attention to the question of the ontology of language and rather special theses in the sphere of linguistics. The rigorous link between the very structure of Traditionalism and the structure of language has already become the subject of scholars' attention.[56] At the same time, it has consistently been made clear that far from any philosophy of language is compatible with Traditionalism; instead, Traditionalism is compatible only with a philosophy of language which proceeds from the indelible, "magical" connection between word and object, name and person, signifier and signified, and which rejects nominalism and the doctrine of the arbitrariness of words that is characteristic of the modern paradigm of thinking. In one way or another, the question of the relation between language and extra-lingual reality has among all the prominent authors of the Traditionalist orientation been resolved from the standpoint of Platonic ontologism, which is rooted in the conviction, traditional for all peoples, that names correspond to reality and that there is a magical link between them. Nikolai Bezlepkin, a contemporary scholar of the philosophy of language and professor at Saint Petersburg University, notes:

---

56 Alexander Dugin, "René Guénon: Traditionalism as a Language" in *Passages: Studies in Traditionalism and Traditions*, vol. 1 (PRAV Publishing, 2023), 17–56.

In the philosophy of name, there is the quite definitively cited thesis that man is not free in naming and cannot give just any name that comes to mind to express the essence of an entity. He must listen to the thing, hearken to its self-revelation, heed what it says to him. A name is only essentially substantive when it presents the self-revelation of a thing. "In this sense," as Sergius Bulgakov noted, "the thing names itself."[57]

Alongside this central question, reflection upon which dates back, if not to the hymns of the ancient East, then in all likelihood to Plato's *Cratylus*, two problems unceasingly find their way into the center of attention: the origin of language as such and the metaphysical significance of etymological research and comparative-historical linguistics.

The study of the etymology of words, their inner form (a term coined by Wilhelm Humboldt and Alexander Potebnya which has become commonly accepted in linguistics), as well as toponyms takes the scholar back into the depths of centuries, to the ancient, traditional sources of thinking. In a number of cases, this front is known as "linguistic archeology." The etymology of words has been engaged by thinkers ranging from Joseph de Maistre and René Guénon, Carl Schmitt and Julius Evola, Owen Barfield and C.S. Lewis, Martin Heidegger and J.R.R. Tolkien, to Alexander Shishkov and Pavel Florensky. In a number of cases (Florensky, Tolkien, etc.), such studies have proceeded hand in hand with the development of comparative-historical linguistics: in the 20th century, this meant above all the study of the Indo-European languages, but also the study of other language families, ultimately leading to the reconstruction of macro-families that existed either eight, ten, or even more thousands of years ago. A key role here was played by Vladislav Illich-Svitych, who reconstructed the Nostratic proto-language, which he saw as a means of acquiring initiatic knowledge. We have already had the occasion to make note of the means

---

[57] Nikolai I. Bezlepkin, *Filosofiia iazyka v Rossii (k istorii russkoi lingvofilosofii)* (Saint Petersburg: Isskustvo, 2022), 223.

by which the valuable developmental work of academic comparative-historical linguistics can be employed in the metaphysical constructions of Traditionalism, especially in connection with turning to the inner form of the words of the Indo-European proto-language and the proto-languages of other ancient families.[58]

In both cases, the Traditionalist, "Platonic" paradigm of thinking has required that scholars dismiss evolutionist and nominalist approaches and doctrines and has brought thinkers back to the problem of the "language of Adam," the "paradisal proto-language," the "giving of names," as well as the correlation between human language, the Divine Word, and the "language of the angels" (the mythical "language of the birds"). Hardly a single philosopher close to or upholding Traditionalist positions has avoided deliberations on the reconstruction of the magical language of the First Man. On this was based the whole philosophy of language proper to pre-Romanticism (Johann Georg Hamann, Antoine de Rivarol, Joseph de Maistre), Romanticism (Novalis, Schlegel, Schelling, etc.), neo-Romanticism (Fr. Pavel Florensky, Fr. Sergius Bulgakov, the "Inklings," etc.). In Russia, movement in this direction was complicated by the major international conflict incited in 1912-1917 by the Onomatodoxy (*Imiaslavie*) movement, which attempted to turn the doctrine of the ontological link between the Name of God and God himself into a church dogma. The Onomatodoxy movement exists in different forms in Russia to this day, whereas in Western Europe its analogues are more often settled in esoteric intellectual milieux.

Within the scope of the present article, we will examine some particular milestones in the historical disclosure of the *philosophia linguae perennis* which serve to illustrate the veracity of this approach. German Romanticism and

---

[58] Maxim V. Medovarov, "Dostizheniia i perspektivy izucheniia dal'nego rodstva iazykov: sovetskaia lingvisticheskaia shkola prezhde i teper'" in *Traditsiia: Materialy seminarov po problemam religiovedeniia i traditsionalizma* 2 (Moscow: Eurasian Movement, 2011), 61-68.

its forerunners deserve the greatest attention, since between Hamann and Heidegger we can speak of a common, 200-year-long tradition of prioritizing the philosophy of language. In our opinion, Novalis should be considered the key figure in this respect: for Novalis, authentic philosophy is identical to poetic genius and the magical words of the poet-mage who is capable of creating real things and living individuals through his song: "Poetry is, as it were, the key to philosophy, its aim, and its meaning."[59] Among the sources of his philosophy of language, Novalis deemed his direct forerunners to be Hamann, Herder, Hemsterhuis, Renaissance magic and the Kabbalah of Paracelsus and Sprengel, and the doctrine of the universal sympathy of things, on the basis of which Novalis developed his semiotics. As one modern scholar has noted:

> Lower, physical things were seen as carriers of certain signs, sigmas, and higher, imperishable bodies. These signs were attributed a "miraculous," magical power, for through them it became possible to influence the physical, corporeal world. "Language" turned into a means of magically influencing (casting spells upon) sensory things. Following the ancient magi, Novalis was inclined to acknowledge a mystical, creative power at work in language.[60]

To Novalis we can trace back the thesis that subsequently emerged in Russian philosophy of language: that which is indubitable is expressed (conditioned) through symbol, i.e., such a form of expression, of utterance, is interpreted in the category of miracle. To Kant's question as to how synthetic *a priori* judgments are possible, Novalis responded: by way of magic, synthetic knowledge, and the creation of miracles through the word. Following Hemsterhuis, this thinker drew a connection between the authentic sacred language of Adam and the Golden Age, which is expected to return anew: "Each of its names seems the word of deliverance for the

---

59 Rimma M. Gabitova, *Filosofiia nemetskogo romantizma (Fr. Schlegel, Novalis)* (Moscow: Nauka, 1978), 173.

60 Ibid., 186.

Soul of each natural Body."[61] Thus, according to Novalis, the poet plays a decisive role in history and is potentially capable, through his word, of gathering the dismembered fragments of the fallen cosmos back into one whole.

Alongside his philosophical *Fragments*, the topic of the philosophy of language also resounds in Novalis' foremost novel, *Heinrich von Ofterdingen*, and especially in the above-quoted essay "The Disciples at Saïs." In the words of Vladimir Mikushevich, "the main question of 'The Disciples at Saïs' is the 'surviving hints at a destroyed language,' to the search for which (hints in the plural) all of Novalis' works are devoted."[62] Indeed, Novalis remarks in his essay:

> Especially had the sacred tongue attracted them, which was once the resplendent link between the Royal Men and the Supernatural Regions and their inhabitants, and of which some few Words had remained, according to the report of many legends in the possession of some happy sages among our ancestors. Its enunciation was a miraculous chant whose sounds penetrated deep into the core of each Nature and analysed it. Each of its names seems the word of deliverance for the Soul of each natural Body. These vibrations evoked with generative force images of world phenomena, and one could say of them with truth that the life of the Universe was an eternal thousand-tongued discourse. For in these words all energies, all species of Activity, seemed to be united most incomprehensibly. To search for fragments of this language, or at least for some information concerning it had been the main object of their journey, and the call of Antiquity had led them to Saïs.[63]

The reference to the cult center of Saïs is noteworthy by virtue of the central role that the doctrine of the magical power of words played in the ancient Egyptian tradition. To

---

61 Novalis, *The Disciples at Saïs and Other Fragments*, trans. F.V.M.T. and U.C.B. [Una Birch] (London: Methuen & Co., 1903), 139. It is noteworthy that the Russian edition has "prophetic word" (*veshchee slovo*) in the place of "word of deliverance"; see Novalis, *Genrikh fon Ofterdingen*, trans. Vladimir Mikushevich (Moscow: Ladomir/Nauka, 2003).

62 Novalis, *Genrikh fon Ofterdingen*, trans. Vladimir Mikushevich (Moscow: Ladomir/Nauka, 2003), 245.

63 Novalis, *The Disciples at Saïs*, 139.

this high ontological status of language Novalis contrasted its modern deviation: "Speech is not understood, because speech does not understand itself, and will not be understood."[64] That language has been spoiled in the modern world is an indelible trait of all traditional linguistic teachings.

If Novalis stood at the origins of the German Romantic philosophy of language, then the crowning of this philosophy can in many respects be considered to have been Friedrich Schlegel's lecture course of 1829, cut short on account of his death. This philosopher proclaimed: "the view and assertion that God himself brought language to man, and taught it to him, cannot properly excite any opposition, in so far as all that is good, and man's best and original prerogatives, must in reason be derived from God as their first author."[65] Schlegel recognized that the primal language of Adam has disappeared and been forgotten by mankind:

> Of the language which may have belonged to the first man, before he lost his original power, perfections, and dignity, we are not, with our present organs and senses, in a capacity to form an idea. Indeed, we are no more able to do this than to judge of the nature of the language employed by the eternal spirits for the immediate interchange of their thoughts, which on the wings of light fly instantaneously through the wide expanse of heaven, or of those words, ineffable by any created being, which are uttered by the Deity in His inmost being...[66]

Schlegel was one of the first philosophers of language after de Maistre to make recourse to Traditionalist terminology: "I called language in general — as being the store-house of tradition, where it lives on from nation to nation, and as being the clew of material and spiritual connection which

---

64 Ibid., 92. The Russian edition (fn. 7) yields a different translation: "Language is not known because language cannot be known and does not wish to know." The word for "know" here, used in the sense of "being able to speak [a language]," is *vladet'*, which can also mean "to master."

65 Friedrich von Schlegel, *The Philosophy of Life and Philosophy of Language: In a Course of Lectures*, trans. A.J.W. Morrison (New York: Harper & Brothers Publishers, 1848), 386.

66 Ibid.

joins century to century — the common memory of the human race."[67]

Of fundamental importance is that Schlegel de facto professed the main thesis of Onomatodoxy on the ontological correspondence between name and phenomenon:

> That name by which each living creature is called by God, and designated from eternity, must embrace the sum of its inmost essence — the key of its existence — the reason and the explanation of its being. As, indeed, generally in the Holy Scriptures, so here, also, a high and holy import is combined with the notion of the name. Interpreted, then, by this profound sense and significance, this brief narrative, as I previously pointed out, conveys the idea that by this communication to man by God Himself, of the names of all living things, the former was set up as the lord and king of nature, and even as God's vicegerent over the terrestrial creation. And indeed this was his original destination. If, then, no existing speech or language can afford us an access to this veiled original, now become inaccessible to us, still the idea of one primary language, or, perhaps, of several such, is certainly any thing but devoid of an historical foundation.[68]

This thesis even fully corresponds to the level that modern comparative-historical linguistics would reach 200 years later. Schlegel's penetrating insight is explained in terms of the solid metaphysical basis of his deliberations:

> In this internal alphabet of the consciousness, however, there is one point on which a few words of further explanation are necessary to a right understanding. And it is one of the very highest consequence, since it concerns the final aim or even the first foundation, being nothing less than the center of life and perfection of unity. God, it is said, must form the key-stone in the arch of the whole consciousness; and no other real point of union can be found. But now God is without, or, rather, above, the human mind.[69]

---

67  Ibid., 397.

68  Ibid., 387.

69  Ibid., 444.

An echo of Novalis' ideas could also be heard in the early 20th century in the expression of Otto Weininger (a thinker who had a strong influence on Julius Evola):

> Every word was first created by *one* individual, by an individual above the average, and the same is still the case today... How else should it have been created? The primal words *were* "onomatopoeic" and they incorporated without the will of the speaker, through the sheer intensity of the specific excitement, something similar to the cause of the excitement, while all the other words were originally tropes, as it were, second-order onomatopoeias, metaphors, similes: all prose was once poetry.[70]

If we subtract from this quotation the fragments of the psychologism that was so typical of the turn of the 19th-20th centuries, then we have before us the earlier Romantic doctrine recast in new terminology.

The same can be traced in the English Romantic and neo-Romantic, Platonic philosophy of language ranging from Samuel Taylor Coleridge and George MacDonald to the Inklings circle in the 20th century. All four of the leading Inklings — J.R.R. Tolkien, C.S. Lewis, Charles Williams, and Owen Barfield — maintained that the "language of Adam" had a magical and poetic character and that personal names have a special, sacred status. Without dwelling on the details of their philosophy of language (for which we refer readers to the works of Thomas Shippey, Verlyn Flieger, and other scholars[71]), let us emphasize the key role that Barfield's books played in forming the coherence of other members of the circle's philosophy of language.[72] Extremely

---

70 Otto Weininger, *Sex and Character: An Investigation of Fundamental Principles*, trans. Ladislaus Löb (Bloomington: Indiana University Press, 2005), 120.

71 See Thomas Alan Shippey, *The Road to Middle-Earth* (London: HarperCollins, 2005); Thomas Alan Shippey, *J.R.R. Tolkien: Author of the Century* (London: HarperCollins, 2001); Verlyn Flieger, *Splintered Light: Logos and Language in Tolkien's World* (Kent, Ohio: Kent State University Press, 2002), especially 33-44 on the influence of Barfield's *Poetic Diction* on Tolkien's philosophy of language.

72 Owen Barfield, *Poetic Diction: A Study in Meaning* (Oxford: Barfield Press, 2010), 69-85; Owen Barfield, *Saving the Appearances: A Study in Idolatry* (Middletown: Wesleyan University Press, 1988), 28-35, 133-141, 167-173.

methodologically important is Barfield's doctrine of the cyclical path of mankind from "primordial participating" in things through names to falling away from them in the modern period down to the "final participation" in the new "golden age." Barfield did not hide his doctrine's indebtedness to the fragments of Novalis and Coleridge, and consequently also Hamann, Hemsterhuis, and Schlegel.

In France, the line of the Traditionalist philosophy of language can be traced from the 18th century (Charles de Brosses, Antoine de Rivarol, Joseph de Maistre) through the 19th century (Antoin Fabre d'Olivet, Claude Sosthène Grasset d'Orcet) and up to the time of René Guénon, the key figure of integral Traditionalism. Guénon's article on "The Lost Word and its Signs" emphasizes that at each stage in the degradation of mankind, sacred centers are destroyed and the sacred words connected with them are lost along with their scripts, libations, and sacred items, after which there emerge substitutes in secondary centers and so on down the chain.[73] In another article, Guénon clarified:

> Just as every secondary spiritual center is like an image of the supreme and primordial Center... so every sacred language — or 'hieratic' language if you will — can be regarded as an image or reflection of the original language, which is the sacred language par excellence; the latter is the 'Lost Word', or rather the word hidden for men of the 'dark age', just as the supreme Center has become invisible and inaccessible to them.[74]

Guénon fully shared the traditional, Platonic and Romantic notion of the symbolism and ontologism of the word: "If the Word is Thought inwardly and Word outwardly, and if the world is the effect of the Divine Word uttered at the beginning of time, then all of nature can be taken as a symbol of a supernatural reality."[75] From Guénon's point

---

[73] René Guénon, *Nauka bukv*, trans. Vladimir Bystrov (Saint Petersburg: Vladimir Dal', 2013), 15-27.

[74] René Guénon, *Symbols of Sacred Science*, trans. Henry D. Fohr (Hillsdale: Sophia Perennis, 2004), 44-45.

[75] Ibid., 9-10.

of view, traditional symbols are archetypes of the Incarnated Word: "The primordial Revelation, which, like Creation, is the work of the Word, is also incorporated so to speak in the symbols which have been transmitted from age to age ever since the origins of humanity."[76] Finally, inherent in Guénon's thought is the doctrine of the paradisal ("Syriac") language of Adam, that is the poetic, lyrical, rhythmic language of Earthly Paradise that we encounter among other philosophers of languages from different countries who came close to Traditionalism.[77] All of this allows us to inscribe Guénon's metaphysics of language into the comparative-historical context of the schools examined in this article.

Turning to the materials of 19th-20th-century Russian philosophy, we note that already in the 1860s, Alexander Potebnya modified the teachings of Wilhelm Humboldt and Friedrich Schlegel to finally formulate the doctrine of the inner form of the word, i.e., the conceptual morphological division of the word and, in the final analysis, its root and its origins in proto-language.[78] This achievement, alongside Potebnya's thesis that language and thinking are inseparable, would be actively employed by 20th-century philosophers (Gustav Shpet and Alexey Losev). In parallel, the Moscow Spiritual Academy hosted the development of a Platonic philosophy of language (Fedor Golubinsky, who was involved in Western esotericism and initiatic organizations, and Viktor Kudryavtsev-Platonov) which exerted a direct influence on Vladimir Solovyov, the founder of classical Russian philosophy. Solovyov wrote surprisingly little on the metaphysics of language, but he nevertheless devoted attention to it in his important, unfinished work, *Theoretical*

---

76  Ibid., 11.

77  René Guénon, *Nauka bukv*, 50. William Morris' remark that the Adamic lineage "comes from Damascus, from God," is another hint at "Syria" being associated with the earthly paradise in the secret language of medieval adepts.

78  Bezlepkin, *Filosofiia iazyka v Rossii*, 130-160.

*Philosophy*, in which he noted the ontological quality and authenticity of the word, and thereby rejected nominalism.[79]

The next stage in the metaphysics of language in Russia is associated with Fr. Pavel Florensky and his associates, Fr. Sergius Bulgakov and Monk Andronik (Alexey Losev). Having encountered the Onomatodoxy movement among not entirely literate monks at Athos and in the Caucasus, Florensky and his associates provided the latter with the missing philosophical basis and argumentatively developed the key theses of the movement, the foremost of which asserted that "the name of God is God himself, although God is not only the name."[80] All of the representatives of this school emphasized the magical character of names and referred to a paradisal language of the First Man before the Fall. Onomatodoxy exerted formidable influence on poets like Osip Mandelstam and Nikolai Gumilev, resounding in the latter's poems. Gumilev's poem "The Word" (*Slovo*) can be regarded as a definitive expression of the Platonic and, at the same time, Biblical-Christian faith in the power of the uttered word:

| В оный день, когда над миром новым / Бог склонял лицо свое, тогда / Солнце останавливали словом, / Словом разрушали города. <...> И в Евангелии от Иоанна / Сказано, что слово – это Бог | On the day when God turned His face down to the new world, The Sun was stopped by the Word, Cities were destroyed by the Word. [...] And in the Gospel of John, It is said that the Word is God. |

Bezlepkin remarks on the Traditionalist character of the metaphysics of Onomatodoxy:

> The Athos dispute over the being of God's name, and whether this sacred being affords grounds for asserting that the Divine name is God himself, was centered around the foremost problem of the philosophy of name: the ontological substantiation of the nature of the word. The whole system of philosophical constructions in

---

79 Ibid., 180-200.

80 Ibid., 201-206.

the works of Florensky, Bulgakov, and Losev is based on arguing for the being of the name and is permeated by the conviction that language is the kind of being that intrinsically entails the unity of entity and energy, the synthesis of apophaticism and symbolism, or, in other terms, ontologism and personalism.[81]

This topic is the subject of Sergius Bulgakov's work *The Philosophy of Name*, Losev's book with the same title as well as his article "Thing and Name," and Florensky's grandiose, unfinished work, *At the Watersheds of Thought*.[82] In the latter, following the Stoics and Romantics, Florensky highlighted several layers within the word ranging from the phonetic (the phoneme) to the semantic (the sememe), and concluded that "following terms and formulations, on the next rung of magical power stand personal names."[83] In this work, written in the early 1920s, Florensky reiterated his previous thesis on the magical nature of the word and the Christian understanding of the "grace of magic" that is primordially intrinsic to man. His disciple, Alexey Losev, authored a separate commentary on this point.[84]

Losev's philosophy of naming has been analysed in detail in a book by the Polish scholar and nun Teresa Obolevich, who examines Losev's view that the cosmos is an intellectual Name and that any name has a symbolic and mythical dimension.[85] Obolevich altogether convincingly discovers the origins of Onomatodoxy in the teachings of Plato and Dionysius the Areopagite. This frees us from the necessity of engaging in a separate excursion into Losev's

---

81  Ibid., 217.

82  Pavel Florensky, *Sochineniia v 4 t.*, t. 3(1), *U vodorazdelov mysli* (Moscow: Mysl', 2000), 104-372.

83  Ibid., 241.

84  Ibid., 249-251.

85  Tereza Obolevich, *Ot imiaslaviia k estetike. Kontesptsiia simvola Alekseia Loseva. Istoriko-filosofskoe issledovanie*, trans. Elena Tverdislova (Moscow: BBI, 2014), 205-300. See in Polish: Tereza Obolevich, *Od onomatodoksji do estetyki: Aleksego Łosewa koncepcja symbolu: Studium historyczno-filozoficzne* (Kraków: WAM, 2011).

works, which are a detailed development of Florensky's main ideas already presented *in nuce* in his early speech, "The Universal Human Roots of Idealism." Delivered to an assembly of the Moscow Spiritual Academy in 1909, this speech posed an unprecedented challenge among the church milieu, as it drew direct analogies to traditional beliefs in "pagan" shell. Let us dwell on Florensky's key theses:

> The word of the sorcerer is substantial. It is the thing itself. Therefore, it is always a name. The magic of effective action is the magic of words; the magic of words is the magic of names. The name of a thing is the substance of the thing. In the thing lives the name, the thing is created by the name. The thing enters into interaction with the name, the thing imitates the name. A thing has many different names, but their powers and depths vary. There are more or less peripheral names, and in knowing them accordingly, we more or less know the thing and are more or less powerful in relation to it. The impenetrability of a thing stems from inability to peer inside it, into its concealed core. The deeper we comprehend a thing, the more we can do so. Whoever knows the concealed names of things, for him there is nothing inviolable. Nothing can withstand the one who knows names, and the greater import, the greater strength, and the more significant the bearer of the name, the more powerful, deeper, and more significant is its name. And thus the more hidden it is. A man's personal name is an almost necessary means of leading and magically operating upon him. It is enough to say a name, and the volition is directed into the turning of the world. Sometimes this name-essence is described through enumerating attributes, just as the creational "Let there be!" is dismembered. Then we have an incantation, but its primary form is simply the name.[86]

The philosopher summarizes this passage in one phrasing; "Turning our attention to the philosophy of the name, I will only point out several of its features. Names express the essence of things... Knowing names yields knowledge of things; names are had by things by their nature, *physei*."[87]

---

[86] Pavel Florensky, *Stolp i utverzhdenie istiny: opyt pravoslavnoi teoditsei* (Moscow: AST, 2005), 21.

[87] Ibid., 22.

Here, Florensky refers to Plato's *Cratylus*, which contrasted the teaching that names are given by nature (*physei*) to the idea that names are granted by convention among people (*thesei*, as in the modern liberal theory). Florensky simultaneously appeals to the Stoic doctrine of the *logos spermatikos*, and even develops it to the point of a full homology between seed and the word as it is uttered:

> The ancient view of the name, like any direct view, sees in the name the very knot of being, its most deeply hidden nerve; the name, the ancients thought, is the essence, the spermatic *logos* of the object, the inner reason-essence, the substance of the thing. "The name is a certain true statement of what is inherent to the named thing," says Pachymeres, and further: "Names are declarations of the things underlying them." Therefore, a name is untranslatable into any other language, and in trying to translate it we deprive it of its inherently mysterious force. Having some kind of substantiality, "the name is recognized to be part of the very essence of the person who bears it, for it is through the name that we can transpose his personhood and, so to speak, resettle it elsewhere" (Tylor). A person without a name is not a person, for he lacks what is most essential... The name is the materialization, the clotting of blessed or occult forces, the mystical root by which man is connected to other worlds. Therefore, the name is the greatest and most sensitive part of man. But this is still too little said. The name is the very mystical personhood of man, his transcendental subject. But this, too, does not yet express the fullness of the reality of the name. "The name is a kind of essence that is comparatively independent of its bearer, but is of high import for his welfare and misfortune, as if parallel to the man himself; it at once presents its bearer and influences him" (Giesebrecht). It is not that there is a name with a person, but rather a person with a name. Name is a special essence, predominant above all others, that is living, that gives life, at times beneficent and at others harmful to man.[88]

Florensky highlights names as the supreme class of words that possess a special force:

---

88 Ibid., 23.

> Every name, even if it is not the name of a god, is essentially something divine. But especially divine are the names that belong to the great gods, theophoric names, i.e., god-bearing names which carry grace, transform their bearers, draw them along special paths, forge their fates, protect and guard them. Onomatophores are in essence theophores: name-bearers are god-bearers; in bearing god within them, they themselves are divine, they themselves are gods. The sharper the eyes perceive names (one's own and others'), the sharper is one's self-consciousness. In the ecstasy of creating with names, the theurge becomes aware of himself as god. The whole world is permeated by magical and mystical forces, and there is no thing that would not be entangled in the nets of the mage. The gods themselves possess all because they know the names of all; but no one knows their names. Know their names, and the gods will be at the disposal of the power of man.[89]

Referring to the traditions of so-called "primitive" or "archaic" peoples and ancient civilizations, the philosopher discloses the ineluctable magical force of a name in light of the ontological understanding of its connection with things themselves:

> The name appears twofold in relation to its bearer. First, it represents its bearer, indicating who someone is and then what he is. Secondly, it stands in a certain separation from its bearer, influencing him, at times as a sign of things to come, at times as a tool of slander, and finally as a tool of invocation. This influence can be good or bad, in accordance with the will of the bearer and what goes against it. But just as the name harbors mystical energies, so can these energies be used from the outside. For the sorcerer, the one who invokes another's name, it brings well-being and power when he conjures higher beings, but it can also cause his death. Hence the numerous taboos on names — prohibitions on uttering certain names. Such are the names of diseases, dark forces, or "obscene" words. One can call upon a name and perish upon failing to wield it. Finally, the almighty Name of God gives complete power over all of nature, because in the Name is revealed to the invoker His divine energy and divine assistance. Thus, "for primeval mankind, the name bears a demonic character" (Giesebrecht)…

---

89 Ibid., 24.

This belief is by no means limited to individual parts of the world, but rather can be discovered almost everywhere.[90]

Hence, Florensky cites the rites of naming known throughout the peoples of the world's traditional order, as well as rites of passage and initiation that involve changing or granting a name, which emphasizes the indivisibility of word and reality:

> The name of a thing is the idea-force-substance-word that establishes for such thing a unity of essence in the diversity of its manifestations, a unity that maintains and shapes the very being of the thing. In that this is so, it stands to reason that a change in the deepest essence is a change in the religious content of a thing, hence a change in the *situs* of a thing in the eternal order of the world beyond and a change in the name of a thing must necessarily correspond to each other, like an object and its shadow... For ancient consciousness, name and essence were not two mutually conditioning phenomena, but one, the name-essence, so changing one means, *ipsa re*, changing the other: after all, the name-essence is mysteriously present in the name-sound. The sound of a name is a transubstantiated sound, for in it the supersensible is corporeally and physically embodied. Therefore, it would be most correct to say that a change of essence-name is to be found in any change of sound-name.[91]

Let us note that this speech was uttered three years before the Onomatodoxy movement appeared; thus, Florensky's philosophy of language chronologically preceded this current, which emerged independently of his own philosophy and only subsequently merged with it.

Bezlepkin furnishes a detailed reconstruction of Florensky and Losev's metaphysics of language:

> A name is a kind of "semantic center" that presents itself to people through some kind of enigmatic essence. In thinking through names, they pose many questions which pertain to the essence of a person, pointing to something greater than the individual alone — the family, lineage, traditions. Proper names, in Florensky's opinion, manifest reality and are themselves reality.

---

90  Ibid., 25.

91  Ibid., 26.

Names form their bearers, every name is a special, closed world. They are invariants of personalities, they express personality types — the foremost lines of personal structure are in their individual totality, hence they contain predictions of fate and biography. Spiritual essence is comprehended by empathy and intuition, not statistics. "Thinking in names" is opposed to the rationalistic reflection that explains personal categories in terms of analytically enumerated attributes. These philosophers believe that another feature of the name, unlike the word, is its energy. The inner core of a name is shaped by a force, an energy, which the name acquires and is charged through its otherness among the various layers of being. According to Losev, possession of this energy makes a name active, effective, and capable of transforming and creating things through immaterial energy. Therefore, "knowing the correct names of things means being able to wield things. To be able to wield names means to think and operate magically."[92]

Hence, Bezlepkin presents what Bulgakov and Losev saw as the symbolism and apophatic nature of names:

> Losev posits that essence is completely inexpressible through verbal definitions, whereas symbol allows for the maximal possibility of expression. A name fully imprints the ineffability of its essence and, consequently, it is a symbol that points towards an inexhaustible source of ever new discoveries of essence. The symbolic character of the word already underscores that a given word is a name. Word-symbols are essentially, above all, names... In Losev, unlike in modern logical constructions, the subject of the name is the *eidos* (idea) of an entity, which is indivisible from its *eidos*. The naming, or energy, of an entity is the semantic picture that is born in the process of thinking of matter in terms of one or another subject.[93]

At the same time, this perspective observes an ontological hierarchy of the cosmos as presented in the traditional (and medieval) picture of the world, such as in Dionysius the Areopagite. In this hierarchy, *eidos*, symbol, and myth appear to be three rungs in the revelation of the essence

---

92  Bezlepkin, *Filosofiia iazyka v Rossii*, 211.
93  Ibid., 212.

of a thing, and above ordinary words stands the Name that has been forgotten by fallen man:

> Losev substantiated the being of a higher state of the word, of the knowledge and self-knowledge of man. On this level, he believes, there can be no talk of a multiplicity of essences, only one essence: the Primal Essence that is adequately replicated in other-being; in other words, there exists one Word, one Name. In a dialectical manner, the philosopher thus proceeds from physical subject back to that which dwells in the final intellectual depth of each and every name: the ontologically first Name, the Divine Word.[94]

This idea was subsequently developed in Russia by Alexander Bashlachev in the 1980s (his poem *The Name of Names*) and by Vladimir Mikushevich in the 2000s-2010s (the difference between the Word and the Unsaid). Even Fr. Georges Florovsky, who was hostile to Platonism and critical of Florensky, was compelled to acknowledge that Onomatodoxy was correct in its posing of the question of the philosophy of language and as a counterweight to positivism: "Modern linguistics is inclined to recognize these 'natural' names, i.e., to recognize the existence of a certain 'supra-language.' In general, modern philology puts forth a number of properly theological problems and it is aware of this, but in order to solve them, or even to pose them properly, one or another linguistics is completely insufficient."[95]

Recently, one of the greatest philosophers of language drawing on traditional metaphysical notions has been Vladimir Mikushevich (1936–2024), who developed his doctrine on the word and language over decades. In one of his early collections of aphorisms (*Fragments* in the spirit of Novalis), we encounter a definition of the essence of man through speech, word, and language:

> The Word is the only level of which man is worthy. Man partakes in nature just as the Word partakes in meaning. The

---

94 Ibid., 219.

95 Georgy Florovsky, *Pis'ma k bratu Antoniiu* (Moscow: Saint Tikhon›s Orthodox University of Humanities, 2021), 192-193.

Word figures only in triunity. The Word is born of the Whole that is not exhausted by Itself. The Whole in the Word: for the Word the Whole is Spirit. The Sign is assigned to the Whole, the Word is born by the Whole. Meaning is an object's participation in the Word.[96]

Contrasting the integral Word to its oblivion and to the positivist, nominalist substitution of numerous empty words, Mikushevich articulates:

> Not finding the Word, science substitutes meaning with denominating. In the Word is manifest the Whole as Whole. Symbol corresponds to the Whole, and in the Word is the Whole itself... Outside of the Word, an object is incomprehensible. To know means to name. Naming is approximate, like any sign; truth is only in the Word. False names do not take root, correct names become worn out... Wherever is the Whole, there is the Word. The Word has no need for meanings, meanings need the Word. The Word gives to every one of Its Own meanings an unrepeatable degree of original being in the hierarchy of the Whole.[97]

As we can see from even this small excerpt, Mikushevich continues the tradition of Onomatodoxy, concretizing and deepening its conclusions by erecting a hierarchy of words in language in terms of their participation in the primal and forgotten Word.

In the next volume of his philosophical fragments, this thinker once again brings into focus the coincidence between word and thing in the *eidos*, in the symbolic quality of the word:

> The meaning of being is truth: the coincidence of meaning and subject in the idea. The meaning of being is to give a sign: the relation of the individual to the Whole. The meaning of being is the Word: the Whole's bearing testimony of Itself... The Word is the symbol of symbols; the revelation in the Word is alike the Hidden that is behind the impossibility of a creature perceiving all of its meanings simultaneously. Hieroglyph points to the Word, the symbol draws towards the Word. The Word

---

96 Vladimir Mikushevich, *Probleski* (Tallinn: Alexandra, 1997), 111-112.
97 Ibid., 113.

is one and unique, while symbols differ... The world is a text, being is the Word. In every Word is the echo of prophecy... The source of myths is language. Myth is the spread of language over the universe. Myth is the Unsaid in language... The Word Itself bears witness to Itself and has no need for other witnesses. Language is founded on trust in the word, that is, in faith, without which he who speaks would not understand himself, not to mention others.[98]

Let us direct our attention here to how the author introduces two new metaphysical categories in his philosophy of language. The first of them is myth (which correspondences to Losev's doctrine): "Universalia are not as much idea as they are myth: the presence of a thing in being. Without myth, a thing does not exist."[99] The second is the Unsaid (a notion which comes close to the "Unmanifest" in René Guénon), which is also interpreted as the silence (Greek *hesychia*) that is above words: "The meaning of hesychasm lies in that Christ was silent on Mount Tabor, for the light of the Divine is the Word itself."[100]

Insofar as Mikushevich adheres to the Orthodox Christian tradition, he seeks, following his Russian predecessors, the grounds for his philosophy of language in the Gospel, while taking into account Heidegger's innovations in posing the question of language as the "house of Being":

> Preceding the sign is the Word which is confirmed by signs (Mark 16:20). The letter is at its core a sign... The shepherds wanted to see the "word that has been" (Luke 2:15)... The Word is designated by letters, while a hieroglyph is the designation of the Unsaid. If, according to Martin Heidegger, thinking is the dictation of the truth of Being, then myth is the very truth of Being insofar as man is capable of accommodating it.[101]

---

98 Vladimir Mikushevich, *Pazori* vol. 1 (Tallinn: Alexandra, 2007), 38, 55-56, 172, 202.

99 Vladimir Mikushevich, *Pazori* vol. 2, 184.

100 Ibid., 234.

101 Ibid., 10, 94.

Finally, in his last book, *Noetic Force* (*Umnaia sila*), Mikushevich presents the outcome of his philosophy of language, incorporating a summation of it in the introductory "theses on creationology":

> The interaction of the secret and the manifest shapes being; being's testimony of itself is the Word. The Word designates Being. The Word preserves the correlation between the secret and the manifest. We do not know all the meanings of the Word, for there is no number to these meanings. Not one word is the Word, but the Word can manifest in every word. Linguistics studies words, philosophy thinks the Word. We come to know the meanings of the Word in time. But by the time we learn them, some meanings have become obsolete, while others have discovered new meanings. The inexhaustibility of knowing is the Secret, and the testimony of the Secret is the Unsaid. The Unsaid leads to the Word, the Word is intuited in the Unsaid. The Unsaid is a series of meanings in time, the Word is the simultaneity of meanings. The Word is operative, which means that the Word wields energy; the energy of the Word is a noetic force. The Unsaid attracts, for it is in the Unsaid that the energy of the Word makes itself known. The Unsaid coincides with the Word until the Word becomes manifest in Revelation. Creation is the interaction of the Word and the Unsaid.[102]

Here, the philosopher uses the Losevian method of the "dialectics of myth," applying it to the interrelationship of the categories of Word and Unsaid, manifest and unmanifest (to use Guénonian terms). The concluding thesis that creativity is the manifestation of the interaction of these categories comes especially close to the British Inklings' philosophy of "sub-creation." Thus, Vladimir Mikushevich demonstrates the open, heuristic possibilities of the traditional philosophy of language even in our time.

Among Russian scholars, there persists the incorrect opinion that the Onomatodox philosophy of the word was known only in Russia. Nikolai Bezlepkin writes:

---

[102] Vladimir Mikushevich, *Umnaia sila: opyty po issledovaniiu tvorchestva* (Moscow: Iazyki slavianskoi kul'tury, 2022), 13.

> Establishing the relationship between name and thing appears to be the most important point exhibiting the fundamental difference in understanding cognition between Russian and Western European philosophy. As A.F. Zamaleev underscores, unlike the Western European tradition, which closed cognition within the boundaries of the mind, i.e., took it to be not an aspect of existence, but exclusively as logic and rationality, Russian philosophy has proceeded from the fact that being constitutes knowledge as its awareness.[103]

Without a doubt, this is not the case, for the tradition founded on the ontological and magical connection between word and thing, name and bearer, is, although first articulated by Plato, to be found among all the peoples of the world; moreover, it has been typical of Western thinkers of the Traditionalist camp to no lesser extent than among their Russian counterparts. It is no coincidence that Italian Evolian Traditionalists have long since put Evola, Florensky, and the British Inklings in one line, as their approaches to language and word do indeed coincide. Unfortunately, even in the 20th century specialists in different countries tended to be generally unfamiliar with other schools' philosophy of language, which led to a mutual ignorance of each other's works. Our present article attempts to partially fill this gap and draw attention to the isomorphic character of the philosophy of language common to the "Platonists" and Traditionalists of different countries.

This isomorphism is closely bound up with structuralism as a worldwide paradigm in the 20th century. This period saw a tendency towards connecting the traditional view of the historical development of language with the achievements of structuralism. This meant seeing the structures of languages, especially lingual universals, as the altogether stable and most ancient core, as living testimonies to the proto-language of the most ancient epochs. Consistently following this path meant transforming structuralism from a gnoseological theory into a metaphysical one. In the field of comparative

---

[103] Bezlepkin, *Filosofiia iazyka v Rossii*, 227.

religious studies, this step was taken by René Guénon and Mircea Eliade, who granted the most important structural elements of the world's religions the ontological status of the Primordial Tradition. In linguistics, a similar step was taken in several countries independently. In Germany, such was the case with studies in prehistory among a whole range of authors from Oswald Spengler to Herman Wirth. In England, analogous studies were undertaken by John Tolkien, an outstanding Indo-Europeanist and Germanist, whose materials on reconstructing the early Indo-European proto-language remain unpublished to this day. In Russia, the preconditions for the structuralist "injection" into the tree of traditional thought had already been prepared over the whole course of Russian intellectual history. Hence, at virtually the same time, the Russian emigration saw the release of the works of the Eurasianist linguists, Nikolai Trubetzkoy and Roman Jakobson (whose philosophical views have been described by Marlene Laruelle and Patrick Sériot as ontological structuralism), while at the same time, in the Soviet Union, Pavel Florensky and Alexey Losev succeeded in bringing together elements of structuralism and phenomenology with Neoplatonism, Orthodox metaphysics, and the heritage of the French Traditionalists (Florensky, for instance, was familiar with Fabre d'Olivet's esoteric works on proto-language).

In the late 20th century, the center of studies in the metaphysics of language passed to scholars engaged in comparative-historical linguistics and questions pertaining to the linguistic kinship between language families and macro-families. Closest of all to the Traditionalist and Platonic positions were the adepts of reconstructing the most ancient macro-families (the so-called "Moscow school," although it was represented in the US as well as around the world), who essentially upheld the Romantic view of language as a real "thing" that is genetically descendant from an ancestral language, whereas the majority of their

American "deconstructionist" opponents treated language as a structure that can easily and arbitrarily be transformed into another. The former ("Moscow") school's ontological approach to studying the distant kinship of languages bears traits of a certain "affinity" with Traditionalist views on the question, whereas the positions of the latter school of "skeptics" are essentially related to philosophical agnosticism, Kantianism, and Marrism, i.e., the extreme disintegration of the metaphysics of language. In the early 20th century, Vladimir Ern aptly called the first approach "realism" (in the medieval Scholastic sense) and the second "illusionism."

It is another matter that studying the proto-language of mankind from the Traditionalist standpoint lies, after all, on a different ontological level than that of academic comparative linguistics, even if it uses the latter's furnished results and developments. In reconstructing individual roots and morphemes, the linguistic school concerned with the distant kinship of languages does not formally claim or strive for any metaphysical explanation of phonetic composition — this is the domain of strictly Traditionalist studies in the spirit of "sacred science." On the other hand, it is no longer possible to approach the proto-language on the level of the early 20th century, ignoring the dictionaries and databases of proto-language families and macro-families (as is the case with archaeological and genetic data) reconstructed by scholars like Sergey Starostin. The unjustified mixing of these two levels of study, or the rejection of one or the other, leads to extremely undesired consequences. "Profane" science should not be discarded at the outset; rather, it should be ontologized and sacralized. Refusing to recognize the merits of the "Nostratic" school and refusing to use its reconstructions of the most ancient proto-languages, most importantly its method (the consistent development of which turns out to be the method of ontological structuralism), would mean rejecting the objective, rigorous, and accurate study of the proto-language of mankind in favor of subjective fantasies. Adopting the main methods and results of the theory of distant linguistic kinship, it becomes a matter of conceptualizing the reconstructed word forms by the methods of sacred science. At the same time, it bears remembering that the maximum that academic linguistics is capable of, both now and in the future, is reconstructing several dozen words and morphemes of a depth of no more than 40,000 years. However, between such an historically ascertainable state of language and Tradition's primordial-paradisal language of Adam, known also as the "language of the birds," the "language of the angels," the "language of Enoch," etc., there still lies a qualitative difference — an ontological chasm which can in no way be overcome by academic methods, but rather only by "magical" methods. We find indications of this among all of the 17th-20th-century thinkers mentioned in this article. It is likely that this is what Illich-Svitych wanted. But then a fully-fledged synthesis of academic comparative studies and Traditionalist "sacred science" would ultimately be manifest as the entelechy of their own inner development.

Thus, studying the etymology of words and names and tracing the fates of ancient proto-languages is, through the Traditionalist approach, not simply a fruit of historical curiosity or the discovery of our distant ancestors' picture of the world, but a relevant argument in "philosophical" (metaphysical) argumentation pertaining to some of the most important concepts in Tradition, such as the "forgotten word," the "language of Adam," and the "language of the birds." When it comes to employing language to the end of spiritual self-realization on the path of initiation, the imperative remains Illich-Svitych's iconic quatrain carved on his grave in the Nostratic language: "Language is a ford across the river of time. It leads us to the abode of those who have passed. He who fears deep waters cannot make his way there."

*Translated by Jafe Arnold*

# TELLING THE ORIGIN: LANGUAGE, MYTH, AND THE SACRED

## Andrea Scarabelli

As a product of the Origin – as anything else, after all – and by telling the Origin, language goes back to its own foundation, fares *à rebours* to earn a new founding essence. It rediscovers its own ancestral essence, which it had actually never abandoned, for such an essence is what constitutes its fundamental value. This was described by Attilio Mordini in his *Verità del linguaggio*, an attempt to investigate the linguistic device beyond those profane philosophies that reduce it to a neural impulse or make it a convention among others, in obedience to the miserable dogmas of "social contractualism." To the contrary, according to Mordini, "the human word has lost none of its evocative power for the very fact that it has remained traditional notwithstanding whatsoever degeneration."[104]

Obviously, the topic is extremely vast. How might we guarantee ourselves theoretical access to the bond that stands between the Origin and the narration of the Origin? We can, for example, begin from our own origin, on the individual level.

### We Are Born (at least) Thrice

Let's play a game: let's think about our birth – or, better, about all the times throughout our lives that we have imagined how we were born. At the age of four or

---
104 Attilio Mordini, *Verità del linguaggio* (Rome: Volpe, 1974), 25.

five we believe to have been brought to our parents by a stork. At the age of seven or eight, however, we discover that the stork is a fairy tale: the *truth* is that we were born from a tender embrace between our mother and father. We have no reason to doubt that this is the case – the narrative, after all, comes from our parents themselves. Only a handful of years later we come across yet another *truth*, this time having to do with genetic codes, ova and suchlike, which relegates the former two to mere stories. They are three *figures of narration*, three *narrative devices* that, one after the other in quick succession, establish our *being-in-the-world*, in the Heideggerian sense, placing its source in a very distant past. Although they are very different from each other, they have some common features: firstly, their truth value is *absolute until proven otherwise*, until it is ousted by the following one, without a solution of continuity; secondly, their truth value has a guarantor, a *fons* (there is no truth that is not posited by someone); thirdly – and this is the most important element – all three deal with the mystery of the Origin, rewritten from time to time starting from what we know about ourselves and the surrounding reality. In the first narrative device, we live in an enchanted world – therefore, birth is a fairy-tale event. In the second one, it is instead an emotional bond that is projected to the beginnings. In the last one, finally, it is science that sets the rules. In fact, we were born (at least) thrice – and, therefore, we existed three times: as fairy-tale creatures, as children, and as a conglomerate of atoms and molecules. When we speak about birth, we speak about ourselves. Language comes from the Origin and returns to the Origin, retelling it, mythically re-establishing it – here lies the meaning of what we usually call *sacrality*. More than being a conventional repertory of symbols, as linguistics likes to parrot, "mankind's word in its most intimate essence is divine".[105]

---

[105] Ibid, 22.

*Telling the Origin: Language, Myth, and the Sacred*

Besides, we could ask ourselves: what about birth itself? What a question! Since we are all within the scientific paradigm, *we know very well how things went* – at least until another hermeneutic figure comes along to overthrow the preceding one. Then we will be reborn for the umpteenth time, regenerating ourselves and opening the enigma of the Origin by means of the *clavis universalis* of language. Who knows, maybe the much-besmirched stork will still have a role to play. From a hermeneutic standpoint, *everything is possible*. And every Beginning is always a New Beginning. We will discuss this further.

In fact, this innocent game has been played since the beginning of time. Its name is *myth*, and it basically tells us two things: first of all, that the fundamental *quid* of mankind is narration, and that therefore it is impossible to think of man without language; secondarily, that concepts such as origin, birth, *telos*, and destination do not exist outside of this context. It is this device that *establishes* both the Origin and the subject who interprets it, two polarities which do not exist "in themselves" but are constituted as such always and only within their dynamic exchange. This narrative device, a middle term between subjectivism and objectivism, creator and destroyer of worlds, of universes of meaning, suggests something essential to us: we have actually never stopped creating myths, not even while lingering in a modernist paradigm which seems to want to present the bill to mythology once and for all, closing the era of the stork forever.

To pose the question of myth in these terms means to give up seeing language as an exclusively human factor. Over the last two or three centuries, opposing the *trahison des clercs* denounced by Julien Benda, it has been mostly poets who have become catalysts of such a *worldview*. One above all is Jorge Luis Borges, whose compositions are archetypal atlases containing the symbols of traditions far-off from each other in space as well as in time. The librarian from

Buenos Aires wrote: "I believe that the poet's work is of a passive nature; we receive mysterious gifts and try to give them a shape, but we always start with something which is different from ourselves, something that the ancients called the Muse, the Jews the Spirit, and Yeats the Great Memory. Our contemporary mythology prefers less beautiful names, such as subconsciousness, the collective unconscious, and so on, but it is always the same thing."[106]

The poetic word is not an arbitrary summation of symbols, but the translation into everyday language of a repertory of symbols which are rooted in Tradition. Borges himself expressed this very eloquently in one of his poems:

> Like alchemists
> who looked for the philosopher's stone
> in elusive quicksilver,
> I shall make ordinary words
> – the marked cards of the sharper, the people's coinage –
> yield up the magic which was theirs
> when Thor was inspiration and eruption,
> thunder and worship.
> In the wording of the day,
> I in my turn will say eternal things.[107]

To understand how much myth – and the sacred space that it establishes – is present today, perhaps it would be beneficial to return to its fundamental components with reference to the reflections of a whole series of authors coming above all from philosophy, anthropology, and the history of religions. A comparison of their fundamental positions on the subject will allow us to identify the structural and nuclear constituents of what may be defined as the *mythographic device*.

---

[106] Jorge Luis Borges and Osvaldo Ferrari, *Conversazioni*, vol. I, ed. Francesco Tentori Montalto (Milan: Bompiani, 2011), 219.

[107] Jorge Luis Borges, *Browning decide di essere poeta*, in *Opere*, vol. II, ed. Hado Lyria and Domenico Porzio (Milan: Mondadori, 1986), 669.

## The Secret of a Stork

What do myths speak of? Of what is primordial, of what is the "primal-in-order": in the words of Carl Gustav Jung and Károly Kerényi, myth speaks "of the origins or at least of what is original."[108] Of birth, in short: all myths open with theogonies and cosmogonies, i.e., re-readings of an Origin *removed* from understanding and, precisely for this reason, *open* to narration. As a necessary condition of our *being-in-the-world* as mythopoetic entities, the Origin never ceases to enshroud itself in an unfathomable mystery, the nature of which is not chronological but *ontological*. The custody of this mystery is tradition, and "language is tradition,"[109] as the aforementioned Mordini wrote in unequivocal terms.

The time of which mythographic language speaks is not the linear or "Oedipal" one, but is *qualitatively* different; it is the *illud tempus*[110] or fundamental time, never restricted to the beginning of days but re-enactable through ritual and the sacred repetition of the Origin itself: "The Primordial," writes Alain de Benoist, is not what "is situated in a past which comes before history," but rather that which "may always open itself up in the present moment precisely because it does not belong to the order of human temporality."[111]

In the world of myth, the origin is thought of in a very peculiar way; unknowable from a chronological standpoint, it may nonetheless open itself up ontologically at any moment, inaugurating, as the historian of religions Joseph

---

108 Carl Gustav Jung and Károly Kerényi, *Prolegomeni allo studio scientifico della mitologia*, trans. Angelo Brelich (Turin: Bollati Boringhieri, 1972), 21.

109 Mordini, *Verità del linguaggio*, 51.

110 Cf. Mircea Eliade, *Trattato di storia delle religioni*, ed. Pietro Angelini (Turin: Bollati Boringhieri, 1999).

111 Alain de Benoist, *L'impero interiore*, trans. Debora Spini and Marco Tarchi (Florence: Ponte alle Grazie, 1996), 21.

Campbell wrote, a *sacred* and *ritual* temporality in the name of eternity, neither meant as an absolute future nor as something torn off from time: "Eternity is that dimension of here and now that all thinking in temporal terms cuts off."[112] If investigated chronologically, however, it remains unknowable, going on to constitute the Great Immemorial. It may indeed be narrated but it will always escape our gaze, exactly like – to use two famous traditional metaphors – the hub of the wheel, which, despite being the efficient and final cause (reminiscent of Dante's "love that moves the Sun and the other stars"), does not participate in the movement, or like the hinge of the door, which remains still even when the door slams.

The absolute Origin, so to speak, does not participate in the above-described man-birth dialectic, which does not involve man and birth "in themselves" but the *narration* of birth and the *narration* of the here and now. The pristine Origin remains unknowable. It is not by happenstance that the mythographies of every latitude and longitude of the world open with an abrupt fracture, the breaking of a stasis, an abysmal interruption of something which existed before. Such a rift begets a polarisation, yielding, as *caput mortuum*, a series of pairs of opposites whose dynamic exchange and interrelation – which is symbolic before being material – constitutes what we usually define as "world history." At that point, the Origin falls silent, supplanted by a "second birth," which is the raw material of myth. And also of language, which may however be revived by those who, in the wretchedness of the present, are not forgetful of its holy roots: "The word is always rich in its evocative power, and the wiseman who treads the traditional path can always make this power re-emerge within himself

---

[112] Joseph Campbell, *Il potere del mito*, trans. Agnese Grieco and Vittorio Lingiardi (Vicenza : Neri Pozza, 2012), 115. [Joseph Campbell with Bill Moyers, *The Power of Myth* (New York: Anchor Books, 1991)].

and open himself up to the primitive efficiency of sacred language."[113]

Historians of religion have referred to this "second birth" in various ways. According to Campbell, for example, myth is not the "ultimate truth" about things (if this expression means anything) but "the penultimate truth – penultimate because the ultimate cannot be put into words. It is beyond words, beyond images, beyond that bounding rim of the Buddhist Wheel of Becoming"; hence it is no coincidence that, in order to define it, the historian of religions uses the image of the wheel, which we mentioned earlier, and then concludes: "Mythology pitches the mind beyond that rim, to what can be known but not told."[114] Analogically, the aforementioned Jung and Kerényi distinguish a first phase of the original reality from a second one (which constitutes the subject of the history of religions), making appropriate distinctions between the two: "The *first* phase, in truth, is not yet a phase. It is the primordial basis, the beginning, the origin as the first spring and the first rising, that is to say, precisely what all mythologies speak about in the language of the *second* phase."[115] It is indeed possible to speak about it, after all, but *always and only* within a different paradigm.

Campbell's "ultimate truth" and Jung and Kerényi's first phase hint to the genetic whereabouts of myth and language, to which both would like to go back. And so, the impossibility of such a return is what gives rise, in a hermeneutic and dynamic way, to the mythographic device, one of whose fundamental elements is *oblivion*. This is why the ancient world did not see truth as an exact representation of reality but as *a-letheia*, as the "undoing" of oblivion, as anamnesis.

---

113 Mordini, *Verità del linguaggio*, 114.
114 Campbell, *Il potere del mito*, 249-250; [Campbell, *The Power of Myth*].
115 Jung and Kerényi, *Prolegomeni allo studio scientifico della mitologia*, 40.

*Telling the Origin: Language, Myth, and the Sacred*

## The *Logos* of *Mythos*

Walter Otto wrote that the language of myth has to do neither with the scientific representation of reality nor with a particularly developed imagination; it is neither subjective production nor mimetic faculty, but translates "the very revelation of Being": it "grips man in his entirety and shapes his existential attitude."[116] Mircea Eliade moves within the same horizon, writing that, far from bending to other figures of truth, "myth establishes absolute truth," constituting "the exemplary model not only of rites, but also of any significant human activity,"[117] from economics to the management of daily affairs, from sexuality to politics. An approach that starts from an idea of totality, so to speak, "more total" than that of the paradigm to which it is usually opposed, that is, *logos*.

*Mythos* and *logos*, language and Origin, are ways of participating in the game of the world from many outlooks which are irreducible to a common denominator and yet bound to the same genetic location, if it is true that, as already highlighted on various occasions, "a language is a tradition, a way of feeling reality, not an arbitrary repertory of symbols."[118] Their opposition is judged absolute only within a paradigm that has distorted them both: "*Mythos* and *logos* are not, as our current historians of philosophy claim, placed into opposition by philosophy as such," Heidegger says, for their Manichaean opposition happens only within a space "where neither *mythos* nor *logos* can keep to their original nature."[119] At that point, the language of *mythos* is

---

116 Walter Friedrich Otto, *Essais sur le mythe* (Paris: Allia, 2017), 134.

117 Mircea Eliade, *La prova del labirinto*, trans. Massimo Giacometti (Milan: Jaca Book, 2002), 142.

118 Jorge Luis Borges, *Prologo* to *L'oro delle tigri*, in *Opere*, vol. II, 452.

119 Martin Heidegger, *Che cosa significa pensare*, trans. Gianni Vattimo (Milan: SugarCo, 1978), 97; [Martin Heidegger, *What Is Called Thinking?*, trans. J. Glenn Gray (New York: Harper Perennial, 2004), 10].

## Telling the Origin: Language, Myth, and the Sacred

reduced to a more or less plausible story, to a fable useful only to support a reason, at the same time taking on the characteristics of a defeated enemy, *becoming mythological*, proposing itself as the only narrative device in a world that has now dismissed myths forever, reducing them to silence. What ensues is the irreparable rift denounced in *Verità del linguaggio*: "Where the fire of the word is extinguished and the tradition of mankind is interrupted, the life of the spirit is quenched or falls asleep, the oneness of life in its multiple manifestation is quenched or falls asleep."[120]

Thus we enter the domain of philosophy, initially hybrid and shadowy, and later increasingly closed into a system which cuts ties with the common origin about which Heidegger spoke. And yet, while this happens, the feeling of the loss of something fundamental arises, and we discover that "what precedes philosophy, the trunk for which tradition uses the name of 'wisdom' and from which this soon-withered bud sprouts, is for us, very remote descendants – according to a paradoxical inversion of time – more vital than philosophy itself."[121] Once bridges have been burnt, a hieratic difference emerges between *logos* based on *de-monstration* (i.e., mediate showing) and *mythos* founded on *monstration* (i.e., immediate showing), on adherence to the phenomenon (*phainomai*, what "shows itself," what opens itself up to light, what is *e-vident*, i.e., outwardly seeable). It has not only the power to explain, but also the power to *clarify*, not by doubling the world in theories or analyses, but by becoming one with it: "The fluidity of the primordial mythological state presupposes a unity with the world, a complete interpenetration with its aspects."[122] According to Otto, even psychological interpretations are not able to do justice to this peculiarity of it: "Myth is not born from

---
120 Mordini, *Verità del linguaggio*, 56.
121 Giorgio Colli, *La nascita della filosofia* (Milan: Adelphi, 1975), 116.
122 Jung and Kerényi, *Prolegomeni allo studio scientifico della mitologia*, 143.

the dreams of the psyche, but from the lucid gaze of the spirit open to the being of things."[123]

Let us turn back to the game with which we began our rapid survey of language's expression of the Origin. Saying that one was born from a stork or from a combination of chromosomes is not neutral, but has several backlashes on the subjective level. To an origin (past) corresponds an identity (present). The same happens in the case of *mythos* and *logos*, with their respective languages: if the latter crystallises reality in a *world picture*[124], the former grasps its metamorphic, agonal and tragic essence, in a perpetual distancing and return to the beginning, through the mechanism of repetition, of the calendar. In this worldview, man is not subject *to* history but is the subject *of* history: "archaic man certainly has the right to consider himself more creative than modern man, who sees himself as creative only in respect to history. Every year, that is, archaic man takes part in the repetition of the cosmogony, the creative act *par excellence*."[125] Archetypal reiteration and the new year, repetition and variation on a theme: the truth of mythical language is contained in the mystery of music. And the same goes for poetry. If, as Borges said, "the word was in the beginning a magical symbol that the wear and tear of time has depreciated," then it is up to the poet "to give back to the word, at least partially, its very first and now hidden virtue."[126] For the Argentinian writer this was a real obsession, so much so that elsewhere he inspiredly

---

123 Walter Friedrich Otto, *Theophania. Lo spirito della religione greca antica*, ed. Alberto Caracciolo (Genoa: Il Nuovo Melangolo, 1996), 73.

124 Cf. Martin Heidegger, *L'epoca dell'immagine del mondo*, in idem, *Sentieri interrotti*, ed. Pietro Chiodi (Florence: La Nuova Italia, 1998); [Martin Heidegger, "The Age of the World Picture" in idem, *Off the Beaten Track*, trans./ed. Julian Young and Kenneth Haynes (Cambridge: Cambridge University Press, 2002)].

125 Mircea Eliade, *Il mito dell'eterno ritorno*, trans. Giovanni Cantoni (Milan: Rusconi, 1975), 113; [Mircea Eliade, *Cosmos and History: The Myth of the Eternal Return*, trans. Willard R. Trask (New York: Harper Torchbooks, 1959), 158].

126 Jorge Luis Borges, "Prologo" to *La rosa profonda* in *Opere*, vol. II, 661.

wrote: "The roots of language are irrational and of a magical nature. [...] Poetry wants to return to that ancient magic. Without fixed rules, it makes its way in a hesitant, daring way, as if moving in darkness. Poetry is a mysterious chess, whose chessboard and whose pieces change as in a dream and over which I shall be gazing after I am dead."[127]

In the paradigm of *logos*, however, things change radically, both in relation to the subject and to the experience of truth: after all, as already said, the subject *consists* in *its* truth. The *aletheia* of myth is overwhelmed by the notorious *adaequatio rei et intellectus*. If the language of the former sees man as actively taking role in the unveiling (*aletheia*)[128], the latter promotes a subject based on the Cartesian image of the world, which opposes *res cogitans* and *res extensa* as ultimate terms – with theism as a guarantor, notwithstanding those who believe that modernity is atheist – irreducible to any further decomposition. There is an innerness, the rational-volitional subject, contrasted with an outerness, an object opposed to it (*ob-jectum*; *Gegen-stand*) whose main attribute is extension. The flow of space-time is crystallised, and the "true language" – the practice of "telling the truth" – no longer requires "participation" in the unveiling, but rather the right accordance (*adaequatio*) between *res cogitans* and *res extensa*. The next step will be, needless to say, the subjecting of the *res extensa* to the work of the *res cogitans*, its transformation into a *Gestell*, a lifeless structure and a resource to be exploited[129], under the banner of an unparalleled will to power.

---

127 Jorge Luis Borges, "*Prologo*" to *L'altro, lo stesso* in *Opere*, vol. II, 9. For an anagogical reading of poetry see, amongst many others, Guido De Giorgio, *Dio e il Poeta* (Milan: La Queste, 1985).

128 Cf. Martin Heidegger, "*La dottrina platonica della verità*" in idem, *Segnavia*, ed. Franco Volpi (Milan: Adelphi, 1987).

129 Cf. Martin Heidegger, "*La questione della tecnica*" in idem, *Saggi e discorsi*, ed. Gianni Vattimo (Milan: Mursia, 1976); [Martin Heidegger, *The Question Concerning Technology and Other Essays*, trans. William Lovitt (New York: Harper Perennial, 2013).

## The Midnight Sun – Telling Myth in Modernity

The idea of the shared origin of *mythos* and *logos*, with their respective languages, often yields unexpected outcomes, one of which is the proliferation of studies on myth precisely in the era of the "disenchantment (*Entzauberung*) of the world" of which Max Weber spoke.[130] In the heart of modernity, which relegates everything that is not enlightened by Reason to obscurantist barbarism, we witness a second birth of myth – and, *therefore*, of man – in authors who intend to look out onto that sunken world in a free and non-ideological manner. Here myth appears, *for the first time*, as an object of study, dissectable and decomposable. From this standpoint, ancient myths exist *only* in the fantasy of modern men, who subject them to the norms of the *logos*, thereby distorting them.

By increasingly materialising, modernity turns to once again to become mythographic. Its crisis accelerates this process, bringing the language of myth "to the surface, like treasures, [...] when time falters from its foundations, under the nightmare of an extreme danger."[131] Then it is studied, but no longer "acted out." We speak about it continuously, moving away from its original and auroral horizon: *telling myth – as well as the sacred – is possible only on the condition of having left its fundamental dimension*, which "has only become intellectually familiar to us to the extent that it has also become existentially foreign to us."[132]

It is, moreover, inevitable that an era of crisis – and every crisis has repercussions on language, mutilating its ability to shape reality – should return to the track of *mythographic speech*, especially considering the fact that it has its roots in mankind itself. This was noticed by

---

130 Cf. Max Weber, *La scienza come vocazione e altri testi di etica e scienza sociale*, ed. Pietro Di Giorgi (Milan: Franco Angeli, 1996).

131 Ernst Jünger, *Il trattato del ribelle*, trans. Francesco Bovoli (Milan: Adelphi, 2001), 60.

132 de Benoist, *L'impero interiore*, 76; [de Benoist, *Empire of Myth*, 77].

Mordini, according to whom "at the origin of every living language there is a religious tradition. This proves once again, in our opinion, that language cannot be merely a human invention."[133] Jean-Jacques Wunenburger echoed this in affirming that the mythographic paradigm conveys an image of the world not bound to sensitivity or rationality, but qualitatively different. In its domains, according to the French philosopher, "there really exists a symbolic insight, a supersensory perception, which has as its correlative a supersensory reality."[134] Man knows – and therefore *tells* – reality to the extent that he develops himself in an operational and transformative perspective. The conquest of the Self is equivalent to knowledge of the world, according to an image of myth *sub specie interioritatis* also shared by Campbell, in which language once again plays an essential role: "myths are metaphorical of spiritual potentiality in the human being, and the same powers that animate our life animate the life of the world."[135] The *living words* of myth do not allude to the Self *or* to the world, but to *both* polarities, captured in a dynamic and *poietic* game incapable of polarising itself into oppositions, referring to specific "planes of consciousness": "There is the plane of consciousness where you can identify yourself with that which transcends pairs of opposites."[136]

There is no heaven or hell that does not have a corresponding state of the Ego which may be reached through transformation – all the testimonies which we have briefly recalled herein agree on this. This is why myth thwarts the claustrophobic notion of the "historical man" with an image of man which has never been decided once and for all, that of a man who can realise himself

---

133 Mordini, *Verità del linguaggio*, 113.

134 Jean-Jacques Wunenburger, *La vita delle immagini* (Milan-Udine: Mimesis, 2008), 96.

135 Campbell, *Il potere del mito*, 54; [Campbell, *The Power of Myth*].

136 Ibid, 84.

in different directions. Myth tells – or rather, *sings*, like the severed head of Orpheus – of a man open to the world and to himself – *as above, so below*. A man whom *logos*, after having severed its own mythographic origin, took charge of extinguishing. Only at that point did the discourse on myth and the sacred begin in the sense of recounting them. All that remained was the golden mark of etymology, combined with the archetypal dimension of the word, to recall the existence of a different type of language: "If the etymology of words is their history, the symbolic meaning is their soul. [...] To resort to etymology is in a certain way to approach the oneness from which words branch out."[137]

In the Midnight of History (Parvulesco), when traditional language is silenced, mythology emerges as an *object*, a standstill of authentic myth, which sinks like the lost continent of Atlantis. Then, however, it will return, reminding us of the possibility to make up our minds and decide upon ourselves and the world, and leaving us with the only prospect of starting over again, retelling a thousand and one times that original laceration, in the awareness that "thanks to myth, man keeps himself at the point where mankind and Being meet." By revisiting its narrative figures, man "[acquires the power] to appropriate for himself the very meaning of his being and to lift himself up to the level where he goes beyond himself... The man who 'recovers' the original myth installs himself back in himself. He returns to the source for a new beginning."[138] He returns to speak, as is natural, the Language of Beginnings.

*Translated by U.X.A. and Jafe Arnold*

---

[137] Mordini, *Verità del linguaggio*, 23-24.

[138] de Benoist, *L'impero interiore*, 29; [de Benoist, *Empire of Myth*, 24].

# A FEW REMARKS ON THE SPIRITUAL IMPORTANCE OF LANGUAGES

## Tamás Bencze

The first and most direct experience is that *I am*. With careful and intuitive observation, I become aware that I am not fully and absolutely myself. The experience is real, but not complete, and the fullness is substituted by a dreamlike condition; something illusory takes the place of completeness. Instead of entirety, there is something finite; totality is replaced by the state of being deprived, the absolute is transmuted into the relative, being *in sē* is converted into being *in aliō*, the autonomous has been modified into something changeable, reflected, and mortal. This being so, I have the possibility of leading myself back to the original state. Leading myself back to the original state means leading *being* back to the original state. When my spiritual realisation is accomplished, being is Awakened. To reach this Aim, I need more and more knowledge, more and more power. This is the real and true *causātiō* of dealing with any topic, such as thinking, language, and languages.

Thinking about Tradition and Metaphysics is always more than fiddling with serious matters and toying with important ideas. It is never just an encyclopaedic enumeration; it is no mere cataloguing of ideas or describing the facts of the world in scientific fashion. It is rather a series of acts of power and *mageia*, it is transcending life and death, it is fighting against weakness, demons, bonds, habits, fear, wrong views, restlessness, emotionality, and other kinds of dark forces which want to block the Light of the Centre and keep the individual on the plane of being that is only terrestrial, permeated with the subterrestrial. And the fight is getting tougher and tougher.

As the *kali-yuga* — the Dark Age — is reaching its final phases, the question of language, first and foremost, arises as the *use* and *misuse* of spoken and written words. What is involved in the latter aspect goes well beyond such phenomena as "abusive language" or the "problems of the programming language of humanoid robotics." In our times, there seem to exist two kinds of clearly distinguishable races that do not "speak the same language" at all.

The misuse of language is connected with the race which can be characterised by the term *deorsum cōgitāre*, "to think downwards" — this means the complete lack of the natural ability to do the *askēsis* of thinking in the true sense of the word. As thinking is the primary function of consciousness today, it is the individual experience of involution and degression, the individual who with the totality of his being keeps thinking and living downwards into his subhuman states. This is the consequence of the fact that a representative of this race can no longer experience himself as himself, in his own relation, he can no longer experience himself *secundum se*, "according to himself," he can only do so *secundum quid*, "according to something"; he needs something else for his self-experience, so that he can point to himself as the subject of that something else: this something else is, on the one hand, the functions and actions of consciousness connected with the human form of being, and, on the other hand, objective reality as the existential support of this secondary experience.

"Thinking downwards" will obviously lead to *deorsum vīvere*, to "living downwards" — this refers to a life occupied solely by trivial actions, without acts in the Guénonian sense of the words; it refers to the existence of *rhetoric* and the lack of *persuasion* (Michelstaedter); it is *ontic* rather than

## A Few Remarks on the Spiritual Importance of Languages

*ontological* (Heidegger); a life that is modern — changing according to each and every current of mania — and not traditional; a life ruled by *Anātmā*, the real principle (*Ātmā*) modified and of reduced intensity; it is the life of the *paśu*, a life analogous with that of a sacrificial animal, a life that totally lacks the principle of *Paśu-Pati*, that is the Lord of *Paśu*, who is *Śiva*.

Life is multi-layered, and the principle of *bios*, the principle of life, includes several principles: first, the principle of — as Georg Simmel puts it — *Mehr-Leben*, "more of life." Life, when it is truly itself, can be grasped as part of a current that exists both before and after life, characterised by continuous regeneration, which gives way to a vitality: in life with some kind of form. In the human form of existence, for example, an individual wants to live more fully, ever more intensely and extensively, ever more vividly, more beautifully and more luminously. At the same time, life is constantly seeking to overflow itself, and this has two directions and two qualities: on the one hand, it sinks into decline, ageing and death. On the other hand, life has the possibility of freeing itself from itself by aiming at terrains *above* itself, leaving what is more of life and reaching what is more than life, *Mehr-als-Leben*. This is the transcendent affirmation of life that is foreign to the representatives of *deorsum cōgitāre* and *deorsum vīvere*.

The type of man in question keeps indulging in speaking without saying anything essential. He speaks in this manner and speaks a lot. He does not seem to be aware of the biblical formula, "let thy words be few, for [...] a fool's voice is known by multitude of words,"[139] which also reflects the fact that this type has been here for a long time now.

Heidegger is lenient in describing "idle talk" (*das Gerede*) as characterized by uprooted understanding (*entwurzeltes*

---

139 Ecclesiastes 5:2-3.

*Verständnis*) and groundlessness (*Bodenlosigkeit*).¹⁴⁰ He also says, however, that

> discourse is what it is, i.e., it forms a sphere of *understandability*, whenever there is a γένεσις of a σύμβολον, whenever a *being held together* occurs in which there also lies an *agreement*. Discourse and word are to be found only in the occurrence of the symbol, whenever and to the extent that an agreement and a holding together occur... What Aristotle sees quite obscurely under the title σύμβολον, [what he] sees only approximately, and without any explication, in looking at it quite ingeniously, is nothing other than what we today call *transcendence*. There is language [*es gibt Sprache*] only in the case of a being that by its essence transcends.¹⁴¹

This type of race is completely blind to anything metaphysical. The Buddha also made such a distinction: "And I saw sentient beings with little dust in their eyes, and some with much dust in their eyes; with keen faculties and with weak faculties, with good qualities and with bad qualities, easy to teach and hard to teach. And some of them lived seeing the danger in the fault to do with the next world, while others did not."¹⁴²

There is a clear and self-evident correspondence between this race and the diminishing light of truth. Julius Evola writes that "the evasive breed of man displays a natural tendency towards lying, often gratuitously so, for no real reason."¹⁴³ Otto Weininger connects lying to the lack of ability to remember and the incapacity for truth. "Liars have a bad memory," he says, or in more serious

---

140 Martin Heidegger, *Sein und Zeit* §35.

141 Martin Heidegger, *Die Grundbegriffe der Metaphysik. Welt – Endlichkeit – Einsamkeit*, 3. Auflage (Frankfurt am Main: Vittorio Klostermann, 2004); idem, *The Fundamental Concepts of Metaphysics: World, Finitude, Solitude*, trans. William McNeill and Nicholas Walker (Bloomington: Indiana University Press, 1995), 446-447.

142 *Majjhima Nikāya*, 26.

143 Julius Evola, "La razza dell'uomo sfuggente" in *L'arco e la clava* (Rome: Edizioni Mediterranee, 2000); idem, "The Breed of the Evasive Man" in *The Bow and the Club*, trans. Sergio Knipe (London: Arktos, 2018), 31.

## A Few Remarks on the Spiritual Importance of Languages

cases they "nearly 'have no memory' at all."[144] What is more, they can lie while they think they are telling the truth, and the more faithfully they "believe to hold themselves to the truth, the deeper their mendaciousness sits."[145] "The future is not yet true," he adds later, yet "the past is true. The lie is a will to exert power over the past."[146]

Truth, in Latin *vēritās*, is *alētheia* in Greek, which shows the hidden, concealed, covered aspect of truth, something that is related to the *sterēsis* of Aristotle, something one is deprived of. "Truth itself is something stolen... it ultimately demands the engagement of man as a whole,"[147] Heidegger says, and adds that statements are true if they are discovering (*entdeckend*) and false if they are covering over (*verdeckend*).[148]

According to the Gospel, *unum est necessarium*, one thing is needed only: Truth. And when Truth arrives in the home of Martha and Mary, Martha abandons herself to culinary activities, while Mary sits down to focus. Horizontal activities and "small talk" conceal the truth, whereas vertical acts and the spiritual use of language reveal it.[149]

So, we can say that it is he who remembers – remembers his own centrality, remembers his origin – lives in the spirit of truth; and, also, anything that has sunk into oblivion and remains in the waters of forgetfulness cannot be true. The Sanskrit word for truth is *satya*, which is related to *Sat*, "being" and "essence," which refers to the fact that what is not essential is not true, and discourse neglecting essential problems is also untrue.

---

144 Otto Weininger, *Sex and Character*, trans. Robert Willis, Chapter 6.

145 Ibid., Chapter 12.

146 Otto Weininger, *On Last Things*, trans. Steven Burns (Lewiston, Queenston and Lampeter: Edwin Mellen Press, 2001), 89.

147 Heidegger, *Die Grundbegriffe der Metaphysik*, §8c.

148 Heidegger, *Sein und Zeit*, § 44b.

149 Cf. Luke 10: 38-42.

## A Few Remarks on the Spiritual Importance of Languages

Let us note here in passing that the Latin word *moralis* was coined by Cicero from the Greek *ēthikós*, but the two terms are used differently: morals are related to customs, to the specific habits and characteristics of an *ethnos*, the genius, the regulating spirit of a people, which prevails over a long period of time and in a particular place. While *ethics* is related to philosophy, whose name — and origin — is *ēthike philosophia* in Greek, or "moral philosophy" in English. In the context of *ēthike philosophia*, it should be mentioned that it is impossible to give any ethics or morality an absolute philosophical foundation, because, by not linking it to metaphysical principles, morality can only have a relative, social significance and cannot respond to the criticisms that come from an age in which man is increasingly detached from the transcendent, in which all values are collapsing. To shed the fullest light on this issue, reference should be made to *yōga*, the *aṅga*s or "members" of the classical practice circles of *rāja yōga*, and especially to the first two. *Yama* means cessation; it refers to that which is to be ceased. *Niyama* refers to what is not to be eliminated, but rather to be strengthened. What the *yama* and *niyama* prescribe is not a prohibition, not a duty, not an obligation. Observance of moral and ethical rules is not meritorious in terms of spiritual realisation. No one anywhere in the world is credited with avoiding something or doing something according to *yama* and *niyama*. Adherence to moral and ethical rules is relevant, but it is raised differently here. This importance is rather conceived and understood in the sense of raising awareness of dangers. Just as the buoy on the water indicates the obstacle, the dangerous area, so all the *upāṅga*s or lower members of *yama* and *niyama* indicate the danger for the one who is engaged in realisation, calling his attention to increased caution and concentration.

The proper use of language pertains to the race which can be described by the term *sursum cōgitāre*, "thinking upwards." To think upwards or towards the Centre, to use the cognitive-mental powers (*shakti*) to get back to the Origin and never to think and live towards the periphery without ruling over the downward movement, and never to perform *katabasis* or *dēscēnsiō* without total control over the act. This means engaging in *jñāna tapas*, the *askēsis* of thinking in the truest sense of the word. The right and true use of language and thinking involves the want of *transcendentia* and *transcendentale*. "*Was gross ist am Menschen, das ist, dass er eine Brücke und kein Zweck ist*" – "What is great in man is that he is a bridge and not a goal," says Nietzsche.[150] Let us add that none of the representatives of this race aims to become the *Übermensch* in the Nietzschean sense of the word. The right and true use of language belongs to the *homō uranicus*, the *homō viātor*.

\*

Thinking, feeling, and will are all infected by *saṁsāra*, but not to the same extent. As has been mentioned before, thinking is the least contaminated of the functions of consciousness. Not all mental processes and phenomena can be considered thinking, however.

The automatic, spontaneous, and destructive flow of associations in the mind, the ensemble of states and processes in which there is a chaotic and bluntly swirling tumult of monologic flows, words, thoughts, images, forms, gestures and other kinds of barely conscious fragments — a phenomenon in which there is little real awareness — is not real thinking, and it cannot be transmuted into real thinking; it simply has to be eliminated.

The mental process of problem-solving and solving a task, finishing an assigned piece of work, although it is intensive, is not thinking either; in the Italian language, however, the word *pensare* ('to think') involves the idea of *task* or *duty*, as it is in connection with the Latin word *pēnsum* ('task').

---

150 Friedrich Nietzsche, *Also Sprach Zarathustra*, Vorrede, 4.

Moreover, its intensity has the wrong direction: it leads you away from the Centre.

One of the books of Oliver Napoleon Hill, an American who joined the "self-help movement," was *Think and Grow Rich*, hence "positive mental attitude" or "positive thinking" as the flat, psychologizing antithesis of "negative thoughts," which is demonically individualistic as a whole, and its potential benefits are clearly incapable of transcending anything more than sociological frameworks. The thousands of "realise yourself" books and lectures that have been published since then have one problem: they are not about self-realization at all. According to "positive thinking," you should have an "optimistic disposition" in every situation. However, a person who is truly autonomous, truly oriented towards the optimum, is neither an optimist nor a pessimist.

It is *cogitātiō rationalis discursīva*, rational-discursive thinking, that can be transformed, it is that which is capable of — by revitalizing, reanimating and intensifying it — transmutation in the sense of transcendence, movement upwards, and the resulting thinking will be *cogitātiō intellectuālis intuiva*.

According to Massimo Scaligero, if you have a firm intention in your thinking, it can be changed back into living thinking, in which the object and the subject will be one and the same. He says, "*afferrando il proprio pensare, l'uomo può giungere a sperimentare come impersonale attività il pensiero soprarazionale, o cosmico, che ha pensato e pensa il creato,*" – "by grasping his own thinking, man can manage to experience the superrational or cosmic thought, which has thought, and thinks creation, as his own activity." He adds, "*ascesi vera è quella del pensiero che si voglia talmente nella determinazione di sé, da superare il limite della riflessità,*" – "true ascesis is that of the thought that one wants so much in self-determination that it surpasses

## A Few Remarks on the Spiritual Importance of Languages

the limit of reflectivity."[151] (This is very similar to Simone Weil's observation that in real prayer, something is prayed for at the beginning, and if prayed for intensely enough, the object of the prayer eventually disappears.)

*

When science takes a bird's-eye view of itself, it is called the "science of science," or metascience; metatheories are concerned with the investigation of the theories themselves. Metalogic, for example, is the metatheory of logic; metaphilosophy, the "philosophy of philosophy" which investigates the nature of philosophy. Likewise, meta-research looks at questions concerning research methods from a higher angle, for instance in health care, to find the most efficient research methods which provide reliable and reproducible answers.

In metaphysics, however, the prefix *meta-* refers to the domain beyond *physis* or *gnatura* – indeed, the word "nature" originally had an initial *g-*, as it meant everything that is involved in *genesis*; it referred to the being of beings, all the states of existence that constitute universal manifestation. Similarly, metatheology deals with Metatheos in the sense of the *Übergöttliche Gottheit,* as it was put by Meister Eckhart, that most universal thinker in Christianity from whom, it is said, God did not conceal anything.

In metaphysics, you expand your horizons to the utmost. Thus, we can say that language is not a primordial reality. It is already a consequence. As regards their ultimate essence, however, languages are principally of metaphysical origin and secondarily of cosmic origin. Language is the consequence of the fact that the Centre distances Itself from Itself (*glottogenesis*), as Guénon says, by the radiation

---

[151] Massimo Scaligero, *Trattato del pensiero vivente* [A Treatise on Living Thinking], 17, 19.

of the Principle, by "the *fiat lux* of Genesis."[152] It is this radiation that makes all linguistic phenomena, even oral articulation, possible.

Language, however, has its limits. This is because it has the particular function of serving human beings: communication, the expression of ideas, play, and emotional release are all carried out by conventional symbols, whether spoken, manual, or written.

Most words and concepts are *heteronomous*, that is they can be defined with the help of *other* words and concepts. We can say, for example, that an angel is a spiritual being serving as a divine messenger and intermediary. However, some of the concepts are *autonomous*, which means that they can be defined or determined only with themselves, only by the same words, like *God is God*. If *other* concepts were to be used, this would lead the explanation away from the concept. This is the only case in which tautology is not a mistake.

What is essential cannot be put into words. Metaphysical Awakening, for example, is inexpressible; it is indeed beyond expression.

Between the self as subject and the self as person, from the person's viewpoint, there is a distance, and realisation can be understood as the elimination of this distance. In several traditions, there appears the image of a Deity moving, as it were, into a person. In Islam, for example, according to an *ḥadīth qudsī*, God says of the aspirant who approaches Him by devotion that through the unifying power of love, "I become his hearing with which he hears, and his sight with which he sees, and his hand with which he strikes, and his foot with which he walks." According to Ibn al-'Arabi, this nearness represents the highest level of human existence, and he says, "now he hears through God, whereas

---

152 René Guénon, *Symbols of Sacred Science*, trans. Henry D. Fohr (Hillsdale: Sophia Perennis, 2004), Chapter 8.

## A Few Remarks on the Spiritual Importance of Languages

before he heard through his own hearing." In terms of true self-knowledge, self-translation, and self-identification, the aspirant is constantly coming to *limits* which he must go beyond. The existence of such limits is well illustrated by the following. "What, then, is time?", asks St. Augustine, "If no one ask of me, I know; if I wish to explain to him who asks, I know not."[153]

"*Wovon man nicht sprechen kann, darüber muss man schweigen,*" says Wittgenstein, "What we cannot speak about we must pass over in silence."[154] The term *sirr*, meaning 'secret' or 'mystery' in the ṣūfī tradition, refers to the boundary between the person and the divine principle. The secret of the true ṣūfī and God, for example, is the quality of the aspirant by which he earns the rank of ṣūfī. Beyond the boundary, according to Hindu tradition, is "that which cannot be expressed by human voice, but by which human voice is possible at all... that which cannot be heard by the ear, but by which hearing is possible at all" (*Kena-upaniṣad*).

This means that what cannot be formulated, what cannot be articulated, can be *pointed at*; however, when *beweisen* or *demonstrare* is impossible, then *aufweisen* or *monstrare* nevertheless becomes possible.

What has been said here gives the definition of *exoteric* and *esoteric*. In a sacred doctrine, anything that can be and is expressed is *exoteria*; everything that is closer to the Centre and cannot be put in words is *esoteria*.

This, of course, must be divided from *taboos*. Modern science goes so far as to speak of "metaphysical risk." People, they say, constantly censor the language that they use because of social constraints on the individual's behaviour wherever it can cause discomfort, harm, or injury. Taboos also arise when people deal with sacred persons, objects,

---

153 St. [Aurelius] Augustine, *Confessions*, trans. J.G. Pilkington, Book XI, Chapter XIV, 17.

154 Ludwig Wittgenstein, *Tractatus Logico-Philosophicus*, trans. D.F. Pears and B.F. McGuinness (London: Taylor & Francis e-Library, 2002), 7.

and places. The reason for taboos of this kind is what is called "metaphysical risk."

It also has to be separated from what is called "inner speech" or "interiorized speech." According to modern psycholinguistics, the so-called "egocentric speech" of a child turns into inner speech when the child reaches school age.

So, all that is *in sē esoteria, in aliō* manifests itself as *exoteria*. *Esoteria* can be reached, but only through *exoteria*; so, if you are a spiritual aspirant, you have to be more and more able to grasp *exotery*. The essence of *exoteria* is that it represents *esoteria* in an appropriate and worthy way. *Exoteria* can represent itself in symbols — mostly visual symbols — as well as doctrines and inner experiences.

The creation and self-distancing of the Principle is inexpressible. Still, there are some exoteric elements of doctrines related to it. In the Hindu tradition, an exceptional and singular self-creation involving all creation is the first creative act: "In the beginning this world was Brahma," says the *Bṛihadāraṇyaka-upaniṣad*, "it knew his Self only [and said], 'I am Brahma!', and by this, All were created." According to *Genesis*, "*Ēlōhim* creates with the Divine Word, by the decree of God (*'āmar*)". In the Islamic tradition, too, creation is God's pure, self-creative command (*al-amr*), which, according to the *ṣūfī* tradition, is renewed with every breath (*anfās*). In the context of breath, it should be noted — and here it is worth noticing the common root and thus the common origin of the ideas carried by the words — that it is the cosmic exhalation (*exspīrātiō*) which, along with the cosmic inhalation (*īnspīrātiō*), refers to the double movement of spirit (*spīritus*) and breath (*spīrātiō*), also expressed in the double spiral (Greek σπείρα, Latin *spira*). This breath is the "breath of life": God, having created man, "breathed into his nostrils the breath of life, and man became a living being"; "the breath of God has created me," says Job, "and the breath of the Almighty gives

## A Few Remarks on the Spiritual Importance of Languages

me life." The *Gospel* speaks of a λόγος that is principial, in power, facing God, and divine. In the Egyptian tradition, Amun, who is higher than the Heavens and deeper than the realm of the dead, also creates with his mouth, and what he decrees has regulative power over everything and everyone, even the gods. According to the Apsaalooke (Crow) Indians, the Creator began to create, also with his mouth, because he wanted to talk to someone. And according to the Maya, in the beginning, when everything was still, silent, and motionless, and the vault of the sky was empty, there were only the creators, Tepeu and Qucumatz, who were sitting and thinking: what they thought and said came into being.

Silence is more primordial than the Word. "Strange men," he said, "what a way to behave! I sent the women away mainly so that they would not cause such a tumult, for I have also heard that it is necessary to die in reverent silence. So keep quiet and endure."[155] It is worth mentioning that this is Socrates speaking, specifically before his soul embarks on its posthumous journey.

"If ever I have spread out a tranquil heaven above me, and have flown into mine own heaven with mine own pinions: If I have swum playfully in profound luminous distances, and if my freedom's avian wisdom hath come to me:- Thus however speaketh avian wisdom: - 'Lo, there is no above and no below! Throw thyself about, outward, backward, thou light one! Sing! speak no more! - Are not all words made for the heavy? Do not all words lie to the light ones? Sing! speak no more!'"[156] These are the lines of Nietzsche, a thinker who ended his life in an atypical stupor upon having reached, like Hölderlin, Weininger, and Sartre, a limit he could not control. Guénon's words about anti-tradition and counter-tradition are relevant here: whoever illegitimately arrives at a frontier, a gate (*porte*), without the necessary qualifications, will find it closed

---
155 Plato, *Phaedo* 117e.
156 Friedrich Nietzsche, *Thus Spoke Zarathustra*, Part 3, "The Seven Seals," 7.

and will have to turn back; but then he will no longer be a mere profane person, but will become a sorcerer or magician operating in the domain of the subtle possibilities of the inferior order ("*un sorcier ou magicien opérant dans le domaine des possibilités subtiles d'ordre inférieur*"[157]).

Silence is the same as "emptiness," *śūnyatā*. It would be a mistake to associate the metaphysical meaning of the idea of emptiness (*śūnyatā*) in Buddhism with the philosophical "nothingness," "nihilism," the relative or the phenomenal in any way, instead of with the concept of fullness (*aśūnyatā*); another pair of concepts necessary for understanding is that of possibility (Latin *potentia*), the power of the tendency towards realisation, and actuality (Latin *āctuālitās*), the realisation of possibility. Now, using these pairs of terms, the following definition can be given: emptiness (*śūnyatā*) refers to the emptiness of actuality and its fullness of potentiality, and fullness (*aśūnyatā*) refers to its fullness with actuality and its being free from potentiality. Contrary to popular belief, in the case of Far Eastern — especially Chinese and Japanese — artworks of a sage with a large belly, the large belly does not represent the "enjoyment of life," it rather expresses "emptiness" and, above all, that he has power over it.

Buddhism speaks of *ārya* silence (*ariyo tuṇhībhāvo*, pāli): "*mā ariyaṃ tuṇhībhāvaṃ pamādo, ariye tuṇhībhāve cittaṃ saṇṭhapeti, ariye tuṇhībhāve cittaṃ ekodibhāvaṃ karohi, ariye tuṇhībhāve cittaṃ samādahāʾti*" – "remember the *ārya* silence, steady the mind in the *ārya* silence, make the mind one in the *ārya* silence, concentrate the mind in the *ārya* silence."[158] This is *dhyāna*, meditation with the fullness of existence. Well, words or silence? I must get back to *the point where both words and silence originate*.

---

157 René Guénon, *Le Règne de la Quantité et les Signes des Temps* (Paris: Gallimard, 1970), Chap. 38.

158 *Saṃyutta Nikāya* 21.

*A Few Remarks on the Spiritual Importance of Languages*

\*

The history of languages is the unquestionable evidence and the indisputable proof against all the varieties of "evolutionism," the elixir for the poison of the modern belief in never-ending "progress." Archaic languages were much more complex than later languages. With respect to the vocabulary that carries spirituality, supra-philosophical philosophy, and the expressibility of cosmicity, Sanskrit surpasses every other known language. The dictionaries of Böhtlingk-Roth and Monier-Williams, which are by no means the complete vocabulary of Sanskrit, contain some 60,000 verb roots. The stock of words employed by Sanskrit is not completely known, but we are aware of the fact that it is potentially unlimited.

Prof. Srinivasa Varakhedi, Vice-Chancellor of the Sanskrit University of Karnataka in Bengaluru, Karnataka, India, has said that cultivating science in Sanskrit opens up new dimensions because, for example, the terminology of a science such as quantum physics is not only easily expressed in Sanskrit, but is rooted in it, as has been confirmed by several non-Indian experts. Of the modern languages, there are no accurate counts of the number of words used in the English language; however, English is estimated to have approximately 200,000 words. The second edition of the 20-volume *Oxford English Dictionary* contains full entries for 171,476 words in current use and 47,156 obsolete words, and there are said to be about 616,500 word forms in these volumes. Sanskrit, on the other hand, probably has over 4 million words. Sanskrit has tens of thousands of words related to spiritual life, while English excels in nautical terms.

Languages, like everything else, are subject to the erosive and destructive forces of time, which manifests itself in the disappearance of various linguistic carriers. The so-called *duālis*, for example, which was used with the singular and plural, has disappeared from the English language. The form *wit* in Old English meant "we [two]," *wē* meant "we [three or more]"; *ʒit* had the meaning of "you [two]," *ʒē* signified "you [three or more]" — the *-t* at the end of *duālis* forms was derived from the numeral *two*.

In the Hungarian language, there were several past tense forms with different meanings. "He wrote" / "he had written" was expressed by *íra, írt, ír vala, ír volt, írt vala,* and *írt volt*. What we know from written texts is that in the 16th, 17th, and 18th centuries, all these forms were used; in the 19th century only four of them were used, and since the early 20th century Hungarians have been using only one of these forms.

There are no longer any words that are coinages. New roots in languages have not been born for at least three thousand years. New phenomena are expressed with, for instance, grammatical shifts, semantic shifts, shortenings such as acronyms, alphabetisms, initialisms, or backformations. The term "teflon" was a computer-generated name, in which one can recognize the words "tough" and "nylon."

Many more examples could be mentioned, but it can be seen that there is no automatic ontological ascent; things descend of their own accord, they move away from the Centre, from their own principle. We can speak of an *involūtiō*, not an *evolūtiō*.

\*

As far as the problem of *translation* is concerned — which has been very important since Cicero, Saint Jerome, or Goethe — let us make a few remarks. The science of translation today is a branch of applied linguistics, and translation theory is its basic component. Translation theory, on the one hand, mainly examines the problems of translation primarily on the basis of the material provided

## A Few Remarks on the Spiritual Importance of Languages

by translation practice; in other words, it is descriptive. On the other hand, it is prescriptive, since it can provide some guidance on how to translate correctly.

Regarding interlingual translation, we have to say that being an eminent expert in both the source language and the target language is not enough, if the translator does not understand the key concepts and what the whole text is about. What is more, it is not the two languages that count, but the actual representation of the two languages in the texts, in the source text and in the target text.

*Equivalence* is of prime importance; the two texts must be equivalent in value, so any time there is some loss during the translation process, the translator must outperform the original text at certain points. This is called "dynamic equivalence." In cases where translation must be strict, exact and precise "formal equivalence" must be preferred, according to linguist, Bible scholar and translator Eugene Nida.

To achieve equivalence, some basic words should not be translated. *Ātmā* or *Logos*, for example, should never be translated in any target language. In these cases, the translator should write notes about the word where it first appears in the source text, and it is not a problem if a note takes up several pages.

Despite the best intentions, there will always be errors in translations. One example can be the following. "Go then, and make disciples of all the nations, giving them baptism in the name of the Father and of the Son and of the Holy Spirit" was translated from the Latin "*euntes ergo docete omnes gentes, baptizantes eos in nomine Patris et Filii et Spiritus Sancti.*"[159] The English version is not correct, whereas the Latin sentence is not flawless either; nevertheless, the original Greek sentence is right when it uses εἰς / *heis* meaning "into"; *in nomine* really means "in

---
159 Matthew 28:19.

the name of," but *in nomen* signifying "into the name of" would be the perfect translation, as *baptismos* is initiation *into* the *name*, into the inner, principal Essence of God.

One also has to be aware of the fact that the text in the source language can contain errors. This is an intralingual deterioration of text due to unknown reasons, of which one can only guess that such might be because of lack of understanding over time, fear, or a desire to modernize. An example of this is as follows. "And they had then an important prisoner, whose name was Barabbas. So when they came together, Pilate said to them, 'Whom will you have? Barabbas, or Jesus, who is named Christ?'" – "*Habebant autem tunc vinctum insignem, qui dicebatur Barabbas. Congregatis ergo illis dixit Pilatus: 'Quem vultis dimittam vobis: Barabbam an Iesum, qui dicitur Christus?'*"[160] The clause "who is named Christ" is a telltale addition to the name which in this form is not only unnecessary, but distorts the sentence as well, because one feels something should be added after the name *Barabbas*, too. The solution to the problem is the following. The Latin text was translated from a Greek version which had already been changed. Some priests might have become afraid of the fact that both persons are called *Jesus*. One of them is Jesus, who is Barabbas, the other is Jesus, "who is named Christ." If we add that Barabbas means "son of the father," one no longer wants to find the "historical facts" about a "criminal" named Barabbas, as the whole parable regains its light and symbolic value. It turns out that it is a teaching that gets us back to the original distinction between *only life* and *more than life*, a teaching that can serve as a starting point for immersive contemplation.

---

160 Matthew 27:16-17.

# THE FOUR LEVELS OF MEANING: POLYSEMIC HERMENEUTICS OF TRADITIONAL TEXTS

## Sebastiano Fusco

> *O voi che avete li 'ntelletti sani*
> *Mirate la dottrina che s'asconde*
> *Sotto 'l velame de li versi strani*
>
> O you who have sound intellects
> consider the teaching that is hidden
> behind the veil of these strange verses
>
> - Dante, *Inferno* IX: 61-63

### Four Worlds and Four Meanings

Understanding any text that conveys a fragment of traditional wisdom cannot be separated from consideration of the *polysemism* typical of this class of works. It is not simply a matter of attributing specific meanings to symbolic structures: for example, one writes "breath" and means "spirit." One must keep in mind the overall layers of meaning that overlap and are woven into the structure of the work itself. Only in this way will it be possible to also understand the "operational" meaning of the teachings imparted by traditional doctrines.

This is particularly true for Judaism, which is based on the polysemous explanation of the Torah, and generally of the complex array of Scriptures. I do not want to go into a matter so dense and complex and so rich in the highest religious sense, which urges the utmost respect. I only want to point out how the vast majority of the texts of traditional mysticism and spiritual doctrine were written with the same polysemous approach in mind and should therefore be interpreted in accordance with it. In the field of Jewish mysticism, moreover, Kabbalah introduces, as we shall see, an additional complicating (or enriching, depending on your point of view) factor.

Many authors have gone to great lengths to describe the meaning of the Torah's "layers." Moses de Leon, to whom we owe the systematization of much of the Zohar, identifies four layers of meaning specified (on the basis of a Talmudic legend, *Chaghiga* 14b) in the word *Pardes*, which means "garden" but to which is given the sense of "Paradise." In Hebrew, *Pardes* is spelled with the four consonants *Peh*, *Resh*, *Daleth*, and *Shin*, and the four letters are the initials of as many words: *Pehsat, Remez, Derasha, Sod*, each of which conveys a meaning that can be translated respectively: *simple, symbolic, religious, esoteric*.

These are the four levels of which the Torah is composed. The first, *Peshat*, is the literal one: these are the narrative events recounted in the text, from which information about Israel's history, ethical and moral teachings, as well as liturgical precepts and rules of behavior, can be gleaned.

The second level, expressed by the word *Remez*, uses images and episodes in the text in the guise of symbols to represent something else. For example, in Genesis 18, Abraham, during his wanderings to the Promised Land, saw three men in front of his tent. He gave them water to wash themselves, and his wife Sarah prepared meat and bread. The three wayfarers rested and ate, then, as they left, assured that Sarah would have a son the following year. Sarah laughed because she was too old to have a child. Then the travelers responded by saying that nothing is impossible for God. A whole series of symbols is present here. The three men are three angels, meat and bread are the nourishment of the soul, and Sarah's laughter is the

## The Four Levels of Meaning

anticipation of the joy of motherhood: the child was born and was named Isaac, that is, "God's Smile."

The third level, expressed by the word *Derasha*, is the religious-homiletic level. It expands and comments on every verse of the Bible, in every possible way, mainly using the tools of reason and logic according to rabbinic common sense. The purpose is mainly to clarify the ethical and legal aspects of the precepts that the Torah prescribes for Jews, but it gleans from them many teachings that would benefit all mankind if it listened to them.

The fourth and final level, related to the word *Sod*, is the esoteric level from which teachings and precepts are drawn for the mystic's meditations and contemplations. The Bible verses become, to those who know how to read them in this way, true "milestones" that guide them along the path of spiritual elevation.

The Kabbalists added – as a further complication – to these levels a fifth one, that is, the analysis taken to the extreme of every single word in the sacred text (indeed, every single letter), on the basis of the combinations and permutations implemented through the rules defined by *gematria*, *notariqon*, and *temurah*, which are the hermeneutic systems used in Kabbalah. Gematria is the study of the numerical value of a word or phrase, compared with others having the same value. Notariqon examines a word or phrase and replaces its letters according to fixed rules in order to find new meanings. Temurah breaks down a word or group of words and sees what new words or phrases can be formed by recombining the same elements.

The texts of many traditional doctrines, such as Alchemy, for example, as well as Kabbalah, were written with such layers of meaning in mind and can only be understood superficially if one is not aware of this. Consider, for example, the different meanings given in the Hebrew texts to the term *Ruach*, which is generically translated as "spirit" or "breath." This is understood initially as *Ruach Elohim*, the "Spirit of God" who "hovered over the waters" of Genesis. Then it indicates what is, for example in the *Shepher Yetzirah*, called "air," in the sense of "primordial air" or the Platonic Idea of Air. From this derives the air understood as a constitutive element in a sense similar to that defined by Aristotle. The last meaning is finally that of "air" in the proper sense. But there is also another stratification related to the divisions of the Whole into the categories of space, time, and man. In this way, *Ruach* is the breath or "blow" in man, the air in space in the sense of atmosphere or "wind," and flow in time. In man himself, *Ruach* is not only the breath but, on a higher level, the rational spirit and, even higher, the intellect.

These overlapping meanings of the term *Ruach* are remote, and can be found in the metamorphoses of the ancient Indo-Aryan root *rh-* inherited by Sanskrit *ruh*, Greek *rei*, and Latin *ruo* until descending into modern languages, as in English *run*, French *courir*, Italian *correre*. It also runs through the Gospel of John, where Christ is attributed the words, "No one can enter the kingdom of God unless they are born of water and the Spirit" (John 3:5), and even better immediately afterward, "The wind blows wherever it pleases. You hear its sound, but you cannot tell where it comes from or where it is going. So it is with everyone born of the Spirit" (John 3:8), where in one sentence the three senses of *Ruach* are united: Air, Word, and Spirit.

In Jewish tradition, the ordering principle for distinguishing meanings is the attribution of each to one of the Four Worlds indicated by the Kabbalah, namely *Atziluth*, *Briah*, *Yetzirah*, and *Assiah*. These are the partitions into which the Whole is divided, seen as the four stages of Creation, namely *emanation* (Atziluth), *appearance of the formless* (Briah), *formation* (Yetzirah), and *action* (Assiah).

## The Four Levels of Meaning

Proceeding from the bottom and rising up by progressive refinements, the first world is that of Assiah, the universe of matter and energy (action) in which the Divine Will takes substance. In the human microcosm, it corresponds to the organic body. The universe of our senses and with it, Malkuth, the last Sephirah of the Tree of Life, are representations of Assiah. Here, the divine Ideas initiated in Atziluth, the highest of the four worlds, take concrete form. The essential bricks with which what is conceived by the Divine Will is built are the Primordial Elements: Water, Air, Fire (Judaism does not add Earth, which, according to Kabbalah, is not a single substance but a compound).[161]

Above that is Yetzirah (the second world from below or the third world from above, depending on where you start), which is the World of Formation, in which the forms that will be filled with matter in Assiah are engraved. In man, it is the world of thought in which logic and intelligence operate and in which the creative power of imagination (the main ingredient of every magical operation, according to a phrase attributed to Paracelsus) is manifested.

This is followed by Briah, the World of Creation, in which the blueprints or "matrices" of the forms to be engraved in Yetzirah are drawn. Roughly speaking, it is comparable to the world of Platonic Ideas. In man, it corresponds to the spirit, which is superior to the intellect but inferior to the soul.

Finally, the highest world is Atziluth, the seat of the Sephiroth, the "logical partitions" used by Kabbalists to frame the Whole, in which subsist the divine ideas that give rise to all creation. It is unattainable and incomprehensible to the human mind, but flashes of the Creator's own Thought emanate from it. In man, it corresponds to the soul. It represents the ideas that are in the Divine Mind, without which nothing is possible in any of the lower

---

161 Following the Bible: "Now the Earth was *formless* and *empty*" (Gen 1:2). It possessed two qualities, therefore it was not a single substance.

worlds. The different worlds should not be thought of as successive stratifications, but as interpenetrating one another. In reference to these concepts, the metaphor of the Great Architect is often used. The Architect is the one who conceives the idea of a house (*Atziluth*), determines its style and size (*Briah*), draws its plan (*Yetzirah*), gathers the materials, and has it built (*Assiah*). The building thus created is the *Adam Qadmon*, the Heavenly Adam, which, in certain interpretations, is likened to a fifth world.

## Two Different Ways of thinking

To fully decipher such a complex scheme, simple human reason, which we rely on for our earthly activities, is not sufficient. Kabbalists often repeat the exhortation, "Understand through Wisdom and be wise through Understanding." The reference point here is the names of two Sephiroth, *Chokmah*, "Wisdom," and *Binah*, "Understanding." These constitute the second and third Sephirahs of the Tree of Life and, together with the first one, *Kether* ("Crown"), form the triangle at the apex of the Tree that identifies the higher world of *Atziluth*, in which the intentions of the Creator are manifested.

The terms "Understanding" and "Wisdom" denote two different mental activities. Their premise is Knowledge, represented by *Daath*, the non-Sephirah of rational faculties, which in the Tree of Life diagram is placed immediately below *Binah* and *Chokmah*, in the middle between these two. *Daath* represents notional knowledge, that is, the collection of the cognition and information we need to begin any path. These data that we have collected must first be *understood*: we must study them thoroughly to realize their significance within the framework of our reference doctrines, that is, the so-called "esoteric" teachings, which go beyond the superficial sense of things studied by "secular" science. The latter is not to be despised, but we must realize

## The Four Levels of Meaning

that it deals with a different category of being than that on which the attention of those seeking transcendence is focused. But understanding the known data is not enough: it is necessary to look beyond them, refining the mental capacities that enable us to peer beyond the appearance of things in order to grasp their exact nature and thus attain that capacity which is traditionally called Wisdom.

Between Knowledge (*Daath*), Understanding (*Binah*), and Wisdom (*Chokmah*), there is a substantial difference in level that I will try to illustrate by venturing a metaphor. Imagine that I am a lecturer intent on describing an orange to an audience of Eskimos who have never seen one before and do not know what it is. First, I show them a slide of an orange. The Eskimos will deduce that the orange is a sphere characterized by a deep yellow color. This is the level of cognition that in the Kabbalah is called "Knowledge" and in the Tree of Life is symbolized by *Daath*. This is how we know the things of this world: not in their true essence, but as their representation seen from afar, like a projected image. Plato also said this in the Myth of the Cave: we are unable to perceive the true reality of things, but only their shadow cast by the sun beyond the threshold of the cave in which we dwell, and which represents our world.[162]

To make it clearer what an orange is, I then pull one out of my pocket and pass it around the audience. Those present, handling and weighing it, will realize that it is a fruit, that its surface is not smooth but wrinkled and porous, and that it has a fragrance and several other characteristics that distinguish it precisely as an orange. This is the second level of cognition: from *knowing*, that is, from learning of the existence of a thing, we have moved on to *"comprehending,"* that is, understanding its nature (*intelligere*, in Latin). We learn, in other words, that it is a fruit with

---

[162] Plato, *Republic* 514-520.

all that goes with it. In the Kabbalah, this level is called "Understanding" and is symbolized by the sephirah *Binah*.

Now, my Eskimos know that there is such a thing as an orange and that it is a fruit, but in order to learn its true nature, they need to see what it looks like inside: that is, they need a knife to cut it open and reveal its internal structure. This knife is the intellectual faculty called "Wisdom," symbolized by the sephirah *Chokmah*. It is the faculty of our deep thought that "cuts" entities so as to bring their intimate essence to light. It constitutes the utmost that human thought can reach by its own strength: beyond it, there is only Enlightenment, which, however, is the exclusive gift of God, who grants it only to those who will Him with choices often incomprehensible to us mortals.

To understand how to use our intellectual faculties to achieve Wisdom, we must take into account the different modes of human thought. There are two fundamental ones which are active in the normal state of consciousness, and they are generally defined as "verbal" and "imaginal." They are allocated in the two different hemispheres of the brain: the left hemisphere is responsible for the functions associated with language, while the right one deals with the interpretation of visual information and spatial processing. Binah is the Sephirah that is placed at the top of the Left Pillar of the Tree of Life, and therefore, it is the one under which so-called "verbal thought" falls, which occurs when we think in words as if we were conducting a conversation with ourselves. This is an empirically verifiable and measurable type of thinking: when we employ it, we tend to speak silently within ourselves, and some specific muscles contract as if we were actually delivering our "inner speech." These muscle movements, however slight, can be recorded and studied. This is why rationalist and materialist philosophers barbarously call such thinking "brain-gland secretion." Such a structured mode determines a fundamentally logical-sequential form of thinking, since verbality itself requires precise scanning in time and adherence to logical-formal rules. This is the reason why Binah's activity is often associated with the term *measure*, as it is the mental activity that is mainly applied to quantitative evaluations. This kind of thinking can serve to "understand" a phenomenon, that is, to define the laws that govern it and the ways in which it develops, going so far as to predict its consequences, but it does not provide what is traditionally called "Wisdom," that is, the profound knowledge that transcends quantities and highlights the qualities of phenomena. This is identified with Chokmah, the name of the Sephirah under which falls the other kind of thinking we are able to pursue, the one termed "imaginal."

In this second case, thought does not proceed sequentially but evaluates multiple elements together and is expressed not by formulating words but by evoking images and sensations. It is a very different modality from verbal thinking, one that is characterized by its "plasticity": mental images, in fact, can be easily modified, restructured, and adapted to the concepts we want to express. Furthermore, they often emerge spontaneously from deep within, without a deliberate act of will on our part, and present themselves for our evaluations.

For psychologists, mental images are either a kind of code-thinking that our brains rely on to depict certain stimulations, or (without one excluding the other) they are an "interface" that the brain uses to make certain stimulations more processable. Kabbalists, and generally those who follow traditional doctrines, see it very differently. For them, images may be tools we deliberately use to get in touch with levels of existence other than the "normal" one, or (again without excluding the other concept) they may be "messages" that come from our deepest inner selves.

In the traditional universe, there is, in fact, no real distinction between the inner and the outer, since the

Whole is conceived as One Thing in which the product of the imagination merges with the results of the senses. It is for this reason that, in order to understand the Whole and grasp the hidden meaning of the Universe, time, and human presence, the ancient initiatory schools urged the magician to peer within himself: at the bottom of man's consciousness the infinite is, in fact, dissolved.

*Gnothi seauthón*, "know thyself," was intimated by Apollo's oracle at Delphi. *Noli foras ire... in interiore homine habitat veritas* was recommended St. Augustine, because perfect knowledge of the absolute can be acquired by gathering within oneself and listening, like Socrates, to the voice of the *daimon* that speaks from deep within us. This voice always speaks the truth, since its word is *the* Word, *Verbum Dei*: it is an act with creative value, similar to those by which the God of the Bible formed the world and gave life to all things by formulating their names. Note the subtlety of the terminology employed by Augustine: the phrase "*in interiore homine*" does not translate, as I often see done, "in the interior of man," but "in the inner man," that is, in the reflection of God that dwells within us, that was breathed into Adam when the Creator blew His spirit into his nares (Genesis 2:7) transforming what was a *Golem*, that is, a mud puppet, into a living being. It is this divine spark that connects the creature to the Creator and must be sought assiduously, through the active way of the warrior and the magician or through the passive way of the ascetic and the mystic, to achieve transcendence.

### The Wisdom of Silence

The Kabbalistic saying, "Understand through Wisdom and be wise through Understanding," seems to indicate the need for an alternation between the two types of thinking we have described. In fact, it is a matter imposed by the very nature of the human mind. "A great power of imagination is the fundamental prerequisite for practicing Magic," goes the aforementioned Paracelsian phrase. This refers to the creative imagination, what Dante called *alta fantasia*, and which allows one to form mental images on which to concentrate, meditate, and finally practice contemplation.

This is achieved through a particular state of mind, in which images can be "fixed" to make them the object of special operations. It is a state in which the mind empties itself completely of all thought and becomes like a *tabula rasa* on which anything can be engraved. It can be considered an extreme mode of "thinking in images," or as the second way of the functioning of our mental faculties. For Kabbalists, it is one of the attitudes governed by the Sephira *Chokmah* (at the top of the Right Pillar of the Tree), while Western esotericists generally refer to it as the "*state of Silence*" and Zen adepts as "*mental emptiness*," that is, a special inner disposition in which the mind is cleared of all thought until the mind itself, detached from attention, remains completely unperturbed.

Nothing should break the silence, not the smallest sporadic thought, not the most trivial sensation of the body (precisely in order to stop feeling the weight of the physical body, yogic-type exercises are practiced). This is a difficult condition to achieve and even more so to maintain, and how to achieve it is one of the first things taught in magical apprenticeship. Practitioners must be able to do Silence within themselves at all times and in all situations. In magical Silence, the imaginative faculties live as detached from the self, in the guise of tools that can be used on command. This is not simply an operative state, but also a defense system. In Silence, one is extremely vigilant, inwardly on guard, lest fears, doubts, worries, and anxieties (as well as instinctive body sensations) rob us of inner imperturbability and peace of mind. To arrive at the Silence, it is necessary to completely master the power of concentration, so that if doubt or trivial thoughts enter our mind, the power of concentration will nullify them; if fear enters our mind,

## The Four Levels of Meaning

the power of concentration will drive it out. Concentration and Silence are the tools through which one nullifies the unenlightened, dark, and destructive thoughts of which we are victims every moment of our lives. A point must be reached where these thoughts are discarded, not deliberately (for that would nullify Silence) but by an instinctive and automatic mechanism, which annihilates them before they come into consciousness, like an ever-vigilant sentry killing the enemy before he can approach the edge of the fortress.

There are specific trainings designated to achieve this state of mind. The "silence," initially, will be maintained for a few moments, because the mind generally reverts instinctively to verbal processing, usually thinking something like "I finally did it!", and this injects a thought into the mental void. In this case, you need to return to silence, try to maintain it as much as possible, until again it falls apart. This is the oscillation alluded to in the transition from *Chokmah* to *Binah*, expressed by the phrase "Understand through Wisdom (*Chokmah*) and be wise through Understanding (*Binah*)." It is only through daily, continuous, and totally partken exercise that consistent periods of "Silence" can be achieved. Help comes from techniques such as contemplation of a mandala, or continuous listening to a rhythmic sound such as a tambourine, or from physical movements such as the so-called "ecstatic dance" practiced by the revolving dervishes or the rhythmic head swings adopted by Kabbalists.

The faculties at the psychic level that are employed for these operations are taught and developed through apprenticeship and exercises in concentration, meditation, and contemplation. These are not synonymous terms, but indicate quite distinct activities. With *concentration*, one learns to create a form with the imagination at the mental level and, at the same time, educates the will not to detach itself from it, to the exclusion of all other thought. One usually starts with the simplest thing, such as a dot first drawn on a sheet of paper and then only imagined, and proceeds with gradually more complex forms: a line, a geometric figure first flat and then three-dimensional, up to a structurally complicated object. Western esotericists often use to imagine a rose; Kabbalists visualize a letter of the Hebrew alphabet as a three-dimensional structure.

At the same time, *meditation* exercises are performed: one considers the intrinsic value of the figure one is imagining, the meaning of a line, the significance of a triangle or cone, how it arises, how it can develop, what valences can be attributed to it. When you then move on to a more complex object, such as a rose, you try to sense its intrinsic qualities, such as the scent and shades of colors, the thorniness, the softness of the petals, and so on. At the same time, one imagines that the object is projected against the background of infinity and tries to penetrate its intimate essence: that is, one analyzes not a single rose, but "roseness" as a whole, trying in a sense to grasp the Platonic Idea of the *rose*.

With *contemplation*, which is practiced only after being well mastered in the previous two stages (it often takes years), it is assumed that the object being contemplated has its own consciousness and awareness and is able to interact with our being. At this point, what one imagines is no longer a simple object, but a figure with deep and complex meanings, such as the image of a god, or something with deep symbolic meaning such as Hebrew letters. One seeks to penetrate and fully absorb the values expressed by the sacred image, not by offering oneself passively as is the case in mysticism, but by seeking them with an inner motion of the spirit and, in the case of contemplation as it is understood by Magic and Kabbalah, coming to *determine* them in order then to be totally understood by them. According to a motto in vogue among occultists, "We concentrate with the enlightened focus of the mind; we meditate with the expanding vastness of the heart; we contemplate with the satisfying unity of the soul." Again, these are the three degrees of the path: Knowledge → Understanding → Wisdom.

While Kabbalists imagined the letters of the Hebrew alphabet as "thought-forms," seeing the letters in increasingly complex aspects and with ever broader symbolic attributions, the theurges of antiquity employed divine or heroic figures with whom they proceeded to identify themselves. The Kabbalists pursued a progressive raising of self-consciousness through the four increasingly elevated worlds conceived by the Kabbalah: from the "earthly" world of *Assiah* to that of *Yetzirah* and then to that of *Briah*, all the way to the threshold of the inaccessible world of *Atziluth*.

Operationally, this is no simple procedure: the two modes of human thought are, in fact, not reconcilable with each other, for one excludes the other: verbal thought excludes imaginal thought, and the awareness of *Binah* erases that of *Chokmah*, and vice versa. They are two opposites: thesis and antithesis. It is necessary to implement what the alchemists called *coincidentia oppositorum* by activating the non-Sephira *Daath*, which is intermediate between *Binah* and *Chokmah*, but lower down. Simple Knowledge (*Daath*) can then become Understanding (*Binah*) and aim to become Wisdom (*Chokmah*).

For this, however, it is necessary to go one step further, deeper. Below *Daath*, there is the Sephirah of the heart, *Tiphereth*. At one time, the heart of man (*lev* in Hebrew) was considered the seat of the higher mental activities, those to which it was necessary to appeal when, having attained Knowledge and Understanding, one aspired to Wisdom, reconciling Chokmah with Binah in the supreme mental balance. This is the mental operation referred to by the alchemists as "transferring the sense of self from the brain to the heart." In Kabbalistic language, it means that awareness, once the balance between verbal thought and imaginal thought (*Binah* and *Chokmah*) is achieved, is transferred into *Tiphereth*, the Sephirah of the heart, which is the vertex of the triangle of the Tree of Life corresponding to the entrance into the World of *Briah*. This is the world of Ezekiel's vision, in which the Throne of Glory is located, and the *chasmal*, the "glow of glowing amber" that announces the prophetic vision, is manifested. It is the World of Creation, where the blueprints or the "matrices" of the forms to be engraved in *Yetzirah*, are drawn. It is comparable to the Platonic world of Ideas. In man, it corresponds to the spirit, which is superior to the intellect but inferior to the soul. One can enter it only after obtaining the perception of the special state of supersensibility in which the subsequent operations aimed at obtaining the power of Formation that was granted to Abraham will be implemented. This special state, which is achieved through contemplative operations, that is, through a special mental discipline, must be preserved and "fixed": it must become almost the habitual state, or at any rate, one that can be recalled at any time. The alchemists called this procedure "extraction of Mercury from the mine."

This is a psychic state in which sensitivity, which is normally turned outward, is instead focused totally toward our inner self, a "reversal of the self" that is clearly expressed by the Hebrew language (a most powerful tool at our disposal as far as knowledge of the transcendent is concerned, comparable to mathematics for knowledge of the physical world). What the Kabbalist seeks is the "house of God," which in Hebrew is spelled *Beth El*. To find it, one must reverse the letters of the name: we then have *El Beth*, which is pronounced *lev* and means "heart." The House of God identifies itself with our heart. In other words, it is by reversing our sensibility from the outside to the inside that we will find what we are looking for. This is an identical procedure to what the alchemist Fulcanelli refers to by the term *bouleversement*.

## The Magic of Images

In this procedure, imagination is of paramount importance. The *Sepher Yetzirah* says that the inner image must be "engraved" and "sculpted," alluding to two stages of inner visualization in the procedure by which it is evoked – in what Dante calls "high fantasy" (*Paradiso* 33:142) – to form an image laden with meanings that we want to explore and begin to meditate on. The image must imprint itself on the inner layer of our mind as if engraved there, so that we can observe it for as long as we wish, examining every detail. It must be "fixed" within us like an inscription chiseled on marble, recallable at all times and under all circumstances, even if we no longer have before our eyes the actual model from which we drew it (a concrete object, the illustration of a book, a human figure, anything else). Put like that, it sounds simple, but in fact, it is an extremely difficult procedure that requires long training and rigorous mental discipline.

After "carving" the symbolic image, we must "sculpt" it. That is, we must eliminate all mental matter in excess of the image itself: that is, nullify any spurious thought or figuration or emotion not inherent in the object of our meditation. The image must acquire three-dimensional characteristics, as if it were a statue carved from a block of marble. We must be able to rotate it in our mind, shaping it with our imagination as if it were a chisel, and be able to observe it both as a whole and highlighting its details and components. It is an even more difficult technique than the first, and to learn to perform it with ease requires activating a special state of mind which can not only be recalled, but stabilized and easily "turned on" whenever desired. It takes years of constant practice before appreciable results can be achieved, unless we resort to dangerous "shortcuts" that are implemented by manipulating the mind through para-hypnotic practices, as in shamanic procedures or in the case of collective ceremonies along the lines of the *macumba*, or even worse, through the use of psychotropic drugs. Without the help of an expert person, the almost inevitable outcome of using these shortcuts is mental disintegration or the onset of paranoid pathologies whose existence we didn't even suspect.

It should be kept in mind that for Kabbalists, the shape of the letters acts subliminally on the minds of those who see them written or visualize them, breaking through the barrier of rationality to engrave itself, without our being aware of it, in the deep layers of our consciousness. This is why scribes had to adhere rigidly to strictly codified rules in tracing them, and those that did not conform were deemed "invalid" or, in certain cases, even dangerous. There is nothing particularly strange about this: even today we use specific graphic signs to elicit particular emotions. In many cases, nonverbal communication is more efficient than verbal communication. This is trivially demonstrated by the widespread use, popularized in an extraordinarily short time, of so-called emoticons that are largely supplementing, if not replacing, written words. But in the case of the letters of the Hebrew alphabet, there is added to these considerations a sacral dimension that descends deeply into our unconscious. In this regard, let us quote a sentence from Carl Gustav Jung:

> Do we really understand what we think? We only understand thought as a simple equation, from which nothing comes out except what we put into it. That is how the intellect works. But beyond that, there is a thinking in primordial images – in symbols that are older than historical man; that have aggregated with him from the earliest times, and, alive in eternity, have surpassed all generations and still form the basic ground of the human psyche. It is possible to live life to the full only when we are in harmony with these symbols; wisdom consists in returning to them. This is neither a matter of belief nor of knowledge but of our thinking's adherence to the primordial

images of our unconscious. They are the source of all our conscious thoughts...[163]

This is exactly what the polysemous structure of traditional texts tends toward, namely, the awakening within us of what Jung called the primal images of our unconscious. I would like to mention that such polysemic writing is not only characteristic of Kabbalah or Jewish mysticism; in fact, it is present in the whole vast category of writings based on traditional doctrines, from Alchemy to Hermeticism, from courtly literature to allegories of love and so on. The noblest example that comes to my mind is the *Divine Comedy*, which Dante himself in the dedicatory epistle of the *Paradiso* to Cangrande della Scala calls "*polìsema*, that is, of several senses." And in the *Convivio*, he explains that the different senses attributable to works of this kind are the *literal*, the *allegorical*, the *moral* and the *anagogical*: the latter "is when spiritually a writing is set forth which, by the things signified, signifies of the supernal things of eternal glory."[164] These are manifestly the same categories of meaning encapsulated, as already explained, in the Hebrew term *Pardes*.[165] The classic example of the four interpretations is *Jerusalem*, which in a literal sense is a city in the Middle East, allegorically it is the symbol of the monotheistic religion, morally it is the soul that believes, and anagogically it is the "heavenly Jerusalem," the image of the Kingdom of God. It is by inviting the reader to seek the latter sense that Dante himself exhorts, "O you who have sound intellects / consider the teaching that is hidden / behind the veil of these strange verses" (*Inf.* ix, 63)[166]. The same

---

163 Carl Gustav Jung, *Modern Man in Search of a Soul*, trans. William Stanley Dell and Cary F. Baynes (London: Kegan Paul, 1933).

164 "*È quando spiritualmente si pone una scrittura la quale per le cose significate significa delle superne cose dell'etternal gloria.*"

165 A term derived, like the Italian *Paradiso*, from the Iranian voice *Pairidaeza*, which is Indo-European in origin.

166 "*O voi ch'avete li 'ntelletti sani / mirate la dottrina che s'asconde / sotto 'l velame de li versi strani*".

exhortation is addressed, more succinctly, by the author of *Sepher Yetzirah* (i, 4): "Discern with Wisdom and measure with Understanding."

Those who have a modicum of acquaintance with magical literature will have realized the similarity of these doctrines to so-called Invocational Magic, that is, the practice of leading angels and devils into one's presence (more the latter than the former, to tell the truth). The points of contact are manifold: the rituality, which in its approach to the sacred goes beyond the liturgical sphere and borders on a kind of "mystical mechanics"; the formal prescriptions, such as the obligation to celebrate in a special place, wear white robes, prepare the body with special exercises; the specific gestures, such as head motions and hand posture; and, above all, the constant recitation, to the point of exhaustion, of long verbal formulations, often in unknown languages or expressed in words that are "barbaric," i.e., incomprehensible and transfigured to the point of becoming "names of power." All of this concludes with the appearance of mysterious figures with whom one can engage in dialogue. Even Moshe Idel, one of the leading living Kabbalah experts, in an interview, after making a point of emphasizing that he "is not a mystic," indulged in a disturbing statement: "In Kabbalah, language coincides with reality, *a concept that is becoming increasingly obvious to all of us.*"[167]

*Translated by U.X.A.*

---

[167] Moshe Idel, "La mistica del comprendere", *Pagine Ebraiche* (09.07.2012). My italics.

# COSMOGONY AND ANTHROPOGONY: SYMBOLS, LANGUAGE, AND SACRED MUSIC IN THE VEDIC TRADITION

*Nuccio D'Anna*

A long series of sacred traditions of both West and East configure sound within the ambit of a fundamental creative dimension. According to Marius Schneider[168], at the origins of the Vedic tradition there appears an "Undefinable Sound" often represented in this archaic ontology as a symbolic "Solar Sound," or otherwise as the "Sun of Truth," *Satyam Sūryam*. It is the "Unhearable Sound" designated in the Vedas as Brahman, the Nirguna Brahman of Vedānta, the "Brahman Without Qualities" or "Without Form", the absolute Truth which on the human plane corresponds to the gap that is created between the birth of an idea and its hearable formulation,

---

168 The essay by Marius Schneider that is analysed here, "*Musique et langage sacrés dans la tradition védique*," was read and widely discussed at the Second Convention of the Tessinese Institute of Higher Studies held in Lugano in 1971, where it was greatly appreciated by all the Orientalists who were present. It was later published as part of the special issue of *Conoscenza Religiosa* 1(1973), 112-145, which also contained the first Italian translation of the 14 *Yoga Upanishads*. A total of 15 articles by Schneider, dedicated to the study of various aspects of musical symbolism, appeared in this journal. A complete autobiography of the great ethnomusicologist up to the year 1969 may be found in Robert Günther, "Special Bibliography: Marius Schneider", *Ethnomusicology* 13:3 (1969), 518-526. The present study intends to highlight the doctrinal and harmonic background that fuelled Schneider's reflections on Vedic cosmogony and anthropogony. The quotations of the German scholar's text, without references to writings, pages, and places, are taken from the Italian version which appeared in *Conoscenza Religiosa* and was edited by Elémire Zolla.

## Cosmogony and Anthropogony

since, Schneider explains, sound is nothing else than "the relationship that runs between thought and imagination." In the Vedic world, it is the song of the Supreme Being to determine the cosmic manifestation, because singing is the very substance of any sacrifice, while the ritual which leads to the intonation of the Holy Chant or *Sāman*[169] is traditionally identified by the term *Ṛta*, which means at once "Truth," "Law," and "Cosmic Order." It is a truth that reveals a full adherence or identity with the cosmic order and can be expressed only through sacred praises and sacrificial chants which interpret its intimate "acoustic form." In the Vedic texts, *Ṛta* is often juxtaposed with *Satya*, the "Truth," or maybe more appropriately, the "Knowledge of Truth," since *Satya* and *Ṛta* are, as Jeanine Miller explains[170], respectively the "essence of what exists" and its "activity," its *modus essendi*. The *Bṛhadāraṇyaka-Upaniṣad* explains that "*satyam* consists of three syllables. *Sa* and *yam* represent truth. The syllable *ti* is outside of this truth. But such deficiency is compensated by the fact that it is 'surrounded by truth.'"[171] *Ṛta* is therefore also

---

169 The Indian liturgical tradition distinguishes between *Ṛc*, the recited verse, *Sāman*, the stanza or sung verse, and *Yajus*, the murmured verse. The *ṛc* root carries a meaning that includes "song," "splendour," and "hymn of praise," and therefore appears linked to a remote background signifying "light." The *Chāndogya-Upaniṣad* (I, 1, 3) repeats: "this *udgītha* is the most essential of all essences, the supreme, the pre-excellent, the octave." Marius Schneider explains that "the ritual chant (*sāman*) is the relationship (the rubbing) of the two poles of life: *sā* ('she') and *ama* ('him')."

170 Cf. Janine Miller, *The Vedas: Harmony, Meditation and Fulfilment* (London: Rider & Company, 1974). This is an important book that develops with rich doctrine the previous intuitions of *shrī* Aurobindo which appeared from 1914 to 1917 in the journal *Arya* of Pondicherry, later continued in idem, *Le Secret du Véda* (Paris: Fayard, 1975). Other texts by *shrī* Aurobindo may be found in *Hymns of the Atris* and *Selected Hymns*, included in the first part of idem, *The Secret of the Veda* (Pondicherry: Shri Aurobindo Ashram, 2003). As an introduction, Jean Herbert, *L'interprétation psychologique du Veda selon shrī Aurobindo* (Paris: Dervy-Livres, 1979), may also be useful.

171 Marius Schneider, *La nascita musicale del simbolo*, in Id., *Il significato della musica* (Milan: Rusconi, 1979), 109.

the ritual action performed in perfect harmony with the Cosmic Order and with the supreme knowledge which realises its universal spiritual meaning. The *RigVeda* (I, 24, 8) reminds us that "the Dawn follows the way of the *Ṛta*, the right way which it has always known, and does not go beyond its boundaries. The Sun follows the path of the *Ṛta*." In Marius Schneider's words intended to explain the connection between "rhythm and sound" as well as that between "image and light," which is fundamental to his system: "when talking about the *Ṛta* that is part of the primordial world, what is described is a luminous mass that radiates invisibly from the bottom of the *Ṛta*." In the second volume of his fundamental monograph on the god Varuna, Heinrich Lüders[172] could affirm that this Vedic god, always considered as the keeper, warranter, and ruler of the cosmic order, celestial harmony and moral law, while governing the world through the *Ṛta* simultaneously "*does* [= creates or composes] *the chants*" without which ritual sacrifice cannot nourish the existence of the cosmos. As *dhṛta-vrata*, "he whose law is firmness" (root *dhṛ*, from which *dhṛta*), Varuna establishes the cosmic order, creates the rhythms which scan its regular unfolding, sets the path of *Sūrya*, and corroborates truth, since Varuna is also the keeper of *Satya*.

According to Schneider, the primordial Brahman, absolutely devoid of any form and often represented in Schneider's writings as an original "Unhearable Sound," is

---

[172] Heinrich Lüders, *Varuṇa*, 2 vols. (Göttingen: L. Alsdorf, 1951-59). This work, carefully followed by Schneider in his other writings as well, overturned the hypotheses about the Vedic god which had been circulating for a long time in the texts of those scholars accustomed to making said god a never-extant "naturalistic hypostasis" by slavishly following the postulates of 19th-century positivism. For a correct description of this god, cf. also Jan Gonda, *Les Religions de l'Inde*, 2 vols. (Paris: Payot, 1962), vol. I, 93-106. On the role of this divine form in the Indian philosophy of the time, cf. Nuccio D'Anna, *I cicli cosmici. Le dottrine indiane sui ritmi del tempo* (Genoa: Edizioni Arya, 2023), in which the spiritual reality which corroborates these particular doctrines is explained.

conveyed by the *akāsha*, the "ethereal space"[173] which the *Jaimiṇīya-upaniṣad-brāhmana* (I, 23) identifies as *Vāk*, "she who holds all worlds united together" (RV, X, 125, 8). From this "ethereal space," that bases its creative power in the *Ṛc* (the recited verse), Brahma, the creator god, arose, and in turn he originated Marīci, "Ray of Light," who in turn begot Kashyapa, one of the primordial 7 *Rishi*s who is regarded as the founder of the "solar essence" which has intimately substantiated the cosmos ("That splendour of yours, oh Kashyapa, whose essence is light, all that brightness which is begotten, oh Shining One, in which the 7 Suns set at once" - AV XIII, 3, 10). In some ways, it may be said that the *akāsha* "includes" *in principiis* the elements which substantiate the whole cosmic manifestation, on both the "subtle" level and the corporeal one. It is a quintessential reality that on the material plane underlies the primordiality of sound amongst the sense qualities, and it is possible to transpose it by analogy onto higher levels, such as, for instance, the unmanifested or the "subtle" order. It is from this quintessential reality that the *mahā-bhūta*, the "substantial elements" or "primal archetypes" which inform every aspect of manifestation, take consistency.

According to Schneider, the unexpressed and "formless" Brahman is followed by a second Brahman identifiable with the god Brahma, symbolically born in a lotus flower, who gave rise to the world of forms by sacrificing and practising the most austere ascetic disciplines. Therefore, the god Brahma personifies the perceptible sound conveyed by *air*, the first constituent element of the cosmos, the basis of every sound which makes possible this very same first determination of it. According to Schneider,

> this part of the primordial world is the starting point of the language of mystical syllables whose ritual execution occurs by cycle V, but which in the concrete world practically represents

---

[173] According to the traditional etymology, *ākāsha* comes from *ā* + *kāsh-* which gives "splendour of light," "space," and "luminous ether."

## Cosmogony and Anthropogony

the entirety of the primordial world. The *AUM* syllable is here pronounced on the characteristic tone of this cycle. It is called the "white syllable," and it is emitted by breathing out and purifying oneself. Conversely, the *HUM* syllable, called "blue," is emitted by breathing in, and in doing so man swallows the *H*, the spiritual sound par excellence [...]. The Brahman exists because when Brahma withdraws his breath he swallows and annihilates the world of *Māyā*, that is, Non-truth, and when one withholds one's breath a void is produced inside oneself, and therein one grasps the immutable Truth.

The second Brahman constitutes a veritable "archetypal form," the principial unity which, notwithstanding its pristine and original purity, already represents a departure from absolute truth. According to the Hindu tradition, in fact, every "form," however elevated, constitutes in itself a splitting or a sundering from the undefinable primordial Brahman and already belongs to the world of *māyā*, i.e., is already sunken into the illusion of becoming, ensnared in the incessant need for completeness. Therefore, one of the attributes of Varuna as ruler of the cosmos is *Jālavant*, the "Owner of the Net" (= *jāla*), the patron of the "magical force" which permeates the universe, identified as the *māyā* with which Varuna builds the worlds. For the latter very special aspects, Ānanda K. Coomaraswamy, in a 1933 article[174] in which he studied the meaning of the terms *māyā*, *deva*, and *tapas*, believed that *māyā* is also the supreme "creative art" of Varuna, the "magical force" which wholly substantiates the moulding action of the god in his function as Universal Sovereign (*Samrāj*).

Schneider considers the purely acoustic dimension to be the fundamental characteristic of the primordial world. In this original sonic reality, permeated by an "Unhearable

---

174 Cf. Ananda K. Coomaraswamy, "On Translation: Māyā, Deva, Tapas", *Isis* 19:1 (1933), 79-91. The monograph by his friend Heinrich Zimmer, *Maya. Der Indische Mythos* (Stuttgart: Deutsche Verlagsanstalt, 1936), remains important. The topic was also discussed in M. Schneider, "Origin of the Symbol in the Spirit of Music", *Diogenes* 7:27 (1959), 39-62.

Sound" or by what he calls "Silent Sound," the first hearable formulation consisted in its syllabic scansion, in which the individual syllables are symbolically represented by the 7 Ŗishis[175], the "Sonic Lights," the "meters of poetry," as Schneider interprets by closely following the traditional symbolism which teaches to rediscover the primordial experience of the unitary "light-sound." The Rishis are the "Guardians of the Sun" (*ye gopāyanti sūryam*, RV, X, 154, 5), the "Great Seers of Yore" (*sahasranīthāh*), those who have "seen and heard" the divine Revelation of non-human origin (*apauru-sheya*), the holy Knowledge or *Shruti*. The vision of the Vedic Rishis appears therefore very peculiar. What appeared before their inspired eyes was a cosmos shining with "sound and light," which in itself constituted a "heavenly vision" echoing divine rhythms and melodies. It was a continuous and uninterrupted hierophany that revealed the intimate spiritual essence with which the cosmos is permeated, and which requires being nourished with sacrifice and ritual singing. To use the terms employed by Jan Gonda[176] in his fundamental study on the "vision" of the Vedic poets, originally the Rishis "established a special

---

[175] The etymology of the term *Ŗishi* is uncertain. If we connect it to the Avestan *ərəšiš*, we get the meaning of "ecstasy". Indologists derive it from the Vedic root *ṛṣ*, which in turn comes from *dṛś*, "to see," from which also comes *ṛṣhi-kṛt* ("he who shows," otherwise "he who sings the sacred hymn"). As we can see, there is a strong substrate pertaining to "light" also underlined by the fact that the term *riksha* (the stars of Ursa, always considered the abode of the Vedic Rishis) might derive from the root *arch* or *ruch*, "to shine," "to illuminate," "to sparkle," whence *archis*, "light" or "ray of light," and *arka* "hymn," "praise," "shining song," or even "thunderbolt." On the relationship between *arch* and "singing," cf. A. Coomaraswamy, "Beauté, Lumière et Son", *Études Traditionnelles* (1937), 51-60. On the complex traditions concerning the Vedic Rishis we follow J. E. Mitchiner, *Traditions of the Seven Ŗṣis* (Delhi: Motilal Barnasidass, 1982); C. B. Pandey, *Ŗiṣis in Ancient India* (Delhi: Sundeep Prakashan, 1987).

[176] J. Gonda, *The Vision of the Vedic Poets* (The Hague: De Gruyter Mouton, 2011). On some related terms (*svar, svardṛś*, etc.), cf. L. Renou, "Sur quelques mots du ŖigVeda", *Journal of American Oriental Studies* 85:1 (1965), 83 ff. More generally, to follow the passage from the Vedic experience of the celestial Powers to the contemplation and worship of their individual "formulation," it remains important to refer to Marila Falk, *Nāma-rūpa and Dharma-rūpa* (Calcutta: Calcutta University, 1943).

## Cosmogony and Anthropogony

manifestation of the *Ṛta*, the regular, normal, true and harmonious fundamental and 'natural' structure of the universe, that which underlies and determines the cosmic, mundane and ritual events, and gave rise to the dhītih, the 'vision.'" As we can see, a principial and pre-formal dimension of the cosmos seems to emerge with sufficient clarity, skilfully combining sound and light, that is, the principial pair which is placed at the foundation of every sacrifice as it "establishes a transaction between the sonic form and the material form of the symbol,"[177] as Schneider further explains. This is the dimension that he repeatedly designates as *"acoustic substance."* It is not the corporeal reality that in Indian doctrines has always been indicated by the binomial *nāma-rūpa* ("name and form": cf. *Muṇḍaka-Upaniṣad* I, 9), the modalities of the sensitive manifestation which Schneider interprets both as "light and image" and as "rhythm and sound." In this context, we can also emphatically highlight the sheer sonority that substantiates the sacrificial chants and praises, which are always modulated on the acoustic essence of the cosmos. As Schneider takes care to explain, "once they come out of the *akāsha* element, that is, of absolute truth, the ideas become audible syllables and forms upon entering the 'air' element. At first only thought of, ideas are then pronounced and become sonic. From this comes a conception of the Creator whose nature is a blow, wind, a whirlwind, a word, a song or a mouth which utters the world." At another one of his important conferences, in which he wished to explain the cosmogonic role played by the Dawn (= *Ushas*) in the Vedic tradition, Schneider further specified:

> since such natural sounding rhythms, still so close to the ultimate truth, cannot yet be embodied in melodies or verses, we are justified in assuming that they were understood as pure, monotonous, but well-qualified temporal divisions (similarly to what happens for the rhythms of drums). Mono-tonous, however,

---
177 Schneider, *Il significato della musica*, 107.

does not mean monotony in the current sense of the term, but rather a prolonged stay on the same tone. The *Shatapatha Brāhmana* (VIII, 2-6 e X, 3) enumerates a long list of such rhythms [...]. The original rhythms are therefore not examples of precise creatures, but pure acoustic forms of activity over time, which forego the created object.

We are at the dawn of creation, in the spring of cosmic manifestation, when from the first two modalities of manifestation, that is to say, from the pair of "rhythm and sound" or from that of "image and light," there arises the principial unity of "sound-light"[178], whose possible formulation can only be purely acoustic. It is the highest one of the "forms" preceding any other possible determinations. And yet, despite its absolute non-expressivity, in still being a "form," it already belongs to the sphere of conditioned manifestation, to *māyā*.

In order to explain what some Indian cosmogonic texts symbolically call the "weaving of the world" (a formulation which uses a symbolism present in the same way in many other spiritual traditions), and wishing to highlight the acoustic foundation which, in his opinion, remains the deepest "substance" of the universal manifestation, Schneider starts by describing the beginnings of the world, the midnight, the winter of creation, the cosmic reality which on the spatial plain refers to the cardinal North and to the astronomical centrality of the North Pole. To reconstruct the original cosmogonic system, he uses a symbolic grid which, like the classical *tetraktys* of ancient Pythagoreanism, develops from 1 to 10 according to a musical scale corresponding to the first 10 sounds of the harmonic series (fig. 1):

---

178 This is a fundamental theme in Schneider's deliberations on the harmonic foundations of cosmogony. An extensive discussion is found in Schneider, "Le basi del mondo luminoso-acustico e sua concretezza apparente", *Conoscenza Religiosa* 1 (1982), 52-71.

*Cosmogony and Anthropogony*

|  |  |  |  |  |  |
|---|---|---|---|---|---|
| primordial, acoustic world | | 1 | I | sound (sun-thunder) inaudible (*akasha*) | |
| | do | 2 4 5 | II | air, respiration, dualism | constant *Rta* |
| | sol | 6 | III | sky, primordial ocean, earth (fire in the waters) - invisible light | |
| | | 7 | III ½ | (= 7) tongue S, H, SH, wet heat | |
| | do | 8 | IV | 1st cycle – milk ocean - 1st theme deep sleep | |
| concrete world | | 9 | | opening of the cosmic egg, winter, midnight, birth and infancy, amphibians | |
| | mi | 10 | V | center of the universe, twilight, dream, sun in the morning star, fish, birds | |
| | sol | 11 12 | VI | ossification, petrification, precious stones, sacrifice dualism-opposition, ambivalence - sickle of moon – puberty serpent, theft of fire, flood - creation of current humanity - double sex divided in two | new *Rta* |
| | | 13 | VI ½ | dawn (filter, tissue), marriage sound-light | |
| | si | 14 15 | VII | morning, spring, second birth, full consciousness | |
| | do | 16 17 | VIII-IX X | full day midday, summer solstice | |

Figure 1

Elsewhere, describing the relationship between the zodiac and the harmonic system, he adds that the planet Saturn is equivalent to the 11th harmonic, Jupiter to the 13th, Mars to the 15th, Venus to the 17th, Mercury to the 19th, the Sun to the 20th, while between Venus and Mars there is the 16th harmonic, corresponding to the Moon and to the Earth. Then, following a harmonic series corresponding to

## Cosmogony and Anthropogony

the order of the planets described in ancient cosmogonies, he attributes a vowel-sound to each planet: the deep U to Saturn, Y to Jupiter, O to Mars, I to the Sun, È (grave) and É (acute) respectively to the *Stella Matutina* and *Vespertina*. In a well-known 1960 article about the "harmony of the spheres" and the metaphysical foundations that substantiate its complex symbolic formulation[179], Schneider noted the interchangeability of the harmonic value of the letters of the Greek alphabet with the planets and notes of musical systems. Assuming that each planet can yield a sound relatable to that of the zodiacal sign in which its main "planetary house" is located, Schneider obtained an extraordinary interpretive grid that gives foremost meaning to the relationships which link the 7 planets and the 12 constellations of the zodiac to the musical notes, and even to a possible cosmogonic perspective unfolding itself, as witnessed by many stellar calendars of ancient civilisations, starting from the summer solstice and the corresponding zodiacal sign of Cancer:

> **Sun** = Leo = F
> **Moon** = Cancer = D flat
> **Saturn** = Capricorn = E flat; and Aquarium = G
> **Jupiter** = Sagittarius = B flat; and Pisces = B
> **Mars** = Aries = C; and Scorpio = F sharp,
> **Venus** = Taurus = E; and Libra = D or Virgo = A
> **Mercury** = Gemini = A flat; and Libra = D or Virgo = A

The result is the following series of notes which, as a veritable "holy series," not only finds correspondence in the yearly rhythms and in the zodiacal signs, but is also able to explain the origin of its own disharmony starting, as Schneider further specified, "from a series of harmonics or

---

[179] M. Schneider, "Die musikalischen Grundlagen der Sphärenharmonie", *Acta Musicologica* 1:2 (1960), 136-151 [Italian translation in idem, *Il significato della musica* (Milan: Rusconi, 1996), 205-227]. Also see idem, "Il mito del mondo primordiale e l'armonia delle sfere", *Conoscenza Religiosa* 1 (1983), 1-10.

hypertones which begins from D flat, that is, from the sign of Cancer (summer solstice), but which was overshadowed by its late insertion into the system of the seven notes":

**Summer**: D flat., F, A.
**Autumn**: D, F sharp, B flat.
**Winter**: E flat, G, B.
**Spring**: C, E, A flat.

By means of these correlations, Schneider was able to outline an interpretive grid capable of nourishing an essentially symbolic attitude to knowledge, and even to substantiate "from within" the Hellenic speculations pertaining to the so-called astronomical science of the Pythagoreans, whose doctrines about the *kosmos* were, on the other hand, deeply permeated by speculations about the "harmony of the spheres."

What is of interest here, however, is the series of the proposed grid which goes from 1 to 10, because it is the one which shapes the original acoustic structure of the world. From the "Unexpressed" and "Principial Sound," the universal manifestation unfolds up to its extreme degree of petrification and crystallisation, according to a gradation outlined by Schneider as a dualism which finds its most precise symbol in the pair "music and stone."[180] In a 1950 essay[181] studying the existing relationships between melody and language in Chinese music, Schneider specified that, in the ancient worldview, words always have the purpose of revealing the sonic substance of things. Their rhythm is the very essence of virtue, not a mere symbol of it. Not only that, but this point may also help us understand

---

180 Cf. M. Schneider, "La coppia simbolica 'musica e pietra': Saggio di decifrazione di un pensiero filosofico espresso con un simbolo di natura rituale", Conoscenza Religiosa 3 (1971), 201-213; idem, "La notion de temps dans la philosophie et la mythologie védiques" in Istituto Accademico di Roma (ed.), Eternità e Storia. I valori permanenti nel divenire storico (Florence: Vallecchi, 1970), 203-214.

181 Cf. M. Schneider, "La rélation entre la mélodie et le langage dans la musique chinoise", Annuario Musical V (1950), 62-69.

another peculiarity of the Vedic civilisation. Here, poetry and music did not constitute the fleeting delight of a court elite, but were part of a very sophisticated sacred knowledge transmitted mainly, if not exclusively, in the sacerdotal class. They were a "form of wisdom" that shaped both the divine plain and the cosmic one. Originally, music, poetry, and singing constituted a fundamental aspect of sacrificial life, and therefore, in the context of the sacerdotal "families" listed in the *RigVeda*, the knowledge of their spiritual "essence" and of the ritual background which corroborated the recitation of compositions constituted "almost necessarily" a path to immortality.

The different "levels" of manifestation to which we are hinting may be divided into two groups. Schneider explains: "The primordial world extends itself from 0 to III½. It is outside of time and space. With cycle IV, time and space are formed during the winter and at the midnight of creation: this is the first winter solstice, the childhood of the Anthropocosm." The image that emerges has a very complex descriptive value. If we consider it, for example, from the perspective of the doctrine of cycles, which is so perfectly ingrained within the whole Hindu cosmogonic system, then there is a manifestation moving away from the origins, which are symbolically placed on the winter solstice, that ends its materialisation on the summer solstice, the "summer of creation" which closes the cosmic manifestation with cycle X. Afterwards, as Schneider explains, there is a "relapse" in cycle IV, since it is here that the original condition of "deep slumber" takes place. It is the cycle characterised by the "primordial Waters," given that the "Creative Word," *Vāk*, is "clad in water" and its "abode is in the waters" (RV 125, 7-8), and is therefore the same power of revelation of *Āditi* both in its purely acoustic, pre-formal and "subtle" dimension, and in its corporeal and

## Cosmogony and Anthropogony

concrete one.[182] Therefore, the *RigVeda* can thus enjoin the primordial *Rishi*: "Speak three words [preceded by light, or] that project light (*jyotir agrāḥ*), that milk the udder which sheds honey" (VII, 101, 1). As we can see, "water" is revealed as the vehicle of the "creative presence of the sound," the mystery contained in the sacred syllable *AUM*. Schneider explains:

> this extension of the syllable *AUM*, seat of all forces, is expressed by the following formula: *AUM* has two heads, three feet, four horns and seven arms. That is to say, it has its origin in the dualist centre of the primordial world which reckons three and a half sounds. They are the three *more*[183], the movements of thought plus the expiatory sound. But the total duration, that is, its extension in the spatial and temporal world, consists of seven times.

Thus, we find ourselves in the reality known in the *RigVeda* as the "unknowable flow of the waters," which are therefore likened to *Vāk*, the "Creative Word" considered by tradition to be the Firstborn in the sound waves of the primordial Ocean. This is also why Lao Tzu could point out that the murmur of water promotes meditation because the water element symbolically leads back to conditions similar to those of the primordial world. It is still an original state in which, as the *Atharva Veda* explains, *Vāk* reveals itself through a sheerly euphonic expressive form since it, the Word, was originally "full of water" and language was scanned on the rhythms of a cosmos still governed by the "acoustic substance" with which it was permeated from the beginning. Since the syllables that constitute the framework

---

182 Cf. L. Renou, "*Les pouvoirs de la Parole dans le RgVéda*" in idem, *Études védiques et pāninéennes*, vols. I-V (Paris: De Boccard, 1955), vol. I, 1: "*Les spéculations védiques [...] reposent sur une sorte de primat de la parole [...] un mot tel que vāc n'est autre que l'équivalent de logos: c'est le prototype d'ātman-brahman.*" Cf. also Ch. Malamoud, *La Déesse Parole dans le Veda: un corp fait de mots* in C. Conio (ed.), *La Parola creatrice in India e nel Medio Oriente* (Pisa: Giardini, 1994), 35-42. Also see Marila Falk, *Il mito psicologico dell'India antica* (Milan: Adelphi, 1986), 49 ff.

183 The term *more* used by Schneider refers to the modalities of controlled thought during the phases of yogic breathing: inhalation, stasis and exhalation.

of the stanzas and verses through which *Vāk* is articulated have simultaneously a phonetic and a numerical value, each sacred recitation reveals itself as the truthful "forming form" of a cosmic environment deeply pervaded by sounds, rhythms, and numbers (= first principles = archetypes), which is only graspable by means of a complex symbolism combining euphony and arhythmosophy.

According to the *RigVeda*, *Vāk* bestows the word upon the gods so that they can reveal the "thought of the Waters enshrined in their own name." As we can see, for the Vedic Rishis and *Kavis* (who are not coincidentally defined as "Keepers of the Sun" in RV X, 145, 5), it is not a question of abstract compositions or poetic assonances which are entirely outward and transient, but of grasping the melodic rhythms and the "sonic substance" which give consistency to cosmic phenomena and are perceived on the bodily level merely as noises of waters, voices of animals, the roar of the thunder or of the downpouring rain. To put it with Schneider, ritual music "sings of heat or dampness, fire or water by performing these elements, before these rhythms achieve concrete existence. Before the waters appeared, there was the murmuring of the waters. In the night of creation, the effect foregoes the cause; time is retrograde."[184] The primordial rhythm always refers to a spiritual meaning because it is "a typical musical event, a contemplation strongly connected to the object or an antinomian feeling," as Schneider further explains. Therefore, the Vedic language of the origins "naturally" transfigured itself into a hymn of praise or into a song raised to an immaculate cosmos and to the supreme Brahman whose most truthful reality could only be grasped through sacrifice. On the other hand, the world had not yet ossified into its transient and phenomenological appearance, and in the eyes of the Vedic Rishis, the world constituted a hierophanic reality, it revealed the "holy texture" of which it was totally informed. Likely

---

184 Schneider, *La notion du temps dans la philosophie et la mythologie védique*, 206.

also due to these aspects, in the temple of Chidambaram in Tamil Nadu, Shiva, venerated from time immemorial as the god who creates the world by means of dance, and therefore also considered the patron of music, is represented in 108 postures assumed while dancing which, at the same time, symbolise the 108 rhythms of the sacred chant, the 108 syllabic formulations of "mystical language," and the 108 paths which lead to liberation. As we can see, this interpretive grid tends overall to give meaning not only to the corporeal manifestation, but also to what we can define as an genuinely archaic anthropogony. Therefore, still using Vedic symbolism, Schneider explains:

> In the primordial world, cycle II represents the nose, the blow, breathing, the consonance of the octave, which constitute the seat of sound dualism. Cycle III is the purely acoustic heaven and earth, the mouth of this world: the palate is the sky, the lower part of the mouth is the earth, and between the two the whirl of the primordial sea resonates. In these waters are found all creation and all the future functions which in cycle III½ will be pronounced by the tongue. Cycle II is the mouth of the first sacrifice.

This principle of creation is "comprehended" or "preserved" in the Cosmic Egg, the *Brahmanda*, of which *Hiranyagarbha*, the "Golden Germ," represents the "enlivening principle" and in a way the "creating principle," given that its sphere of action is that of the world of the "subtle" manifestation, where the pre-formal root of what is lived or grasped (by analogy with the daily bodily experience) as a "sound vibration" or a "light wave" is experienced. For this series of reasons, in Hindu mythology Hiranyagarbha is always placed in relation with the "Cosmic Waters," in which Brahma lays down the "germ" which will become the Cosmic Egg. Therefore, Hiranyagarbha is also likened to the god Brahma himself, who in this case takes the appellation of *Nārāyana*, "He Who Moves [or Floats] on the Waters." However, Schneider specifies that we must distinguish yet another very particular aspect of such symbolism:

## Cosmogony and Anthropogony

the primordial head enclosed in the World Egg is not identical to the head of the Anthropocosm realised in time and space. This is a product of the primordial head. The Anthropocosm is a phenomenon of *māyā*, that is, of the world of Non-truth, which gives birth to a heaven and an earth, respectively above and below the foregoing acoustic heaven and earth, always constituting the centre and embryo of the universe. The new heaven and the new earth are formed from the two parts of the cloven Egg.

Returning to the grid of fig. 1, Schneider explains that there is a precise relationship between the indicated cycles, the "stages" of "thought," and astronomical references: "between cycles III and IV are the 3½ measures: the three stages of thought corresponding to the three letters of the syllable *AUM* plus the exhalation time. These three stages appear in our system as cycle III½, but the *Upaniṣads* teach that the duration of these 3½ beats is rhythmically worth 7 beats." This is an important notation that allows Schneider to move directly to the explanation of the symbol that the Vedic texts describe as the "texture of the cosmos." At the origins of the special reality drawn in his grid, in fact, what Schneider calls "the inner or primordial 7" was created by the gods by intoning a 7-beats song. Most likely, this archaic sacrificial chant must be identified with the *sapta vānīh* spoken of in the *RigVeda* (I, 164, 24), interpreted by the ancient commentator Sāyana as the "7 voices" or the "7 metres," then also explained by Hermann Grassmann in his *Wörterbuch zum Rig-Veda* as *Liedformen*.[185] Going deeper into the interpretive levels, and adhering to the classic translation by Karl Geldner[186], we can affirm that these are the "7 names of the cosmic Cows" corresponding, in Schneider's terms, to the "7 sound rhythms of the Heavenly Lights," since the Vedic *gauh*, *go* (= "cow," "milk-cow") also

---

185 H. Grassmann, *Wörterbuch zum Rig-Veda*, 4 vols. (Wiesbaden: Otto Harrassowitz, 1955 [1873]), 1257.

186 K.F. Geldner, *Der Rig-Veda aus dem Sanskrit ins Deutsche Übersetzt*, 4 vols. (Cambridge: Harvard University Press / Wiesbaden: Otto Harrasowitz, 1951).

## Cosmogony and Anthropogony

indicates the "celestial light" (but also the "ray of light," the "heaven" or the "thunderbolt") poured throughout the cosmos by Āditi, the "Heavenly Mother," which symbolises Endless Light and Universal Knowledge.

The Vedic Rishis symbolically sang the freeing of the "cow-lights" from the Cosmic Cave upon the appearance of *Ushas*, the Dawn of an enlightened and pure consciousness, the time when the Seers intone their prayers, raise chants to the gods, operate sacrifices, and the divine light regally abides within their hearts like the "cow in the stable." For this reason, the *RigVeda* recalls that "the power of *Vāk* revealed itself in the seat of the Cow" (*pade go*, III, 55, 1), likened here to *Āditi Sahasrākṣarā* (the "Heavenly Mother of the Thousand Syllables"), which connects in an absolutely evident way *Vāk* with the cosmic light and with the infinite creative potentialities of *Āditi*. All this may help us to understand without excessive difficulties even the passage in the *RigVeda* (VII, 84, 4ab) which recalls the impartation of the god Varuna to the Rishi Vasiṣta: "the Cow bears 3 times 7 names." We are at the heart of the spiritual symbol that substantiates the "sound-light" pair, which is fundamental to understand the Schneiderian cosmogonic system. In fact, is *Vasiṣta*, on the one hand, as a *Rishi* is "he who is himself light" or "he who has light in himself" (*svabhānavah*), on the other hand, as the son of the divine couple *Mitra-Varuna* (= "day" and "night")[187] he has also always been considered by the Vedic tradition (RV, VII, 33, 11 e 13) as the "light-bringer" (= *Ushas*, the "Dawn").

The *Rigvedaprātiṣākhya* (III, 7) specifies: "They say that [there are] 3 positions of the voice: grave, medium and supreme, each one with 7 tones [*yama*]. The 7 notes are the 7 tones [*yama*] or they are different." On a cosmological level, all this corresponds to the spiritual dimension which

---

187 Schneider, *Il significato della musica*, 35.

## Cosmogony and Anthropogony

also includes the "polar" symbolism of the constellation of Ursa, the *sapta ṛiksha* (= the 7 Rishis dwelling in the 7 stars of Ursa, each of them having the Pole oriented from his star seat during a particular cosmic phase), the 7 original rhythms, the 7 metres of archaic poetry, the 7 notes (*svarna*), the 6 x 7 "chant styles" (*bhāsa*), and even the 7 positions taken by the tongue when it emits the sounds S or SH. "This is the moment," Schneider explains, "when Non-truth (dualism) begins to conceal the Truth to make our concrete world arise." In this regard, it may be useful to remember that in the *Atharva Veda* the 7 Rishis are depicted as the "weavers of Dawn," that is, as the "Sonic Lights" which the *RigVeda* describes as they intone their song on the "7 threads of the shuttle." What is meant here are the stanzas or *Sāman* sung by the priest *Udgātṛ* ("He Who Sings Aloud"), who represents or personifies *Sūrya*, the "Spiritual Sun" which, as *Gandharva*, is also the original source of the "music of the spheres." The song of the *Sāman* is symbolically regarded as "the spool that weaves the primordial sacrifice" because, as RV X, 130, 2c further explains, "these are the rungs. They sat on the seat and made the spools to weave with the *Sāman*." Wanting to give meaning to these symbolic structures, Schneider adds that "*Sāman* is the sacred formula raised to its highest level. It is the essence of sacrifice, being the full consent to the offering of the 'life breath' by means of sound. The two most revered forms, the *Rathantara* and the *Brihat*[188], are the secret formulas which, like a sailing boat, are headed towards the gods." In order to understand symbols that are so particularly linked to the mystical-sacrificial experience of the primordial Rishis, one must bear in mind that whereas in the *RigVeda* the stanza is identified with *Vāk* and the *Sāman* with the "life breath," elsewhere the stanza is likened

---

[188] The *Rathantara* is sung at midday during the oblation of *Soma*, while the *Brihat* has the task of conveying the spiritual force of *Vāk* and is articulated on a rhythm of 36 syllables which remodulates *ad hoc* the symbolism of the 360 degrees of the cosmic circle.

to hearing and the *Sāman* to thought. These are liturgical "forms" that underline the simultaneously creative and formative function of the *Sāman* which, as "sound rhythm," is interwoven, like the "life breath," with the cosmic Order.

It is precisely due to this sacrificial "essence" that the *Sāman* "nourishes" the gods and facilitates their existence. Precisely because of this complex liturgical and ritual basis Schneider recalls that "the hymns of the *Sāman Veda* [are] composed of mystical syllables. This ancient chant is related to the doctrine of the vowels and creative syllables that in Vedic psalmody (of which they constitute the whole text, or in whose text they are interspersed) allow for 'reaching eternity,' provided that they are uttered with the "right intonation."[189] As we can see, what emerges by following the grid provided by Schneider is a precise scheme combining cosmogony, musical notes, celestial constellations, sounds, phonemes, and cycles of manifestation. We must keep firmly in mind that up to cycle IV we are still within the scope of the *Ṛta* and the purely acoustic primordial world. This is the pre-formal sphere, which follows the dimension of the Unexpressed and the Metaphysical Zero (= Sanskrit *kha* which, as Ānanda K. Coomaraswamy explained in an unsurpassed study[190], symbolically also indicates the hole or void of the hub of the cosmic wheel), when the "mouth of the Anthropocosm is shut" and silence reigns before any articulation of sound. It is the world of the first principles that, starting from the Unhearable Sound (cycle I), through the archetypal principle which takes concreteness by means of the air element (*vāyu*) and the rhythmic breathing on the vibrations of what Schneider defined as the original "acoustic substance" (II), then flows into the primordial

---

189 Schneider, *Il significato della musica*, 199-200.

190 Cf. A.K. Coomaraswamy, "*Kha* and other Words denoting Zero, in connection with the Metaphysics of Space", *Bulletin of School Oriental Studies* VII (1934), 487-497. An in-depth examination of the metaphysical foundations of this doctrine is found in his posthumous work, *Tempo ed Eternità* (Rome: Mediterranee, 2013), 19-35.

Ocean, where light still remains invisible and the tongue articulates sounds on 7 beats (III). Each one of these three cycles belonging to a pre-formal plane is based on a sacred phoneme, *A, U, M*, plus the half measure of the expiration time. On the cosmic plane, between cycles III and III½, are also to be placed the polar constellations of Cygnus and Ursa, which characterise a remote, initial era of cosmic life. In the "intermediate world" that takes form between cycles III and III½, Schneider also places the Milky Way, given that the myths of the origins and many sacrificial songs tell of a time when the Sun still travelled along the Milky Way, the ancient "Way of Ursa," as it is called in the *Atharva Veda* (18, 2, 31), before the Sun changed its path and inaugurated a new cosmic cycle by settling along the current *Via Solis*. We are at the winter solstice, at the midnight of creation, until cycle IV concludes the first part of this process of manifestation which, beginning from the original world of the Unexpressed, will lead to the "Ocean of Milk" and the "hatching" of the Cosmic Egg. We are under the sign of Aquarius, since "from the four rivers or the four holes [of the sky] the 'sonic waters' of the Ṛta pour onto the land and the Ocean." According to Schneider, cycle IV also marks "the cosmic position of *AUM*. It lies on the border between Truth and Non-truth and in our concrete world it is the only possible formulation of Truth." The concrete world begins to emerge: a "new *Ṛta*" is formed which replaces what Schneider had previously defined as the original "constant *Ṛta*." This is the "new *Ṛta*" which will give shape to the corporeal world and in turn will conclude its existence after a complete revolution of the *Rota Mundi*, at the midday of the world and on the summer solstice.

The following cycle V begins on the autumnal equinox, which in many traditions marks the beginning of the sacred calendar and ceremonial activities. The Sun illuminates the *Stella Matutina*, and sacrificial hymns are sung starting at dusk. The constellation of Pisces shines in the sky. But it is with the subsequent cycle VI that the life of the universe begins. It is the time of the crystallisation of the original creative impulse, and the law of bodily existence is dualism or ambivalence. The male-female human pair is born, the Moon scans its rhythms starting from the crescent, and fire and water oppose each other, breaking the primordial unity constituted by the symbolic synthesis of "fire-water" or "rhythm in sound." The zodiacal sign is Aries, which marks some aspects of important spiritual traditions. Between cycles VI and VII we find cycle VI½, because starting from the initial twilight the movement of the *Rota Mundi* has led us to the dawn, and to the birth of the "light-sound" on which many symbols and many archaic liturgies are arranged. The Vedic Rishis, the "Sonic Lights" who at the beginning of everything had "seen and heard" the divine Revelation which wholly informs the cosmos, offer up hymns of praise to *Ushas*, "the Dawn rising from the East / just like the poles are raised for the sacrifice" (RV, IV, 51). This is the spiritual light that sustains the cosmos and can only shine by means of the recitation of prayer. In this perpetual sonic sacrifice that nourishes the existence of the cosmos, the Rishis are assisted by two deities. The first is Rohita, the "Bull of Chants," who has the primary function of extending the "texture of light" generated by sacrifice to the bodily manifestation as well. The second is B*r*haspati, the "Lord of Chants," of the "Creative Word" and of "Prayer," the god who opens up the Cosmic Cave with the ritual cry emitted from his 7 mouths and his 7 rays, and who, with the refulgence of the Sun evoked by his praises, rips the veil of darkness which enshrouds the manifestation. When B*r*haspati climbs onto the "bright chariot of the Order" he beats down the demons and opens the "yard of the Cows," thus allowing the "divine light" (*svarvid*) to flow into the cosmos. Revealingly, the Vedic term used in this context by the primordial Seers is *arka*[191], which means both "shining song" and "thunderbolt" — which implies an "almost physical" power of the sacrificial chants and prayers which symbolically operate as the purifying and demiurgic force of fire, *Agni*, the triumphal splendour which springs from the Spiritual Sun, *Sūrya*. The chant raised by the *Rishi*s and by the genuine "celestial projection" (= *Ecclesia Spiritualis*) constituted by the protective deities (*Bṛhaspati* and *Rohita*) of the liturgical chant and sacrificial prayers, dissolves every form of darkness, makes light triumph, gives rise to a different cosmic reality, and creates a new "harmonious form" by means of the wedding of Truth and Non-truth, of Heaven and Earth. In traditional arts and crafts, the divine principle of this renewed unity is revealed especially in the cloths obtained by skilfully intertwining the weft thread with the warp thread. The symbolic archetype of traditional weaving is the bond fastened by the "Spiritual Sun" (= *Sūrya*) with the cosmic manifestation through a ray-thread (= *sūtrātmā*, the "spiritual thread") which links the various worlds and thus establishes "a warp thrown from afar on which these threads are woven" (AV, X, 8, 38). The *sūtrātmā* represents therefore the "ray of light" which comes down from heaven and, uninterruptedly conveying divine "blessings" into our world, stabilises the cosmic harmony and allows mankind to regain its original condition.

Cycle VI½ prepares cycle VII. After dawn comes the morning, the spring of the year. The sacred calendar and the liturgy begin their festive scanning on the spring equinox. The primeval age of this cycle is youth, and the rites are those which celebrate the initiations of the young, second birth, and spiritual transfiguration. The Pleiades shine in the sky and, together with the appearance of Arcturus and Orion, mark the beginning of the calendar of the

---

[191] About this term cf. L. Renou, "Les pouvoirs de la parole dans le Ṛgvéda" in idem, *Études védiques et panineénnes*, 6-7: "Le mot arka [...] est ambigu entre les valeurs de 'lumière' et de 'chant.'"

civilisation sung by Hesiod at the daybreak of the Hellenic world. The main zodiacal constellation for orientation can only be Taurus. One of the most important symbols of this cycle is the ceremonial Chariot (= *jyotīrathā*, "bright chariot") which is found as a fundamental element in many rituals, religious and cultural systems of archaic civilisations. The *RigVeda* enjoins us to symbolically get onto the chariot since "in crossing the oceans, your chariot is the wide-oared boat of the sky" (I, 46, 8), where what is meant by "ocean" is the intermediate region placed by the archaic cosmogony between Heaven and Earth, and what is meant by "chariot" (= *ratha*) is the sacrificial action, considered from time immemorial as the most suitable vehicle which allows the Vedic Seers to cross the celestial world. According to many myths, with cycle VII, with its spring equinox marked by the appearance of the Pleiades, there begins scansion of time according to the symbolic "7 days" of creation. At first, we find the "sonic light of the *Ṛta*" (0). Schneider specifies that in this original dimension "God speaks the light first. This sonic light can be nothing else than sunlight because the Sun is created only on the third day." The "sonic light" corresponds to the harmonic sound 7. Then creation proceeds with the sky (1st day), the earth (2nd), the Sun (3rd), fish and birds (4th), terrestrial animals (5th), mankind in paradise (6th), and in the end the Sun on the horizon (7th). As we can see, the *Rota Mundi* unrolls following the laws of cyclical development, and each phase or position marks an entire era of the universal manifestation with its own specific duration, its own cognitive aptitudes, and even different "forms" of corporeal beings. In the end, with the remaining cycles VIII, IX, and X, the whole cycle of manifestation reaches its conclusion; it is the fullness of the day and the year. The world is now firmly arranged around the corporeal and sensible reality. Now the dominant geometric figure is the square, which, with its stability and fixity, reveals the distance from the inaudible primordial "thunder-sound" and the full adherence of this cycle to the element Earth, *Prithivī*. We are at the midday of the world and almost everywhere the liturgical calendars celebrate the New Year on the summer solstice, under the constellation of Cancer. As Schneider further explains, at this point "the world gets gradually bigger, it has moved so far away from its origins that the primordial world has become almost imperceptible. The constant and eternal sound of the *Ṛta* of cycles III and III½ is no longer heard." The recitation of the sacred monosyllable *OṂ*, which upholds and nourishes the order of the cosmos and has guided its development from its origins up to its extreme bodily manifestation, must now reverse itself and become *MUAH*, the "lowing of the Cow," that is, the original "light-sound," because it is precisely the ritual recitation of this syllable that allows the triumphal ascent of the Sun. Following the teaching of the *Upaniṣads*, Schneider explains that the reversal of the primordial sacred syllable *AUṂ* also brings about a different symbolic-ritual system: the phoneme *M* represents heaven or the primordial world, *U* the intermediate world, and *A* the earth. The recitation of this formula, like a "celestial boat" or the ritual "chariot" intoned by the Rishis, allows souls to be transported from the concrete world to that of the origins, where, as the *RigVeda* explains, "the Sun shines thanks to the song born from the Truth." In the cosmogonic outlook outlined by Schneider, this is the "Sonic Sun" or "Unhearable Sound," the "Truth spread out like the Sun" (*satyaṃ tatāna sūrya*: RV, I, 105, 12), the one sung by the Rishis at the origins of the cosmos.

Hitherto, we have seen how, in many points of his discussion of Vedic cosmogony, Schneider has indicated some particularities of the sound *SH*, linking it to the creative function of the sacrifice of *Soma* and to the fact that, according to tradition, such a sound "starts off from the tongue of *Soma*." This is a typical expression of the

## Cosmogony and Anthropogony

*RigVeda* meant to show the god while he "carries this hissing sound from cycle III to cycle VII. In doing so, he plays the role of the cosmic tree that unites the cycles through the common centre of the concentric circles," as Schneider explains at the beginning of the section which analyses the *cakras* and their symbolic function. This is the rite through which *Soma* clears the "Cosmic Cave" while the *Sāman* is sung. Its psalmody is entrusted to the *Udgatṛ*, who loudly intones the *udgītha*, the second verse of the holy quatrain. According to the *Brāhmana* texts, the gods carry out the squeezing of *Soma* when the god, with his "thunder voice," places himself at the service of *Sūrya*, the "Spiritual Sun": by means of his sacrifice, *Soma* allows the "rays of light" to impregnate the cosmic manifestation. The ritual lasts five days while the Rishis, the "metres of poetry", with their incessant singing make the nectar obtained by grinding the plant between the two squeezing stones flow into the sacrificial vase, since, as ritual traditions make sure, "the sacrifice of *Soma* purifies from all sins."

On the microcosmic plane, the function of the hissing sound *SH* is essential. When it appears in cycle III½, it already resonates as a synthesis of its constituent phonemes *S* and *H*, and such a particular function is confirmed by the doctrine of the seven *cakras* (= "wheels"). In the context of this cosmogonic and sacrificial scheme, indeed, according to Schneider the *cakras* correspond not only to the cycles which unfold after the closure of the "primordial world of Truth," from cycle III to IX, that is to say, the period which begins on winter solstice (= coccyx) and ends with the spring equinox (= larynx), but also to some "subtle" points of the human body analogically corresponding to physical organs and to a series of special sounds conveyed by the letters of the Sanskrit alphabet. Schneider explains:

> the starting point is the *Parabindu*, an unhearable geometric point of threefold nature that forms a unity. This *Parabindu*, by splitting, manifests itself (1) as *nada*, which is the undifferentiated

189

sound, (2) as *bindu* (nasal exhalation), and (3) as *bīja* (root of consonants). The whereabouts of these three elementary data is cycle III, where they constitute the equilateral triangle called the triangle of the divine vow to create the world. The three corresponding sounds are A-KA-THA of the primordial world.

Let us now try to understand the meaning of the three pre-formal conditions which result from the split of the *Parabindu*, the primordial Unhearable Sound which Schneider likens to a geometric point (maybe relying upon Euclidean geometry, in which the point is maximal simplicity, what has no parts). Meanwhile, it should be noted that *nada-bindu-bīja* form a triangle whose creative virtualities are realised in the *matrikah*, the first principles that transcend the forms of manifestation, the archetypes of every sound and every phenomenon which, precisely by virtue of their inexhaustible generating power, give rise to words (*sabdah*). *Nada* is the "subtle" sound that allows ritual mantras to be absorbed into the Principle or Absolute. According to some commentators on Kṣemarāja (975-1125), perhaps the most important disciple of the great Abhinavagupta, it would be the primordial "resonance" (*paradhvani*) of "vibration" (*spanda*) which permeates *Paravāk* (the "Supreme Word") and gradually congeals into a "drop" (*bindu*) of pure phonic potentiality. Therefore, *nada* appears as the very essence of all *mantra*s and foregoes any form of differentiation and even the slightest formulation. In turn *bindu* (= the "drop"), as Andrè Padoux explains, is the "subtle sonic vibration that follows the bindu in the *uccāra* (= ritual repetition) of the OM,"[192] and each one of its sound

---

[192] A. Padoux, *Mantra Tantrici* (Rome: Ubaldini, 2012), 19. Cf. also idem, *Recherches sur la symbolique et l'énergie de la Parole dans certains textes tantriques* (Paris: De Boccard, 1963). An essential text remains that of Pio Filippani Ronconi, *Vāk. La Parola primordiale* (Marina di Patti: Pungitopo, 1987), in which see part IV, 65-102: "La teoria della Parola e del Linguaggio nella meditazione filosofica indiana." The doctrinal background of these Tantric doctrines had already been illustrated by Arthur Avalon in *The Garland of Letters* (Madras, 1955) (Italian translation: A. Avalon, *La Ghirlanda di Lettere. Studi sul Mantra-Shāstra*, (Rome: Mediterranee, 2012).

## Cosmogony and Anthropogony

articulations also includes *A* and *HA*, the initial and final letter of the Sanskrit alphabet. In graphic terms, it is the point that represents the presence of Shiva within each *mantra*, so that the union of *bindu* and *nada* corresponds to that of Shiva and his energy. It is the "light" and its "vibrating resonance," as explained by Lilian Silburn. On the ritual plane, *bindu* goes beyond the level of simple "nasal exhalation"[193] and, indeed, continues unto the moment of breath stillness because, as Jayaprakāśa further explained in his *Śivayogagaratna* in the 16th century, it corresponds to the *M* of the *haṃ* syllable of the word *haṃsa*.

The third "elementary datum" of the Schneiderian scheme is constituted by *bīja*, which here fulfills the function of the "root of consonants." Still following the explanations of the phonetic doctrine of the masters of Kashmir Shaivism, each *bīja* corresponds to a deity of whom it represents the subtle "essence," the spiritual background. Therefore, *bīja* stands at the remote origin not only of the consonants which reveal a particular aspect of "subtle" and pre-formal reality, but also of every sacred formulation and every aspect of reality presided over by this or that deity (= *bīja*).

*Nada, bindu* and *bīja* constitute what Schneider calls the "triangle of the divine vow to form the world," that is to say, the symbol which in the *Tantrāloka*, Abhinavagupta's masterwork[194], is also known as the "triangle of desire" or of "desire-time" (*kāma-kāla*). Some Kashmir Shaivite traditions explain that at the top of the "triangle of desire-time" stands the Sun, while at its left tip there is fire, and at its right tip stands the Moon, three symbols likened respectively to the knowing subject, knowledge, and the known object (cf. Lilian Silburn). Each of these three symbols corresponds

---

193 This is underscored by Marius Schneider, who on this point seems to accept the hypotheses of some modern scholars of Kashmir Shaivism.

194 We follow the version edited by Raniero Gnoli, *La Luce delle Sacre Scritture* (*Tantrāloka*) (Turin: UTET, 1972). Cf. also its important epitome, *Essenza dei Tantra* (*Tantrasāra*) (Turin: Boringhieri, 1960).

to a letter of the Sanskrit alphabet, and all three letter-sounds, A-KA-THA, are arranged on the three sides of the triangle. Schneider explains:

> Each of the three sides of the triangle contains 16 sounds and in each corner there is a sound. 51 sounds in total. The series of 16 sounds of the first side of the triangle, containing 16 vowels, begins with the letter *A*; the second side begins with *K* [up to the letter "*ta*"] and the third with *Th* [up to the letter "*sa*"]: *AKATHA*. *A* is the acoustic form of the larynx, *KA* that of the heart, and *THA* that of the navel. Here is the world that the Creator forewished: the triangle *AKATHA* forming a navel, a heart, and a larynx, of which the Creator himself is the head containing the sonic idea.

In this way, the three "archetypal" letters arranged on the sides of the triangle virtually "contain" all the letters of the Sanskrit alphabet — as if to say that the three letters virtually include the totality of the degrees of the cosmic manifestation. The result are three "orders" of letters, each of which includes 16 sounds, which entails the overall sum of 48 letter-sounds (16 vowels + the two series of 16 + 16 consonants), to which Schneider also adds the three sounds kept in the three corners of the triangle. In Kashmir Shaivite traditions, however, it is more common to add to the 48 sound-letters only *HA* and *KṢA*, that is to say, respectively, the letter of the "creative" or "initial power" which manifests itself eminently in the emission (*ḥ*), and the final letter symbolising the "reabsorption" of the whole manifestation. In total, the outcome is 50 sounds, or sacred letters, first principles, universal archetypes. As we can see, in this tradition the "triangle of desire" is also conceived as a symbol built on a geometric and phonetic order capable of explaining some aspects linked to the figure of the Anthropocosm: the letter *A* corresponds to the open mouth (*adbhuta*); I to creative will (*iccha*); U to the immaterial moment which determines the manifestation (*unmeṣa*). Together, *A*, *I*, and *U* constitute the framework

## Cosmogony and Anthropogony

of reality; they are the acoustic archetypes which shape the cosmos, which constitute its "sonic texture."

According to Schneider, at the point when *nada* reveals the will to manifest itself, it is perceived in the form of a sonic spiral S which the Hindu tradition has always depicted as a coiled snake: *kundalini*.[195] This is one of the most characteristic symbols of Tantric spirituality, and it indicates the ways in which *shakti*, the divine energy or power, is found in man and how it can be awakened by making it ascend through the *sushumnā*, the "axis of light" which, according to the mystical physiology of Tantrism, allows its passage from the ascetic's heart to the *cakra* located above the head. Schneider believes that the vibratory movement of *kundalini* unfolds along a precise inner "path", which the phonetic foundation of Schneider's system allows to follow even in its individual stages:

> Coiled in primordial slumber, it rises during cycle III½ with a hiss (S) corresponding to the coccyx *cakra* (of the Anthropocosm), and, after having gone through the sex, the heart and the larynx by following a helical line, it reaches the tip of the tongue. At this point the forehead and the nose oppose the spiritual sound H to it, and then the snake withdraws and falls back into sleep.

In the Kashmir Tantric system, which seems to fully substantiate Schneider's reflections, the "divine energy" contained in the *Mūlādhāra-cakra* (from *mūla*, "root," and *ādhāra*, "support") is awakened to rise towards the navel and then flow into the heart, from where it is then gathered into the larynx, the *chakra* which, developing some symbolic data from the Tantric tradition, Schneider believes he can identify as the "gate of liberation." At this point, the forehead (*bhru*) and the nose position the spiritual sound H opposite to the *kundalini*, which blocks the latter's ascent

---

[195] Lilian Silburn's *La Kuṇḍalinī ou l'énergie des profondeurs* (Paris: Les Deux Océans, 1983), based entirely on Kashmir Shaivite literature, particularly on the writings of Abhinavagupta and his most important students, is a text that is rich in doctrine.

and causes it to fall back into the initial sleep. Schneider teaches that in this process

> the original vowel is O, which occupies the centre, that is, the heart. It is the generating vowel that, by cleaving (like the *Parabindu*), yields A and U. When *Kundalini* awakens with the sound SH (7 on the left), it passes through all the consonants, that is, through the various *chakras*, starting from the coccyx up to the heart, starting from the labial consonants and ending with the guttural ones. In the heart, the inner sounds begin to become perceptible, thus, passing through the second vowel, Y, *Kundalini* reaches the gate of liberation, which is the mouth where the vowels are produced. Here the cloth of the Dawn is woven. And S on the tip of the tongue meets H which comes out of the nose. In ritual singing, the highlighted consonants or vowels are always essentially those on which one wishes to act. When the vowels are acquired, the whole body becomes more sonic, the consonants gain a body. K becomes KA, TH becomes THA, etc. The AUM formula divides itself in the following way (6). It is AUM (sh) when heading from *māyā* to the truth, whilst it is SH-MUA when it creates the world.

In this process of awakening, the forehead plays an essential role, because it is the seat of the sounds H, voiced S, and Ksh. When the sound H + Ksha is pronounced, it yields the formula Haṃsha [= the primordial white swan], which reversed gives So-Hama. In this way, the outlined process appears twofold: on the one hand, there is the original Unhearable Sound, which, in manifesting itself, gradually leads to the sensible reality — according to a process outlined by Schneider in his previous study about the symbolic pair "music and stone"[196] —, on the other hand, there is the "reabsorption" which from the corporeal world ends in *Nirguna Brahman*, the "Brahman Without Qualities" or "Formless Brahman."

We conclude with the words with which Marius Schneider himself ties together his important study:

---

[196] Cf. M. Schneider, "*La coppia simbolica 'musica e pietra': Saggio di decifrazione di un pensiero filosofico espresso con un simbolo di natura rituale*", Conoscenza Religiosa 3 (1971), 201-213.

even the *yogi*, who in order to obtain contact with the Truth eliminates every thought and every visual representation, proceeds through ten degrees of meditation. The first two degrees sound *ciñi* and *ciñini*, the third is a bell sound which gives fatigue, the fourth a seashell sound which inspires doubts about the concrete world. The fifth degree's sound comes from a stringed instrument which irritates the palate. At the sixth degree, hands are clapped, which makes it possible for the *yogi* to drink the suprasensible world. The seventh degree transmits esoteric knowledge to him with the sound of the flute. At the eighth degree, a drum inspires him with sacred speech. Thanks to another drum, at the ninth degree he acquires invisibility, and eventually, at the tenth degree, a thunderclap introduces him to the absolute truth of Brahman.

*Translated by U.X.A.*

# GIORGIO COLLI, JULIUS EVOLA, AND HELLENIC MYSTERIOSOPHY: CAN LANGUAGE AND WRITING BE TRUTH-MAKERS?

*Giovanni Sessa*

### A Premise

The themes of language and writing, as well as their relationship with "truth", have played a central role in modern thought. The debate about these issues animated neo-positivism, and resurfaced, in a peremptory manner, in Wittgenstein and in the philosopher who most influenced the theorisation of the twentieth century, Martin Heidegger. Important traces of such theoretical congeries are alive in Lacan, in his attempt to deconstruct Freudian scholasticism, and their echo resonates in Jacques Derrida and, more in general, in the "French school".[197] Language and its theoretical implications were also debated in twentieth-century Traditionalist thought, in particular by Julius Evola: albeit not central to his system, this theme nonetheless accompanies Evola's "guiding ideas". It was in his artistic and philosophical phase that the Roman thinker clearly asked himself questions about the problem of the relationship between "truth" and its expression, particularly in *Phenomenology of the Absolute*

---

[197] Cf. Jacques Derrida, *Il fattore della verità*, trans. Francesco Zambon (Milan: Adelphi, 1978).

*Individual* and in his theoretical writings on art.[198] In the pages that follow henceforth, we will try to compare the theses of Evola with those of the philosopher and philologist Giorgio Colli (1917-1979). The latter is known to the general public for having edited Friedrich Nietzsche's *opera omnia* in Italian together with his student Mazzino Montinari.[199] His philosophical thought is still today, several decades after his death, surrounded by the deafening silence of academic criticism, as it is the bearer of a vision of life centred on a radical questioning of contemporary common sense, aimed at recovering the original Hellenic *Wisdom*.[200] In his speculative path, the themes of *expression* and language, even in its written form, have a decisive role. Because of this, in the comparison between the two it is behoveful to start from Colli's theses and, more in general, from the analysis of the intellectual "climate" which emerged in Italy in the attempt to overcome Giovanni Gentile's actualism. As for what concerns Colli, we will rely upon two recent publications of great critical importance dedicated to his thought.[201]

---

198 Cf. Julius Evola, *Fenomenologia dell'individuo assoluto*, introductory essay by Massimo Donà (Rome: Edizioni Mediterranee, 2009); Id., *Teoria e pratica dell'arte d'avanguardia*, introductory essay by Carlo Fabrizio Carli (Rome: Edizioni Mediterranee, 2018).

199 For Colli's intellectual biography, cf. Federica Montevecchi, *Giorgio Colli. Biografia intellettuale* (Turin: Bollati Boringhieri, 2004).

200 For the philosopher's works, cf. Giorgio Colli, *Filosofia dell'espressione* (Milan: Adelphi, 1969); idem, *Dopo Nietzsche* (Milan: Adelphi, 1974); idem, *La Nascita della filosofia* (Milan: Adelphi, 1975); Id., *La Sapienza greca*, 3 vols. (Milan: Adelphi, 1977-1980); idem, *Scritti su Nietzsche* (Milan: Adelphi, 1980); idem, *La ragione errabonda*, ed. Enrico Colli (Milan: Adelphi, 1982); idem, *Per una enciclopedia di autori classici* (Milan: Adelphi, 1983); idem, *La natura ama nascondersi. Physis kryptesthai philei*, 2nd ed., ed. Enrico Colli (Milan: Adelphi, 1988); idem, *Zenone di Elea* (Milan: Adelphi, 1998); Id., *Gorgia e Parmenide*, ed. Enrico Colli (Milan: Adelphi, 2003); idem, *Platone politico*, ed. Enrico Colli (Milan: Adelphi, 2007); idem, *Filosofi sovrumani*, ed. Enrico Colli (Milan: Adelphi, 2009); Id., *Apollineo e Dionisiaco* (Milan: Adelphi, 2010); idem, *Empedocle*, ed. Federica Montevecchi (Milan: Adelphi, 2019).

201 Cf. Vv.Aa., *Esprimere il vissuto: la filosofia di Giorgio Colli*, ed. Ludovica Boi, Giulio M. Cavalli, Sebastian Schwibach (Naples: La scuola di Pitagora-Istituto Italiano per gli Studi Filosofici, 2023); Ludovica Boi, *L'aurora inapparente. Upanishad, Bruno e Böhme nella metafisica giovanile di Giorgio Colli* (Naples-Salerno: Orthotes, 2024).

For Evola we will prevalently use works that have focused on his philosophical-artistic period.[202]

## Colli, Evola, Ultra-Actualism, and "Italian Ideology"

Colli interprets the Pre-Socratics as *mystics* and compares their theses with doctrines of the Lutheran heterodoxy: "Between the ancient wisemen and the 'mystics' who came after the Pre-Socratics, Colli sees a substantial air of akinness".[203] The *Wisemen* were bearers of a *mystical experience* in which man came to identify himself as God. Such an experience was attained in the *innerness* of the individual soul. In this, the Turinese philosopher, as observed by Ludovica Boi, was indebted to the exegeses of archaic religious phenomena which matured in the German countries between the end of the nineteenth century and the beginning of the twentieth, in particular towards the readings of Paul Deussen, Karl Jöel and Erwin Rohde. The Collian view, therefore, gives way to a gnoseology hinged on feeling and insight. In it, what plays a foremost role are the vitalist conception of matter and spirit, the centrality of the movement of the subject towards the principial dimension in order to realise god-individuality, the immediacy of supreme knowledge, and the rethinking of the modern notion of subject. Heed, however, that Colli's mystical comparativism

---

202 Cf. Gian Franco Lami, *Introduzione a Julius Evola. Un passo per la vita, un passo per il pensiero*, foreword by Giuliano Borghi (Rome: Volpe, 1980) [new edition: *Arte e filosofia in Julius Evola*, ed. Giovanni Sessa (Rome: Fondazione Evola-Pagine Editore, 2017)]; Roberto Melchionda, *Il volto di Dioniso. Filosofia e arte in Julius Evola*, foreword by Giano Accame (Rome: Basaia, 1984); Giovanni Damiano, *La filosofia della libertà in Julius Evola* (Padua: Ar, 1998); Massimo Donà, *Un pensiero della libertà. Julius Evola: filosofia e magia al cospetto dell'impossibile*, in Julius Evola, *Fenomenologia dell'individuo assoluto* (Rome: Edizioni Mediterranee, 2009), 13-33; idem, *Apologia dell'immediato. Itinerari evoliani* (Rome: InSchibboleth, 2020); idem, *L'irripetibile. Il paradosso di Dada* (Rome: Castelvecchi, 2020); Romano Gasparotti, *L'individuo assoluto e la magica potenza dell'immagine*, in Julius Evola, *L'individuo e il divenire del mondo* (Rome: Edizioni Mediterranee, 2015), 11-23; Michele Ricciotti, *Provare l'Io. Julius Evola e la filosofia* (Rome: InSchibboleth, 2020).

203 Boi, *L'aurora inapparente*, 19.

is not merely historical, but phenomenological in the sense suggested by Eliade, as well as genealogical.

For this reason, the experience of the Turinese philosopher can be read as a moment in research which had its antecedent in the rethinking of Gentile's actualism, of which Evola was the undisputed protagonist. The volumes produced by Evola in his strictly philosophical period, between 1917 and 1923, were significantly affected by the historical "circumstance" in which they were produced and represent a confrontation with Italian neo-idealist culture, in particular with the philosophy of Giovanni Gentile, as Roberto Melchionda acknowledged. In the present writing we do not aim to summarise the positions of magical idealism, but we want to indicate the existence of a *fil rouge* which is present, karstic and underground, in authors of an actualist formation or school, which links such authors to Hermeticism and the Hellenic worldview. A *fil rouge* that later resurfaced also in Giorgio Colli, who had no relationship with actualism. It is not by chance that Melchionda, in his exegesis of Evola, tended to valorise the actualist contribution, diluting the controversies which until then had been dividing Evolians and Gentilians, which also emerged in the light of the Traditionalist thinker's distancing himself from the Castelvetranese philosopher, as Evola remarked in *The Path of Cinnabar*.[204] It is worthwhile to reckon that the Gentilian "precedent" arose from a radical rethinking of the "Italian speculative tradition", which started from Renaissance thought and in particular from Giordano Bruno.[205] Furthermore, illustrious scholars were trained in

---

204 Cf. Melchionda, *Il volto di Dioniso*; Julius Evola, *Il cammino del cinabro*, ed. Gianfranco de Turris, Andrea Scarabelli and Giovanni Sessa (Rome: Edizioni Mediterranee, 2018), 95-127, in particular 103, in which we read: "In Gentile there was, moreover, a smoky pomp and an unbearable paternalistic pedagogism." About the Evola-Gentile relations cf. Hervé A. Cavallera, "Giovanni Gentile, Ugo Spirito e Julius Evola: un incontro possibile?", in Vv.Aa., *Studi Evoliani 2015*, ed. Gianfranco de Turris, Damiano Gianandrea and Giovanni Sessa (Rome-Carmagnola: Fondazione Evola-Arktos Editore, 2016), 124-139.

205 About this, it is important to remember that Gentile's interest in Bruno and the Renaissance is attested by several reviews and a series of very important

actualist culture, including Carlo Diano, a scholar of Greek culture and historian of religions who, like Evola in his philosophical period and Colli, questioned the primacy of the Aristotelian act towards power, interpreting the former as *periechein*, "what enwraps" the otherwise non-normable *dynamis*, always *at work* in the *physis*.[206]

I believe that this stream of thought, which seems to have found its land of choice in Venetia (I refer, amongst others, to the *ultra-actualist* speculative experience of Andrea Emo[207]), should become an essential point of reference for

writings. We would like to point out, first of all, Gentile's editing of the *Dialoghi italiani* of the philosopher from Nola, which resulted in the Laterza publications of the *Dialoghi metafisici* (1907-1925) and the *Dialoghi morali* (1908-1927). It is also important to mention the essays *Giordano Bruno nella storia della cultura* dated 1907 [latest edition: Agira: GAEditori, 2018], *Lo svolgimento della filosofia bruniana*, and the now classic *Veritas filia temporis*, both dated 1912 [now in: *Il pensiero del Rinascimento* (Florence: Sansoni, 1940)]. Furthermore, Gentile dealt on several occasions with religious themes and did not disdain critical confrontation with the doctrine of the Mysteries in the ancient world, with anthroposophy and with oriental philosophy. This is clear by reading Giovanni Gentile, *Ritrovare Dio. Scritti sulla religione*, edited by Hervé A. Cavallera (Rome: Edizioni Mediterranee, 2021). According to Corrado Claverini, the second exegetical "paradigm" of the Italian philosophical tradition may be traced back to Gentile. The latter, since 1897, with his *Rosmini e Gioberti* took up and originally reworked Spaventa's theses. Compared to the Abruzzo native, Gentile integrated the important figure of Genovesi into the course of Italian philosophy. The thinker from Castelvetrano would have liked to complete the work of his predecessor, developing it as "it was necessary to abandon the attitudes of mere doxographic erudition together with the most brazen ideological operations" [Corrado Claverini, *La tradizione filosofica italiana. Quattro paradigmi interpretativi* (Macerata: Quodlibet, 2021), 10]. It was a question of filling the "gaps" left by Spaventa in his history of Italian thought. For this purpose, the philosopher of the pure act committed himself, between 1904 and 1915, to drafting files relating to the history of Italian philosophy for the publisher Vallardi. The last one, about Lorenzo Valla, came out in 1915. Compared to the forerunner, the difference is evident: "In Gentile we start from the Middle Ages, analyse Renaissance humanism in depth, and deal with some Neapolitan thinkers who lived between Vico and Galluppi" (Ibid, 11). In any case, it was Eugenio Garin who brought the actualist's work to a conclusion and, in 1947, his *Storia della Filosofia italiana* — which, to date, has had several editions — was published.

206 Cf. Carlo Diano, *Opere*, ed. Francesca Diano, with contributions by Massimo Cacciari and Silvano Tagliagambe (Milan: Bompiani, 2022).

207 Cf., amongst the many posthumous writings of the Venetian philosopher, the sylloge *Quaderni di metafisica 1927-1981*, ed. Massimo Donà and Romano Gasparotti, foreword by Massimo Cacciari (Milan: Bompiani, 2006).

reading Evola beyond the "masks" which he himself assumed or which were attributed to him, indispensable for unveiling his deep and living "face". The cited thinkers do not aim, *sic et simpliciter*, to reduce the "Italian speculative tradition" to the mere historico-political dimension, but they discover its theoretical assumptions — so relevant in the logical works of Gentile himself[208] — aimed at questioning any form of dualism. It is no coincidence, therefore, that in Diano and Emo we can see a clear debt towards Leopardi[209], towards

---

208 The fourth interpretive canon of Italian thought, after those of Spaventa, Gentile, and Garin, is attributable to Roberto Esposito who, in 2010, published the work *Pensiero vivente*, whose central argument was widened in 2016 in the following work *Da fuori*. The philosopher presents here a reconstruction of Italian philosophy from Renaissance humanism to the contemporary *Italian Thought*: according to Esposito, Italian philosophy is a *philosophy of resistance* as shown by the exiles of Dante and Machiavelli, the burning at the stake of Bruno and Vanini, the trial of Galilei. Gentile himself, who for part of his life was a *state philosopher*, ended his days murdered. Furthermore, "since its outset [...] life, politics and history constitute the scrolling axes of a thought which is largely external to the transcendental plague in which the most conspicuous and influential part of modern philosophy remains entangled" [Claverini, *La tradizione filosofica italiana*, 106]. Esposito believes, and this marks the distance of this paradigm from the previous ones, that the discourse on Italian philosophy must be made in "territorial" terms, not in national terms. Although the nation-territory distinction appears to us at least captious, we share Claverini's position when he claims that in the epoch of globalisation the non-chauvinist recovery of specificity, including philosophical specificity, is a valid antidote against the *pensée unique*. Evola, Emo, Diano, Colli, as Leopardi himself, may be included, given the biographical features which distinguished them, among the *philosophers of the resistance* against the era when they were fated to live. About Evola's biography we refer to Andrea Scarabelli's essential work, *Vita avventurosa di Julius Evola* (Milan: Bietti, 2024).

209 Cf., about the subject, Carlo Diano, *Commento a Leopardi*, ed. Francesca Diano and Gaspare Polizzi (Milan-Udine: Mimesis, 2023). In these pages, the poetry-music contraposition, that is to say the contrast "between life and form [...] the vision of the relationship between the Dionysian and the Apollonian of Nietzsche", is evident in Leopardi (Ibid, 14). This is the central theme in the Diano's whole production: the form, the Aristotelian act, what "enwraps", hides the event, the *dynamis*, the original possibility-potency of the *physis*, which mankind and the entities are always hanging on to, as in the attunement of the absolute individual. The thinking feeling of the great man from Recanati recovers the 'mystical' dimension which, given Colli's lesson, characterised the vision of reality typical of the *Wisemen*. In his verses, as the editor remarks, lives the *Soul* told by Jung and, more recently, by Hillman: "Mysticism resolves the conflict between the self and the world with total annihilation, whether in God, or in the Infinite, or in eternal nothingness. Or in that silence to which every word tends" (Ibid, 55).

*Giorgio Colli, Julius Evola, and Hellenic Mysteriosophy*

the latter's tragic humanism — which, as noted by Cacciari, is a real fundamental trait of "Italian thought"[210] —, together with an original rereading of Nietzsche. Considering the aforementioned reasons, it should be remembered that it

---

210 As for what concerns this phase of Leopardi, see his *Thoughts*, published posthumously in 1845, many of which were extracted from the immense theoretical laboratory represented by the *Zibaldone*, whereas others were instead written and revised several times. In the volume, the philosopher-poet from Recanati dealt with men and their conduct in society. According to Sergio Solmi, these pages are characterised by an "iciness" always accompanied, take heed, by the meticulous precision in the description of the socio-political mechanisms of contemporary social relations. This is why the aphorisms of the Recanatese resemble Emo's scathing judgments. Leopardi looks at reality, human and political relationships, on the basis of his vision of life, making use of a Machiavellian and anti-Christian point of view. The antiquity-modernity dichotomy is subordinated to the criticism of contemporaneity, dominated by "economic wisdom", by the triumph of "Gazette" truth, by the aspiration to organise every spiritual activity in an industrial way. In a page of the *Zibaldone*, Leopardi presents a conception of time very close to Emo's and Evola's spherical one: past and present are not understood in oppositional terms, but in terms of an effective copresence, "as if sparks that never go out might really escape from the fire of time, almost as moments of an eternal return" [Cesare Galimberti, *Fanciulli e più che uomini*, in Giacomo Leopardi, *Pensieri* (Milan: Adelphi, 2008), 183]. On these theses, Leopardi's thought manifests its essential vocation as a *philosophy of the few* and a *philosophy of the order*. The concordance between Leopardi, Diano, Emo, and Colli seems to us to be the result of a philosophical and aesthetic formation, aristocratic in the spiritual sense; the "good" man of the *Thoughts* is the posthumous man, "oppressed by rampant vulgarity, excluded from the possibility of acting and almost of living, he however retains [...] the terrible privilege of seeing, of knowing and of not prostrating himself before the 'barbarising' mistakes of the times" (Ibid, 185). Leopardi's position has naturally re-emerged, on several occasions, in the tradition of Italian tragic humanism: typical examples were Michelstaedter, Rensi and Martinetti. Furthermore, the Leopardian lineage of Emo's thought (that of Evola was certainly not direct, but mediated by his "authors") seems to us to clearly show itself in the conception of the absolute presented in the *Night Song of a Wandering Shepherd in Asia*, freed from the ultimate foundation as a chasm that welcomes and annihilates everything, a "horrid, immense abyss" but the same time a place of the "force" which produces and destroys everything, as it happens to the *absolute* individual, whose path is hyperbolic, aporetic, inconclusive. We report the comment by Sergio Givone in *Storia del nulla* [(Rome-Bari: Laterza, 2006), 143]: "This is not nihilism, but enigmatic thinking, abysmal thinking [...] Nothingness makes things be what they are: fragile, ephemeral, mortal, but precisely for ithis reason worthy of being loved in their reality between a double negation. Reality without foundation, without beginning, and without any principle other than nothingness". Words that are therefore also valid to define the essential moment of the *ultra-actualist* philosophies of Emo and Evola. About this, also cf. Giovanni Damiano, *Leopardi, il poeta* (Rome: Altaforte, 2022).

was a thinker belonging to the actualist school, Guido Calogero, who realised the significance of Evola's theoretical proposal, so much so that he invited the latter to submit a contribution for the prestigious German magazine *Logos*, to which, amongst others, Husserl and Cassirer both collaborated. Contrariwise, a negative judgement on Evola was expressed in a review of his *Essays on Magical Idealism* written by Ugo Spirito.[211] Actually, this apodictic and ungenerous judgement has had a long-lasting effect on the reception of Evola's philosophical thought. Things began to change by the end of the 1970s, as Giano Accame recalled, at the same time — and it is not a coincidence — with the "Nietzschean reflowering, which began with Colli and Montinari's critical edition"[212], of the work of the German thinker for the publisher Adelphi.

Given this change in the cultural climate between the 1970s and the 1980s, if Evola may have seemed delirious when, at the end of the 1920s, he predicted the realisation of philosophy in Hermetic practice, in 1975, one year after the death of the theorist of magical idealism, Giorgio Colli "with a precious booklet titled *La nascita della filosofia* made the same concept, partly taken up by Nietzsche, widely acceptable".[213] Colli, according to Accame, could have become an exceptional dialoguer, Evola's "travelling companion", as he was shifting the interest of the cultural debate towards the world of the *Wisemen* and of Hellenic mysteriosophy, through a method of investigation in in which philology and philosophy once again became twinned in an unusual way. One of his students, Angelo Tonelli, rightly noted that Colli, around the age of twenty, already had a clear idea of what his theoretical-sapiential development would

---

211 Ugo Spirito, *Rassegna di studi sull'idealismo attuale*, IV, in *Giornale critico della filosofia italiana*, XVIII: 2 (March 1927) [now an appendix to Evola, *Saggi sull'idealismo magico*, 189-197].

212 Giano Accame, *Nota sull' "Evola moderno"* in Melchionda, *Il volto di Dioniso*, 12.

213 Ibid, 15.

be: "In the name of a mysticism — propitiated by a youth self-initiatory experience and maybe by contacts unknown to us with some personalities of the initiatory *milieu* — corroborated by a solid faith in the *lógos* illuminated by a sense of mystery".[214]

Colli's thought, marginalised by "intellectual correctness" and academia, enters, by full right, into the ranks of the Italian *philosophy of resistance* (which we mentioned in footnote), a resistance to the dominant power on both the political and intellectual plane. Whoever wants to free Evola from the "ghetto" to which he has been relegated by prejudiced critics and "Evolomaniacs", must "give breath" to his pages, put him into conversation with the great thinkers of the twentieth century, read his pages "heretically", showing faithfulness to the substance of his theses and not simply to the letter of the Traditionalist *vulgate*. In this sense, the Evola-Colli comparison is essential.

## Hellenic Mysteriosophy: A First Exegesis of the Evola-Colli Relationship

Amongst the exegetes of the two thinkers, only Gianni Ferracuti seems to have noticed this cruciality.[215] Fifteen years after Colli's premature death, in a volume dedicated to the philosopher from Turin, he wrote that Colli, just like Evola,

---

214 Angelo Tonelli, *Una meteora sapienziale*, in Vv.Aa., *Il giovane Colli. Atti del simposio in onore di Enrico Colli curatore delle opere postume di Giorgio Colli* (Lugano: Agorà & Co., 2014 [now, with some changes, in Vv.Aa., *Trame nascoste. Studi su Giorgio Colli*, ed. Clemente Taufari and David Beronio (Genoa: AkropolisLibri, 2018), 233-236, here 236]. The author recalls how a sort of brotherhood was formed around Colli, made up of the students most sensitive to his thoughts, and how this survived, after the death of the philosopher, for a certain period of time around his son Enrico: "A sort of enthusiastic and Dionysian sapiential *synousía* was born, a memorable *bohème* with dialectical challenges [...] of which Enrico, blood heir of the philosopher-wiseman, became for us, his thought heirs, the fundamental centre of gravitation" (Ibid, 235).

215 Cf. Gianni Ferracuti, *La sapienza folgorante. Introduzione a Giorgio Colli*, presentation by Luigi Chiocchini (Rome: Settimo Sigillo, 1994). The second chapter, "Shamanism and philosophy", in which emerges the Colli-Evola comparison, is now in, Vv.Aa., *Trame nascoste*, 252-269.

requires a profound change in his reader, "involving him in a complex network of enigmas: instead of plainly exposing a philosophy to him, he places him in a philosophical situation, of which he often hides the interpretive keys".[216] More specifically, Colli, referring to a Nietzsche purified from Wagnerian teleologism, has shown a new path: "Living itself as a method of knowledge; experience as a source, as a richer deposit than simple words".[217] Heed that such *livedness* leaves no room for *Erlebnis* (i.e. "aliveness") but is indicative of *contact*: "The real moment of experience in which the distinction between subject and object has not yet been produced".[218] This lemma indicates "reality as absolute, independent from any human presupposition".[219] Philosophy arises beyond common sense perception, from exceptional moments: "When the conscious person seems to open up to superior forms of lucidity [...] where 'objective' classifications and separations appear senseless".[220]

Such "moments" have nothing to do with a "return to the past", with reactionary nostalgia. The path to the absolute is *in the present, always possible*, in the sense that Klossowski attributed to this expression, on the basis of the exegesis of Nietzsche's *spherical*, not at all cyclical, temporality.[221] The Hellenic auroral philosophy was "expression of the moment, of the *contact*", and was transmitted orally as realised, *lived* knowledge, a knowledge which became *Wisdom*. It escapes the sight of the historiographical, analytical method, of that merely humanist philology aimed at universalising the

---

[216] Ferracuti, *La Sapienza folgorante*, 13.

[217] Ibid, 15.

[218] Ibid, 16.

[219] Ibid.

[220] Ibid, 17.

[221] Cf. Pierre Klossowski, *Nietzsche, il politeismo e la parodia*, trans. Giuseppe Girimonti Greco (Milan: Adelphi, 2019). The author upholds that "the superhuman announces itself as a new maturity of the spirit returned to the *ever possible*" ( Ibid, 39).

cognitive datum which is, on the contrary, always individual, a *phenomenological* conquest of the *person*. The epistrophic movement to which Colli invites us is the reconquest of the divine which is within us *ab initio*: "The divine that manifests itself is the core of Greek Wisdom and the foundation of divination"[222], as Evola recalls in *Ride the Tiger* when speaking about the complementarity of Apollo and Dionysus: "The two divine figures are neither opposed nor confused, but articulated around the central axle of the ecstatic experience".[223] In it, the logocentric distinctions imposed by the principles of identity and non-contradiction are eliminated, a fundamental outcome also reached by Evola's philosophy.

Dionysus is the *contact*, while Apollo manifests it through the words of the Delphic Pythia which simply make allusions based on paradox and enigma. Dionysus is the dazzling eye exposed on the *totality* of life, the haughtiness of sapiential knowledge: it requires the silence of the subject, of the distinguishing modern conscience, the overcoming of the border which in *representation* divides, first and foremost, the subject from the object. In ecstasy, defined by Colli as mystical and by Evola as Hermetico-ascetic (mysticism and asceticism refer, in this context, to the same experience), one "expands the scope embraced by his awareness and forms another image of himself"[224]; it is a *reinstatement*. What exists, *physis*, the cosmos, manifests the divine that only in it lives and pulsates. For this reason, Colli writes: "Dionysus is the god of contradiction [...] of everything that, manifesting itself in words, is expressed in contradictory terms. Dionysus is the impossible, the absurd that proves true with his presence".[225] Orpheus represented the mediator

---

222 Ferracuti, *La Sapienza folgorante*, 28.
223 Ibid, 29.
224 Ibid, 31.
225 Colli, *La Sapienza greca*, vol. I, 15.

between the Dionysian *contact* and the Apollonian *expression*: he symbolises the paradox of the polarity and unity of the two gods. Ferracuti notes that the same vision is present in Evola. The latter wrote: "There does not exist a world of the 'phenomen' [...] and behind it the true, impenetrable reality, the essence; there is a single datum that presents different dimensions, and there is a hierarchy of possible forms of experience".[226] The origin thrives, never normable, only in the entities, according to both Colli and Evola in his philosophical phase; potency comes true in acts, essence in existence. Potency, "in her freedom [...], 'She who plays' [...], makes the world of *samsara* appear [...], manifesting herself within it".[227]

Ferracuti glosses: "The absolute place, outside of time but recoverable, is grasped by breaking the chains of individuality, thanks to Mnemosyne, memory".[228] We distanced ourselves from this experience since, at an early time, the "love for wisdom" took written form, separating itself from *contact*. Therein lies the "problem" of language. The Collian-Evolian lived experience is inexpressible. It is witnessed in life. Philosophy, after Socrates, is decadence; it has become worldly, aimed at the search for power over the world. Rhetorical knowledge has dissipated the *livedness* of *Wisdom*.

## About Wisdom and Philosophy

In any case, for Colli as well as for Evola, both philosophers of great calibre, philosophising — as Carlo Sini reminds us, as far as the former is concerned —

---

[226] Julius Evola, *Lo yoga della potenza* (Rome: Edizioni Mediterranee, 1968), 250 [latest edition, introductory essay by Pio Filippani-Ronconi (Rome: Edizioni Mediterranee, 1994]. The very same conception may be found in the pages of J. Evola, *Autobiografia spirituale*, ed. Andrea Scarabelli (Rome: Edizioni Mediterranee, 2019), 83-84.

[227] Evola, *Lo yoga della potenza*, 41.

[228] Ferracuti, *La Sapienza folgorante*, 37.

## Giorgio Colli, Julius Evola, and Hellenic Mysteriosophy

was, at its origin, a lifeboat on which the *mythos* found shelter; a lifeboat which nowadays is sinking. Colli, in his *La nascita della filosofia*, understood that one can return to *Wisdom* only through philosophy, thus also through language, provided that we succeed in rewriting the relationships that link it to philology.[229] In Colli's thought, *Wisdom*, as Federica Montevecchi holds, is symbolised by Dionysus put to death by the Titans, an enigmatic topic to which the world of expressions leads back.[230] Colli does not start either from the present or from Aristotle to cast his gaze on the pre-Platonists, but he believes that it is necessary to refer to what preceded them. This is the *descending path*, as noted by Montevecchi.[231] In Greece it had this articulation: divination, enigma, dialectics and, finally, philosophy. The latter could simply hint at the origin, not fully express it. Colli's philosophy is configured as an *ascending path*, in that he enters a route opposite to that followed by the *ratio*. The decisive point is given by representation understood

---

229 Cf. Carlo Sini, *Giorgio Colli e l'origine del sapere*, in Vv.Aa., *Trame nascoste*, 23-37.

230 Even in the early Evola, the Dionysian *potestas* has a central role; indeed, it represents knowledge. Cf. Evola, *L'individuo e il divenire del mondo*; idem, *Par delà Nietzsche*, in 900. *Cahier d'Italie et d'Europe*, n. 2, Cahier d'hiver 1926-1927, ed. "La Voce" C. Malaparte and M. Bontempelli [now in Julius Evola, *Oltre il superuomo. Scritti su Friedrich Nietzsche 1926-1973*, ed. Giovanni Perez, trans. Laura Cametti and Giovanni Perez (Rome: Fondazione Evola-Pagine Editore, 2017), 51-66]. The same positions, albeit mitigated, return in Julius Evola, *Cavalcare la tigre*, introductory essay by Stefano Zecchi (Rome: Edizioni Mediterranee, 1995), and in idem, *Dioniso e "la Via della mano sinistra"* in *Vie della Tradizione*, III, n. 10, April-June 1973 [now in Julius Evola, *Ricognizioni. Uomini e problemi* (Rome: Edizioni Mediterranee, 1974), 79-84]. The last two publications testify how Evola, at the end of his speculative journey, returned to look with interest at Dionysus, already central to the overcoming of logocentrism in his philosophical works. About the value of this divine figure in Greek tragedy, cf. Davide Susanetti, *L'altrove della tragedia greca. Scene, parole e immagini* (Rome: Carocci, 2023). By the same author, about the connections between Mysteries and philosophy, cf. *La via degli dei. Sapienza greca, misteri antichi e percorsi di iniziazione* (Rome: Carocci, 2017).

231 Cf. Federica Montevecchi, *Giorgio Colli e lo specchio di Dioniso*, in *La società degli individui* 14, 2022, 35-44 [now in Vv.Aa., *Trame nascoste*, 123-137].

as *repraesentatio*, re-evocation, the outcome of a "mystical" feeling.[232]

Deep knowledge is not exhausted by empirical immediacy, it alludes to something foreign to Kantian space-time but, as owned by "memory", it lives within us. Colli shows how the logical categories of the "necessary" and the "contingent" depend on an original *coincidentia oppositorum*, revealed by the *contact*, another name for the Hermetic asceticism to which Evola refers.[233] Alessio Santoro has shown that the criticism of reason in the Turinese philosopher — as in

---

[232] About the centrality of the recovery of mysticism in Colli, as we have said, not different from "asceticism", cfr. Ludovica Boi, *Alle radici della "vissutezza"*. *Colli e Böhme*, in Vv.Aa., *Esprimere il vissuto*, 135-155. The *Wisemen* and Böhme lived, according to Colli, an extra-representative experience, a cosmicisation of interiority. An experience that may not be communicated, even though sometimes it happens, as happened to the theosophist when he began writing *Aurora*, to be *stricken* by "expressive urgency" (Ibid, 142). Colli shows particular interest for the metaphysics and cosmology of Böhme. Reality, for the German, is the result of the process of self-revelation of the *Ungrund*, a groundless beginning which "transcends the very plane of being as what, in its most proper essence, is no essence at all" (Ibid, 145). This element has within itself a will that induces it to manifest itself. It is not mere quietness and transcendence, but yearning, "a spur to exist" (Ibid.). All opposites already are in the beginning, starting from being and nothingness, unity and multiplicity, essence and existence. Böhme's mystical "abandonment" hints to the "*reintegration* in the cosmic order, is the consummation of the illusion of the two" (Ibid, 152), which is experienced as *livedness*, through the body. Both thought and the beginning have corporeal feature and, just as for the Wisemen, the *Geist* is given in the *Leib*. Essence and existence, beginning and *physis*, say the same thing. A groundless beginning like Evola's freedom, which shows itself in the corporeality of entities. Cf., furthermore, Boi, *L'aurora inapparente*. About the silencing of the animated "matter" implemented by Patristics and mediaeval Platonism cf., Davide Ragnolini, *Hyle. Breve storia della materia increata* (Soveria Mannelli: Rubbettino, 2023).

[233] Massimo Cacciari is of the same opinion. The *immediate* to which Colli refers coincides with substance, but not in the sense of *ousía*, since "the immediate may not be predicated-defined unless it is transformed into the object of mediation. Representation may not therefore define the immediate that it presupposes as its own 'foundation', but only express it". Massimo Cacciari, *Della cosa ultima* (Milan: Adelphi, 2004), 450. The escape from the *contact* is achieved by the concept, by the principle of identity, beyond which Evola placed himself: but, take heed, in the subject-object gnoseological dualism occurs the "reflux" which re-proposes the memory of *contact* through the renunciation of the overwhelming arrogance of the concept. In this must be noted the importance of philosophising for Colli and Evola.

Evola as well — cannot be reduced to irrationalism, but starts from reason itself and uses its tools, firstly logic and language, to induce a rapprochement with *Wisdom*. Colli relativises the cognitive role of the subject, a "partial and provisional point of view on the world".[234] *Expression* is the definition attributed by the thinker to connections detached from the subject, which are the "manifestation of something else from which the expression has distanced itself and which it will never be able to recover — 'immediacy'".[235] In the *Introduction* to *La Sapienza greca*, indeed, Colli argues that the subject is in what the subject sees, Dionysus is inside the looking glass, as Montevecchi comments.[236] With this, the dualistic distinction between foundation and phenomenon is abolished. In the Dionysian reality, playful dimension, gratuitousness and command resolve themselves into one another. The world presents itself as a "child's regiment"; it is *dynamis*, tragic power-possibility. The mirror reflects the image of the Other that we always are. For this reason, *Wisdom* is a confrontation with the enigma, is a descent into the labyrinth. As Ferruccio Masini recalled, the *philosophy of expression* is meditation on the enigma.[237] Wise is he who knows how to "bear" the tragic side of life and of "wonderful" nature: the mirror, in which the one breaks into the many, refers to the non-representable, to no-entity, to nothingness. It is form without any forms; for this reason, it is necessary, beyond any historical determinism, to consider the present as an eternal beginning, an incorruptible moment. The enigma tears open a gap that is, at once, both open and barred. Both open and barred even in language. According to Masini, *primitive remembrance* is a look into the abyss that

---

[234] Alessio Santoro, *Una lettura colliana del verbo essere nel De interpretatione di Aristotele*, in Vv.Aa., *Esprimere il vissuto*, 65-83, here 81.

[235] Ibid.

[236] Cf. Montevecchi, *Giorgio Colli e lo specchio di Dioniso*, 132.

[237] Cf. Ferruccio Masini, *Il filosofo e l'enigma*, in Vv.Aa., *Giorgio Colli. Incontro di studio*, ed. Sandro Barbera and Giuliano Campioni (Milan: Franco Angeli, 1983), 63-70 [now in Vv.Aa., *Trame nascoste*, 111-122].

opens up in the fabric of time; it is a threshold of mystery. It expresses a reason that is not foreign to animality, to Nietzschean and Greek corporeality. For the early Greeks, every word was a sign of this ever-quivering life, which is always *at work*. Hence Colli and Evola's interest in music, which is capable of tearing away the web woven by concepts and of bringing out the *immediacy* in which nothing is really annihilated. In it, time and eternity are given at once.[238]

## Between Idealism, Hermeticism, and the Mysteries

The mysteriosophical roots identified by Colli have their correlation in Evolian Hermeticism. After all, magical idealism has only brought the results of idealism to extreme coherence and surpassed them. In idealist systems, in particular in panlogism, on the sidelines of the dominant and evident rational system and modern *ratio*, the legacy of Hermeticism also arises.[239] Massimo Donà argued that the beginning in Hegel "is set in motion".[240] By whom? By a force that induces it to deny itself. The foundation turns out to be unfounded; it is the power of Nothingness, intuited by Leopardi, which animates the positive. This is because the beginning "is denied by the presupposed potency which requires it to deny itself".[241] The abstract (the beginning) is dominated by a concreteness which requires it to deny itself and unfold itself dialectically in view of the re-appropriating conclusion. In dialecticism, Hegel's

---

238 About this topic, as far as Colli is concerned, cf., Edoardo Toffoletto, "*Il filo unidirezionale del tempo*". La struttura musicale dell'espressione, in Vv.Aa., *Esprimere il vissuto*, 203-232. Concerning Evola and music, cf. Julius Evola, *Da Wagner al Jazz. Scritti sulla musica 1936-1971*, ed. Piero Chiappano, foreword by Massimo Donà (Milan: Jouvence, 2017).

239 Cf. Glenn Alexander Magee, *Hegel e la tradizione ermetica. Le radici "occulte" dell'idealismo contemporaneo*, introduction by Massimo Donà, afterword by Giandomenico Casalino (Rome: Edizioni Mediterranee, 2013).

240 Massimo Donà, *Logos ermetico. Lo "speculativo" hegeliano e la tradizione magico-ermetica come forma stessa della razionalità* in Magee, *Hegel e la tradizione ermetica*, 13-28, here 22.

241 Ibid.

proximity to the theme of the God-World relationship typical of Hermeticism is revealed. The German philosopher certainly cannot eschew thinking God as transcending the world but, at the same time, he thinks God as implicated in the world, as in the attunement of Hermeticism. Donà enters into the living things of the Hegelian *logic of being*, in which the original co-belonging of being and nothingness is effectively sanctioned. In fact, "only nothingness is able to constitute itself as an otherness [...] which is not other"[242], as it is nothing, nothingness of being. Nothingness is the Hermetic absolute, exemplarily thematised in the *Sermons* of the heterodox "Christian" Eckhart. For this reason, every "presence", in the transfiguration of its positivity, is a perfect image of totality, an iconoclastic image, the ephemeral face of the Collian and Evolian Dionysus. With the words of Andrea Emo, a *philosopher of the few*, it is possible to argue that "eternity can only be loved in the form of presence", as it grants to us "the glee [...] of the fragmentary, the episodic, the contingent".[243]

## The Problem of Language in Colli

After this broad but necessary premise on the Colli-Evola proximity and on the positions of *ultra-actualist* thinkers, let's see what Colli and Evola thought, concretely, about language. The young Colli, as we have said, was an attentive reader of Bruno and Böhme: his theses around language and expression owe much to both of them. The Turinese philosopher, on several occasions, focuses on the "violent", immediate aspect of the experience of *contact*, of what he designates as *livedness*. The *Wisemen* of Hellas experienced *contact* in their innerness, and in a tragic way: their souls were prey to conflicting forces, which thrusted

---

242 Ibid, 25.

243 Andrea Emo, *Quaderno 122*, 1951, 13-XI, in Giovanni Sessa, *La meraviglia del nulla. Vita e filosofia di Andrea Emo*, foreword by Romano Gasparotti (Milan: Bietti, 2014), 239.

in the direction of expression, of the need to *say* what had been *seen* and experienced with the body. The *Wisemen* in the schools, with their fellow disciples, mainly used oral language, thus *co-philosophising*. The oral word is alive, it has a greater possibility of transcribing the beginning, the *dynamis*, the power-freedom which inhabits the *physis*. It is no-thing, no-entity which eschews the staticisation of written word and concepts. The writing of the first philosophers, still linked to the enigmatic Delphic dimension, is judged by Colli as the first distancing of the experience of *contact* with the *Grund*, the abysmal bottom of life that precedes the epistemological distinction of subject and object. In it all the dualisms of being-nothingness, essence-existence, phenomenon-noumenon, live in oneness. Yet, to return to testify this intuitive knowledge, the Turinese thinker is aware that language and philosophy itself must be used in order to realise the project of civil *paideia*, which was quintessential for the *Wisemen*. A language, of course, capable of escaping from mere conceptual connotativity.

It is the language that Böhme and Bruno talked about. The former was induced to write his main work, *Aurora*, driven by a *violent tension* after "something" "assailed him *like a shower of water*".[244] The work was meant to be the transcription of previous intuitive experiences, which had revealed to him how the opposites live in one another. The theosophist, despite being aware that writing cannot restore the fullness of intuitive experience, as it is lived intimately and never fully communicable, worked using the only language possible for the purpose: the *imaginal* one: "The evocation of images, employed as metaphors, studs [...] the fabric of the mystic's works".[245] The images aim to bridge the gap that divides the narrator from the reader and arouse in the latter, as Boi recalls, *physical* sensations, which allow him

---

[244] Jacob Böhme, *Theosophische Sendbriefe*, ed. Gerhard Wehr (Freiburg: Aurum Verlag, 1979), letter cited in Cecilia Muratori, *Introduzione*, in Jacob Böhme, *Aurora nascente*, trans. Cecilia Muratori (Milan-Udine: Mimesis, 2007), 29.

[245] Boi, *L'aurora inapparente*, 163.

to approach the reality of the *contact*. Such an experience is conveyed by auditory, tactile and visual sensations. For this reason, for Colli as much as for Böhme, language is a continuously evolving tool, to be subjected to revisions and clarifications aimed at providing it with a "spiral" trend, "spinning wholly around the experience that one would like to try to communicate".[246]

The two thinkers start from the same Hermetic assumption: the divine is within mankind. They also support the mystical identification of soul-cosmos-principle. Truth lies in the "Heart", understood in the traditional sense: "There are not two separate substances, the human and the divine, but a single substance whose constitutive essence lies in giving rise to the illusion of the Two".[247] Such understanding is reached through a long process, exemplified by Böhme's table depicting the "eternal eye". In it, a cross tangential to the representation of the two worlds, of transcendence and immanence, has a "Heart" at its centre. The eye unified by the theosophical path is the "Heart", hinge and point of conjunction between the finite and the infinite, between time and eternity. It is achieved by renouncing *ratio* and using a gaze enlivened by *Verstand*: a cognitive modality that corresponds to what Colli called *livedness*, a unifying gaze on the world. Contrariwise, as Boi points out, what the theosophist designates as *Vernunft* is not equivalent to Colli's *Lógos*, which is "word of life": "It is the whole expression, as a spectacle of appearance coming to the surface from a submerged background, and it is the means through which the search may, at least, begin".[248]

Even Bruno, read by the young Colli, matured a similar vision of language. He used symbolic-imaginative language to define the story of Actaeon, in order to allow its *visualisation*. Words have "illusionistic" force and produce

---

246 Ibid, 169.

247 Ibid, 171.

248 Ibid, 177.

*evidentia*, "which is obtained by exploiting the ability of language to arouse *mental* images in the reader".[249] Language takes on an *emblematic* form in Bruno; it is centred on *deeds*, described or drawn figures which are associated with a Latin motto (there are 28 of them in the *Eroici Furori*). The emblematic function of language alludes to ecstatic knowledge: "Each emblem is an act of recognition through which the *anima mundi* and the individual soul come to recognise their 'dual unity', one being the reflection of the other".[250] Colli never descends into irrationalism, but distances himself from the arrogance of modern reason, which is forgetful that, before *lógos*, there is a *yonderness* which is achieved in *contact*. The unitive relationship of the innerness and the cosmos in Colli is an indisputable answer to the laceration, identified by Löwith in Nietzsche's eternal return.[251] The latter is the Christian-originated distinction between the spiritual interiority and the world that would have led Nietzsche to "experience" nature in terms of mere exteriority. Colli teaches that *innerness*, for the Greeks, meant the same thing as *physis*. If the history of European thought was therefore marked by the transition from Mysteriosophy to philosophy, the latter today might take on the task of making us accomplish the wayfare of return to *Wisdom* through allusive and imaginal language, a language other than that of current theoretical non-fiction.

## The Problem of Language in Evola

As Roberto Melchionda reminds us, the binding and betraying structure of linguistic expression, particularly written expression, was always known to Evola.[252] Since his artistic period, he confronted this theme in a radical

---

249 Ibid, 153-154.

250 Ibid, 155.

251 Karl Löwith, *Nietzsche e l'eterno ritorno*, trans. Sandro Venuti (Rome-Bari: Laterza, 2010).

252 Cf. Melchionda, *Il volto di Dioniso*, in particular 225-227.

way. The apodictic statement "to express is to kill" may be considered as the synthesis of his pictorial-poetical path through Dadaism.[253] He was also aware that, in order to hint to the deep meanings of reality, in every era, even in the Last Age, a reserve language, as Melchionda defines it, is available — a pre-language or, to put it with Fichte, an *Ur-sprache*. It is not the heritage, take heed, of any given people, but a "traditional" legacy: it is the "language of birds", of the Hermetic symbols. The Roman thinker had arrived at this assumption on the basis of the acquisitions of his artistic-philosophical period, thus before his meeting with René Guénon, which took place at the end of the 1920s. The path of the absolute individual led to an ultra-philosophical *novum*, to a praxis, to a free, powerful, and realising *action*. In *The Path of Cinnabar* there is a very meaningful passage for our exegesis, for what concerns language: "no one had ever been interested in investing such non-ordinary and, for many, discredited matter with systematic and dialectical speculative thought, apart from Marcus, von Baader, Hamann and Schopenhauer in some of his essays".[254] Evola refers to the conclusions he reached in *Phenomenology of the Absolute Individual*: it is significant that here he quotes Franz von Baader, a German theosophist who in *Erotic Philosophy* had dealt with language in Hermetic terms.[255]

In his pages, Baader starts from the *Ungrund* as a groundless principle that aspires to grounding, to manifest itself. The principle is stillness that desires generative movement. A stillness that is silence that progressively moves in the direction of sonority, having within itself the inner

---

253 Evola, *Teoria e pratica dell'arte d'avanguardia*, in particular 37-40, 43-45, 147-176. On this topic, we take the liberty of referring to our work: Giovanni Sessa, *L'arte magica di Julius Evola*. "Sule terrazze lunari l'iperbole danza" in *Via della Tradizione* 177, July-December 2019 (Bari: L'Arco e La Corte, 2020), 3-36.

254 Evola, *Il cammino del cinabro*, 107.

255 Cf. Franz von Baader, *Filosofia erotica*, trans. and ed. Lidia Procesi Xella (Sesto S. Giovanni (MI): Jouvence, 2023).

possibility of the Word: "The becoming essence of the inessential [...] is mediated most especially by language".[256] In such a perspective, language is not a conventional sign of reality; rather, the being of the world must be identified in naming, in saying. Baader's thesis has to be placed within the original relationship which, according to the theosophist, is given *erotically*, though not in the Schellingian polarity of attraction-repulsion, but in the androgynous unity of masculine-feminine, and is always *in fieri*. Logic is therefore not a science of the concept but concerns the alchemical principle of individuation of the freedom-power which connotes the *Ungrund*. Language as a mere transcription of reality, of things, has forgotten this deep reality, since, beginning at least from Cartesian philosophy, it has absolutised the male moment to the detriment of the female one. Despite this, even for Baader, as for Colli and Evola, it is only by starting from language that it is possible to recover its founding and revealing power, due to the nostalgic attraction exerted by the principle which always exists within mankind. For the magical idealist this can be achieved either by using symbolic-Hermetic references or by exercising a traditional "pedagogy" operation using the same conventional and degraded language. This is the primary achievement of the absolute individual projected, hyperbolically, towards the principle, exposed to it and to its perpetual *novum*. His free will is *power*.

In the conclusion of *Phenomenology*, where he presents in an articulated way the "proof of Dionysus", which he had already spoken about in *The Individual and the Becoming of the World*, Evola writes: "Trying to make sense of these experiences [...] is certainly difficult and dangerous. In this context [...] intuitive allusions may be useful, such as those of a certain poetry of a semi-enlightening nature, e.g.,

---

[256] Ibid, 43.

Rimbaud".[257] Evola wants to tell us that if the connotative language betrays the metaphysical truth, either we resort to art and symbols, or, as he did in his philosophical works, all that remains, by virtue of the conquest of what we have actually managed to achieve in the path of individual awakening, is the possibility of "charging" the words in use with new force. To do this, Evola used actualist philosophical language, without resorting to the creation of a new theoretical lexicon, as Heidegger instead did. The problem of language in Evola takes the form of an attempt "to make the contents of his thought-experience communicable, understandable and less difficult".[258] In his linguistic option we can identify the desire to communicate with the men of the Final Age, a choice, says Melchionda, based on generosity and humility. He knew that his readers were selected: those who read Evola and, above all, those who continue to do so over the years, testify to a spiritual-existential harmony with the author's thesis. They are *differentiated* readers. Evola approached this very particular kind of reader by implementing, through the "technical" language of philosophy, the "communication of existence" of which Kierkegaard had spoken in the nineteenth century, a communication which aimed at the awakening of both speech and the person at the same time.

Therefore, Colli and Evola deserve "unfaithful" readers who do not halt at the literalist surface of their teaching, but who know how to grasp the "secret fire" which animates their pages.[259]

*Translated by U.X.A.*

---

[257] Julius Evola, *Fenomenologia dell'individuo assoluto* (Rome: Edizioni Mediterranee, 1974), 272 [latest edition, 2009].

[258] Melchionda, *Il volto di Dioniso*, note 2, 227. Oblique is by the author himself.

[259] Cf. Julius Evola, *Fuoco segreto*, introductory essay by Joscelyn Godwin, ed. Andrea Scarabelli, Giovani Sessa, and Luca Siniscalco (Rome: Edizioni Mediterranee, 2024).

# TRUTH AND LANGUAGE: ATTILIO MORDINI'S SAPIENTIAL HERMENEUTICS OF LANGUAGE

*Adolfo Morganti*

> *To Franco Cardini,*
> *who was a disciple,*
> *therefore, a Master*

> *All other animals are instinctively aware of their own natures;*
> *one exercising fleetness of foot, another swiftness of flight,*
> *others their ability to swim.*
> *Man, however, can do nothing unless he is taught;*
> *neither speaking nor walking nor eating.*
> *In short, he can do nothing by natural instinct except weep.*
>
> *-* The Elder Pliny (29 AD-79 AD)

Although he left a profound mark and an important *didaché* of students behind him, as well as a decades-long presence within the world of Italian traditional culture, Attilio Mordini (1923-1966) is still little known, especially outside his native country — despite the fact that he taught at the University of Kiel in Germany, as well as in Italy itself. This is due to certain dynamics of the Italian traditional context — both Catholic and non-Catholic — in the second postwar period.[260]

---

[260] Although such would be useful, a historical-doctrinal reconstruction of the theses and fruits of the Italian "traditionalist" world (a term which we will not use any further herein due to its structural ambiguity, preferring instead the clearer and simpler term "traditional") in the second postwar period is beyond the scope of the present writing. Nevertheless, there is at least one text we shall indicate for those who would like to delve deeper into the history of 20th-century traditional Italian culture: P. Tosca, *Il cammino della tradizione e altri scritti*, integrated 2nd ed. (Rimini: Il Cerchio, 2005) – this volume also contains a vast series of bibliographical references useful for personally retreading those tortuous, arduous paths which will better resonate with the Reader.

Therefore, a substantial rediscovery of this unusual figure, that of a mid-20th-century "aloof scholar" who went almost unnoticed in the eyes of a society like the Italian one — which has changed too quickly and has, furthermore, typically been careless towards its best men — seems increasingly important to us.

A central aspect in the teaching of Attilio Mordini is the providential function and metaphysical depth that he attributed to language. His certainty of this dimension stemmed from a thorough knowledge and exegesis of the Biblical tradition and the ensuing Catholic and Eastern Christian cultural traditions, with particular attention to the ancient and medieval epochs. In his teaching, such an acknowledgement is both the foundation of a broad inter-cultural and inter-religious analysis, which partially anticipated the developments of the Second Vatican Council as to the recognition of the providential value of the various spiritual traditions of mankind, and the basis of an in-depth mythical-symbolical analysis of European popular literature, particularly fantasy literature and cinematography.

As the third chairman of the *Identità Europea* association, the author of the present writing has had the honour of starting and leading a "cultural workshop" dedicated to Attilio Mordini, which as of today has been active for more than 10 years, and has coordinated the reprinting of some of his most important works and critical essays through the publishing house Il Cerchio.

## Attilio Mordini:
## A True Life is an Uncomfortable One

Attilio Mordini di Selva was born on 22 June 1923, into a Florentine family (his father was a colonel in the army). He was first educated by the Piarists and later by the Salesians of Don Bosco, and since his adolescence he showed a strong religious feeling, along with a turbulent character which led him to despise inner compromises and lukewarmness. Although slightly maimed in one foot due to a streetcar accident, at the beginning of the Second World War he enlisted as a volunteer in the Third Anti-Aircraft Legion of Genoa. With the breakdown which followed the Armistice of Cassibile on 8 September 1943, he returned to Florence, where, faced with the doleful spectacle of three German soldiers singlehandedly occupied the headquarters of the local army corps in his city, he ran to enlist again, serving in the engineering department of the 4th Panzer Pionier Division, which was engaged in Ukraine at the time. Once back in Italy after being wounded at the front, he had the will to enlist once again in the National Republican Guard, and for this reason, at the end of the war, he was jailed for one year in the Murate prison in Florence, on slanderous charges from which he was later fully acquitted. Because of the extremely harsh conditions and beatings he had to endure in jail, he contracted tuberculosis, which would later lead to his premature death.

After the war, Mordini resumed his university studies in Foreign Languages at the University of Florence, where he graduated with honours and defended his thesis in German literature (under the supervision of the Italian Germanist Vittorio Santoli) about Stefan George, a poet with strong links with the beginnings of the "Conservative Revolution." During the same period, while he was staying in Rome as a guest of Father Alighiero Tondi S.J. (who went down in history as "the Communist Jesuit"), he attended courses at the Pontifical Gregorian University and entered the Third Order of Saint Francis under the name Brother Alighiero.

In the postwar cultural scene, Mordini contributed to the renowned magazine *L'Ultima*, founded by Giovanni Papini, and collaborated with the Florentine cultural milieu that passed down the cultural and spiritual legacy of its founders: the Catholics of the "New Cloister", amongst whom were Father Balducci, David M. Turoldo, Mario

Gozzini, and Reverend Divo Barsotti. He also collaborated with the circles of the Jewish-Christian alliance and those around the peculiar scholar of psychology and meditation who was Roberto Assagioli, and published many articles in various traditional Catholic publications, such as: Primo Siena's *Il Carattere*, published in Verona; Fausto Belfiori's *Adveniat Regnum*, published in Rome; Giovanni Allegra's *Il Ghibellino*, published in Messina; and Silvio Vitale's *L'Alfiere*, published in Naples. Yet, he always knew how to remain an "aloof scholar," as he was indeed defined.

He made pilgrimages, according to the ancient wont, to La Verna, Lourdes, San Giovanni Rotondo, and St. Michael's Cave in Gargano.

After 1955, Mordini taught Italian as a lecturer at the University of Kiel, and during his stay in Germany he contributed to the theological and religious studies journal *Kairos*, published by the Benedictine monks of Salzburg, and to *Antaios*, founded in Stuttgart by Ernst Jünger and Mircea Eliade. He was in a collaborative and epistolary relationship with important personalities of the Italian and European cultural world — "refractory" and not only — of the second postwar period, including Giano Accame, Gianni Baget Bozzo, Titus Burckhardt, Alfredo Cattabiani, Julius Evola, Adolfo Oxilia, Silvano Panunzio, René Pechère, Pietro Porcinai, Sergio Quinzio, and Adriana Zarri. His correspondence is now preserved in Rome at the archives of the Ugo Spirito and Renzo De Felice Foundation.

After having faced a life of woes and sorrows with an ascetic and warrior attitude, he eventually died in Florence on 4 October 1966, the day of Saint Francis, his beloved patron saint. He was just 43 years old.

Amongst his most renowned disciples, it is worth mentioning Ennio Ciliano, Primo Siena, Giovanni Cantoni, Luigi De Anna, Franco Cardini, Fausto Belfiori, Paolo Caucci, and Marco Tangheroni. Inasmuch as one can recognise pupils by already knowing their master, the reverse is also true, hence the keen reader will need no further words and will not be floored upon discovering that the developments of the Italian degeneration after 1968 brought some of Mordini's early pupils to positions which were not only different, but in many respects even opposite and far away from those of their master.[261]

In the following decades, the city of Rome saw the establishment — albeit shortlived — of a Centre for Traditional Studies named after Attilio Mordini, which also published its own magazine, *Excalibur*, from whose pages Paolo Galiano and Mario Polia began to make themselves known.[262]

## Silence and Heart

*Militia est vita hominis super terram*

- Job 7:1

After the Second World War, Italy remained submersed for a long time — likely until the end of the 20th century — in a cultural climate that saw Italian Catholicism increasingly

---

261 See L. Copertino, *SpaghettiCons. La deriva neoconservatrice della destra cattolica italiana* (Rimini: Il Cerchio, 2008).

262 The magazine *Excalibur* had a limited run. Although it had only 14 issues published between 1976 and 1980, it became a main reference for a "traditional Catholicism" utterly alien to Lefebvrian (Marcel Lefebvre's) and Plinian (Plinio Corrêa de Oliveira's) "traditionalist" temptations. In 1978, the two leading authors of the magazine, namely Paolo Galiano and Mario Polia, began to reprint some important articles by Attilio Mordini, amongst which we highlight "*La tradizione e la genesi del tradizionalismo attuale*" and "*Premessa agli incontri con le tradizioni d'Oriente*," as well as articles about various aspects of Mordini's thought written by P.F. Zarcone and E. Santacroce. On the occasion of the 15th anniversary of Mordini's death, *Excalibur* published a special issue (no. 3-4, 1980, which was the very last issue of the magazine) entirely dedicated to him. After 1980, thanks to Mario Polia, the experience of *Excalibur* gave rise to *I Quaderni di Avallon* (later simply *Avallon*), published by Il Cerchio starting with issue 1, 1982, running to a total of 56 issues published between 1980 and 2007.

divided between a liberal-bourgeois Christian Democracy and a number of circles which were quickly being absorbed by the cultural and political Marxism embodied by the Italian Communist Party (which was the largest Communist Party in the West). This process would reach its culmination in the 1970s, especially with the double defeat represented by the 1974 and 1978 referendums, respectively on divorce and abortion.[263]

In such a swampy scenario, while pursuing his inner pilgrimage in search of a true, virile, chivalric[264] form of Catholicism, Attilio Mordini always drew inspiration — a few decades ahead of the rediscovery triggered by the Second Vatican Council — from the *depositum sapientiae* of the Church Fathers, the first thousand years of the undivided Church, the millennium of the Christian Middle Ages, the social archetypes that the *civitas Christiana* reaffirmed before the Protestant laceration – priests, warriors, and peasants.[265] At the same time, following the teachings of the Fathers to the end, he opened his eyes to the value of the great spiritual Traditions of mankind, which were understood as being providential preparation for the Incarnation of the Fullness of the Word: in properly Patristic terminology, *propaideia Christou*.

Starting from this spiritual and cultural horizon, Mordini's works (some essays and a much greater number

---

263 On this historical season of Italian Catholicism, see A. Del Noce, *I cattolici e il progressismo* (Milan: Leonardo, 1994); idem, *Il problema dell'ateismo* (Bologna: Il Mulino, 2010); idem, *Il suicidio della rivoluzione* (Milan: Rusconi, 1992); see also E. Corti, *L'epoca di Paolo VI* (Chieti: Solfanelli, 1978); idem, *Il fumo nel Tempio* (Milan: Ares, 2022).

264 There is no room here for a detailed definition of the meaning that the adjective "chivalric" had within Attilio Mordini's experience, in which it played a fundamental role. In order to approach this topic, see A. Saenz, *La cavalleria. La forza delle armi al servizio della verità inerme* (Rimini: Il Cerchio, 2000).

265 About this functional tripartition, see G. Dumézil, *L'ideologia tripartita degli indoeuropei* (Rimini: Il Cerchio, 2014); O. Niccoli, *Sacerdoti, guerrieri, contadini. Storia di un'immagine della società* (Turin: Einaudi, 1979); and G. Duvy, *Lo specchio del feudalesimo: sacerdoti, guerrieri e lavoratori* (Rome-Bari: Laterza, 1998).

of articles) analysed in a decisively *non*-individual synthesis the rise and fall of European civilisation from its origins to his time, when the dissolution that today, 60 years later, is overwhelmingly widespread, was then already blatantly dawning. He thus continued, with strong bravery and intellectual freedom, the cultural and spiritual lineage of the great post-1789 anti-revolutionary tradition, the one that inspired popular armed responses to the French Revolution and subsequent liberalism throughout Europe – from Joseph de Maistre to Luis de Bonald and Juan Donoso Cortés[266], but also Gustave Thibon[267] and Augustin Cochin[268] – which demonstrated its foretelling keenness in having critically examined the first phases of the rise of modernity and identified its dissolutionary and nihilistic essence from its very beginning.

> Theologically a Thomist, but spiritually a Franciscan (he was in fact a member the Third Order of the Friars Minor), Mordini was also a devotee of Saint Ignatius and an admirer of the Society of Jesus, and to those who objected that Franciscans and Jesuits did not seem, during the events of the centuries of the history of the Church, to have ever liked each other, he replied by citing Ignatius' autobiography and highlighting the meeting in Ignatius' thought of Franciscan spirituality with Cusanian and Erasmian spirituality, which would inspire Charles V himself. Now that a Jesuit has become pope under the name of Francis, all this has taken on a surprising relevance. Attilio was very attentive to the signs represented by coincidences, references, more or less astonishing syntonies, and indicated them (perhaps sometimes even smiling a little about them) to his friends as

---

[266] Regarding Joseph de Maistre, it is essential to know his *Essay on the Generative Principle of Political Constitutions* [in Italian: *Saggio sul principio generatore delle Costituzioni politiche e delle altre istituzioni umane* (San Marino: Il Cerchio, 2012)]. See also Louis de Bonald, *Le leggi naturali dell'ordine sociale* (Crotone: D'Ettoris, 2020); and Juan Donoso Cortés' immense *magnum opus*, *Saggio sul cattolicesimo, il liberalismo e il socialismo* (Rimini: Il Cerchio, 2007).

[267] See Gustave Thibon, *Ritorno al reale. Prime e seconde diagnosi di fisiologia sociale* (Milan: Effedieffe, 1998).

[268] See Augustin Cochin, *Le società di pensiero e la Rivoluzione francese. Meccanica del processo rivoluzionario* (Rimini: Il Cerchio, 2008).

a "gracious" gift from the Divine Providence to help us read both our personal history, our time, and its process.[269]

At the heart of his proposal to *return to the roots of Europe* lies an organic and sacralised conception of Culture which shuns any Protestant anthropocentrism and Enlightenment-bequeathed intellectualism in order to embrace the human being in its wholeness (body, soul, and spirit) while acknowledging its transcendent Origin, its transcendent purpose; a *Culture* which is linked to *Cultivation* — of oneself and of the things of the world —, and to the centrality of the *Cult* (Worship).[270] Such is a truly universal Culture, whose weaving of values was normative for all times and civilisations (with the exception of modern civilisation, the only one which stubbornly wanted to establish itself on the *naught*) thanks to the providential action of the *Seeds of the Word*, and which found its ultimate fulfilment in the *revelatio secunda*, the Magisterium of the Incarnated Word, as handed down by the Holy Scripture and Tradition.

As another great European in eternal exile, the Romanian author Vintila Horia, wrote: "I am my books. Everything else is literature." In the case of Attilio Mordini, however, this does not mean that his *lifestyle* was superfluous. Instead, it means that his personal testimony draws worth from his going beyond himself, and from being able to retell today, here and now, universal truths whose origin would have been defined by Mordini's contemporary, non-Christian thinker, Julius Evola, as "non-human," being actually "much more than human." This is the function of traditional culture, today as yesterday: it is the transmission of *meaning* and *vocation*. And the whole of Attilio Mordini's essayistic production fully embraces this vocation to *kenosis*, to "self-emptying" aimed at facilitating a "self-filling" from a wholly Other source and

---

269 M.C. Camici and F. Cardini, *Attilio Mordini, il maestro dei segni* (Rimini: Il Cerchio, 2016), 15. Hereinafter, we will regularly make reference to this little-known but very important essay.

270 A. Mordini, *Verità della cultura* (Rimini: Il Cerchio, 1995), 9.

power. After all, this is none other than the well-known "traditional anonymity": *Adamo me fecit* is found carved on the facades of the most ancient Romanesque cathedrals that overlook the shores of our seas.

The typically chivalric ability to hold together in a very tight and fruitful synthesis the transcendent level of spirituality and the historical level of cultural action in the world is therefore one of the most important keys to understanding Mordini's work today, as illustrated by the following twofold quotation, taken from one of his works that is often vainly indicated as a "minor" one:

> Decadence and the fall below the human level correspond to an outright law, a natural and physical necessity which finds likeness in the law of gravitational attraction. The offspring of Cain flees more and more from the presence of God, but each distancing increases the decadence, yielding a further distancing. The law of guilt, which begets new guilt by accelerating its course in moving away from God, immediately reveals an increase in weight, and therefore in speed, directly proportional to the ever-increasing distance between the sinner and his Creator. And this is in a manner perfectly analogous to the law of falling bodies, according to which a weight, while falling, increases in proportion to the algebraic square of each meter of its fall... It is the law of material weights and, analogically, of materialistic progress, which increases in proportion to the algebraic square of the results achieved, from time to time, by the previous century.[271]
>
> *Hylic* progress — that is, progress which tends towards materialism (and is therefore atheistic, at least in practice) — always proceeds by setting each generation, from century to century, against the works of their fathers. Think of the rebellion of the nationalist sovereigns of the Middle Ages, such as the Sovereigns of the House of France, against the authority of the Holy Roman Emperor, which was later followed by the rebellion of the Princes who fought, in their turn, against the national monarchy; the further step was the French Revolution, that is, the struggle of the bourgeoisie against the nobility. It is the third estate that revolts against the nobles, and shortly afterwards there is the

---

271 A. Mordini, *Il mistero dello yeti alla luce della tradizione biblica* (Milan: Società Editrice Il Falco, 1977), 55.

revolution of the fourth estate, of the proletariat, against the bourgeoisie, against the third estate! And the forces called into play become more numerous from time to time, and their social and economic doctrines also become more and more *quantitative*, in a progressive quantification of democracy through *universal suffrage*. It is the multiplication of revenge, and therefore of malediction, in a truly *progressive* and... *liberal* way![272]

## A Thoroughly Modern Question: What is Tradition?

*Tradition* is a crucial word that has been bogged down for too long in rivers of descriptions, and proportionally to falsifications, deformations, and diversions along the flow; being itself the Way, straying from it is enough to wreck whole existences and generations. Here language plays its ability to elevate itself to the Otherness. Mordini worked a lot on this term, both philologically and in daily militancy; from the point of view of a needed rectification of the term, and after decades of idealistic, superhumanistic, and Masonic aberrations, we owe to him a precious and integral "return to the Real."[273]

According to Mordini, *Tradition* (and here the term should, for once, be rightfully written with the uppercase initial) is the expression of God's unknowable but providential and continuous presence in the history of humankind and of the assistance of his living Word bestowed to all men and civilisations, in different forms according to quantitatively and above all qualitatively different degrees, but absolutely culminating in the Revelation warranted by the pact with Abraham and his offspring, crowned by the Incarnation, Death, and Resurrection of the Son, the Word of God made man, the Redeemer of the world.

---

[272] Ibid., 57-58.

[273] On this fundamental topic, see Camici and Cardini, *Attilio Mordini, il maestro dei segni*, 35: *Tradizione. La parola e la cosa*; also see M. Polia, "Tradizione: il significato di un termine", *I Quaderni di Avallon* 10 (Rimini: Il Cerchio, 1986), 13.

*Truth and Language: Attilio Mordini's Sapiential Hermeneutics of Language*

Mordini was fully aware that the gnoseological level of his research (achievable with the main tools of reason, history, philology, archaeology, anthropology, and, as he had intuited, genetics) was destined to remain humanly limited and cannot be sustained and perfected except by Faith and Grace. This fundamentally and unequivocally distinguishes Mordini's research from solicitations of the Gnostic-Masonic type: it bears strongly underscoring that his vision, according to which in all religious or mythical-religious traditions one finds a living and, on different levels, authentic divine inspiration (which makes all nations co-participants, on different levels and to different extents, in the project of Revelation),[274] has nothing to do with an esoteric vision which leads to a kind of indifferentism.

Mordini was rather close to the concepts of *Prisca Philosophia* and *Religio Perennis* which are reflected, according to an explicitly apocalyptic and prophetic reading, in Nicolaus Cusanus' fundamental work, *De pace Fidei*, without which neither Erasmus of Rotterdam nor Ignatius of Loyola can be understood. The cues offered to Mordini by authors such as René Guénon or Julius Evola — of whom he was declared a "follower" by reviewers or critics who were not very earnest, and even less honest and prepared — were always welcomed by him "in the light of the Creed." It is still true that he was an attentive, critical, generous, unprejudiced reader and that, in general, he fought against the systematic denigration of esoteric culture — to which he was conceptually alien, but which

---

[274] It bears repeating, especially for those who — often in perfect good faith and historical ignorance — are convinced that the Christian Tradition in Europe begins and ends with the Council of Trent, that such renewed awareness does nothing else than fully resume the teaching — forgotten by the loss of Universality following the end of the Middle Ages — of the Church Fathers of the 1st millennium, prior to the great schism between the Christian East and West. For an introduction to this theme, see M. Polia, *Il seme e la pienezza* (Rimini: Il Cerchio, 2000), and the wide set of Patristic quotations on the subject collected therein.

he nonetheless knew well — then practised especially in the context of Marxist historicism. And although he had some connections with the "traditionalists" of his time, such as Élemire Zolla, he wished to clearly distinguish himself from them while accepting with loyalty and generosity the confrontation of his ideas with those who, in a spirit of intellectual honesty, even if from very distant positions, proposed such to him.

In his writings — not only organic essays, but also notes and letters — he began the interpretation of "signs" which he would later call "playing with symbols," or an "earnest game," as he claimed when writing to Sergio Quinzio. The latter — an official of the Italian Financial Police, then perhaps not yet 30 years old — visited Attilio Mordini more than once in his studio in Florence, often accompanied by his brother Patrizio. A great sympathy immediately took shape between the two, who, almost the same age, had begun at the same time and with the same passion and devotion an eschatological reading of the Holy Scripture and history. While there were many syntonies between them, there were also some differences. For both of them, the Kingdom of God was not to be understood merely as a sublime and personal spiritual fulfilment, for it was a real Kingdom, a real Communion, the City of God, the "Dominion" of the Lamb, an eschatological, concrete resurrection of bodies, a resurrection "which cannot be understood without flesh and bones, without blood and limbs," as Saint Jerome put it. For both of them, faithfulness to the Church did not lie in following it in its updating and adapting itself to the times, but in an obedient, ever-renewed and deepened listening to the Word for its fulfilment: it was *scientia Crucis*, without much mediation by erudite philologists and fashionable "theologians." However, they did not agree on the value of symbolic language, or on the concept of myth, which for

Mordini was an essential message, the primordial guardian of truth[275], whilst for Quinzio it was, instead, a mostly neglible tale. Nor did they agree on the religion-faith-culture nexus: Quinzio considered such to be almost a hybrid, whereas Mordini saw it as the central heart of the great apologetic and missionary work of the Greek Patristics and, in modern times, as the source and strength of a tradition which has to be bequeathed in order to thwart the loss of the identity of peoples and of the sovereignty of individuals.

The "earnest game" that he spoke about with Sergio Quinzio always remained for Mordini a model of contemplation; a contemplation which is "game" and "science," or even, as he recalled quoting Saint Bernard, the "only absolutely indispensable science."

Sometimes the "masters of the game" seem to be children, even more than the initiates or the mystics or the great metaphysicians he was reading. As he said, a model for him was even his own feeling as a child, such as when he used to return to the city in the evening after long excursions on the hills of Fiesole with youngsters led by a "cool" (*ganzo*, which in the spoken Florentine of that time meant "likeable, brave, and entertaining") priest — when he perceived, step by step, the One who "spoke behind him" during that simple yet vivid experience of the beauty of the sunsets over the flowing Arno river: "As if Jesus walked with me behind those crumbs of beauty that I gradually encountered." Thus, his inspirers remained all those children who are "not troubled by pseudo-rationality," or "by the short-sightedness of calculating reason," children for whom "the horizon line is simply and directly the Mysterious," the Infinite which offers itself in the finite, a "direct and blissful living experience," a "daily wonder" which resembles

---

275 "Moreover, mythos, in its original sense, means 'word inherent to the fact' and therefore 'announcement.' Such was therefore the Annunciation to Mary, the announcement of the Incarnation, of the 'Word made flesh,' to which all the myths of the pre-Christian Tradition tended, precisely to be incarnated in Him." (Mordini, *Verità della cultura*, 53).

the path of wisdom and which is preserved, "saved," in that "inner childness" that is properly characteristic of the personality and actions of every creative genius. "The secret of genius is to preserve childhood, the disposition of childhood throughout one's life," wrote Pavel A. Florensky from the Solovki Gulag on the Solovetsky Islands in May 1937, a few months before being executed by firing squad for "counter-revolutionary crimes."[276]

Mordini read and interpreted in this spirit the fairy tales that for centuries have spellbound children, transporting them to another plane of being and, without pretending to explain everything, provided those who listen to them with silence, rest, and witness of the Beyond.[277]

Attilio Mordini certainly recognised the ever-growing gap between contemporary culture and the religious worldview, given the extreme difficulty that today's men have with listening to the language of symbols and the sacred. However, he declared himself undisposed to wait-and-see solutions, more or less syncretic irenicism, as well as uncritical conservatism. He argued for the urgency of not giving up on the future, of establishing new educational structures and projects, of giving life to some institutional realities suitable for conveying a Christian renewal, without fear of denouncing the compromised and debased state of the already existing ones. He had few hopes, but he believed that it was necessary to fight the banalisations

---

[276] For obvious reasons of space, here we offer a short summary of the much broader analysis written by Maria Caterina Camici and Franco Cardini in *Attilio Mordini*.

[277] The reference is to A. Mordini, *Il segreto cristiano delle fiabe* (Rimini: Il Cerchio, 2007), where, alongside classical fables, he interpreted Ingmar Bergman's *The Virgin Spring* under the same lens. For those who wish to delve deeper into the profound cultural and spiritual meaning of this "call from the beyond," besides "Le terre dell'Altrove. Fantastico ed immaginario", I Quaderni di Avallon 28 (Rimini, 1992), it is necessary to refer to J.R.R. Tolkien's essay "On Fairy-Stories," accompanied by a befitting meditation on G. Spirito O.F.M. Conv., *Tra San Francesco e Tolkien. Una lettura spirituale del Signore degli Anelli* (San Marino: Il Cerchio, 2018).

and rhetorics of conservatives and progressives alike, "forms that sounded empty," in order to make the wonder of the Word heard aloud: he was also willing to suffer and "cry out to the other shore" until his last breath, as he said, what he thought would "serve" such an end, even at the risk of misunderstandings and scandalised refusals. "It is beautiful to bear the cross and see others happy, to feel that that happiness is made of our cross as of a still fertile and giftful wood," he wrote in the summer of 1958.

When he passionately suggested to believers not to despise the riches of truth, doctrines, and rites present in other religious traditions, it was certainly not to downplay the missionary action of the Church which received from Jesus the mandate to announce and bear witness to the Good News of the Incarnation of the Word, of Jesus' Passion and Resurrection. Understanding the figure and "likeness" of what is Christian in the pre-Christian is and in fact has been a way that can open the heart and mind to the mystery of the God who comes to "dwell among men" and to change history. Mordini's so-called traditionalism hoped for and practised — and in this he was not alone — something close to the themes that later, in the Second Vatican Council, appeared innovative and "revolutionary" precisely to most of those "progressive" Catholics who hated tradition.[278]

In the early 1960s, for as long as he could, Attilio Mordini spent a lot of time, almost all of his time, sowing, without thinking about the fruit. In the Japanese samurai tradition, which has clear origins in Zen, this is defined by the locution *mu shotoku*, which means "without a spirit of profit." Let us therefore reread the Parable of the Sower with the spirit of someone who knows that his days are numbered: he knows well that the quality of the soil on which the seed he throws falls will determine whether this seed will bear fruit or not, or will simply die; at the

---
278 See note 17.

same time, he can neither know nor dominate the quality of the land on which he historically finds himself living, walking, and therefore also sowing; he is entitled only to the freedom of the act of sowing, that is, to invest all his energy so that the seed entrusted to him may go far and find a greater patch of fertile ground. The sower, therefore, does not dwell on the fruit, but on the prize that his vocation will bring to him at the end of time, based on which he will be judged, according to what is taught to us by the Parable of the Talents.

At the beginning of the 1960s, Attilio Mordini found himself almost naturally surrounded by a good group of young people who had spontaneously gathered around him, just as in the *Universitates* of the Middle Ages were the students who chose their *Magister*. We have already mentioned the names of that early generation of Mordini's students, and the generation of the writer of the present text — that of today's 60-year-olds — owes to many of them the orientations for not getting lost, and the examples of dignity and freedom which have allowed us to not be ruefully reduced to doing politics in an equally rueful and useless conservative party.

## *Semina Verbi*

> *The man who does not see the signs or, worse, opposes them, closes himself into his own immanence. Bereft of their apophatic help, he will not be able to open the way which leads him through himself, and therefore will not get into what gravitates within his person.*
>
> Stanisław Grygiel, *Dialogando con Giovanni Paolo II*

*En arché:*

    **1** In the beginning was the Word,
       and the Word was with God,
       and the Word was God.

**2** The same was in the beginning with God.
**3** All things were made by Him,
and without Him was not anything made that was made.
**4** In Him was life,
and that life was the Light of men.
**5** And the Light shineth in darkness,
and the darkness comprehended it not.
**6** There was a man sent from God,
whose name was John.
**7** The same came as a witness
to bear witness of the Light,
that all men through him might believe.
**8** He was not that Light,
but was sent to bear witness of that Light.
**9** That was the true Light
which lighteth every man
that cometh into the world.
**10** He was in the world,
and the world was made by Him,
and the world knew Him not.
**11** He came unto His own,
and His own received Him not.
**12** But as many as received Him,
to them gave He power to become the sons of God,
even to those who believe on His name,
**13** who were born not of blood,
nor of the will of the flesh,
nor of the will of man,
but of God.
**14** And the Word was made flesh,
and dwelt among us,
and we beheld His glory,
the glory as of the only Begotten of the Father,
full of grace and truth.
**15** John bore witness of Him
and cried, saying, "This was He of whom I spoke,

> 'He that cometh after me
> is preferred before me,
> for He was before me.'"
> **16** And of His fullness
> have we all received,
> and grace for grace.
> **17** For the law was given by Moses,
> but grace and truth came by Jesus Christ.
> **18** No man hath seen God at any time;
> the only begotten Son,
> who is in the bosom of the Father,
> He hath declared Him.[279]

We will not spend many words on the common heritage of *Homo religiosus*[280] in relation to the causal link between the Word of God and Cosmogony[281], a link preserved by the mythical memory of any religious Tradition worthy of being handed down, and therefore worthy of being called such.[282]

The link between the Power of the Word of God and the Word-Language of Mankind is less obvious today, due to the gradual and extremely strong *impetration* of contemporary humanity, which moreover characterises the latter's sad loss of identity. Yet, it is universally clear how the metaphysical dignity of Mankind is immediately lifted, as soon as Mankind itself is created, to a rank that the Islamic tradition defines as "caliphal," and the great linguistic

---

[279] John 1:1-18 (KJ21).

[280] On this term, see J. Ries (ed.), *Le origini e il problema dell'Homo religiosus* (Milan: Jaca Book, 1989).

[281] In the Christian Tradition, the primary reference is to Genesis: 1 and 2:1-4b, in which the *dixit* of the Creating Word of God resounds ten times, and His consequent *benedicere* three times.

[282] For a swift introduction to the mythical wisdom relating to Cosmology in the different religious Traditions, it is useful to read M. Marchetto, *Miti stellari e cosmogonici* (Rimini: Il Cerchio, 2012). The relationship between Cosmogony and History is well explored in G. Géorgel, *Le quattro età dell'umanità. Introduzione alla concezione ciclica della storia*, revised 2nd ed. (Rimini: Il Cerchio, 2022).

and symbolical wisdom of J.R.R. Tolkien as "sub-creative." As Genesis 2:15 immediately reminds us: "And the Lord God took the man and put him into the Garden of Eden to till it and to keep it." The role of Mankind is therefore not merely conservative or contemplative[283]: it must "cultivate" — and therefore perfect — the Garden already perfectly created by God, i.e., the *Cosmos*, by *acknowledging* the fabric and Laws of Creation, *inserting* itself into them and *modifying* them with its own original and unique contribution: "[19] And out of the ground the Lord God formed every beast of the field, and every fowl of the air, and brought them unto Adam to see what he would call them; and whatsoever Adam called every living creature, that was the name thereof. [20] And Adam gave names to all cattle, and to the fowl of the air, and to every beast of the field..." (Genesis 2:19-20). God therefore entrusts Man, through the latter's *language*, with the task of *defining the name*, that is, the *intimate identity*, of every created thing, and therefore *acknowledges forthwith the cosmic ordering function of language, blessing it*.

This entails the "dominion" of man over Creation, understood *not* in the Protestant and liberal sense as a right to private property free from any bond other than the individualistic one of increasing profit, but in a purely chivalric sense, as wardenship and protection of the divine harmony of Creation itself: "In the Book of Genesis 1:26 we read that on the sixth day God quoth: 'Let Us make man in Our image, after Our likeness; and let them have dominion over the fish of the sea, and over the fowl of the air, and over the cattle, and over all the earth and over every creeping thing that creepeth upon the earth.'"[284]

---

283 "We must remember, however, that the order of salvation not only presupposes creation, but rather begins with it. The Symbol of faith refers us, in its conciseness, to the whole of the revealed truth about creation, to discover the truly singular and exalted position which has been given to mankind." (Saint John Paul II, Homily of 9 April 1986)

284 Ibid.

A passage like the latter is too often diluted in a superficiality of convenience or habit, but Mordini restores it through an *Auctoritas* of undying value, to its full anthropological and metaphysical meaning:

> According to Saint Bernard of Clairvaux, to say that man is created in the image of God means that the Lord gave him free will. To say that he was created in the likeness of God means that, upon being created, he also received the natural sake of goodness. This likeness — again according to Saint Bernard — was lost with the sin of Adam, whilst the image remained. It follows that man, although capable of determining himself for the good, is not always capable of attaining it, since his nature is tainted... Therefore the likeness is restored onto the image by means of the exercise of the virtues of Christian asceticism.[285]

This, and nothing less, is the immense and eternal ontological root of the metaphysical dignity of human language, shattered — but not lost — after the Fall (cf. Genesis 3: 23-24) and the crumbling of Babel (cf. Genesis 11: 6 ff.), and therefore even today. Thus follows the needfulness — even before the usefulness — of Mordini's systematic work on the essential Oneness of every aspect of human culture, and on the linguistic roots of the terms that we use daily, in the meanwhile cherishing the early and conspicuous part of Georges Dumézil's philological and anthropological work[286]: "It follows, then, that since the Word is One, then the cult is one, the culture is one, and the cultivation of the land is one, even if now, after the sin[287], cult, culture

---

285 Mordini, *Verità della cultura*, 61.

286 Regarding the work of the philologist and historian of religions Georges Dumézil, see J.C. Rivière, *Georges Dumézil e gli studi indoeuropei. Una introduzione* (Rome: Settimo Sigillo, 1993), and Dumézil's own most popular work, *The Tripartite Ideology of the Europeans*.

287 With the term "sin," Mordini alludes to the metaphysical breaking that is revealed in the expulsion of Adam and Eve from the Terrestrial Paradise (Genesis 3: 23-24), a theme which traditional Cosmogonies preserve, each according to its own mythical language. On this topic, see G. Géorgel, *Le quattro età dell'umanità*, 111, with the additional annotation that such a "fracture" produces, both in the Bible and in the religious experience of humanity, an epochal and symptomatic "confusion of tongues."

*Truth and Language: Attilio Mordini's Sapiential Hermeneutics of Language*

and cultivation are three very distinct things, but always well unified in the act of religion and rite."[288]

Mordini's meditation on the metaphysical value of Language finds its culmination in the essay *Verità del linguaggio*, completed in 1957 after three years of intense work, but published only in 1974.[289] It is a text of interesting theoretical difficulty, which presupposes that the Reader has not only decent preparation in both logic and *thēos*-ology, but also offers the rare privilege of speaking clearly, in a synthesis that is both evidently provocative towards contemporary "scientific" linguistics and implicitly accusatory towards the Christian for his ignorance of his own Tradition, which, like every aspect of the human mind, is almost always the fruit of a free choice:

> However disfigured by incorrect use in common language and marred as a consequence of sin, the word of man is divine in its most intimate essence; but this divinity must be felt and tasted in wisdom, in the most intimate flavour of each syllable in the light of revelation. Already the wisemen of the Upanishad sought the deep meaning of words in the relationship of their sound with the essence of the signified thing.[290]

In reference to the pristine Christian Tradition, he makes even clearer: "The Fathers of the Church themselves could not but savour words, for Christianity is precisely the religion of the Word, and in their works they were generous with interpretations which were overall similar to *nirukta*. In a certain sense, we could say that if the etymology of the words is their history, the symbolic meaning is their soul."[291] Furthermore: "Contemplating is therefore also seeking, and with the Grace of God reacquiring, the meaning of our

---

288 Mordini, *Verità della cultura*, 12.

289 By the publisher Giovanni Volpe and with a foreword by Father Raimondo Spiazzi O.P. (Rome, 1974).

290 A. Mordini, *Verità del linguaggio* (Rome: Volpe, 1974), 22.

291 Ibid., 22-23.

words in His Word, for the effective restoration of the Kingdom of Heaven in ourselves and in the world."[292]

Thus, the "body" of Language, constituted by the wholeness of the organic plurality of the individual Words which compose it, has its own genealogy, its own historical identity, condensed in its own etymology, a genealogy that is therefore "animated" by the depths of the *symbolic meaning*. And just as we cannot overlook the historical and corporeal concreteness of a given entity of reality in order to know it – under the burden, otherwise, of infinitely misshaping such a given entity's meaning according to the weak and fleeting wills of whomsoever, thus killing it — likewise, *not noticing*, or worse, *refusing to acknowledge* the symbolic whatness of said entity means consciously using it as a dead body, a dissectible and perfectly mute corpse.

Proceeding with a deep respect for the historical identity of each word involves knowing how to look back to the thousand-years-long history of its roots. For this reason, Mordini used to proceed from the Roots of individual words, generally harking back to Semitic, Ural-Altaic, Indo-European, and Chinese protohistory, in order to bring to light the given word's deep meaning, beyond any deformation induced by the nominalistic ideology which stands at the very core of modernity. In this way, he brought his analysis back to the same paths that the best contemporary History of Religions had for some decades already begun to trace.[293]

However, when the body of Language is bereft of its symbolic soul, then it is, as we have already said, a meaningless corpse, a victim disposable to any kind of abuse. Hence today's need to underline *what it means*

---

[292] Ibid., 26.

[293] We already hinted at Dumézil's work (see note 27). Herein, in juxtaposition with Dumézil, it is enough to mention the names of Mircea Eliade (1907-1986) and Cardinal Julien Ries S.J. (1920-2013), a direct student of Eliade and late Professor of History of Religions at the Catholic University of Louvain.

to open the inexhaustible Book of Symbols. In truth, recognising this need already means, on the one hand, escaping from the horizontal prison of modernity, and at the same time forcing oneself to acknowledge that the whole path of human culture, with so-called "Western modernity" as the only exception, has been sustained by the use of religious languages deeply imbued with symbolic meanings, consciously invoked and handed down.[294] Here it is not just a matter of taking note of the "polysemy of symbols," but of becoming aware that the dynamics of the symbolical-hermeneutical work is etymologically *sapiential* and constitutes a Ladder to Heaven. It is enough to recall the summary that Dante Alighieri gives us in the *Convivio*[295]:

> To convey what this means, it is necessary to know that **writings can be understood** and ought to be expounded **principally in four senses.**
>
> 3. **The first is called the literal**, and this is the sense that does not go beyond the surface of the letter, as in the fables of the poets. **The next is called the allegorical**, and this is the one that is hidden beneath the cloak of these fables, and is a truth hidden beneath a beautiful fiction…
>
> 4. Why this kind of concealment was devised by the wise will be shown in the penultimate book. Indeed the theologians take this sense otherwise than do the poets; but since it is my intention here to follow the method of the poets, I shall take the allegorical sense according to the usage of the poets.

---

[294] On this theme, see A. Morganti, "*Attilio Mordini, maestro dei simboli*" in *Terra Insubre* 99 (2021), 63; a very stimulating summary has been written by F. Zambon, *Allegoria. Una breve storia dall'antichità a Dante* (Rome: Carocci, 2021), which is particularly attentive to the complex *didaché* that from pre-Christian Western antiquity reaches the end of the Middle Ages. The only limitation shown by this work is a perceptible difficulty in distinguishing precisely between the two concepts of "allegory" and "symbol," sometimes presenting them as almost interchangeable, which is obviously not the case.

[295] Dante, *Convivio*, II, 1, 2-6 (English translation by Richard Lansing), the boldenings are ours. On the subject of the fourfold interpretation of Scripture, an extremely useful summary is H. de Lubac, *Esegesi medievale. I quattro sensi della Scrittura*, 3 vols. (Jaca Book: Milan, 1986-1996).

5. **The third sense is called moral,** and this is the sense that teachers should intently seek to discover throughout the scriptures, for their own profit and that of their pupils...

6. **The fourth sense is called anagogical, that is to say, beyond the senses**; and this occurs when a scripture is expounded in a spiritual sense which, although it is true also in the literal sense, signifies by means of the things signified a part of the supernal things of eternal glory...

At the risk of being once again uselessly repetitive, experience has taught us that it is always more than appropriate to repeat that these "four senses" must be understood as *simultaneously co-present* in living Language, leaving to each person's ability the freedom to understand their total, orderly complexity, or at least a part of it; and even in the case — which is common nowadays — of voluntary blindness or *a priori* refusal to open the intellect to the supraliteral senses of reality, such complexity remains intact and eternally accessible to *healthy intellects*.[296]

At this point, it might perhaps be better understood how Attilio Mordini discerned that "culture can never be reduced to an individual fact,"[297] for "religious man [...] is not just anyone who is gripped by sentimentality for divinity, but he who is ordered to *religio*, that is to say to the natural and sacred tradition of the forefathers"[298] – "just as it is inconceivable for a cult to not be expressed in a culture, which, if halved, may save individual souls from hell through the binding and loosing of Peter, but not the

---

[296] On this topic, see M. Schneider, "*Natura ed origine del simbolo*", *Conoscenza religiosa* 4 (1971), 313; P. Florensky, "*Il dizionario dei simboli*", *Conoscenza religiosa*, 2 (1977), 103; J. Vidal, "*Ermeneutiche del simbolo*", *Atopon* 1-2 (1992), 34 and 1-2 (1993), 27; G. Durand, "*Il simbolo come ricerca del sacro*", *Atopon* 1-2 (1993), 85; H. Bissonier, "*L'educazione al sacro. Valore pedagogico del simbolo*", *Per la filosofia* 29 (1993), 63; P. Filippani Ronconi, "*Mondo simbolico e mondo reale*", *Letteratura-tradizione* 6 (1999), 2; J. Ries, "*Simbolismo ed esperienza religiosa*" in idem, *L'uomo religioso e la sua esperienza del sacro* (Milan: Jaca Book, 2007), 55; F. Cardini, "*La virtù dei simboli*" in *Luoghi dell'Infinito* (October 2017), 22.

[297] Mordini, *Verità della cultura*, 38.

[298] Ibid., 41.

*Truth and Language: Attilio Mordini's Sapiential Hermeneutics of Language*

whole world with its institutions according to the *Charitas* of John; and it is of such *Charitas* that our culture must be substantiated."²⁹⁹

In another passage, Mordini endeavors to hone in even more on the ascetic and chivalric nature of the cultural *opus* in our time: "We repeat that culture consists in gradually becoming aware of how mankind's work tends to be formed for cult [worship] by the order of the rite in the Sacraments instituted by Christ and enlivened by the Holy Spirit."³⁰⁰

## Conclusion: *"I Fought the Good Fight"*

We entrust the conclusion of this invitation to rediscover the *example* of Attilio Mordini — even before the invitation to read his writings —, to the following words of one of his pupils, who is today certainly the most renowned one: the historian and scholar of the Eurasian world Franco Cardini. To him, in turn, we ourselves owe 40 years of the example of freedom, bravery, and teaching love for Europe and its cultural and spiritual roots, while recognising ourselves with fondness and pride as a further link, however frailsome and modest, in this same long chain:

> When Giulio [Schettini] abandoned our patrol, the latter had already dispersed, frayed and pulverised. A strong core remained, held together by deep bonds of personal friendship and gathered around the memory of another friend who had died prematurely (at the age of about 44): Attilio Mordini, a former war volunteer in Russia and then in the Italian Social Republic, a very talented scholar of Germanic philology under the guidance of Vittorio Santoli, a Franciscan tertiary, a Catholic and collaborator of Rodolfo Oxilia in the editing of Papini's *L'Ultima*.
>
> I owe Attilio a gratitude that is difficult to put into words: I owe him for having taught me to read Thomas Aquinas and Dante; for having earnestly introduced me to the great world

---

299 Ibid., 43.

300 Ibid., 55.

of Austro-German culture (from Prince Eugene, to Mozart, to the Habsburg tradition); for having inspired me with a severe and deep love for Europe, freeing me from the Risorgimento-inspired and nationalist temptation represented by the "vulgate" of the Italian Social Movement; for having introduced me to an intimate understanding of Judaism and Islam as sister religions of Christianity; for having taught me the rudiments of the symbolical reading of Christian art and liturgy that I would later — as a scholar of the Middle Ages — yieldingly verify; for having helped me to read — and disenchant — authors such as Evola and Guénon, who constituted the "esoteric temptation" of the young people of my political wing and of my generation, who were indeed members of a minority party but had to bear an additional burden insofar as they did not accept, as a minority within a minority, the Mazzinian and Gentilean *Weltanschauung*.

Mordini provided us with the essential keys for a tight, non-hysterical, non-preconceived critique of modernity, very different in quality from the heavy and cumbersome esoteric Spenglerianism of Julius Evola's *Revolt Against the Modern World*, our Bible at the time. Mordini introduced us to the reading of authors such as Burke and De Maistre; he led us to interpret that same fascist experience to which his youth choices had brought him, and to which he remained morally faithful (and that was, for him, a way of giving meaning to his own life: jailed after the war for crimes he had never committed, in the inhuman conditions of his imprisonment he contracted tuberculosis, which would lead him, albeit 20 years later, to his death), certainly not — in Croce's terms — as a moral illness itself, but as the tragic outcome of the ethical, institutional, and social crisis which had stricken the whole of contemporary Europe with the First World War, and which had then turned into the *Totentanz* which overwhelmed the whole continent.

In this sense, Mordini's traditionalism, although not resulting in an orderly and coherent teaching — after all, his early death did not give him enough time to adequately develop and formalise his thought — allowed us to glimpse the way out of the provincialism of the Italian Social Movement, indicated to us the horizons of a universalism strongly anchored to Europe and the Mediterranean (and very similar, in many ways, to the most serious core of Giorgio La Pira's ideas), and freed us from the ghosts of political nostalgia, nationalism, and racism. It was, again, Mordini who in the early 1960s informed us about structuralism — when no one or very few people in Italy were talking about it —, distinguishing its outcomes in, respectively, linguistics and anthropology; it was he who first introduced us to the works of Mircea Eliade and Georges Dumézil; it was he who spoke to us about Wittkower, Krautheimer, Panofsky and the "Warburg school." I still remember as a splendid season those long months between 1961 and 1962, which coincided with the very first student occupations of faculties in which our patrol took part, albeit in a critical and painful way (and in quite profound disagreement with the line officially chosen by the party, entrenched on its side in a short-sighted and provincial anti-communism, that is, the party in which we, notwithstanding everything, still recognised ourselves)...

In those months, during the daytime, there were lessons by Sestan, Cantimori, Contini, Longhi, Pugliese Carratelli, Garin, and in the evening, the simple and warm hospitality of Attilio's studio in Via San Gallo awaited us, with long conversations until late, and the common reading of essays and texts often alternated with long pauses for meditation and even prayer. Mordini was an older brother and a spiritual guide to us: around him, in many ways, we constituted a true community, an Ivory Tower. Of that legacy — focused on a strong meditation around the *philosophia perennis* and enlivened by an intense and devoted Mariological reflection — I still live today. Without a doubt, I have also contracted limitations and errors from that intense teaching, from which it has been painful for me to free myself later, and from which perhaps I have never completely freed myself. But I think back to it with the affection and gratitude that are due to men, things, and circumstances without which — for better or for worse — we would not be what we are.

Attilio left in 1963 for a long period of teaching at the University of Kiel. [...] Mordini returned to Florence a few months later, ever more in love with "his" Germany, but disappointed by the academic environment, which was even there neither too generous nor, ultimately, free. The effort sustained during those months of intense work, and perhaps also the climate of northern Germany, healthy but too rigid, had the upper hand over his tired body. In fact, he passed away shortly afterwards, on 4 October 1966, the day of that Francis of Assisi who had been his spiritual model and whose habit he had worn, as a tertiary. Exactly one month later, on 4 November, the terrible and memorable flood of the *Arno* hit Florence. For our small community, the coincidence of these two events was a sign that would remain engraved in our memory for the rest of our lives. We felt, then, that a page of our existence had been turned forever."[301]

For the sake of all this, in 1995, the Identità Europea association inaugurated its first "cultural workshop" dedicated to Attilio Mordini, whose aim is to ensure the availability of Mordini's major writings through reprints, commentaries, and new editions. If in the last 25 years we have been able to witness a certain renaissance of Mordini's legacy, then this has been possible thanks to this effort, which is still ongoing. The publication in 2016 of the *Introduction to the life and work of Attilio Mordini* edited by Maria Caterina Camici and Franco Cardini, entitled *Attilio Mordini, il maestro dei segni*, perhaps represented its highest point.

## Epilogue

"Man speaks, and when he is hungry he asks for bread, when he needs joy he asks for wine, when he needs comfort he asks for love; man speaks, and here, we repeat, is the possibility of his salvation. Man speaks, and when he wants justice he asks for blood; unbeknownst to himself, he pronounces the great truth of Golgotha. Man reads, and when he cannot read he listens in amazement. Man writes, and when he is not even able to write his own name, he draws the sign of the cross."[302]

## Postscript: A Bibliographic Contribution

Works by Attilio Mordini:

- *Il segno della carne*, written under the pen name Ermanno Landi, Florence, 1956, new ed.: Chieti, 2023;

---

301 Quoted from F. Cardini, *L'intellettuale disorganico* (Milan: Nino Aragno, 2001).
302 Mordini, *Verità del linguaggio*, 29.

*Truth and Language: Attilio Mordini's Sapiential Hermeneutics of Language*

- "Il lavoro in luce cristiana", entry in the *Moderna Enciclopedia del Cristianesimo*, Edizioni Paoline, Turin, 1963;

- *Dal mito al materialismo*, Florence, 1966; now its two constituent parts are published separately: *Verità della cultura* (Rimini, 1995), and *Il segreto cristiano delle fiabe* (Rimini, 2007);

- *Verità del linguaggio*, Rome, 1974;

- *Il mito primordiale del cristianesimo quale fonte perenne di metafisica*, Milan, 1976, new ed.: Rimini, 2020;

- *Il mistero dello yeti alla luce della tradizione biblica*, Milan, 1977, latest reprint: Siena, 2012;

- *Il tempio del cristianesimo*, Rome, 1979, new ed.: Rimini, 2006;

- *Francesco e Maria*, Florence, 1986;

- *Il cattolico ghibellino*, Rome, 1989;

- *Passi sull'acqua*, Rome, 2000;

- *Povertà regale*, Florence, 2001;

- *Giardini d'Oriente e Occidente*, Rome, 2008;

- *L'ordine costantiniano di S. Giorgio. La regola di S. Basilio e altri scritti di simbologia e cavalleria (1960-1964)*, Palermo, 2017;

- *INRI. Il mistero del Regno*, Siena, 2021.

It is worth noting that most of Attilio Mordini's books were published posthumously. As often happens to those who shun the Ring of Power and do not like to be in the spotlight, someone eventually realises their value only after they have died in silence and solitude.

*Translated by U.X.A.*

# NEO-ARCHAIC TERMS IN THE THEOLOGY OF CONTEMPORARY SLAVIC NATIVE FAITH

*Veleslav Cherkasov*

> *True Tradition is the transmission of living Fire, not the preservation of ashes.*

In the present essay[303], we use the term "neo-archaic" to designate an undertaking which is ongoing in the society of our days — particularly in Slavic Native Faith [*Rodnoverie*], but not only — namely, a transgressive attempt to transition to a new spiritual paradigm by means of overcoming the rigid, dead, clerical schemas surviving from the era of totalitarian religions as well as the simulacra of the Postmodern era. In the broad sense, we call "neo-archaic" any ideas or the expressive forms embodying them, regardless of the sphere of life to which they pertain, which are adequate to the demands of our time and are based on archetypal forms, archaic myth, and traditional culture as a whole (in our case, Slavic culture).

---

303 This text is based on two original papers: the first, "The Neo-Archaic in the Theology of Contemporary Slavic Native Faith," was presented on 18 May 2024 at the conference "Phenomenon and Meaning: Towards the Phenomenology and Semantics of the Word," held at the Moscow State Institute of International Relations (MGIMO) under the Ministry of Foreign Affairs of the Russian Federation, on the panel "Myth and the Sacred in the Contemporary Religious Culture of Russia"; the second, "The Concept of the *Koshchnyi* Age," was presented on 30 June 2024 at the seminar "Slavic Eschatology in Mythology and Today" organized under the aegis of the journal *Veshchii: Almanac of Slavic-Russian Tradition*.

### Neo-Archaic Terms in the Theology of Contemporary Slavic Native Faith

From our point of view, in contemporary Slavic Native Faith, the neo-archaic represents a kind of challenge, which includes an aesthetic dimension, that has been posed to society and to the dominant religious and pseudo-religious systems within it (including those which have discredited themselves, have been hopelessly profaned, and have lost any relevance). In our understanding of the word, neo-archaic should be distinguished from all the pseudo-traditional and pseudo-Slavic "cherry-pickings" that are spiritually fruitless, vulgarly primitive on the aesthetic plane, and branded with commercial aims in modern society. In the latter category we count the pseudo-folklore ensembles wearing plastic *kokoshniki*-headdresses, the vast majority of urban "folk holidays," other similar "festivities," the obsessive replication in the mainstream media of "folk" templates with cartoon bears, costumed Cossacks, Russian vodka, matryoshkas and balalaikas, as well as simulacra in the likes of the so-called *Slavic-Aryan Vedas*[304] which present our ancestors as aliens who came to Earth from other planets on spaceships, and so on.

Let us turn to a direct examination of cases of neo-archaic terminology that can be found in the milieux of contemporary Slavic Native Believers [*Rodnovery*]. It bears preliminarily noting that the world history of the development of ideological systems (whether the ideology of communism, the Christian religion, or, for instance, Hegel's philosophy, not to mention countless local subcultures) glaringly shows us that any sufficiently developed political, religious, or philosophical system needs its own special means of self-expression and over time forms its own, sometimes unique conceptual language. In some cases, old words and notions are given new meaning, while in others, neologisms are born, some of which subsequently become common usage in the rest of

---

304 The *Slavic-Aryan Vedas*, which are included on the Ministry of Justice of the Russian Federation's list of extremist materials, are comparable to many other "conspiracies" widespread among contemporary pagans in the West.

society (one such case is contemporary society's widespread use of terms and expressions from ecclesiastical vocabulary or from once "secret" thieves' slang). In contemporary Slavic Native Faith, neo-archaic manifestations are to be found first and foremost in specific Rodnovery terms that have spontaneously appeared over the last three decades and which — although they are based on well-known roots in the Old Russian language (not to be confused with the Old Church Slavonic language, which was artificially created to suit the needs of the church) — are, with rare exceptions, neologisms. The exceptions are represented by words which existed in the past, but whose meaning has changed to a greater or lesser extent within the framework of Native Faith discourse.

## Rodnoverie

The term *rodnoverie*, "Native Faith," is itself a neologism referring to the native (*rodnaia*) and ancestral (*rodovaia*) faith of the Slavs, which is natural (*prirodnaia*), indigenous (*rodnaia*), and of the folk (*narodnaia*). The root term *rod* ("tribe," "clan," "kin," "lineage") comes from the Old Russian родъ (cf. Greek ένος, γενεά, ἔθνος), and the term for "faith" or "belief," *vera*, comes from the Old Russian вѣра (cf. Greek πίστις).[305] We introduced this term in 1999, initially in the form of the adjective *rodnovercheskii*, that is "pertaining to the native [*rodnoi*] faith of the Slavs." In Oleg Trubachyov's opinion, it is conceivable that the word *rod* "is related to the Armenian *ordi*, 'son,' the Hittite *ḫardu*, 'great-grandson,' and goes back to the Indo-European *\*ǝordh-*, 'high, grown,' hence Russian *rasti*, 'to grow,' Latin *arbor*, 'tree.' Thus, this word can be traced back to the Proto-Slavic *\*ordъ*."[306]

---

[305] M. Vasmer, *Etimologicheskii slovar' russkogo iazyka* [*Russisches etymologisches Wörterbuch*], vol. I (Moscow: Progress, 1986), 292; ibid., vol. III (Moscow: Progress, 1987), 490; I.G. Cherkasov (Veleslav), *Osnovy slavianskogo rodnoveriia* (Moscow: Institute of Humanitarian Studies, 2022), 21.

[306] Vasmer, *Etimologicheskii slovar'* III, 491.

### Neo-Archaic Terms in the Theology of Contemporary Slavic Native Faith

In our *Foundations of Slavic Native Faith*, it is said of the native faith of the Slavs as it presents itself in the present time: "Slavic Rodnoverie brings together the traditional beliefs of the Slavic peoples that originated in the pre-industrial and, in the very least, the archaic era of the differentiation of the Slavic branch of the Indo-European language tree. Rodnoverie is founded on the natural and ancestral values which have stood the tests of time and have not lost their relevance in modernity."[307] The very term *rodnoverie* "means the native [*rodnaia*], that is, the original faith of the ancestors, fidelity [*vernost'*] to their ethical precepts, as well as reasonable trust [*doverie*] in the life and spiritual experience obtained by the people on its historical path, which is open to any person who is sufficiently involved in the traditional culture of this given people."[308]

Before the emergence of the term *rodnoverie*, the names most commonly used by Slavic pagans to refer to their spiritual tradition were "natural faith" (*prirodnaia vera*), "folk faith" or "faith of the people" (*narodnaia vera*), and "native faith" (*rodnaia vera*), which, so it seems to us, do not require any special clarification. However, it is of interest that one of the first to use the terms "natural faith" and "faith of the people" for Slavic paganism was Mikhail Ivanovich Kastorsky (1809-1866), a Russian philologist, pedagogue, ethnographer, translator, doctor of philosophy, and professor of world history at Saint Petersburg University. In his *Outlines of Slavic Mythology* (1841), he wrote the following:

> We [...] have accounts of our people from the time when it still had, so to speak, primordial customs and, as it were, was still forming its Religion — these tales are precious to all of the native inhabitants of Europe. These primordial customs and life of the Slavs, imbued by pure nature itself and even determined by it, are nothing other than a celebration of the natural faith [*prirodnaia vera*] that constitutes the essence of the Religion of our ancestors [...] And so it is left to us, having laid out the

---

307 Veleslav, *Osnovy slavianskogo rodnoveriia*, 20.

308 Ibid.

foundations of the root features of the character and life of the Slavs, to thereupon affirm them, as was once the case in reality, with the seal of the faith of the people [*vera narodnaia*].[309]

Speaking of the rebirth of Slavic paganism, it is impossible not to mention the Polish Slavist, archaeologist, folklorist, ethnographer, and dialectologist Zorian Dołęga-Chodakowski (*né* Adam Czarnocki, 1784-1825). His controversial dissertation, *On Slavdom before Christianity* (*O Sławiańszczyźnie przed chrześcijaństwem*, 1818), was one of the first works to challenge the then current notion of the "benefits" that the imposition of Christianity allegedly brought to Poland (which in his time was part of Russia), and this work proved to be a precursor of the later Slavic movements. He argued that Christianity was an alien religion which destroyed the characteristic traits of the Slavs and their cultural achievements, but certain elements associated with earlier beliefs had been preserved in folk culture, the large-scale study of which would enable fostering a genuine spiritual renaissance of the nation. Thus, Dołęga-Chodakowski was one of the first to openly call himself a pagan and call for returning to the original religion of the Slavs, thereby forever inscribing his name in the scrolls of history as one of the first heralds of modern Slavic Native Faith. The influence of his ideas is clearly visible in, among other things, the terminology used by the members of the Sacred Circle of Worshippers of Światowid (*Święte Koło Czcicieli Światowida*) founded in Poland in 1921.

### Kolovrat

Unlike the word *rodnoverie*, the word *kolovrat*, which contemporary Slavic Rodnovery call the round, swastika-like symbol with eight rays bent either clockwise or counterclockwise, has been known for a long time, although it wasn't applied to this particular symbol. It is enough to

---

309 M.I. Kastorsky, *Nachertanie Slovianskoi Mifologii* (Saint Petersburg: E. Fisher, 1841), 100-101.

recall, for example, Evpatiy Kolovrat, who is mentioned in the *Tale of Batu's Destruction of Ryazan* (the surviving copies of this literary monument are part of the manuscript collections of the 16th-18th centuries). According to the *Tale*, Kolovrat was the name of the legendary Russian hero who fought against the Mongol-Tatars in the 13th century.

The word *kolovrat* comes from the old word *kolo* which, according to Vladimir Dal's *Interpretive Dictionary of the Living Great Russian Language*, means "circle, circumference, ring, loop, hoop," and further: "to turn something, to spin around, to encircle, to rotate... *Kolovratnyi* — that which rotates, circles, spins around; *Kolovratnost'* is the quality or state of being rotary... *Kolovorot, kolovrat* — axle, capstan, standing shaft with levers for lifting a load, pulling a seine, etc."[310]

As for the history of the emergence of the *kolovrat* symbol, the following was told to me in person by the late Ladomir (Fyodor Nikolaevich Razoryonov), the high priest of the Golden Kolovrat community, in 1998. In the early 1990s, Dobroslav (Alexey Dobrovolsky), Selidor (Alexander Belov, the founder of Slavic-Gorits martial arts), and Ladomir decided to choose the *kolovrat* as the symbol of the renaissance of the Slavic pagan movement. They saw it as a double solar symbol designating the twofold increase of the power of fire and the Sun. The "double cross"[311] they chose was based on the scholar Boris Rybakov's description of a "calendar" depicted on a "vessel for divination" from Lepesovka in Volhynia (4th c.) as well as an even older vessel from Almásfüzitő (18th c. B.C.E., from the Bell Beaker culture on the territory of modern Hungary), which has "signs of the 12 months and four solar phases."[312] On

---

310 Vladimir Dal', *Tolkovyi slovar' zhivago velikoruskago iazyka*, vol. II, 2nd ed. (Saint Persburg/Moscow: Izdanie knigoprodavtsa-tipografa M.O. Wol'fa, 1881), 138.

311 Cf. M. Vasmer, *Etimologicheskii slovar' russkogo iazyka* [*Russisches etymologisches Wörterbuch*], vol. II (Moscow: Progress, 1986), 372-373.

312 B.A. Rybakov,"*Kalendar' IV v. iz zemli polian*", *Sovetskaia arkheologiia* 6:4 (1962), 66-89; idem, *Iazychestvo drevnikh slavian* (Moscow: Nauka, 1981), 323-325.

both "calendars," among other symbols and patterns, were two oblique crosses which the academician associated with the month of June (*kresen'*) and the summer solstice (*Kupala*). The founders of the Rodnovery symbol placed one cross on another and had an eight-pointed figure, the protruding ends of which they proposed to bend "clockwise," that is in the direction of the visible movement of the Sun across the sky. As a result, the eight-pointed swastika symbol that we know as the *kolovrat* appeared. Dobroslav was the first to suggest using the *kolovrat* (in unity of form and name). Three Soviet flags hung out on the streets for state holidays were taken down, the hammers and sickles were removed from them, and yellow braid was used to sew a large round *kolovrat* in the center of them.

After some time, as not uncommonly happens among passionary people, the three of them parted ways due to differences in their views on the fate of the movement (or perhaps it would be more accurate to say that their characters didn't come together). Ladomir (Razoryonov) subsequently plunged into personal spiritual seeking, changed his last name to Ozaryonov, and in 1998 he passed along to me his *bratina*-bowl (a two-handed ladle carved out of linden wood by Dobroslav's son with kolovrats depicted on both sides) as well as his community's standard with the *kolovrat* (one of the original three) for the ritual needs of my community (founded in 1998 as *Satya-Veda*, called *Rodoliubie* since 1999). It was then that he told me the above-mentioned history of this symbol. Later, on top of the *kolovrat* sewn with yellow braid, I sewed a *kolovrat* of the same shape, cut from a single piece of yellow fabric, under which the original braid patches were preserved — it is in this form that the banner still exists today.

The first books whose covers depicted the *kolovrat* were Dobroslav's pamphlets, self-published (*samizdat'*) in 1988. The first official publication bearing the eight-pointed, rightward-turning, yellow *kolovrat* on a red background was Vadim Kazakov's *Imenoslov* (Book of Names, 1994).[313] My first book with the *kolovrat* on the cover (gold embossing on black boomvinyl) was published in 1998, exactly 10 years after Dobroslav's first book.[314]

Among contemporary Rodnovery, there is the persistent idea that the *kolovrat* is one variation of symbols of the Sun and the Year-Wheel (eight-spoke wheel) depicted in motion, in a cyclical dynamic. The *kolovrat*-wheel is seen as consisting of a periphery, which is eternally in motion, symbolizing the Great Turning of all beings and matter in the circles of time, and a motionless center symbolizing the sacred spiritual center: the Axis Mundi, invisible to the corporeal eye, runs through it, while the Rotating (Great Return) proceeds around it.

A similar interpretation of swastika symbolism has been found in the works of the Traditionalist philosophers René Guénon and Julius Evola. In *Symbolism of the Cross*, Guénon remarked:

> the *swastika* is essentially the "sign of the Pole." If it is compared with the figure of the cross inscribed in the circumference of a circle, it will be seen that these are really equivalent symbols in certain respects; but in the *swastika* the rotation around the fixed centre, instead of being represented by the circumference, is merely indicated by short lines joined to the ends of the arms of the cross and forming right angles with them; these lines are tangents to the circumference which mark the direction of movement at the corresponding points. As the circumference represents the manifested world, the fact that it is as it were "suggested" (or "understood") indicates quite clearly that the *swastika* is not a symbol of the world, but rather of the Principle's action upon the world. If we relate the *swastika* to the rotation of a sphere, such as the heavenly sphere, upon its axis, it must be supposed

---

313 V.S. Kazakov, *Imenoslov. Nepolnyi spisok imen slavianskikh s tolkovaniem znacheniia i proiskhozhdeniia* (Kaluga: Zolotaia alleia, 1994).

314 A. Arinushkin and I. Cherkasov (Veleslav), *Zov Giperborei* (Moscow: Gil'-Estel', 1998).

as traced in the equatorial plane, and then the central point, as already explained, will be the projection of the axis on this plane which is perpendicular to it. As for the direction of rotation indicated by the figure, its importance is only secondary and does not affect the general meaning of the symbol; in fact both forms are found, indicating both clockwise and anti-clockwise rotation, and this need not mean that it is always intended to establish an opposition of some kind between them. It is true that in certain countries and epochs schisms from the orthodox tradition may have occurred, and the schismatics, in order to manifest their antagonism, may have deliberately given the figure an orientation contrary to the one used in the environment from which they separated; but this in no way touches the essential meaning, which remains the same in all cases. Besides, the two forms are often found in association, and they can then be regarded as representing one and the same rotation looked at from each of the two poles.[315]

## *Kolokres, Kologod*

Later, in the time of the early Rodoliubie circle (the early 2000s), there arose the terms *kolokres*, which refers to an equal-armed cross inscribed into a circle, an archaic symbol of fire and the Sun[316], and *kologod*, the Rodnovery name for the Year-Wheel and the cyclical time of the traditional worldview that determined the structure of the folk calendar with its cycles of agrarian, pastoral, artisanal, and other signs, holidays, and rituals. The Rodnovery calendar itself is sometimes called the *kologod*.

## *Bratina*

The word *bratina* has in contemporary Slavic Rodnoverie only somewhat undergone a change in meaning. The *Russian Traditional Life* encyclopedic dictionary reports that the Old

---

315 René Guénon, *Symbolism of the Cross*, trans. Angus Macnab (Ghent: Sophia Perennis et Universalis, 1996), 55-56

316 Ariel Golan, *Mif i simvol*, 2nd ed. (Jerusalem: Tarbut; Moscow: RUSSLIT, 1994), 122.

Russian *bratina* (its first mention belonging to the 16th century) is "a dish for serving and drinking mead, wine, and beer (for drinking 'for the whole brotherhood [*bratiia*]')." It is described as:

> A wooden or metal vessel of spherical shape with a wide neck fixed to a lower base. Wooden bratinas were turned on a lathe from burl, rhizome, or a whole piece of wood, and covered with paintings or carvings... Metal bratinas were stamped out of a sheet of copper, silver, or tin. Copper bratinas were tinned from the inside, and sometimes from the outside. They could be smooth or spoon-shaped, i.e., their walls could have vertical bulges or bubbles alternating with depressions. An ornament made via engraving or chasing technique was applied to the metal bratina. In the 17th-19th centuries, the bratina was used in the villages and towns of the northern provinces of European Russia.[317]

In contemporary Slavic Rodnoverie, "*bratina*" most often refers to a traditional *kovsh*-cup/ladle with two handles which can conveniently be passed from hand to hand around in a circle during ritual libations offered to the Gods and ancestors.

### Trebishche, Treba, Kapishche, Kap'

Some terms associated with pagan rites can be interpreted in different ways not only among Rodnovery themselves, but also in the scholarly literature. One example of this is how one dictionary of the Russian language in the 11th-15th centuries defines the meaning of the word *trebishche* as a "sacrificial altar," whereas *A History of Russian Art*, a textbook used in art courses at universities, takes *trebishche* to mean a pagan sanctuary or shrine as such: "Pagan cult places — *trebishcha* — were round earthen platforms where idols stood and sacred fires were burned. Beautiful and effectively located elevated places were chosen for sacrificial rites. In Kiev, the idol of Perun stood on a hill outside the

---

[317] I.I. Shangina, *Russkii traditsionnyi byt. Entsiklopedicheskii slovar'* (Saint Petersburg: Azbuka-klassika, 2003), 366-367.

prince's court. It is very likely that the Eastern Slavs also had wooden pagan temples."[318]

Vladimir Dal's dictionary defines *trebishche* as "an altar, a place for offering sacrifices to God" and as "a pagan temple, idol, shrine, priestly site, pagan site, sacrum, icon for idol worshippers."[319] The word *treba*, whence *trebishche*, can in contemporary Slavic Rodnoverie designate the specific sacrificial offering to the Gods and ancestors (e.g., a loaf of bread or mead) as well as the whole rite of offering sacrificial gifts. Vladimir Dal's dictionary defines *treba* as "sacrifice, offering" as well as "the conducting of sacrament or holy rite."[320]

In contemporary Slavic Native Faith, across different communities, *trebishche* can refer to a pagan altar, next to which (or on which) revered sculptures are set up, as well as to the holy shrine (*sviatilishche*) in general, particularly the place where people gathered for the rite stand, as distinct from the *kapishche*, the place where the cult statues of the Gods — *kapi* — are set up. The word *kapishche* can mean the whole shrine (this is how contemporary Slavic Rodnovery most often refer to their *sviatilishche* in ordinary speech) as well as the special part of it with the erected *kapi* (or, more rarely, an individual cult statue, an idol, *kap*, or *chur*). In the first volume of his *History of Russian Art since Ancient Times* (1903), A.P. Novitsky wrote:

> *Trebishche* comes from the word *treba*, which has been preserved to this day and means the place where pagan *treby*, or sacrifices, were carried out. *Kapishche* comes from the word *kap'*, which means image, depiction... The suffix *-ishche* ordinarily means a place, such as *pozharishche*, 'place of fire,' or *gorodishche*, 'place of a city,' but sometimes has its meaning expanded: *idolishche*

---

318 M.M. Rakova and I.V. Riazantsev (eds.), *Istoria russkogo iskusstva*, vol. I: *Iskusstvo X — pervoi poloviny XIX v.*, 3rd rev. ed. (Moscow: Izobrazitel'noe isskustvo, 1991), 8.

319 Vladimir Dal', *Tolkovyi slovar' zhivago velikoruskago iazyka*, vol. IV, 2nd ed. (Saint Persburg/Moscow: Izdanie knigoprodavtsa-tipografa M.O. Wol'fa, 1882), 427.

320 Ibid.

means not only the place, but the idol. The word *kapishche* is used in the latter meaning in the chronicles, e.g., where it is said [in the *Tale of Bygone Years* under 6496/988] that Vladimir brought back "two copper *kapishchi*" from Chersonesus [which has been translated as "two copper idols"]. Especially valuable for us in this respect is the famous *Sermon on Law and Grace* by the first Russian Metropolitan, Hilarion, who lived under Yaroslav the Wise: 'We are no longer defending *kapishchь*, we are building churches of Christ.'"³²¹

Among contemporary Rodnovery, *kapishcha* tend to be common (communal) and household (the home shrine or the *krasnyi kut*, the "red corner" in the traditional Slavic home). Some also speak of the "inner *kapische*," the "*Kapische* of the Heart" within man, that is, the invisible abode of the Divine Spirit within each of us.³²²

## *Chur*

The legitimacy of the use of the term *chur* for statues or sculptures is the subject of disputes among Rodnovery. Vadim Kazakov (the former head of the Union of Slavic Communities of Slavic Native Faith), who was from Kaluga, strongly opposed calling ritual statues "churs," as he believed that Chur was exclusively the proper name of the Deity of borders.³²³ In our article "Was Chur a God of the Slavs?", we showed that "Chur" is first encountered as a theonym only in the 18th century, in Lomonosov's *Ancient Russian History*, on account of which we cannot claim with any certainty that the Slavs worshipped a God bearing this name in antiquity.³²⁴ According to our observations, the majority of contemporary Slavic Rodnovery predominantly use the word *chur* in the

---

321 A. Novitsky, *Istoriia Russkago Iskusstva s' drevn'eshikh' vremen'*, vol. I (Moscow: Izdanie V.N. Lind', 1903), 12.

322 Volkhv Veleslav, *Rodnye Bogi Rusi* (Moscow: Velesova Kruga, 2009), 383-386.

323 V.S. Kazakov, "*Chur Velesa i makosh' Svaroga*", VK (7 December 2019) [https://vk.com/@vskazakov-chur-velesa-i-makosh-svaroga].

324 Veleslav, "*Chur — Bog ili net?*", VK (28 July 2022) [https://vk.com/@65162828-chur-bog-ili-net].

meaning of a cult sculpture/statue of a God or ancestor, i.e., an idol or *kap'*, which forms the semantic chain of *chur*, *shchur* ("ancestor"), and *prashchur* ("forebear"), which implies that the indigenous Gods are understood metaphorically as the ancestors of our ancestors.

### Sviato

Contemporary Slavic Rodnovery use the word *sviato* for both a traditional festival holiday, or *sviatoden'* (often timed to coincide with one or another date on the Slavic *kologod*-calendar), and a venerated depiction of a Deity or ancestor (whether sewn, drawn, etc.). In Vladimir Dal's dictionary, we find *sviato* listed as meaning a holiday in general, including the forms *sviatok'* and *sviatden'*, as well as "holy water," as in "the priests walked around with *sviatom'*" (the adjective *sviatoi* means "holy," "sacred").[325]

### Strava

The term *strava*, first mentioned by Jordanes, a 6th-century Gothic historian, in his *On the Origins and Deeds of the Getae*, is interpreted by some Rodnovery in the narrow sense as a memorial feast during a funeral service for the deceased, while others understand it in the broader sense as meaning a ritual feast. In Jordanes' description of the funeral of Attila, we read: "After he was mourned with such lamentations, they celebrated by holding a *strava*, as they call it, on his burial mound, which was accompanied with a huge feast. In combining such opposite [feelings], they express their funeral grief mixed with jubilation."[326]

---

[325] Dal', *Tolkovyi slovar* IV, 161.

[326] In the Latin original: "*postquam talibus lamentis est defletus, stravam super tumulum eius quam appellant ipsi ingenti commessatione concelebrant...*" Russian edition: Iordan, *O proiskhozhdenii i deianiiakh Getov.* "*Getica*", trans. E.Ch. Skrzhinskaia (Moscow: Izdatel'stvo vostochnoi literatury, 1960), 117, 172.

In his 1868 work *On the Burial Customs of the Pagan Slavs*, Alexander Kotlyarevsky noted that the Slavs "to this day use this term to mean: food, a dish, an assortment of dishes making up a meal, and in this meaning it is now used in Polish, Czech, Slovak, Little Russian, and Great Russian. But the use of the word can be traced back to ancient times: we find it in the same form in the monuments of old Czech literature and precisely with the meaning of funeral feast, a feast after death."[327]

Vladimir Dal's dictionary recorded the term as meaning "food, dish, especially of liquid, such as broth or brew" and noted that in some localities it is pronounced *strova*.[328] In Max Vasmer's work, we find the same definition of *strava/strova* along with its attestations in Ukrainian, Belarusian, Czech, Slovak, and Polish. Vasmer traces the word back to *sъtrava*, which is connected to *trava*, "herb," and the verb *travit'*, "to poison, to intoxicate, to exterminate."[329] The actual etymology of this term remains the subject of disputes to this day.[330]

## Trizna

*Trizna* is another term from ancient Russian paganism whose precise meaning and etymology provokes discussions to this day. Some Rodnovery understand it to mean assemblies of warriors during memorial celebrations in honor of the deceased, while others take it more broadly to mean funeral celebrations with feasts and libations, or funeral rites in general.

Unfortunately, the sources do not afford us the possibility of unambiguously determining the ancient sense of the word.

---

327 A.A. Kotlyarevsky, *O pogrebal'nykh obychaiakh iazycheskikh slavian* (Moscow: K.A. Popov, 1868), 39.

328 Dal', *Tolkovyi slovar* IV, 334.

329 Vasmer, *Etimologicheskii slovar'* III, 770.

330 O.B. Bubenok, "Termin 'strava' v "Getike" Iordana (k voprosu o semantike i proiskhozhdenii slova)", *Materialy po arkheologii, istorii i etnografii Tavrii* 16 (2012), 376-398.

*Neo-Archaic Terms in the Theology of Contemporary Slavic Native Faith*

In the *Laurentian Codex* of the *Tale of Bygone Years*, we read the following of the Slavs' ancient funerary customs:

> Whenever a death occurred, a [*tryzno* (variations: *triznu, tryznu*)] was held over the corpse, and then a great pyre was constructed, on which the deceased was laid and burned. After the bones were collected, they were placed in a small urn and set upon a post by the roadside, even as the Vyatichians do to this day. Such customs were observed by the Krivichians and the other pagans...[331]

Commenting on this testimony, Viljo Johannes Mansikka noted:

> *Trizna* is usually taken to mean a war game, a competition, fight, battle, or *pugna* (Latin: fight, battle), *certamen* (Latin: contest) organized to commemorate the deceased at their burial or afterwards on memorial days (cf. Czech *tryzniti* - to torment, to languish, to torture, to beat/hit), or a feast held over a grave that consists of games accompanied by refreshments. Similar *loci profani* (Latin: folk games) organized over the dead in their honor are attested among many peoples, both ancient as well as still living ones.[332]

Sreznevsky's dictionary of the Old Russian language reports:

> *trizna=tryzna* means "fight," "contest," as well as "feat," "award," "religious celebration" and "solemn commemoration in honor of the deceased in pagan Rus'"; *triznik'=tryznik'=tryzd'nik'* means "wrestler," "fighter," as well as "priest"; and *triznishche* means the site of a *trizna*, games, or fights, i.e, an arena, as well as "ceremonial commemoration in honor of the deceased," "struggle (figurative)," and even "trial."[333]

---

[331] Standing Historico-Archeological Commission of the Academy of Sciences of the USSR (ed.), *Polnoe Sobranie Russkikh Letopisei*, vol. 1, *Lavrent'evskaia letopis'* 1: *Povest' vremennykh let*, 2nd ed. (Leningrad: Academy of Sciences of the USSR, 1926), 14. [Translation from: *The Russian Primary Chronicle: Laurentian Text*, trans./ed. Samuel Hazzard Cross and Ogled P. Sherbowitz-Wetzor (Cambridge: Mediaeval Academy of America, 1953), 57].

[332] V.J. Mansikka, *Trudy po religii vostochnykh slavian*, ed. A.I. Alieva, V.Y. Petrukhin, S.M. Tolstaya (Moscow: Forum; Neolit, 2016), 125.

[333] I.I. Sreznevsky, *Materialy dlia Slovaria drevne-russkago iazyka po pis'mennym' pamiatnikam'*, vol. III [publication of the Department for the Russian Language and Literature of the Imperial Academy of Sciences] (Saint Petersburg: Imperial Academy of Sciences, 1903), 995-996.

Vasmer's etymological dictionary offers a more expansive account:

> *trizna*, "contest; feat; award, funeral feast (12th c.); *tryzna* (Svyatoslav's *Izbornik* of 1073, *Laurentian Codex*; cf. Sreznevsky III, 1995), Old Slavic *trizna*, [Greek] ἔπαϑλον, Proto-Slavic *trizna*, [Greek] στάδιον, παλαίστρα, ἆϑλον, *triznodav'ts'*, [Greek] ἀγωνοϑέτης, Czech *trýzeň*, "torment, anguish," *tryzniti*, "to torment, to torture," Slovak *trýzeň, tryznit'*, Polish *tryznić*, "to waste (time)." The Proto-Slavic, evidently, was *\*tryzna*, judging by the West Slavic forms connected by the alternation of vowels with *travit'*, that is, originally "(funeral) refreshments" [...] Others regard *\*trizna* to be the original form — which is less probable — and connect it with Old Icelandic *stríð*, "dispute, war, unrest, torment" [...] [Slavic *\*trizna* might be explained as derived from *trizъ* ("three-year-old," referring to an animal), hence the original meaning of *trizna* would be "sacrificial slaughter of a three-year-old animal" — O.N. Trubachyov].[334]

Let us note that in the late 18th century, Mikhail Dimitrievich Chulkov voiced the proposal that *trizna* might be associated with the number 3 (*tri* in Russian), which figures in funerary rites to this day:

> *Trizna* means a commemoration of the deceased, e.g., on the third day after death, on the ninth (3x3), on the 40th, a year after, and three years afterwards. The ancient Slavs held funeral feasts at graves with food and drink, which many still do in remote towns and villages; they bring cakes, pancakes, fried pies, fritters, bread wheels, and other dishes to the graves or to the church refectory, inviting the priest and the whole clergy, and they eat together.[335]

We encounter another mention of *trizna* in the *Laurentian Codex* of the *Tale of Bygone Years* in the section dated 6453/945, which describes the funerary-burial rites arranged by Queen Olga for her husband, Prince Igor:

> Olga then sent to the Derevlians the following message, "I am now coming to you, so prepare great quantities of mead in the

---

334 Vasmer, *Etimologicheskii slovar'* IV, 102

335 M.D. Chulkov, *Slovar' Russkikh' sueverii* (Saint Petersburg: Shiner, 1782), 249; idem, *Abevega Ruskikh' suverii, idolopoklonnicheskikh' zhervoprinoshenii, svadebnykh prostonarodnykh' obriadov', Koldovstva, Shemanstva, i proch.* (Moscow: F. Gippius, 1786), 300.

city where you killed my husband, that I may weep over his grave and hold [*trizna*] for him." When they heard these words, they gathered great quantities of honey and brewed mead. Taking a small escort, Olga made the journey with ease, and upon her arrival at Igor's tomb, she wept for her husband. She bade her followers pile up a great mound and when they had piled it up, she also gave command that [*trizna*] should be held. Thereupon the Derevlians sat down to drink, and Olga bade her followers wait upon them.[336]

What catches our attention in this passage is the manuscript's testimony that the *trizna* (whatever it might have been) was held after after the burial mound had been piled up and filled, and the funeral feast included copious libations using an alcoholic mead drink, which finds parallels throughout almost the entire Indo-European world.

### *Prav', Yav', Nav'*

In *Foundations of Slavic Native Faith*, in the chapter "The Structure of the Cosmos," we examined in detail the terms *Prav'*, *Yav'*, and *Nav'*, which were put into circulation in the mid-20th century by Yuri Petrovich Mirolyubov and have come to be used by some contemporary Slavic Rodnovery to denote the "Upper," "Middle," and "Lower" worlds (often called the *Nebesa*, "Heavens," *Belyi Svet*, "White World/Light," and *Podzem'e*, "Underworld," respectively).[337]

Let us note that Mirolyubov himself, along with some of his closest followers, imparted a somewhat different meaning to these terms. *Prav'* was understood to be a kind of invisible foundation of the world of *Yav'* (but not *Nav'*!), or was imagined to be the "world of laws" governing visible reality (hence the "Laws of *Prav'*"). In Mirolyubov's words, "People believed in *Yav'*, *Prav'*, and *Nav'*. *Yav'* is actuality, reality, the visible world. *Prav'* is the invisible 'backbone' of reality

---

336 *Lavrent'evskaia letopis'*, 57; *Russian Primary Chronicle: Laurentian Text*, 80 [see fn. 331].

337 I.G. Cherkasov (Volkhv Veleslav), *Osnovy slavianskogo rodnoveriia* (Moscow: Institute of Humanitarian Studies, 2022), 256-326.

to which *Yav'* holds. *Nav'* is the *Yav'* beyond that is void of *Prav'*."³³⁸ Compare this to the remarks of Sergey Lesnoy (Paramonov), one of the first translators and publishers of the *Book of V[e]les* (which was presumably written by Mirolyubov himself): "The ancient Russians [*Russy*] viewed the universe as divided into three parts: *Yav'* is the visible, real world, *Nav'* is the world beyond, the unreal, the world of the afterlife, and *Prav'* is the world of laws that governs everything in the world."³³⁹

In D.M. Dudko's translation and commentary on the *Book of V[e]les*, we read (on "plank" 1): "In vain do we recall our good old times in order to go who knows where. And how we look back and say that we are ashamed to know of *Nav'*, *Prav'*, and *Yav'*..."³⁴⁰ Dudko offers the following commentary:

> *Yav'*, *Prav'*, and *Nav'* are the most important philosophical notions of the *Book of Veles*. *Yav'* is the earthly, material world. *Prav'* is the heavenly, ideal world that governs the world of *Yav'*. *Nav'* is the underworld of death. This corresponds to the universal mythological division of the Cosmos into upper (heavenly), middle (earthly), and lower (subterranean) worlds. The term *Nav'* is related to the Czech *Nav*, that is "underworld," the Old Russian and Bulgarian *nav'e* (malicious spirits of the dead), and the Ukrainian *navka* (/*mavka*), 'forest maiden.'

The text continues: "And how we look back and say that we are ashamed to know of *Nav'*, *Prav'*, and *Yav'* and to know and think both sides of being. Dazhdbog created for us the egg that is the light of the stars and the moon. And in that abyss Dazhdbog hung our earth so that it holds." Dudko comments:

> The myth of the World Egg is universal. Dazhdbog, the Sun, does not figure in Slavic texts as a demiurge, but in Roman

---

338 Y.P. Mirolyubov, *Sobranie sochinenii*, vol. 9: *Slaviano-Russkii fol'klor* (Munich: Verlag Oto Sagner, 1964), 31.

339 S. Lesnoy, *Vlesova kniga — iazycheskaia letopis' doolegovskoi Rusi (Istoriia nakhodki, tekst i kommentarii)*, vol. 1 (Winnipeg: Trident Press, 1966), xxix.

340 D.M. Dudko (trans./ed.), *Velesova kniga. Slavianskie Vedy* (Moscow: EKSMO-Press, 2002), 27-28, commentary on 126-127.

## Neo-Archaic Terms in the Theology of Contemporary Slavic Native Faith

> Mithraism Mithra (the Iranian god of the sun) is born out of an egg (or rock) and creates the world. The idea that the earth is suspended in space without support first appears in Anaximander (6th century B.C.E.). In the Slavs' folk beliefs, the earth rests on the back of an animal (a whale, fish, snake, bull, etc.) or in God's hand.

The text continues:

> Thus, the souls of the forebears shine upon us as stars from Iriy [*Iriy* is paradise, the land to which migratory birds and the souls of the dead fly — Dudko]. *Prav'* was arranged by Dazhdbog in an unknown way, and *Yav'* flows along it like yarn, and it creates our life, and when it goes away, there comes death. *Yav'* is the current created in *Prav'*, and *Nav'* is before it (*Yav'*) and after it is *Nav'*. In *Prav'* is *Yav'*.

Dudko comments further:

> The philosophical foundation of the *Book of Veles* is the doctrine of the three worlds: *Yav'*, *Nav'*, and *Prav'*. *Yav'* is the earthly, material world. *Prav'* is the spiritual world beyond. *Nav'* is the underworld of death. *Prav'* invisibly governs *Yav'*, but not *Nav'*, in which everything dwells before birth and after death. However, paradise, *Iriy*, where righteous souls go after death, belongs to *Prav'*. The source of all three worlds is Svarog, yet *Prav'* is established by Dazhdbog. *Yav'* and *Prav'* seem to be an ordinary idealism of the Platonic type. But alongside *Nav'* they rather resemble the universal myth of three worlds: heavenly, earthly, and subterranean. In particular, they resemble the Scythian variant, where the earthly world of life is contrasted to the two — heavenly and subterranean — worlds of death (but not evil). The Slavs knew the mythological term *nav'* (Czech *nav*, "underworld," Old Russian and Bulgarian *nav'i*, evil spirits of the dead, the Galician *navki/mavki*, forest maidens, spirits of dead girls). But *Yav'* and *Prav'*, like the system as a whole, are only to be found in the *Book of Veles* and in "Mirolyubovian" folklore.[341]

In fact, as we will see below, the word *yav'* [*iav'*[342]] is also well known, and although *prav'* as a proper noun is not

---
341 Ibid., 143-144, 274-275.

342 [Although spelled identically in Russian, we have opted for the alternative transliteration *iav'* in the case of the well-known Russian (and, more broadly, Slavic) word in order to distinguish it from the specifically "quasi-" or "pseudo-mythological" *Yav'* from the *Book of Veles*. — Trans.]

found in Slavic literature (besides one instance in which it was evidently an error), this word nevertheless refers us to the notions of "truth" (*pravda*), "correctness" (*pravil'nost'*), and "righteousness" (*pravednost'*) as well as to rules (*pravila*, both written and unwritten), "direction" (*napravlenie*), and especially "governance" (*upravlenie*) and "rule" or "reign" (*pravlenie*) as carried out by the prince or divine ruler (*pravitel'*). This corresponds to the contemporary Rodnovery notion of the "Laws of *Prav'*," that is, divine decrees (in one way or another manifest in the laws of nature) that govern (*upravliaiut*) the cosmos in what is right and true (*pravda*) as opposed to what is wrong and false (*krivda*, etymologically "crooked"). This is well known to us from Slavic folklore, especially the *Golubinaia kniga* (Dove Book):

> Truth met Falsehood;
> Wherever the hare was white, there was Truth,
> Wherever the hare was grey, there was Falsehood.
> If only Truth could overcome Falsehood [...]
> Truth will be taken by God from earth to heaven,
> And Falsehood will spread throughout the whole earth...[343]

Let us discuss *Prav'*, *Yav'*, and *Nav'* in greater detail.

**Prav'**. The word *prav'* can be found a number of times in old Russian documents, although not as a noun, but as an adverb meaning "correctly," for instance in Luke 7:43 as written in Glagolitic in the *Codex Zographensis* and *Codex Assemanius* evangeliaries: правь сѫдилъ ѥси — "you have judged correctly." The Glagolitic *Codex Marianus* evangeliary has *pravě* (правѣ) written instead of *prav'* (правь), and the *Savva Book* (a Cyrillic manuscript from the 11th century which might have been based on a Glagolitic original) uses the form *pravo* (право).

---

[343] M.L. Seryakov, *Golubinaia kniga — sviashchennoe skazanie russkogo naroda* (Moscow: Aleteia, 2001), 292. Seryakov cites P.A. Bessonov [Bezsonov], *Kal'ki perekhozhie. Sbornik' stikhov' i isledovanie P. Bezsonova*, vol. 2 (Moscow: A. Semen, 1861), 291-292.

The word *prav'* can also be found as a particle meaning "truly, in truth," such as in the *Codex Suprasliensis* (358, 3), dated to the early-mid 11th century, which reads: правь глаголѭ вамъ — "I speak truly to you." However, in the same place in the Gospel of Matthew (18:18) in the *Marianus*, *Zographensis*, and *Assemanius* evangeliaries, as well as in the *Savva Book*, "amen" is written instead of *prav'*: аминъ глаголѭ вамъ. *Prav'* could also figure as meaning *imenno* ("namely," "indeed," "precisely") such as in the *Codex Suprasliensis* (472, 15-16): правь въ истинѫ таци бышѧ — "in truth they were [indeed/precisely/namely] such."

The only time that the word *prav'* appears as a noun was evidently a mistake on the part of the scribe of the *Izbornik* of 1076, one of the oldest dated landmarks of Russian literature known to modern scholarship.[344] On this note, we might also recall other landmarks of juridical-legal thought in Old Rus', such as the *Russian Truth* (*Russkaia Pravda*) and *Righteous Measure* (*Merilo Pravednoe*).[345]

**Yav'.** As for *Yav'*, Vladimir Dal's dictionary knows this word, not in the meaning of a "middle world," but rather as a name for the state of wakefulness, as opposed to slumber or some other altered state of consciousness. Dal' describes *iav'*[346] as "a sober, conscious state, not asleep, non-delirious, and not oblivious or forgetful, in full, healthy mind" and cites the following sayings: "some are asleep, some are in *iav'*," "in sleep happiness, in *iav'* misfortune," "what happens in *iav'* can also be dreamt of," "what is done in *iav'*, one does not fear; what is seen in sleep, one fears."[347] The verb *iavliat'* means "to appear, show, manifest." It is worth noting that Dal' writes *naiavu* separately as *na iavu* — this is not

---

344 Veleslav, *Osnovy slavianskogo rodnoveriia*, 291, with reference to V.S. Golyshenko, V.F. Dubrovina, V.G. Demyanov, G.F. Nefedov (eds.), *Izbornik 1076 goda* (Moscow: Nauka, 1965), 153.

345 Veleslav, *Osnovy slavianskogo rodnoveriia*, 292-293.

346 See fn. 40.

347 Dal', *Tolkovyi slovar* IV, 671.

a grammatical mistake, as it might seem to modern man, who is used to writing the words together seamlessly, but rather testifies to the existence in the still recent past of *iav'* as a masculine verbal noun, from which the modern Russian language (in which *iav'* is feminine) has been left with only the derivative saying "*naiavu.*" Old Russian also knew *iav'* as a saying in the form of ѣавѣ, as did Old Church Slavonic in the form of авѣ, which meant "clearly, openly." For example, in the Glagolitic *Zographensis*, *Marianus*, and *Assemanius* evangeliaries, John 11:54 says that Jesus "no longer moved about openly [ѣавѣ] among the people of Judea," and Matthew 26:73 in the latter three as well as in *Savva Book* says that Peter's speech revealed who he really was: бесѣда твоѣ авѣ та творитъ.[348] In G.M. Dyachenko's *Complete Church Slavonic Dictionary*, we find *proiavlenno* (Проѧвлённо), translating the Greek προδηλῶς, as meaning "clearly, manifestly" (*iavno*).[349]

Vasmer's etymological dictionary presents a wide range of Slavic *iav'*-related terms as well as Indo-European cognates:

> [Russian] *iavit'* [to manifest], *iavliu* [I will show], *iavit'sia* [to manifest (reflexive)], *ob'iavit'* [to declare], *proiavit'* [to manifest], *v'iav'* [really, actually], *naiavu*, *iavnyi* [clearly, manifestly]; Ukrainian *iaviti*, *iaviy*; Belarusian *iava*, "phenomenon," *iavlia*, "appearance"; Old Russian ѣавити, "to show, to appear," ѣавити сѧ [to appear, to manifest (reflexive)], ѣавѣ, "clearly, definitely, openly," ѣавьнъ, "clearly"; Old Slavonic авити, ѣавити [= Greek] δεικνύναι, φανεροῦν, авѣ, ѣавѣ [=] σαφῶς, δῆλον; Bulgarian *iave*, "openly," *iavia*, "I show, I speak," Serbo-Croatian *javiti*, "to declare," *javiti se*, "to announce oneself, to appear," *najavi*, Slovenian *jáviti*, "to report," *jáviti se*, "to show oneself, to appear," Czech *jeviti*, "to show," *v jev*, *na jev*, "openly, publicly," *jevný*, "open," Slovak *javit*, "to show," *jav*, "phenomenon," Polish *jawić*, "to disclose," *na jaw*, *na jawie*, "into the open, in the open," Upper Sorbian *zjewić*, Lower Sorbian *zjawiś*, Polabian *vüöb-óve*, "shows." Proto-Slavic *\*aviti* is related to Lithuanian *ovyje*, "openly," *ovyties*, "to be seen

---

348 Veleslav, *Osnovy slavianskogo rodnoveriia*, 297.

349 G.M. Dyachenko, *Polnyi tserovno-slavianskii slovar' (so vneseniem' v' nego vazhneishikh' drevne-russkikh' slov' i vyrazhenii)* (Moscow: Tipografiia Vil'de, 1900), 520.

as a vision, to be dreamt of," Latvian *âvitiês*, "to talk nonsense, behave stupidly, behave outrageously," Old Indic *āvíḥ*, "clear, striking," Avestan *āvíš*, *āvišya*.³⁵⁰

**Nav'.** When it comes to *nav'*, in some Slavic traditions (above all, among the Czechs), the word *nav'* really did mean the subterranean domain of the dead (although not only such), yet some sources especially emphasize that this is about the abode of "good souls," while other sources demonize entities that come from among the dead (*navei*). The *Etymological Dictionary of Slavic Languages* edited by Oleg Trubachyov offers an exhaustive list of attestations, among which we can highlight the following:

*navъ, *navъjь, *navъja, *navъje: Old Church Slavonic навь, [Greek] νεκρός, [Latin] *mortuus*, Bulgarian *navi*, "evil spirits, e.g., *vily*, *samovily*, three sisters according to some, seven according to others, 12 according to others; they torment birthing mothers when they go into labor, when they're nursing by sucking out their milk, they throw themselves onto mothers and choke them, torturing to the point they lose consciousness... sometimes the mother dies in severe birth pangs. These evil spirits live somewhere far beyond the sea. In order to save a woman in labor from them, spells are cast by various means: they're driven away with an axe, the birthing mother is led through a green wreath, they put tar, onion, and three crushed pieces of coal in a potsherd and smear the birthing mother with this mixture three times with an incantation (conjuring with words). Cf. навιак, dialectal, plural *navi*: "demonic beings: three women who cause a woman to lose consciousness or die during childbirth; the souls of infants who die without having been baptized"; *navi*, *naviatsi*, "impure force, evil spirits," *navi*, plural, "spirits of children who died unbaptized (believed to be in the form of featherless, naked birds who fly on rainy nights and make a special high-pitched sound." Macedonian *navi*, plural, mythical "evil spirits (12 witches who suck the milk of birthing mothers"; Serbo-Croatian *nav*, "*mortuus*, a dead person"; Slovenian *nâv*, "according to pagan beliefs, the soul of a dead person"... Old Czech *náv*, new form *náva*, "a grave, the world beyond, hell," "the netherworld, the kingdom of the dead, the underworld, hell"... Among the ancient Czechs, *nav* meant "dwelling place of good

---
350 Vasmer, *Etimologicheskii slovar'* IV, 540-541.

souls"... Old Russian навь, "dead person, *funus*, corpse, *cadaver*, νεκρός"... [Old Russian] навь (навъ) и навье, "deceased (according to some views, associated with the cult of the dead, capable of protecting and helping the living)"... "a dead person who rises from the grave, an inhabitant of the netherworld"... Serbo-Croatian *navje*: "Hades, Tartarus, the kingdom of the dead"..."the kingdom of death imagined to be beyond the sea — raj, nav (or *navje*) is separated from the earthly abode of people by a 'big water'. Whoever wishes to go there must swim across a river, the celestial sea, or cross a rainbow bridge (the Milky Way)." "In Russian, *nav* means a dead person, especially his skeleton, and in Czech the netherworld of shadows or a paradise, a warm land, where birds spend winter"... Recent years have seen the updated and developed theory that there is a possible connection between the lexeme *\*navь* and the ancient name for a ship (Latin *navis*, etc.). Based on the most ancient notions that the kingdom of the dead is separated from the world of the living by water (a sea or river) across which the souls of the dead are transported on a boat or ship, and taking into account known data on the role of a ship (boat) in funeral rites, particularly among the Slavs, Balts, and Germanics, a connection is proposed between the Slavic *\*navь* and common Indo-European name for a vessel, *\*nāu̯-s*, which takes the meaning of "dead person, death" to be secondary... Trubachyov refs to Polomé's opinion that Indo-European *\*nāu̯s*, "ship, boat," and *\*nau̯s*, "death, dead person," are absolute homonyms, and although he does not consider this to be a final solution to the question, he cites identical derivatives from *\*nau̯-s* I and *\*nau̯-s* II: Indo-European *\*nau̯i̯o*,"ship-like, pertaining to a ship" (present in Creto-Mycenaean, where, however, it means "temple-like, pertaining to a temple") and Slavic *\*navьjь*, "dead person," the latter possibly going back to the meaning of [Russian] *lodochnyi* = "buried in a boat," and *\*nāu̯s* which might have primarily meant "ship of the dead."[351]

*Nav'* is sometimes seen as the personification or embodiment of death, and some see an etymological kinship with the name of a separate deity named in Jan Długosz's (15th c.) list of Polish gods, *Nya*, who is identified with the Roman God of the underworld and death, Pluto (Greek Πλούτων,

---

[351] O.N. Trubachyov (ed.), *Etimologicheskii slovar' slavianskikh iazykov* [*Praslavianskii lekicheskii fond* 24] (Moscow: Nauka, 1997), 49-52.

Latin *Pluto*).³⁵² However, in contemporary Slavic Rodnoverie, this "Lower" World or realm of the dead "beyond the grave" is usually associated with Chernobog and/or the *Koshchnyi* hypostasis of Veles, to which we will turn shortly.

On the whole, the attitude of contemporary Slavic Rodnovery towards the terms introduced by Mirolyubov by way of the *Book of Veles* is not unambiguous. In the late 1990s and early 2000s, interest in the *Book of Veles* in Russia was rather high, and some poetic fragments from it could even be found used in ritual practices, but by the 2020s, only marginals and the ignorant still believe in the book's authenticity. In the meanwhile, however, it bears recognizing that *Prav'*, *Yav'*, and *Nav'* remain to this day perhaps the most effective and most frequently used names for the Heavens, the White Light-World, and the Underworld among Rodnovery (as well as by some outside the Rodnoverie community).

## The Concept of the "*Koshchnyi* Age," "*Koshchnyi* Kingdom," and "*Koshchnyi*" Veles

"*Koshchnyi* Age" (which has already become well-known in the catchphrase "Veles wisdom in the *Koshchnyi* age") is what some contemporary Slavic Rodnovery call the era of spiritual degradation and the maximal alienation of man from Tradition. This sometimes refers to the "reign of quantity" (René Guénon), the "society of the spectacle" (Guy Debord), the "era of Postmodernity" (Alexander Dugin and others), the concept of the "Iron Age" known from the works of ancient authors (Hesiod's *Works and Days*, Ovid's *Metamorphoses*, etc.), and the broadly philosophical sense of sacred rather than material history.

In the article "The Iron Age: The Time of Chernobog," written on 9 June 1998 (according to the date indicated at the end of the article), we read:

---

352 V.V. Ivanov and V.N. Toporov, *"Nav'"* in *Mify narodov mira*, vol. 2, ed. S.A. Tokarev (Moscow: Soviet Encyclopedia, 1982), 195.

In the Iron Age, the righteousness of people passes into decline, the Eternal Wisdom is forgotten and perverted, and people cease to live in accord with the Laws of Svarog. This time sees the maximal distortion of the True Tradition and the triumph of the forces of *Anti*-Tradition; people profess religions brought into the lands by Chernobog. This is the era of the Great Division, when the struggle between Truth and Falsehood is exacerbated like never before. Whether man will enter the next Golden Age of the new Cycle, the Age of *Prav'*, depends on which Path man chooses in this Age.[353]

In the early 2000s, Chernobog, known predominantly from the history of the Western Slavs[354], was by many Slavic Rodnovery identified with the well-known *Koshchee* or *Kashchee* known from East Slavic folklore sources, and the "kingdom of Chernobog" (the "Lower World," *Nav'*) and the "Age of Chernobog" (the "Iron Age" of sacred history) were correspondingly deemed the "*Koshchnyi* kingdom," "*Koshchnyi* age," etc.

According to some of our fellow believers, the tragic passage from the Golden Age to the Iron Age — to the "*Koshchnyi*" age — might be poetically illustrated in the *Tale of Igor's Campaign*: "There Prince Igor climbed out of the golden saddle and into the *Koshchievo* saddle."[355] In D.S. Likhachev's explanatory translation, this phrase is translated as "And now Prince Igor switched from the golden (princely) saddle to the slave's saddle [i.e., from a prince he became a slave, a captive)."[356] The latter translator thus interpreted *koshchei* as "slave," "captive."

---

353 Veleslav et al, *Traditsiia* (Moscow: Institute of Humanitarian Studies, 1999), 92.

354 See Helmold's *Chronica Sclavorum* (12th c.) [Russian edition: Gel'mol'd, *Slavianskaia khronika*, trans. L.V. Razumovskaya (Moscow: Academy of Sciences of the USSR, 1963), 129-130].

355 *Iroicheskaia pesn' o pokhode na Polovtsov' Udel'nago Kniazia Novagoroda-Severskago Igoria Sviatoslavicha, pisannia starinnym' Russkim' iazykom' v' iskhode XII stoletnia s' perelozheniem' na upotrebliaemoe nyne narechie* (Moscow: V' Senatskoi' Tipografii, 1800), 22.

356 *Slovo o polku Igoreve*, ed. Varvara Adrianova-Peretz (Moscow/Leningrad: Academy of Sciences of the USSR, 1950), 88.

## Neo-Archaic Terms in the Theology of Contemporary Slavic Native Faith

In Vladimir Dal's dictionary, we read that *kashchei* is a fairy-tale figure, like the eternal Jew, described with the adjective 'immortal'; the name is probably from Slavic *kastit'* ['to blaspheme, to scold, to besmirch'], transformed into *koshchei* from *kost'* [bone], meaning an excessively skinny, emaciated person, especially an old man, a miser, a stingy person, a usurer poring over his treasure, a smerd, a foul slave. *Kashchei* [is described as] "as short as a fingernail but with a beard down to his elbow and a whip seven arms long." *Kashcheika* — a stingy, very thin old woman [...] [The verb] *kashcheit'* or *kashcheinichat'*, "to be stingy, to be a cheapskate." *Kashcheinichan'e*, "stinginess"; *kashcheistvo* means the same but in a more abstract sense. *Kashcheinik*, — "one who swindles [*kashcheinichaet*]."[357]

Following Dal', Vasmer notes that the word *koshchei* has two meanings of different etymology: "1. 'thin, skinny person, walking skeleton'; 2. 'miser.' Probably from *kost'* [bone]... To the contrary, the Old Russian *koshchei*, *koshchii* means 'lad, boy, captive, slave' — from Turkic *košči*, 'slave,' from *koš*, 'camp, station'... Less probable is Sobolevsky's association with *kostit'*, 'to scold.'"[358] However, some contemporary scholars have substantially critiqued the interpretation of *koshchei* as "captive, slave":

> Scholars attribute the word *koshchei* to the Turkic *košči* (*qoš* + *čy* — actor affix). This word has a whole range of meanings: (1) a plowman accompanying a team of animals (from *qoš* meaning a harnessed team of livestock, ard, plow); (2) someone who accompanies a nomadic convoy, caravan, a drover caring for horses during migration (from *qoš* meaning a nomadic convoy); (3) someone who lives in a temporary shelter (from *qoš* meaning a lean-to or hut set up for temporary housing during migration). The word *košči* is not used in the sense of a captive or save, although a whole range of scholars, including Turkologists (P.M. Melioransky, K.G. Menges), have tried to give it such a meaning.[359]

---

357 Dal', *Tolkovyi slovar'* II, 101.

358 Vasmer, *Etimologicheskii slovar'* II, 362.

359 V.A. Vorontsov, "*Slovo o polku Igoreve*" *v svete podlinnogo istorizma* (Kazan: Intelpress+, 2009), 174.

Scholars have also tried to derive *koshchei* from Russian *koshchunnik* (someone who is sacrilegious, blasphemous, who mocks, ridicules sacred things), from Lower Sorbian *kostlař* ("sorcerer, magician"), or from Proto-Slavic *\*kastь/\*kostь*, a root with clearly negative semantics (cf. *\*pakostь*, "vicissitude"), whence *kastit'*, which means "to dirty, to spoil, to scold, to berate," etc.[360] On this point, let us point out that the notion that the Old Russian *koshchuna* (кощѹна/ коштѧна/коштюна) and Greek μῦϑος ("myth") are identical, an idea which became widespread thanks to the works of Boris Rybakov[361], demands more attentive examination and clarification, since in Old Russian sources the former corresponds to the Greek word only in the sense of "fable, nonsense,"[362] not "myth" in the sense of mythological tale.[363]

At the present time, the hypothesis that *koschei* comes from *kost'*, "bone" (in the sense of "thin, skinny") is perhaps the most widespread and, so to speak, functionally justified (death or the personification of Death is colloquially called *kostliavaia*, "bony"). However, according to Bogumil, "in folk tales, *koshchei* is virtually never described as 'lean' or likened to a skeleton."[364] Yet, Kashchei is described in the form of a skeleton in A.S Kaisarov's *Slavic Mythology* (1807): "Russian mythology describes him as a living skeleton," similar to how Western European mythologists described the enigmatic God (?) *Flyns* (/*Flynt*).[365] Koshchei

---

360 Volkhv Bogumil (B.A. Gasanov), *Koshchei Bessmertnyi. Vladyka zagrobnogo mira v mimologie slavian* [Book II in the series *Chernobog: Obraz, kul't, mif*] (Moscow: Veligor, 2022), 11-25.

361 B.A. Rybakov, *Iazychestvo drevnei Rusi* (Moscow: NAuka, 1987), 314-316.

362 I.I. Sreznevsky, *Materialy dlia Slovaria drevne-russkago iazyka po pis'mennym' pamiatnikam'*, vol. I [publication of the Department for Russian Language and Literature of the Imperial Academy of Sciences] (Saint Petersburg: Imperial Academy of Sciences, 1893), 1308.

363 L.S. Klein, *Voskreshenie Peruna. K rekonstruktsii vostochnoslavianskogo iazychestva* (Saint Petersburg: Evraziia, 2004), 89; Bogumil, *Koshchei Bessmertnyi*, 11-21.

364 Ibid., 10.

365 A.S. Kaisarov, *Slavianskaia Mifologiia* (Moscow: V' tipografii Dubrovina i Merzliakova, 1807), 95.

appears as skinny and boney in the Soviet black-and-white film *Kashchei the Immortal* directed by Alexander Rou and released by Soiuzdetfilm in 1944. In Bogumil's opinion, "it bears concurring that folk etymology links the name *Koshchei* with the word *kost'* [bone] solely for the sake of explaining something that was otherwise unclear and had no basis in folklore tradition."[366]

Nevertheless, no matter what we take to be the original meaning of the word *kashchei/koshchei*, it reflects one or another quality of an entity from the world of the dead or one or another attribute of death (thinness, a state of being restricted, dependence, lack of freedom, meagerness, ritual pollution, desecration, etc., as opposed to attributes of life: stoutness, freedom, generosity, ritual purity, glory, etc.). According to folklore sources, wealth, which is an indispensable attribute of the Lord of the Other World (for he will sooner or later get everything possessed by the living, and even the success and wealth of the living depends, according to the traditional worldview, on the ancestors and the world of the dead), is traditionally associated with the image of "King Koshchei."

It bears noting that *Koshchei* (Кощии, Кощѣи) and *Kosh'kei* (Кошькей, Кошькѣи, with the Novgorodian dialectal reading of *-shch-* as *-shch'k-*) as well as some other personal names can be found more than once in the 12th-century birch bark letters from Novgorod and Torzhok.[367] The name *Koshchei* is also mentioned in the Moscow ink-text birch bark letter No. 3, dating back to the end of the 14th century, which was discovered on 12 August 2007 during excavations in the Taynitsky Garden of the Moscow Kremlin (this is the longest Old Russian text on birch bark known at present).

The term "*Koshchnyi* kingdom" (*Koshchnoe tsarstvo*) has come to be broadly applied to designate the "Lower" World

---

366 Bogumil, *Koshchei Bessmertnyi*, 10.

367 A.A. Zaliznyak, *Drevnenovgorodskii dialekt*, 2nd rev. ed. [including findings from 1995-2003] (Moscow: Iazyki slavianskoi kul'tury, 2004), 49, 205, 456, 674, 750.

(the world of *Nav'*, the Underworld) thanks to the works of Boris Rybakov, who traced this term back to chronicle manuscripts. In the *Novgorod First Chronicle*, in the section dated 989 (according to the Commission List), we read that in 6497:

> Vladimir was baptized, and so was the whole Russian land; and a metropolitan was established in Kiev, an archbishop in Novgorod, and bishops, priests, and deacons in other cities [...] And Archbishop Akim of Korsun came to Novgorod and destroyed the sanctuary [*trebishcha*] and cut down [the idol of] Perun, and commanded that it be dragged out into the Volkhov [river]; they tied it with ropes and dragged it through the mud, beating it with a staff. He commanded that no one should accept it anywhere. Then a Pidblyanin came down to the river in the morning to take his pots to the city. Perun floated up to the pier, and the Pidblyanin pushed him away with a pole and said, "You, Perunishche, have drunk and eaten your fill, and now you will swim away," and <u>ply so sveta okosh'noe [плы съ свѣта окошьное]</u>.[368]

The end of the latter sentence is the subject of controversy, especially the form and meaning of *okoshn'noe*. Is it "*okosh'noe*" that "floated away from the light [i.e., out of sight?]," or is it, as Boris Rybakov interpreted, Perun that floated away "from the light into *okoshnoe*"?

Viljo Johannes Mansikka comments: "The word *okosh'noe* is replaced in the *Sofia Chronicle* with the word *nekoshnoe*. *Nekoshchnyi*, according to Sreznevsky, means 'despised' (*despectus*). According to Vasnetsov (in 'Materials for the Explanatory Regional Dictionary of the Vyatka Dialect'), in the Vyatka Governorate the word has the meaning of a 'mythological being, like a *leshy*, a demon, and is a bad word.'"[369] Bogumil draws our attention to the problematic course of this word's transmission across the different

---

[368] *Novgorodskaia pervaia letopis' starshego i mladshego izvodov*, ed. A.N. Nasonov, M.N. Tikhomirov (Moscow/Leningrad: Academy of Sciences of the USSR, 1950), 159-160.

[369] Mansikka, *Trudy po religii vostochnykh slavian*, 115, fn. 46.

## Neo-Archaic Terms in the Theology of Contemporary Slavic Native Faith

redactions of chronicle manuscripts: in the respective versions of this passage, we find the term rendered as *nekoshchnoe, vkoshnyi (vokosh'nye), okoshnoe, ne koshchnoe, v koshyni, vo koshnoe, v koshnye*, which obviously indicates that the scribes did not understand the text and tried to somehow "mechanically" fix it.[370] Rybakov proposed reading this phrase in the following way:

> On the basis of these variants included in the *Complete Collection of Russian Chronicles*, according to all the manuscripts known at this time, it can be reconstructed thusly: "And it [the idol of Perun] floated from the light into the *koshnoe*, that is to say, into total darkness." The word *koshch'noe* is not in Sreznevsky's dictionary, but the glosses with which the scribes explained it ("total darkness," "netherworld") leave no doubt as to its infernal meaning. This is not the Christian hell, but the Slavic kingdom of the dead, which can be compared with the domain of King Koshchei the Immortal. The kingdom of the dead that the peoples of the South (for example, the Greeks) located in the West, where the sun dies, was among northern-more tribes often associated with the North, with the realm of the polar night and lifeless cold. In Russian fairy tales, the kingdom and crystal palace of Koshchei are located "at the edge of the world, at the very end." It is there, "from the light into the *koshch'noe*," along the current of the Northward-flowing Volkhov, that the wooden idol of Perun, rejected by the village potter, floated away.[371]

Although we cannot be certain that Rybakov's hypothesis is correct, and regardless of how we might interpret this "obscure" place in the chronicle, the application of the term *Koshchnyi* (which resonates with *Kostianoe*, "of bone") to the "Lower" World (the world of *Nav'*, the Underworld) has been affirmed by a number of contemporary scholars of Slavic tradition.

**Koshchnyi Veles.** "Veles is worshipped by contemporary Slavic Rodnovery in his *Koshchnyi* hypostasis as the Lord of the World of the Dead, as well as in his *Dorodnyi*

---

370 Bogumil, *Koshchei Bessmertnyi*, 25-26.

371 Rybakov, *Iazychestvo drevnei Rusi*, 253-254.

guise as the God of wealth and abundance."[372] Let us note that *dorodnyi*, which literally means "burly" and is therefore associated with life force, wealth, and prosperity, is the hypostasis in which Veles is more widely worshipped in contemporary Rodnoverie, compared to his *Koshchnyi* hypostasis as the Lord and Guide of the dead. However, Veles' *Dorodnyi* and *Koshchnyi* guises are seen not as much in opposition as being complementary and, in a certain sense, "flowing" into each other (according to one archaic Indo-European notion, this divine character is, so to speak, the embodied "success" or "fortune" of the *rod*, the visible blessing of the ancestors, which implies and applies to both the living and the dead).

It is no coincidence that some scholars (from the linguist Vasmer to the archaeologist Leo Klein) have upheld the hypothesis that Volos (God of cattle, associated with wealth) and Veles (associated with the world of the dead) are not one but two different Gods. In reality, however, we do not have sufficient grounds to separate Volos and Veles, especially upon taking into consideration the following fact:

> the line between 'the god of the cattle' and the realm of the dead may be explained by the Common Indo-European concept of the nether world as a pasture. The latter has been reconstructed on the evidence of the identical oldest data of Indo-Iranian and Greek traditions. They coincide with the recently studied Hittite rituals and mythological concepts about the nether world as the pastures where the divine herds of the Sun-god and of the king who 'has become god' (i.e. has died) are grazing.[373]

---

372 Veleslav, *Osnovy slavianskogo rodnoveriia*, 581.

373 V.V. Ivanov and V.N. Toporov, "A Comparative Study of the Group of Baltic Mythological Terms from the Root *vel-", *Baltistica* 9(1) (1973), 16; See also: B.A. Uspenskii, *Filologicheskie razyskaniia v oblasti slavianskikh drevnostei (Relikty iazychestva v vostochnoslavianskom kul'te Nikolaia Mirlikiiskogo)* (Moscow: Moscow University, 1982), 56-80; Thomas V. Gamkrelidze and Vjačeslav V. Ivanov, *Indo-European and the Indo-Europeans: A Reconstruction and Historical Analysis of a Proto-Language and a Proto-Culture, Part II*, trans. Johanna Nichols, ed. Werner Winter (Berlin: Mouton de Gruyter, 1995), 722-723.

## Neo-Archaic Terms in the Theology of Contemporary Slavic Native Faith

\*\*\*

And so, let us summate some of the outcomes of the above case studies.

**1.** Over the past 30 years, Slavic Rodnoverie has formed its own terminology and developed its own conceptual language as needed by Slavic pagans to more accurately express certain components of Slavic faith and tradition at the contemporary stage.

**2.** We apply the term "neo-archaic" to the totality of these key ideas and the expressive forms intended to embody them within contemporary Slavic Rodnoverie as a cultural phenomenon. This term refers to contemporary Slavic pagans' conscious and practical turn to ancient roots to reconstruct and conceptualize their living faith without resorting to formally imitating "the olden days." In questions of faith, imitation is practically always a matter profanation.

**3.** Contemporary Slavic Rodnoverie's theology and philosophy are based on traditional Slavic and, more broadly, Indo-European notions. It is the principled return to these root notions that distinguishes Rodnoverie from the whole range of other contemporary religio-philosophical currents which otherwise stubbornly refuse to follow tradition or are adamant on creating their own mythical "histories" which, alleged to have begun back in deep antiquity, are in reality none other than Postmodern simulacra.

*Translated and edited by Jafe Arnold with assistance from Evgeny Nechkasov*

# THE TRADITIONAL UNDERSTANDING OF THE NON-TRADITIONAL

## Maxim Makovchik

> *The Rigveda, the Yajurveda... Vyākaraṇa, Mīmāṃsā, Nāstika... Vedānta, Yoga... The Arthaśāstra, the theory of the Yavanas – these are the thirty-two sciences.*
>
> - Śukranītisāra 4.3.55-59

Every seeker or student of tradition acquires an understanding that is distinct from that which is "usual" or accepted in mass culture to the extent that he is successful. We are speaking here of the acquisition of another worldview – other answers, rejected by modern culture, to the fundamental questions: "Who am I?", "What is the world?", "What is my relationship to the world?" It stands to reason that such a new worldview can, in itself, only be acknowledged as a secondary aim; more precisely, such a worldview comes as a consequence of other, more substantial and fundamental changes that occur internally. By way of illustration, we might consider the Sanskrit terms *āgata* ("one who has departed never to return") or *siddha* ("one who has attained/achieved"). For the person to whom these words refer, life is no longer a mere period of time during which the body exists or a procession of chaotic circumstances, but a path toward and comprehension of that which lies beyond things. For the one who walks such a path, the cosmos is simultaneously a comprehended and incomprehensible mystery which, in some respect, has ceased to be a death sentence or a compulsory chaos; rather, it has become a companion or fellow traveler in a game that is at once within time and extra-temporal. With regard to the advanced seeker, other than the potential reality which can be externally described as "spiritual practice" (meditation, scriptural study, etc.), everyday tasks become for him a practice that is just as significant; in taking on an utterly other quality, these tasks cease to be routine and become matters of import in the highest sense (the sense one finds in scriptures and practices, or *sādhana*, for which it is not so much the visible result which is important, but the internal dimension and its content). Viewed through the symbolism of war, the "conquered world" must in some way be preserved so that it is not lost anew (such a loss is, to a certain extent, possible during the intermediate stages of the seeking). At some point, a person must choose to live differently and protect himself from all that he deems non-traditional – all that is harmful to that Self which he has become and is becoming, and which is untrue from the perspective of his elected principles, thereby violating the order of things. In doing so, he supports the equilibrium between "heaven and earth" in both himself and the world; more abstractly speaking, he maintains the balance of opposed principles. Let us examine the surest error one may commit in this respect.

In dividing all phenomena into "traditional" and "non-traditional," one must establish a boundary between the two concepts. But will this boundary be the same in all cases? Can the answer to one and the same question go eternally unchanged, unbeholden to a context which is never entirely identical to those that have preceded it? It is obvious that any concrete application of principles cannot but vary by dint of occurring at various times and places; however, it is of the greatest importance to recognize that the principle itself remains unchanged when this happens. As a result, in every traditional culture, we encounter the concepts of the "pure" and the "impure," the "worthy" and the "unworthy";

these concepts apply to one or another situation or person depending on the present conditions. And, suddenly, we see that what is righteous and true in one culture may be unrighteous and untrue in another. We cannot speak here of an error being made in one of the two cases, as the rules defining the boundary cannot be deemed erroneous on account of their correspondence to their culture. For the inquirer into this matter, the only valid criterion in making an evaluation is who he himself is.

Is it possible to absolutely and categorically declare something "traditional" or "non-traditional"? Metaphysics differs from philosophy precisely in its lack of static definitions ("this is that"); this is because one can only make such affirmations on the basis of one's observational position. That which, according to the Latin proverb, "is granted to Jupiter but not to the bull" is what it is by virtue of this difference, namely that Jupiter is not the bull, and the bull is not Jupiter. The Apostle Peter writes: "You know that a Judaean is forbidden from fraternizing or communing with a foreigner; but God has made a revelation to me such that I am not to consider a single person as foul or impure." What is it that erases this boundary that defines a being? It is his faith, or his knowledge of the fact that the boundary exists within him and does not constitute an insurmountable external circumstance. But is it possible and necessary, in every instance, to rub out the bounding line between the blessed and the cursed, the permitted and the forbidden? The answer is no: while one in principle, things and people are never equal or identical in context. When one achieves a certain level of understanding, intentions change as well. For example, the desire to "change the world for the better" may dissolve within the understanding that the world is already perfect. But is it possible, after arriving at such an understanding, to follow through with one's choice to improve the world all the same? Undoubtedly. But this would no longer be a compelled reaction (as it was at first); rather, it would be a neutral, fully considered, and unconditioned intention to make the world different, better than it was. Concerning the difficulty of choice, the saying goes as follows: "Everything is permitted to me, but not everything is beneficial; everything is permitted, but nothing must be allowed to possess me." In other words, the intention ceases to possess the person – the person begins to possess the intention.

It would be fair to say that he who strives for the truth is striving for freedom from all boundaries, even though the achievement thereof by no means evokes a freedom – perceived during the early stages of the search as a goal - from any internal or external aspects. "He who knows his limitations without suffering from them is free. He who knows he is sick in the midst of his illness is not ill…" Does a person's need for food and sleep necessarily make him unfree? Obviously, it does not, for such are the conditions of human existence; but even without them, it would be possible for a person to have inner freedom. Any understanding of the potential for achieving inner freedom and advancing toward its realization becomes impossible given a cosmetic, "black and white" relationship with the phenomena of life. One need not perceive limitations as limitations, even if (in a false understanding) they should seem to contradict the fundamental goal of freeing oneself from them. A violation and contradiction may arise due to a false comprehension of that which, in the process of spiritual becoming, must be perceived as a limitation, and that which must not be perceived as such. In pushing this boundary away, a person observes that the unendurable and the ugly no longer exist for him; relative, external criteria are no longer as important as one's intention and choice of perspective, by means of which that which is usually considered cursed may become blessed through an understanding of the context of perception, action, and the ability to direct them. As a result, the degree to which one accomplishes the external aim is no longer taken into account, as it can apparently either be attained or not attained, and people are not always in control of the result. What is important is not that one achieves something externally, but that one achieves a realization of intention; in this sense, the external criteria are no more than a support and a convention for orientation. The internal result is always within a person's power to control, and it is his attainment in this sense which leads to spiritual becoming. The refusal to make such an effort and carry out an action in relation to "objective causes" creates a duality in the Vedic sense. "He who knows does not fall because he is not attached to objects. How can the path of knowledge lead into a ditch?" He who knows will not suffer failure, under the condition that his knowledge passes into action and does not remain a mere verbal construction and self-delusion. One may even say that the full manifestation of this action is the sign of true knowledge.

Considering the fact that every individual is wittingly limited in his capabilities, conditioned by predispositions and susceptibilities of one kind or another, his achievement of the highest aim will practically always be preceded by concepts of the traditional and the non-traditional. Any given phenomenon is equally capable of leading a person either toward ascent or obscuration. But something else is important here: the external perception of any object or action as traditional or non-traditional – blessed or cursed – may often be crucial and correct, but it is nonetheless a convention or, more accurately, a cultural circumstance; it may even be a trapping of traditional doctrine, but it does not always provide the full "instructions" required, due to the impossibility of accounting for all combinations of man's inner nature, place, time, and other contextual data. In the terms given by René Guénon, one must take one's cues from intellectual intuition.

Although it bears absolutely no formal connection to the Vedas, Western philosophy, which is mentioned in the traditional text cited in this essay's epigraph as the "theory of the Yavanas," is nevertheless included in the list of traditional *vidyās* (sciences) alongside the Vedas, the Vedāṅgas, and the Darśanas. This list also includes the Nāstikas – the doctrine of the primacy of causality, nature, and the non-existence of the Īśvara; this school is often considered materialist, and there is a seed of truth in this idea. It may seem that these doctrines' views are non-traditional, but this is not so; not even tradition recognizes the existence of a singular, unerring position as such (i.e., a position of non-relative perception); rather, tradition recognizes positions which are more or less applicable in a given set of conditions. From a different angle, we might speak of a standpoint capable of directing a person and his apperception with a greater or lesser quantity of contradictions within a concrete context. Of Vaiśeṣika – a doctrine of which modern atomism is reminiscent – it is said that one must cast out its particular propositions and accept only the general ones, which do not contradict the specified criterion – *śruti*. This is to say that, under certain conditions, *śruti* (the most profound essence of the Vedas) is contradicted neither by Greek philosophy, nor what is called atomism or materialism. However, it is clear that the overwhelming majority of Traditionalists, or those who adhere to traditions, would be inclined to disagree. But one must remember that the Traditionalist and a person truly adhering to a tradition are often distinct; today, Traditionalism is becoming a certain school of thought with its own worldview and philosophy, which is a far cry, in Guénon's terminology, from attachment or adherence to a concrete tradition. When a person finds himself within a tradition, he rarely has need of the works of the prominent thinkers commonly identified as "Traditionalists." In this case, he is directly collaborating with the subject of their writings. The concepts of "traditional" and the "non-traditional," understood cosmetically as a mere indication of correspondence or non-correspondence with the words of a given thinker, or even with the teachings of a given tradition, possess meaning almost exclusively among Traditionalists. In its own right, this kind of correspondence is undoubtedly valid and justified. But enclosure within Traditionalism, as opposed to a tradition, can easily become an orientation toward description instead of the original itself. This leads to the appearance of polarizing labels, the usage of which causes their wielders – in the absence of adherence to a tradition – to easily lose sight of the most important thing, that is the spirit of tradition, which does not abide by such limitations and labels.

In the highest sense, supposing that all external conditions have been overcome – that is, from the position out of which Tradition itself fundamentally speaks through texts – there are no non-traditional sciences. There are only those sciences which have not been given a traditional application, because traditional knowledge is a knowledge derived from the entire context (primarily that of the knower), the existence of the greatest and most crucial part of which is categorically negated by modern culture. There is no non-traditional music; there is only disharmonious and crude music, as Tradition is harmony and the ability to express that which is most subtle. There are no non-traditional societies, only those where Tradition has fizzled out; such a state of affairs cannot last for long, for Tradition is order and clarity, never an external sign or criterion.

*Translated by Charlie Smith*

# *MOUSEION, KUNSTKAMMER,* AND THE CLASSICAL MUSEUM AS MODELS OF REALITY: THE TRANSFORMATION OF MUSEUM PRACTICES AND OUR IMAGE OF THE WORLD FROM PREMODERNITY TO MODERNITY

*Alisa Zagryadskaya*

The present article is devoted to museum practices in the traditional, modern, and contemporary world. Different types of worldviews correlate with attitudes towards sacred objects, works of art, and the human body in particular ways. "Worldview" here is used in the critical sense encountered in literary studies, where it often describes the way a particular author's perception is expressed in literary devices. Cultural worldviews differ so significantly and at such a fundamental level that it makes sense to talk about them as reflections of differing realities. From this it follows that the "artistic devices" of various cultures become ways of drafting images of the world. The worlds of different epistemes are structured in their own ways: they assign people different roles, and their methods of symbolizing phenomena and gnoseological strategies differ. In this regard, the ancient *mouseion*, the 16th-century *Kunstkammer*, and the modern museum can be seen as microcosms reflecting their respective operating metaphysical pictures.

## The Ancient Mouseion and Ritual

From ancient times, people have created and preserved objects that evidence interactions with otherworldly forms of being. Researchers of "proto-museum" practices note that the first "collections" were formed from relics and trophies offered to the Gods or ancestors. Collecting is sometimes interpreted as a fundamental feature of mythological consciousness, a way of recreating the integrity of the world, its unity.[374]

It is no secret that within the framework of an economy that involves the world of Gods and the dead, votive objects were often made unsuitable for ordinary use. For example, valuable and difficult-to-make weapons were broken and tossed into waters. By destroying, burning, or casting these objects to the bottom of a swamp, these objects were taken out of the everyday world and transported to the realm of the invisible. The non-utilitarian act of expenditure opens the door from the world of necessity to the space of *something entirely different*. Similarly, the concentration of values in a sacred place implied their withdrawal from everyday circulation. Cult objects were used in rituals, the structure of which, depending on the specific tradition, presumed dynamic interactions. A sacred image that had served its purpose in this world (including one that had fallen into disrepair) was also sent "to the other side," i.e., burned or cast into the water.

According to the definition offered by Vladimir Toporov, a scholar of Indo-European mythology, ritual sharply delimits the "naturalness" of existence from otherness, initiating processes of ontologization, personalization, verbalization, and symbolization.[375] This "epochal breakthrough towards the

---

[374] A.A. Bondarenko, "*Antichnyi Museion: rozhdenie muzeia iz mifa i rituala*", Vestnik Sankt-Peterburgskogo universiteta 1 (2007).

[375] V.N. Toporov, "*Predislovie*" in M. Evzlin, *Kosmogoniia i ritual* (Moscow: Radiks, 1993), 18-19.

## Mouseion, Kunstkammer, and the Classical Museum as Models of Reality

iconic"[376] represents the movement from the natural to the cultural, from the profane to the sacred. In the same way, the body, accepting scar-signs, is hewn out of amorphous matter during initiation, when a person becomes involved in myth and the Sacred Time that breaks up profane time (Mircea Eliade). Language, singing, and speech that verbalize communication with the sacred form the basis of those practices that in Ancient Greece were called the musical arts: philosophy, music, science, and poetry. All of these types of votive human activity were services accessible only to the initiated.

The prototype of what we call a museum today was the ancient Greek *mouseion*, although the meanings of these phenomena are fundamentally different. Initially, the word Μουσεῖον denoted the sanctuaries of the Muses, sacrificial altars, or the sacrifices themselves. In ancient Greek, this concept was also related to "gathering" — this could be the name for a procession of the Muses, a gathering of people involved in the performance of a mystery, or just a gathering in general (for example, the "gathering of speeches" in Plato's *Phaedrus*). The valuables brought to the altars of the companions of Apollo, patrons of the sacred arts, also constituted a special "gathering." Thus, we are talking about the most ancient type of sanctuary — an altar in a forest or a rocky grotto — where offerings and sacrifices were made. This is a repository of ancient culture, a place of initiation into ritual, a place for the transmission of the skills used in sacred services. It is therefore understandable why in antiquity the teaching of arts and sciences took place at the temples of the Muses.

Later, in the classical era of Greece, the mouseions became large cultural centers and schools of musical education, which implied a comprehensive education that incorporated the basics of philosophy, rhetoric, politics, and the arts.

---

376 Ibid.

Manuscripts, works of art, and other valuables were also kept there. The famous Library of Alexandria, adjacent to the Alexandrian mouseion, contained hundreds of thousands of scrolls. Although a step towards modern forms of education and museum work had already been taken here, the ancient mouseions retained an essential connection with traditional sanctuaries: there were altars, sacrifices were made, collective meals were held (rituals of joint sacrificial eating for sharing food with the Gods), and all musical activity was votive in nature.

In all of its forms, a museum is, in a sense, a model of the cosmos: it constitutes a representation of the world, its processes, and man's place within it. The ancient mouseion corresponds to the idea of a living, spiritual cosmos, in which man is included, communicating with its pulse through ritual. Therefore, temples of the Muses and Gods naturally coexist with schools, libraries, gymnasiums, and art collections.

## "Religious Art" and Aesthetic Consciousness

The concept of "religious art" would be unclear to a representative of traditional culture, since it has been forced into a separate domain only with the advent of secular art. The very essence of art in traditional culture presupposes a merging with the sacred. As a rule, arts, like crafts, are given by Deities and have their patrons. Songs and dances, images on dishes, protective patterns – all "art" had a more or less obvious sacred meaning, not just the statues of Gods. This becomes clear if we recall the sacred role of theater in antiquity, the collectivity and obligation of theatrical productions, games, and gladiatorial fights. In Greece, the spectator of a festive procession was called a *theoros* – one who contemplates the divine. Thus, "Greek metaphysics still conceives the essence of *theoria*... as being purely present to what is truly real, and for us too the ability to act theoretically is defined by the fact that in attending to something one is able to forget one's own purposes."[377]

Philosophical aesthetics and the phenomenology of art (more broadly, the phenomenology of experience in general) regularly address the topic of the connection between aesthetic and metaphysical experience. The metaphysical element of aesthetic experience has been considered by many researchers of both art and the phenomenology of religion. Whether it is a question of captivating beauty, an unclear languor of the spirit (similar to unfulfilled longing), or otherworldly horror, these experiences pull the perceiver beyond the horizon of the visible and point to something that is never given explicitly in the subject of experience itself. In the worldview of traditional religiosity, the aesthetic is involved in the ontological, since it is connected with the "presence in being" with which the *theoros* is occupied. The primary unity of art, religion and life, which was characteristic of ancient cultures and inertly preserved for some time in the Western medieval world, is a feature of the archaic cosmos, a quality of all traditional cultures.

In the art of the late Middle Ages and especially the Renaissance, a transition was made from images of the real (in the medieval sense of the word "realism" – the most "real reality" is sacred reality) to images of visions of the mind. Once upon a time, a statue of the Deity allowed the Deity itself to be present at the mystery. From the human side, a cult image was a "way out" to the transcendent. It is unnecessary to wander across it with one's gaze, hence the indifference of archaic artists to literal mimesis, as well as the schematism, relative simplicity and "precision" of ancient ritual images. A statue or drawing of this kind represents a door, which might be decorated with carved ligature, but is primarily of interest in the context of opening.[378]

---

[377] Hans-Georg Gadamer, *Truth and Method*, rev. 2nd ed., trans. Joel Weinsheimer and Donald G. Marshall (London: Bloomsbury, 2020), 127.

[378] See Alexander Sekatsky's 2012 lecture "*Opyt sviashchennogo v isskustve*" (The Experience of the Sacred in Art).

The birth of painting is marked by the emergence of space for this-worldly wandering: the space of the imaginary expands, which does not lead directly out of the door, but lulls a person into his own fantasy. Here, aestheticism itself is formed (admiration of form, torn away from the knowledge of the sacred). The image begins to refer solely to itself. The establishment of self-reference is noticeable in the evolution of Christian art, in the transition from medieval schematism to the artistry of the Renaissance where dimension, perspective, confident mimesis of the physical, and portrait resemblance begin to signify mimesis of the psychological. Religious painting by Baroque masters brings the "wandering gaze" to the limit in the Dutch genre of "pictures with flower garlands," where the Virgin Mary or Christ (and sometimes even the image of their sculptures) are framed by flowers, as though lost among roses and tulips.

A number of art theorists (Hans Belting, Walter Benjamin) associate "the shift from the image of the Madonna herself to the image of the idea of the Madonna, to representation" with signifying "the real end of cult images and the beginning of art in the modern sense of the word."[379] Aesthetic experience continues to contain the promise of the otherworldly. However, instead of transporting the viewer beyond the horizon of earthly existence, self-identical art entertains with the decor of a closed "door."

With this change, we are left with a large reception room full of works that invite us nowhere, a repository of art that has lost its connection with life and religious practice – the art museum. In modern times, the self-referentiality of art has led to the emergence of gallery art, created exclusively for galleries. This is pure simulacrum, the opposite of pre-museum art, which was inscribed in the context of religious, social, and cultural life.

---

379  M. Yampol'skii, *Tkach i vizioner: Ocherki istorii reprezentatsii, ili O material'nom i ideal'nom v kul'ture* (Moscow: NLO, 2007), 146.

*Mouseion, Kunstkammer, and the Classical Museum as Models of Reality*

## The Cabinet of Curiosities as a Microcosm of the Renaissance

During the Renaissance, the physical world was rehabilitated in the works of the humanists. Flowing spatiality and temporality acquire clarity, blank spots and lions' dens are banished from maps. This is the time of European expansion to other continents, archaeological excavations that open up a glimpse into ancient history, and the formation of a new class alien to traditional social systems - merchants and bankers. These changes contributed to the growth of interest in the earthly world, antiquity, objects from distant lands, and natural wonders. Man begins to see history and the material world as his spiritual possessions inasmuch as he learns about them through collecting.

The Renaissance formed its reflective "model of the world" in collections of rarities, in the "cabinet of curiosities." "Cabinet" originally referred to a piece of furniture with an abundance of small drawers – a transparent symbol of the emerging classificatory attitude to reality. However, in the Renaissance, the new European reality had not yet assumed total control. The central thread of the Renaissance, the predominant mood, was curiosity and daring (sometimes passing over into Promethean daring), not the establishment of power. Over time, divisions came to be drawn between natural-scientific cabinets of curiosities, *Wunderkammern* with curiosities, *Schatzkammer*-treasuries, and *Münzkabinette* with coins and medals. And yet, for a long time, the "cabinet" included a wide variety of objects. In the collections of rulers, scientists, and aristocrats, one could find minerals, unicorn horns, Roman coins, jewelry and dragon teeth side by side. In an ambivalent, transitional era, contradictory tendencies coexist in much the same way. It is no coincidence that cultural researchers disagree on how to epistemologically classify this worldview – does it belong to the Middle Ages, the Modern Age, or should it be considered separately?

**299**

Rationalistic explanatory moves like experimentation, calculation, and mechanization originated from the Renaissance. At the same time, Renaissance consciousness had a specifically pre-modern European ordering principle that united magic with erudition. Thus, Michel Foucault distinguished the Renaissance episteme from the classical (i.e., the rationalism of the 17th-18th centuries), which is reflected in the Renaissance principle of the coparticipation of language in the world and the world in language. The Renaissance cabinet-microcosm has not yet grown into a full-fledged filing cabinet with numbered drawers. It is accompanied by intuition, according to which the human body is also microcosmic. The representative matrix of stellar anatomy connects the body and the cosmos, suggesting the conformity of human bodily functions with the planets, zodiacal configurations, and the elements.

Humanistic philosophy takes sensory knowledge to be true, and art is interpreted as a way of knowing God, nature, and man. In the Renaissance, aesthetic experiences were closely intertwined with the knowledge of the Good, the sensory with the supersensible, and beauty is identified with truth, which is a guarantee of the truth of art. However, the primacy of beauty gradually paves the way for the affirmation of aesthetic consciousness. Hitherto inextricably linked with the world and considered more of a craft-*tekhne*, art itself now claims a sacred role, and the artist-genius becomes its priest. If art previously assumed its own man-made nature and spirituality from above, then with the individualization of the master, it no longer seeks to hide its man-madeness and "artificiality." From the crucible of ritual sacrifices in which the world and man were created, only subtle fractions of the symbolic remain – volatile elements that settle in works of art and only vaguely refer to the transcendental, non-human origin of creativity and craft.

## The Birth of the Classical Museum

Although galleries and collections have existed since ancient times, the museum in the modern sense was born in the 18th century, when public museums entered common life. One of the first major institutions of this type was the Louvre. Its opening to the public occurred under the influence of the French Revolution, in the spirit of the famous revolutionary thesis that "art should belong to the people." One question that philosophers posed in revisiting the classical aesthetic paradigms was: "Is that which is exhibited in museums brought closer to man, or, to the contrary, is it thereby separated from him even further?"

As a result of the "Copernican revolution's" turn toward the centrality of the subject, the world becomes unstable, and instead of faith and knowledge, diversity and uncertainty reign. Therefore, man takes on the ungrateful task of rationalizing and classifying the disintegrating cosmos with the help of the cognizing mind. Active secularization, the specialization of sciences, as well as the division and dissection of all areas of life, between each other and within themselves, began in the Age of Enlightenment. It is here that public museums begin to emerge – museums of history, natural science, and art. Over time, the chaos of the previous collections (i.e., the chaos of the unknown world) is replaced by the principle of thematic ordering.

The museum becomes one of those spaces that is taken to be transparent to power and knowledge. Like the ancient mouseion, it is an educational tool, but in the case of the classical episteme, it is related to forms of training and discipline. According to Foucault, the museum is an ideological instance that defines the forms of existence and the very corporeality of the individual: "The individual body becomes an element that can be placed, set in motion, connected to other elements."[380]

---

[380] Michel Foucault, *Nadzirat' i nakazyvat': Rozhdenie tyur'my* [Discipline and Punish: The Birth of the Prison] (Moscow: Ad Marginem, 1999), 201.

Museum collections emerged out of private collections, pharmacies, arsenals, and monastery treasuries. Objects are thus excluded from real life, from cult and social circulation, and placed into an environment which is nothing more than a container. This move — the creation of a "special place" for exhibiting — is simultaneous with the process of the formation of aesthetic consciousness, which entails alienation from reality. "The 'aesthetic differentiation' performed by aesthetic consciousness also creates an external existence for itself. It proves its productivity by reserving special sites for simultaneity: the 'universal library' in the sphere of literature, the museum, the theater, the concert hall, etc."[381] Over the course of this institutionalization, a regulated process of interpretation is formed. For example, knowing art shifts toward knowledge about art and historicism, and reading the contexts of a work replaces the act of interaction and contemplation.

By the 19th century, Christian church art, liturgical utensils, and the cult objects of various peoples that had ended up in ethnographic halls, began to be treated like any other objects in a museum. Scholars have defined the latter as "the museum as a colonial space." Discussing the status of sacred objects in the museum environment, Hans-Georg Gadamer wrote: "A work of art always has something sacred about it. True, religious art or a monument on exhibit in a museum can no longer be desecrated in the same sense as one still in its original place. But this only means that it has in fact already suffered an injury in having become a museum piece."[382]

---

[381] Gadamer, *Truth and Method*, 79.

[382] Ibid., 150.

## The Museum of Elemental Fibers and the Panoptic Body

In parallel to the demarcation of the sacred and the artistic, the human body becomes desacralized and loses its cosmic nature. This change in anthropological notions is vividly reflected in the anatomical exhibitions of the Enlightenment and the "cabinets of curiosities" with theatrical dissections. At this time, anatomical science completely changed social views on the body, and the mechanism of the era was mixed with a baroque fascination with the bizarre and capricious. Natural science exhibitions included human skeletons, pickled babies with anomalies, "scientific dummies" of anatomized bodies ("Medical Venuses"), and demonstrations of the circulatory system by filling the vessels with colored wax. The pioneer of these practices was the Dutch anatomist Frederik Ruysch, whose collection made an indelible impression on Peter the Great and was purchased to equip the Russian Kunstkammer, the "Sovereign's Cabinet," as the reformer Tsar wanted to introduce his subjects to an enlightened view of the structure of man.

For centuries, Western medicine was dominated by the theory that humors determine vital phenomena and temperament, an idea which goes back to Hippocrates and Galen. By linking the fluids in the body with the elements, it combines the particular and the universal in a dialogue of substances (the doctrine of *doshas* in Ayurveda and a number of other traditional medical systems are constructed in a similar way). In the era of mechanicism, "the hour of anatomy struck when analysis and mechanicism gave birth to the theory of fibers, which was the result of a long cycle of development, leading to the epistemological victory of the principle of fragmentation."[383] Now, fibers reign as an explanatory model – muscle, bone, nerve. The motor

---

[383] Rafael Mandressi, "*Vskrytie i anatomia*", *Istoriya tela*, 3 vols., vol. 1: *Ot Renesansa do epokhi Prosveshcheniya* (Moscow: NLO, 2024), 253.

fiber becomes the main elementary particle of morphology, launching the work of the "animate mechanism."

Both physical and spiritual processes were associated with the activity of fibers and nerves. Irritation and tension, relaxation and contraction – these are the terms in which the enlighteners described both melancholy and experiments on stimulating frogs' hearts. The philosopher Denis Diderot claimed: "Nerves in the body are the same as a line in mathematics," and they "are the core of any mechanism."[384] The body consisting of fibers is seen as a physical device (this concept is most vividly reflected in the work *Man a Machine* by La Mettrie). It is significant that against the background of interest in "solid parts" instead of liquids, the subject of anatomical research is a dead body in which the movement of humors no longer occurs.

This parceled attitude toward corporeality is the direct opposite of the sacred anthropology of traditional cultures, where the pulse of the cosmos beats in every part of the body. It is no coincidence that the body has historically been a metaphor for society, be it the Vedic system of *Varnashrama-dharma* or the idea of the state body in the European Middle Ages. The sacred and integral body is replaced by a transparent body that can be divided into parts. The principle of holism is replaced by searching out elementary particles and small details. Since every part of the flesh is perceived as a fragment, man himself goes from being a creature through whose spine the Axis Mundi passes to little more than a detail – a sign of the arrival of post-human ontologies.

Anatomy presents the body as completely open, transparent for viewing both from the outside and inside. The main advantage of body dummies and cadavers, that is, bodies that have not been laid to rest in accordance with religious tradition, is the "disclosure of all the most secret details" –

---

384 Denis Diderot, *Éléments de physiologie* (Paris: Didier, 1964), 63-66.

this motif of uncovering is found in the works of all the enlighteners. The new natural scientific principle assumes complete bodily transparency – nudity that goes deeper than the skin. This is the bodily correlate of the "Panopticon," the ideal prison personifying the totalizing control of the new European reality.

Total erotic exposure, carried out with the help of mirrors, is one of the recurring fetishes of courtly libertine novels. An extreme example of the panoptic nature of the body can be found in the works of the Marquis de Sade, who takes Enlightenment epistemological ideas to the limit and removes the veil of illusions from autonomous morality and secular eudaemonism. In one of the most grotesque scenes of the novel *The 120 Days of Sodom*, after all available tortures have been exhausted, the nerves are pulled out of the victim. The finality of this procedure reflects not only the satiety of de Sade's libertine, the origins of which were described in detail by Georges Bataille,[385] but also plays on scientists' obsession with elementary fibers.

"Mechanistic terminology, with its levers, ropes, canals, pulleys and springs, accompanies the gradual descent of anatomists from one level to another in search of the final segment, the part of parts, the initial composite unit. The microscope reveals it to be a thread, a fiber."[386] The same elementary systems of the body as de Sade's were displayed at anatomical exhibitions, where vessels were filled with wax. According to the dark legends of the time, the procedure was sometimes carried out on still living people. Regardless of the reality of these rumors, the intuitions of the first viewers of anatomical exhibitions about (cognitive) violence are quite logical.

---

385 For more on this subject, see Georges Bataille's "Sade and the Common Man" and *Sade and the Sovereign Man*.

386 Mandressi, *Ot Renesansa do epokhi Prosveshcheniya*, 250.

The anatomical cabinet, followed by the natural history museum as part of a new scientific approach, indicates a change in attitude toward nature and man. Strictly speaking, we still live in this parcel paradigm of attitudes toward the body, exposed to all-knowing optics.

## Conclusion

We have outlined how changes in worldview, the autonomization of aesthetics, and the development of the natural-scientific method have led to the emergence of modern forms of museum exhibiting. Even the fact that Postmodern art goes beyond the museum, permeating various spheres of life (design, media environment, street art), and that museums themselves can demonstrate relevant interdisciplinarity and a non-classical approach to exhibiting, does not facilitate any unification of the dismembered parts of human existence. The "total aestheticization" (Wolfgang Welsch) of modernity exists in a desacralized reality, multiplying and shuffling bloodless forms.

In ancient times, valuables were concentrated in the sanctuary because they were sacrificial offerings. In museums, objects are also removed from everyday life, but not to be offered to otherworldly forces, but rather to be put into a "special space." It is generally accepted that a museum which introduces us to the culture of the past is fulfilling educational, conservation, and recreational (in other words, entertaining) functions. Museums do broaden horizons and contribute to the saturation of information, but, unlike the museums of antiquity, they no longer teach anyone the arts, understood as sacred services.

Offering cups were once used in rituals. Weapons were washed in the blood of enemies. Paintings decorated villas and palazzos. In the museum, historical objects are captured and excluded from contexts and deprived of their function.

*Mouseion, Kunstkammer, and the Classical Museum as Models of Reality*

Cult images and objects share the halls with human body parts.

Different traditions have their own stories about the difficult or bad fate of objects. For example, in Shinto beliefs, old abandoned things gain self-awareness, turn into restless spirits called *tsukumogami*, and can turn their wrath on those who damaged them or used them incorrectly. From this point of view, a historical or ethnographic museum can be thought of as a cursed place, full of restless dead and hungry ghosts. Or, in the more sad and realistic conditions of our world, it can be thought of as a deserted space full of discarded clothes, empty husks, and ashes.

*Translated by John Stachelski*

# THE EXISTENTIAL DIMENSION OF TRADITIONALISM IN THE WORKS OF JULIUS EVOLA: TOWARDS THE FUNDAMENTAL PRINCIPLES OF THE BEING OF THE DIFFERENTIATED MAN

*Dmitry Moiseev*

The post-war works of the Italian Traditionalist Julius Evola (1894-1974), in which he transitioned to a position of *apoliteia* (απολιτεία) and fully dissociated himself from the problematics of practical politics, are saturated with the motif of mentorship. He addressed himself to the youth who were undergoing a profound existential crisis as a result of the acceleration of degenerative processes in modern Western societies following the Second World War. The degradation affected practically every key sphere of people's lives – the social climate, personal relationships, spiritual seeking and practices, culture, art, and politics. This state of affairs was particularly oppressive to those few whom Evola called "differentiated men," i.e., those who were born into and matured with a deep feeling of foreignness in relation to the surrounding world, and who had a deep existential longing for "normality." The Italian philosopher argued that these traits were possessed by all "well-born" people prior to the French Revolution.

Taking into account some of Evola's key works during this period (*Ride the Tiger* being of primary importance), this essay attempts to describe the crucial existential prescriptions that the Italian Traditionalist put forth to the alienated youth of the modern world. These possibilities and propositions, posed in the greatest detail by Evola, serve as a pragmatic collection of existential practices (when decrypted from the language of Traditionalism) of colossal practical benefit to modern man. This 'decryption' may be useful to correctly understand the primary impulses behind the Traditionalist metaphors and academic philosophical terminology used by Evola, so as to decode the concrete advice given by the Italian thinker. This is especially important for those among the youth who have yet to reject those false attitudes which have been insinuated via the informational and spiritual infrastructure of modernity.

### The "Man Among the Ruins" in the "World After God Has Died": A Formulation of the Problem

In his post-war output, observing the ongoing process of dissolution in the modern world, Julius Evola addresses those few for whom the very foundations of this new reality seem totally alien. In his book *Men Among the Ruins* (1953), he gives the following diagnosis:

> since the present world looks more and more like a world of ruins, sooner or later the same line of action will assert itself everywhere: in other words, people will realize that it is useless to lean on what still has vestiges of more normal institutions, but which is compromised by several negative historical factors, and that it is imperative to go back to the origins and to start anew from them, as if they towered over history, moving ahead with pure forces along the path of an avenging and reconstructive reaction.[387]

In *Ride the Tiger* (1961), Evola poses the problem with a quote by Robert Reininger: "This is a struggle for the sake of modern man, that man who no longer has any

---

[387] Julius Evola, *Liudi i ruiny* (Moscow: AST, 2007), 13 [*Men Among the Ruins: Postwar Reflections of a Radical Traditionalist*, trans. Guido Stucco (Vermont: Inner Traditions, 2002), 106].

roots in the sacred soil of tradition, wavering in search of himself between the peaks of civilization and the abysses of barbarism, trying to find a satisfactory meaning for an existence completely left to itself."[388] The Nietzschean metaphor of the "death of God" serves as the most important, primary supposition – in a world that has broken ties with all things transcendent, the problem of finding answers to existential questions and developing a creative *modus operandi* reaches its apex. The spiritual maladies of the modern world – socialism, utilitarianism, materialism, as well as the wretched remains of puritanical norms – proffer a mass of "soporific," unsatisfying answers, the natural reaction to which is total nihilism, expressed in the radical jettisoning of artificial and duplicitous values.

The Beat Generation were the harbingers of this radical protest, having spawned a number of ingenious literary works (especially those of Jack Kerouac and William S. Burroughs); however, they failed to provide satisfying answers to essential questions, as they remained mere witnesses and topographers of the crisis within the history of culture. In accurately diagnosing the problem of the absurdities oppressing modern man, the existentialist philosophers also proposed inadequate solutions, which Evola critiques as follows:

> For him [Sartre], man is like someone in a prison without walls; he cannot find, either in himself or outside himself, any refuge from his freedom; he is destined, is sentenced to be free. He is not free to accept or refuse his freedom; he cannot escape it. I have already mentioned this state of the mind as the most characteristic evidence of the specific, negative sense that freedom has assumed in a certain human type in the epoch of nihilism. Freedom that cannot cease to be such, that cannot choose to be or not to be freedom, is for Sartre a limitation, a primordial, insuperable, and distressing "given."[389]

---

[388] Julius Evola, *Osedlat' tigra* (Saint Petersburg: Vladimir Dal', 2005), 29 [*Ride the Tiger: A Survival Manual for Aristocrats of the Soul*, trans. Joscelyn Godwin and Constance Fontana (Rochester: Inner Traditions, 2003), 16].

[389] Ibid., 167 [84].

In this way, man is presented with his own boundless, ineradicable freedom – a freedom of "dereliction," "desperation," "abandonment"; this is a freedom deprived of all meaning. A different mode of existence in a world where absolute foundations and supernatural, superbiological meanings are absent, would be truly unthinkable. What should the rare, "special" or "differentiated" type of man undertake in such a situation? In which direction should he search for foundations that might help him not only to "hold out" in such a world, but also to establish a creative path therein and arrive at a state of existential resilience? For such a person, Evola offers a number of fastidious prescriptions. But, before turning to him, we must analyze some fundamental ontological presuppositions, without which it will be impossible to turn onto the "ascending" path.

## The Spiritual Problem:
### Transcendence Beyond Theism and Atheism

The key, primary trait of Traditionalist ontology that distinguishes it from the first principles of existentialist atheism consists of what Evola calls the "dimension of transcendence" – namely, the immanent feeling given to the differentiated man that there is a "super-world" within the world of the senses. The Italian Traditionalist qualifies that this may serve as a point of support:

> Only this kind of man can use those positive aspects gleaned from the preceding analysis as his elementary basis, because when he looks within himself, he does not find a changeable and divided substance, but a fundamental direction, a "dominant," even though shrouded or limited by secondary impulses. What is more, the essential thing is that such a man is characterized by an existential dimension not present in the predominant human type of recent times—that is, the dimension of transcendence.[390]

The very fact of the transcendent as such being present draws the differentiated man nearer to the man belonging

---

390 Ibid., 92 [47]

to the World of Tradition, for whom the reality of "two natures" (material and super-material) was unremarkable and obvious. The "sense of the dominant" of which Evola writes is something akin to an internal voice of a non-terrestrial order, through which we evaluate our actions. This is expressed in our sensations, dreams, and creative impulses which lead us along the path of self-awareness and toward the formation of a center. Such a perception of the world intensifies the spiritual problem as meticulously described by Evola in *Ride the Tiger*:

> What is the God whose death has been announced? Nietzsche himself replies: "Only the god of morality has been conquered." He also asks: "Is there sense in conceiving of a god beyond good and evil?" The reply must be affirmative. "Let God slough off his moral skin, and we shall see him reappear beyond good and evil." What has disappeared is therefore not the god of metaphysics, but the god of theism, the personal god who is a projection of moral and social values and a support for human weakness. Now, the conception of a god in different terms is not only possible but essential within all the great traditions before and beside Christianity, and the principle of nonduality is also evident in them... Zarathustra in fact announces nothing new when he says: "Everything that becomes seems to me divine dance and divine whim, and the liberated world returns to itself"; it is the same idea that Hinduism casts in the well-known symbol of the dance and play of the naked god Shiva.[391]

From the perspective of this differentiated man, the withering away of Abrahamic, super-theistic religions can only be welcomed. This is the path toward liberation from God as a "center of gravity," opening up the way to a new spiritual substantiality. In rejecting God as an "appendage of morality" that has become a bourgeois "crutch," Evola celebrates the reemergence of "another dimension of reality" – "naked Being," accessible only to the few – in which the "special type" may reinforce himself, "make himself his own." That which is truly transcendent is always immune to destruction.

---

391 Ibid., 107 [55].

The fall of theistic religions and the triumph of a naïve, ignorant materialism in the modern world has resulted in the creation of the necessary conditions for the discovery and liberation of transcendent forces hitherto shackled by dogmas. It is in this that we find a favorable potential, latent in the crisis which has opened up before us; therefore, it is precisely the "seeker" who finds himself in a position "beyond theism and atheism."

To arrive at a comprehension of one's own divinity is to achieve the highest degree of traditional thought that is characteristic of practically all authentic traditions. One may find this kind of thinking in Hinduism and in other ancient religions. It is a solution to the riddle of why the atheist and the materialist always sense "abandonment" and "insecurity," no matter what chimera they might draw themselves for help.

If the theistic God has "died," then the authentic Spirit can never die. This transcendence is our very root – the root of our essential being – and, from birth, we are more involved with it than most others are. The solution and answer to the question, "Why am I?" or "Why are we?", is present in several traditional doctrines – Platonism, Hermetism, and Hinduism. We may briefly describe its metaphysical meaning by recognizing that we chose this for ourselves before being born – the decision was made by that component of "we" which is "unborn," unsusceptible to decomposition. The Hindus call this *karma*; the fatalists call it "fate"; in either case, this is a given of our being, and we live with it.

Our task is to live with it in dignity and to realize our own human potential in the world – to pass, dignified, through our trials, to multiply our spiritual experiences, to learn our lessons; in other words, we are to "be ourselves," to create the situation of our own resilience and indestructibility.

## To Be Oneself in a Cursed Reality: Differentiated Being, Invulnerability, Centrality, Acting without Desire

Now we turn to the Evolian analysis of prerequisites for the creation of a resilient existential situation for the differentiated man. Evola defines the fundamental principle for the individual repulsed by the modern world as "being oneself":

> For now we must set aside such allusions to a higher dimension of experience of a liberated world in order to define more precisely what such a vision of existence offers us in realistic terms. It is, in fact, the principle of purely being oneself. This is what remains after the elimination of what philosophy calls "heteronomous morality," or morality based on an external law or command. Nietzsche said this about it: "They call you destroyers of morality, but you are only the discoverers of yourselves"; and also: "We must liberate ourselves from morality so that we can live morally." By the latter phrase, he means living according to one's own law, the law defined by one's own nature. (This may result in the way of the superman, but only as a very special case.) This is on the same lines as the "autonomous morality" of Kant's categorical imperative, but with the difference that the command is absolutely internal, separate from any external mover, and is not based on a hypothetical law extracted from practical reason that is valid for all and revealed to man's conscience as such, but rather on one's own specific being.[392]

We shall attempt to explain the specificities of what Evola, in his reference to Nietzsche, intends with the term "specific being." He writes that Nietzsche

> did not stop at the physical being when he spoke of the "greater reason" contained in the body and opposed to the lesser reason: that which "does not say I, but is I," and which uses the "spirit" and even the senses as "little tools and toys." It is a "powerful lord, an unknown sage that is called oneself (*Selbst*)," "the guiding thread of the I that suggests all its ideas to it," which "looks with the eyes of the senses and listens with the ears of the spirit." He is not speaking here of the physis but of the "being" in the

---

392 Ibid., 80 [41].

full ontological significance of the word. The term he uses, das Selbst, can also be rendered by "the Self" as opposed to the I (Ich): an opposition that recalls that of the traditional doctrines already mentioned between the supra-individual principle of the person and that which they call the "physical I."[393]

In essence, this "post-script" to the principle of immanentizing the transcendent is elucidated by Evola in his early philosophical works, in his magical idealist period. Acting as a "bridge" between worlds, ferrymen between the "world of ideas" and the "immediately given world," we do not think ourselves exclusively as a body, but as a unity of "body" and "spirit," the "physical I" and "personality." Resting obscurely within this comprehension is a profound individualism, characteristic of Evola's analysis of the anthropology pertaining to differentiated men.

The principle of "being oneself" is linked with the principle of inviolability. Evola clarifies this thought in reference to Karl Jaspers:

> This trial through self-knowledge under the stimulus of various experiences and various encounters with reality may be associated in a certain sense with the maxim of *amor fati* (love of fate). Karl Jaspers has rightly said that this is not so much a precept of passive obedience to a necessity presumed to be predetermined and knowable, as an injunction to face each experience and everything in one's existence that is uncertain, ambiguous, and dangerous with the feeling that one will never do anything other than follow one's own path. The essential thing in this attitude is a kind of transcendent confidence that gives security and intrepidity, and it can be included among the positive elements in the line of conduct that is gradually being delineated.[394]

The Italian Traditionalist introduces the theme of transcendental trust – or a "trust in faith" – into the narrative; this theme stands in opposition to the existential terror characteristic of atheistic existentialism. This is a trust in the world, in life, and in that transcendent force

---

393 Ibid., 81 [41-42].

394 Ibid., 120 [61].

with which we are conjunct. This theme, in turn, stands in conjunction with the aspect of centrality:

> The problem of being oneself has a particular and subordinate solution in terms of a unification. Once one has discovered through experiment which of one's manifold tendencies is the central one, one sets about identifying it with one's will, stabilizing it, and organizing all one's secondary or divergent tendencies around it. This is what it means to give oneself a law, one's own law... It depends on this last trial to resolve, or not to resolve, the problem of the ultimate meaning of existence in an ambience lacking any support or "sign." After the whole superstructure has been rejected or destroyed, and having for one's sole support one's own being, the ultimate meaning of existing and living can spring only from a direct and absolute relationship between that being (between what one is in a limiting sense) and transcendence (transcendence in itself). This meaning is not given by anything extrinsic or external, anything added to the being when the latter turns to some other principle. That might have occurred in a different world, a traditionally ordered world. But in the existential realm under consideration, such a meaning can only be given by the transcendent dimension directly perceived by man as the root of his being and of his "own nature." Moreover, it carries an absolute justification, an indelible and irrevocable consecration, which completely destroys the state of negativity and the existential problem. On this basis alone does "being what one is" cease to constitute a limitation... In a meaningless world, the absolute sense of being depends almost exclusively on this experience. If it has a positive outcome, the last limit falls-away; transcendence and existence, freedom and necessity, possibility and reality coincide. A centrality and invulnerability are realized without restriction in any situation, be it dark or light, detached or apparently open to every impulse or passion of life.[395]

Having isolated a central drive out of the chaos of life and acquired transcendent unity, it is as though we awake to a new life in correspondence with the very essence of our being. It is in this way that "immanentization of the transcendent" is realized – by means of a link between our immediately given being and a transcendent being that manifests in and through us, which is the source of knowledge,

---
395 Ibid., 120 [62-64].

creativity, and, ultimately, truth. For the differentiated man, this comes so naturally that he is capable of giving himself up to the process reflexively; however, the true value which allows one to scrutinize the meaning of being in the world consists in a comprehension of this experiment. Therein lies the key to transformation and departure from the crisis. Turning to the language of eudaimonism, we might refer to this state as "absolute happiness," or as a state of fullness, in which the meaning of life unfolds and becomes apparent in its totality. Terror and the void disappear. The unfolding of this meaning allows for the realization of a *modus operandi* referred to by Evola as "unwilled action." He writes:

> The higher dimension, which is presumed to be present in oneself, manifests through the capacity to act not with less, but with more application than a normal type of man could bring to the ordinary forms of conditioned action. One can also speak here of "doing what needs to be done," impersonally... Such a line of conduct obviously refers to the domain in which one's own nature is allowed to function, and to that which derives from the particular situation that one has actively assumed as an individual... Pure action involves the other kind of pleasure or happiness, which it would be wrong to imagine as inhabiting an arid, abstracted, and soulless climate. There, too, there can be fire and vigor, but of a very special kind, with the constant presence and transparency of the higher, calm, and detached principle—which, as I have said, is the true acting principle here.[396]

Here, Evola directs the reader toward his early work *Tao Tê Ching: The Book of the Way and Virtue* (1923), in which he describes the Taoist principle of non-action, or *wu-wei*. In view of one's non-engagement with the external, immediately given being is the Taoist ideal of man – the "perfect" or "true man" – who gains access to the essence of all things by means of active non-action; in other words, he does so by means of a refusal of teleological action, either directly or conditioned by something other than his essence or Path. In coming to a comprehension of this mysterious force and acquiring the *Te*, the chief virtue of Taoism, the Perfect

396 Ibid., 135 [68-70].

One also acquires a special magical potential for action – an invisible, imperceptible, and practically intangible means of "acting through inaction" (*wu-wei*). The idea of pure action, therefore, is of exclusive importance for the fulfillment of the main maxim of "being oneself." This is an acquisition of harmonious being in which no existential questions remain, at least in relation to oneself:

> the man for whom the new freedom does not spell ruin, whether because, given his special structure, he already has a firm base in himself, or because he is in the process of conquering it through an existential rupture of levels that reestablishes contact with the higher dimension of "being" — this man will possess a vision of reality stripped of the human and moral element, free from the projections of subjectivity and from conceptual, finalistic, and theistic superstructures.[397]

These words sum up Evola's considerations.

## The Specificities of Inter-Sexual Relations: On the Necessity of Exclusive Experience

Everything we have elaborated above relates to the Evolian perception of the individual as a "unitary" being whose initial situation is to be understood as one of inner conflict with the modern, egalitarian, and materialistic world; man is prepared to solve this conflict by acquiring the dimension of transcendence, comprehending it and harmonizing with it. An additional question unavoidably arises due to the anthropological characteristics of the human being: "How might this situation appear if the differentiated man does not wish to undergo this trial alone?"

Evola unfolds this question in *Ride the Tiger* (1961) and *The Metaphysics of Sex* (1958). The question is two-sided, connected both to sexuality in its pure form and to the relations between the sexes. Overall, given definite conditions, Evola sees the creative potential of cooperation between the sexes in the contemporary situation. He notes:

---
397 Ibid., 150 [75].

> Contrary to puritanical opinion, a free sexual life in the case of persons of a certain stature can tell us nothing about their intrinsic value—history is rich in examples of that. What they allow themselves should be measured solely by what they *are*, by the power that they have over themselves. Relationships between men and women, with regard to living together, should be clearer, more important, and interesting than those defined by bourgeois mores and sexual exclusivism, which understands the significance of female integrity in mere anatomical terms.[398]

In light of this observation, the disintegration of the sanctimonious, blind, and limiting sexuality of bourgeois, puritanical morality can only be welcomed. The traditional world always viewed sexuality and its manifestations as a necessary and normal part of life; and sex, in itself, given the presence of an appropriate partner, contains the potential of "rupturing one's existential level." As Evola writes in this regard, "the pure sexual experience also has its metaphysical value, the intensity of intercourse being able to produce an existential rupture of planes and an opening beyond ordinary consciousness. Along with the sacralization of sex, these possibilities were recognized in the traditional world."[399] It goes without saying that Evola is not speaking here of a chaotic "sex in itself," though it bears recognizing that such stages in the maturation of the individual may be acknowledged as something not destructive, but which carries the potential to remove a profound resistance toward this realm within mass consciousness. It is practically impossible to abstract oneself from this due to what Evola calls an "atmosphere of dissipated, erotic intoxication."

Moreover, in the traditional interpretation of the creative relations between the sexes, we may speak here of the magnetism proper to eros which serves as an authentic foundation for any kind of love, be it divine, physical, or a combination of the two. The loss of this natural magnetism leads to a foreclosure on the authentic connection between

---

398 Ibid., 405 [197].

399 Ibid., 409 [198].

man and woman, which supersedes sentimental romanticism. According to Evola, magnetism emerges spontaneously, and whatever happens next "depends on ourselves." In one way or another, this question significantly overcomes the physical surface and bare sexuality. In *The Metaphysics of Sex*, Evola notes that "it is this magnetized imagination or 'exaltation,' rather than the intellect, which acts in lovers... Again we find that the common language of lovers, usually taken as sentimental, romantic, or flaccid, meaningfully relates to this point... The positive and objective content is the obscure feeling, the foreboding, of a shift in the plane of consciousness linked in varying degrees to eros" – and he adds that "operative sexual magic is also based on this,"[400] in that it allows the practitioner to supplement the existential self-manifestation of the individual.

In *Ride the Tiger*, Evola acknowledges that "the present situation excludes the possibility of integrating sex in a life full of meaning within institutional frameworks. So we can only think of certain cases in which, despite everything, favorable conditions exceptionally and sporadically converge."[401] With this, we approach an answer to the fundamental question – what might qualify as creative relations? Evola elaborates that one may transform poison into medicine through

> relationships that, without being superficial or "naturalistic," have an evident character, grounded on the social and ethical side in loyalty, camaraderie, independence, and courage. The man and woman always remain conscious as two beings with distinct paths, who, in the world in dissolution, can overcome their fundamental, existential isolation only through the effect of pure sexual polarity. If there is no need to "possess" another human being, the woman will not be a mere object of "pleasure," a source of sensations that are sought as means to assert oneself.[402]

---

400 Julius Evola, *Metafizika pola* (Moscow: Belovod'e, 1996), 63 [*Eros and the Mysteries of Love: The Metaphysics of Sex* (Rochester: Inner Traditions, 1991), 27].

401 Evola, *Osedlat' tigra*, 409 [*Ride the Tiger*, 198].

402 Ibid., 410 [199].

Additionally, he points out:

> If, however, we do not want to deal with mere concepts, but with their practical application, today I can only refer to sporadic, unusual experiences open only to the differentiated human type, because they presuppose a special interior constitution that survives in him alone. Another presupposition regards the woman: it is that the erotic, fascinating quality widespread in today's environment is concentrated and almost "precipitated" (in a chemical sense) in certain female types precisely in terms of an "elementary" quality. Therefore, in a sexual relationship with a woman, the situation I have often considered would reappear— that is, a dangerous situation that requires a self-mastery, the surpassing of an inner limit by anyone who intends actively to attempt it. Despite a certain exasperation or crudeness due to the different environment, the meanings originally connected to the polarity of the sexes could reappear in this context, if not yet suffocated by the puritan religion of the "spirit," and if they were not enfeebled, sentimentalized, and made bourgeois, but also not primitivized or simply corrupted. These significances are found in many legends, myths, and sagas of very different traditions. In the true, typical, absolute woman, they recognized a spiritually dangerous presence, a fascinating and even dissolutive force; this explains the attitude and the precepts of that particular line of ascesis averse to sex and woman, as if to cut off their danger. The man who has not chosen either to renounce the world or to be impassively detached from it can face the danger and even derive nourishment from the poison, if he uses sex without becoming a slave to it, and if he is able to evoke the profound, elemental dimensions in a certain transbiological sense.[403]

And so, through our interpretation of Evola's positions, we can affirm the following: the drive to overcome existential loneliness is more natural than conscientious asceticism. The differentiated man to whom Evola makes his appeal is no exception. On the contrary, through the development of his own selfhood – an indispensable condition of his survival in a world bereft of orientational points – he will direct himself toward the acquisition of a partner who manifests favorable traits. We may express solidarity with Evola's

---

403 Ibid., 412 [199-200].

position in that the relations leading both sexes "upward" may be founded on obligatory preconditions of friendship, faithfulness, independence, and valor. Each component is of exceptional importance: (1) friendship is the foundation of openness, benevolence, and respect, barring which relationships are impossible; (2) faithfulness is indispensable for the respective partners in a relationship as they concentrate on one another in a conscientious and directed manner, as it is to ensure that there is no dispersion of sexual energy; (3) the partners' mutual independence is important for the reasons we have cited above, including such existential dominants as "being oneself" and the "cultivation of inviolability" – this has equal bearing on both men and women, as Evola non-trivially writes about the necessity of decisively rejecting the "possession" and objectification of one's partner, which otherwise deals a crushing blow to trust and freedom, and this idea is also implied in the component of independence[404]; (4) for the risk-taking associated with it, valor requires first

---

[404] Here, in addition, we must cite a fragment from *The Metaphysics of Sex* in which Evola gives a withering critique of jealousy in intersexual relations: "There are cases in which love's need to possess another being wholly, physically and morally, in the flesh and in the soul, can be explained in its most superficial aspect by the pride of the ego and the impulse toward power. We say 'its most superficial aspect' because these impulses are not primary but rather complex ones formed at the level of the social individual, whose root is more deep and hidden. The *Geltungstrieb*, the need to have worth, the need to enhance one's value in one's own eyes even more than in the eyes of other people, the 'manly protest' that Adler set as a central theme in his analytical psychology, are not so much the causes of neurotic overcompensation as the effects of an inferiority complex. This complex is transcendental in nature, stemming from an understanding of man's inborn privation as a finite being, shattered and problematical, a mixture of being and nonbeing. Eros is one of the natural forms with which man seeks to reduce and suspend this feeling of privation. It is logical that some people strive for self-confirmation and a sense of self-worth through erotic and sexual possession: it gives them the illusion of "being" – and the phenomenology of both jealousy and sexual tyranny arises from it. But, let us repeat, none of this has a primary character; it only concerns transpositions belonging to the sphere of the most peripheral consciousness. A man who limits himself to this level does not understand the ultimate sense and the depth dimension of the impulses that he obeys in these cases; thus, he often nourishes the deflected and distorted compensatory manifestations we have just mentioned. That quite ridiculous thing called the 'pride of the male' is of this sphere." Evola, *Metafizika pola*, 122 [*Eros*, 72].

and foremost that man consciously ceases to be "unitary." As Evola justifiably argues, the ascesis disseminated in relationships throughout the traditional world was perceived as a movement toward security, since all relationships eliminate any threats within themselves, even if those threats should be seductive. Moreover, the potential which is obscured within the qualitative bond between two qualitative people supersedes all known risks.

Finally, the exclusive experiences of which Evola writes are associated with that overwhelmingly rare combination of traits described above. If a "unitary" individual, following the commandment to "be himself," should obtain a partner worthy of sustained connection and, by means thereof, should part with the existential loneliness that has previously defined him, then this event creates a potent emotional impression which in itself reveals his potential to "rupture the existential level" and further reinforce his life potential.

### The Final Trial and the Right over Life

Everything we have elaborated above in drawing on Julius Evola's fundamental works leads us to a key thesis bearing existential connotations: the creative path consists in living, "riding the tiger of time" without departing from the world, but actively transforming the surrounding reality of one's selfhood through one's deeds and personal example. For this to be possible, one must grant himself the "right over life" in a world of ruins, bereft of orientational points and, more precisely, must succeed in the final trial.

This trial stands forth as the eternal temptation to quit, out of one's own volition, this world which so often seems unworthy of our existence in it. The cultural heroes who inspired Evola committed suicide at the age of 23 – Carlo Michelstaedter and Otto Weininger. Evola himself contemplated and prepared himself for that act at the same age; however, his acquaintance with Eastern spirituality (primarily Buddhism) proved fateful, saved his life, and, in the long run, bore a surprising lot of fruit.

When Evola deliberates on this trial in the face of death, one may have total confidence in him. He writes:

> These aspects could provide a positive climate in the modern world for the differentiated man, because that which has been affected only concerns a vision of humanized life devoid of the sense of great distances. He can then consider a particular "contemplation of death" as a positive factor, as a challenge, and as a measure of his inner strength. He can also follow the well-known ancient maxim of considering every day as the last of his individual existence: at the prospect, not only should he maintain his calm, but he should not even change anything in his thinking or acting.[405]

In his allusion to the ancient principle of *memento mori*, Evola argues that adherence thereto constitutes one of the fundamental aspects of existential "indestructibility." On the basis of his own trials, Evola was convinced of the complexity involved in resolving to live in a situation of incoherent chaos, as does the differentiated man. However, in order for one to access what is "greater than life," thoughts of death are of essential importance. Evola recounts the concrete attitudes necessary for "discovering the path into the beyond": one must "contemplate death," live every day in the present (as though each day were one's last), and maintain an orientation toward the "vertical." These are concrete behavioral attitudes which benefit each of us. In the modern, materialist world, a commitment such as this is an existential feat; but, within this complexity, we find a key aspect of the overall prescription. In elucidating his thesis, Evola affirms:

> Elevating oneself above that which can be understood in the light of human reason alone; reaching a high interior level and an invulnerability otherwise hard to attain: these are perhaps among the possibilities that, through adequate reactions, are offered in the cases in which the night journey allows almost nothing to be perceived of the landscape that one traverses, and in which the

---

405 Evola, *Osedlat' tigra*, 445 [*Ride the Tiger*, 216].

theory of *Geworfenheit*, of being absurdly "flung" into the world and time, seems to be true, especially in a climate in which physical existence itself must present a growing insecurity. If one can allow one's mind to dwell on a bold hypothesis— which could also be an act of faith in a higher sense—once the idea of *Geworfenheit* is rejected, once it is conceived that living here and now in this world has a sense, because it is always the effect of a choice and a will, one might even believe that one's own realization of the possibilities I have indicated—far more concealed and less imaginable in other situations that might be more desirable from the merely human point of view, from the point of view of the "person"—is the ultimate rationale and significance of a choice made by a "being" that wanted to measure itself against a difficult challenge: that of living in a world contrary to that consistent with its nature, that is, contrary to the world of Tradition.[406]

## Conclusion

In closing our analysis of the existential aspect of Julius Evola's works, we shall note our key theses and formulate some brief parting thoughts for our readers.

With its fundamental premises (materialism, egalitarianism), the modern world has created an existential situation of crisis in which man, who would perceive the surrounding reality otherwise given other circumstances, finds it impossible to root himself and live creatively. The theistic god is "dead," and attempts proposed by atheists to counteract the crisis are unsatisfactory, as they can all be fundamentally reduced to an attempt at "accepting" the encircling void.

Julius Evola sets the task of helping the differentiated man develop his own path in a world that is alien to him, expressed in the following dimensions: (1) one must recognize the correct ontology, based on an acceptance of transcendence; (2) one must adhere to a clear, existential mode of action, based on the principles of inviolability, centrality, unmotivated action, and "contemplation of death"; (3) in the case of a conscientious rejection of "unitarity," one must agree only

---

406 Ibid., 462 [224].

to a union with a partner who is worthy, who existentially corresponds to traditional parameters.

It is difficult to overestimate the significance of the intellectual and spiritual effort made by Evola within the conditions of the modern world, the crisis of which has only worsened during recent decades. Despite Wittgenstein's early advice that one "should remain silent with regard to that of which it is impossible to speak," the Italian thinker clothes the seemingly inexpressible within a system of adequately simple language, familiar to anyone who has taken even a semester of philosophy courses at university. Evola provides a complex methodology for inner self-attunement which cannot but evoke a response in those whom he deems the differentiated men.

In Evola's later works, the terminological instruments which he had developed over the course of his life and meticulously substantiated in his pre-war works (particularly in his most important book of 1934, *Revolt Against the Modern World*) were put in the service of the best people in this world – young seekers undergoing profound spiritual crises, provoked from both within and without, and persisting in their active quest for internal supports whose infrastructure had been mercilessly ruined by the events of the oppressive twentieth century.

We dare to hope that this essay will serve as a worthy point of entry into the multidimensional and exclusively beneficial thought of Julius Evola for those who have yet to acquaint themselves with it; we also hope that this study will serve as a reminder of the Italian Traditionalist's contributions for those who have already read his most important books. We are certain that these contributions have aided many, as they have us, in our comprehension of the problems of the modern world and of the creative paths leading to their resolution.

*Translated by Charlie Smith*

# ANDRÁS LÁSZLÓ'S FUNDAMENTAL CONTRIBUTION TO METAPHYSICAL TRADITION

## László Virág

Let us begin with the obvious fact that we can trace innumerable manifestations of Tradition, which is synonymous with Truth, in history, in society, in state institutions, in worldviews, in attitudes towards transcendence and immanence, in human habits, in everything that ultimately focuses on some higher, spiritual reality which transcends and determines the whole being of the ordinary man. Underlying all these manifestations are spiritual-religious doctrines, which are not mere theoretical speculations, but manifestations, articulations of existential and self-experiences. It is debatable whether these doctrines are summaries of the different levels and aspects of existential and self-experience, or whether the various manifestations are derived from these doctrines. This does not affect the truth of the statement that, at a given level, doctrines underlie the whole of Traditionalism – "divine" doctrines that guide, orient, and lead man and his world, the whole cosmos, beyond contingencies, impermanence, time and space, and thus provide man and all of existence with a real perspective, a real meaning.

The highest of these doctrines are, without a doubt, those which expound and emphasize the doctrine of Oneness, of "non-duality," which are therefore in this sense "monisms" – not only in relation to the non-duality of the Oneness of God, but also in relation to the non-duality of all being, of transcendence and immanence. Many traditions have this doctrine explicitly at their core, and it is safe to say that ultimately and plausibly only those can be called Traditions in which this doctrine is either emphasized and explicit (i.e., explicitly expounded for the intellectual elite) or can be revealed by an autonomous spiritual activity.

When we have just spoken of the non-duality of all being, we have obviously also referred to the non-duality of consciousness itself, since being and consciousness cannot be separated. And this brings us to one of the cornerstones of the doctrine of traditional monism: the singularity, or more precisely the "non-duality" of consciousness. For nothing can be assumed outside of consciousness. Whatever proposition, opinion, or statement one encounters – be it error or truth –, it is always a proposition, opinion, or statement of *consciousness*. The same is true of any event, experience, perception, etc., that is, of any form of experience: there can only be the momentums of *consciousness* in this respect as well. With regard to propositions, assertions, etc., we may say that they are only momentums of human awareness, but we may also say that any proposition of any man expresses his relation to universal consciousness. And universal consciousness is One, unique consciousness. If we take its absolute singularity, that is, if we experience ourselves as absolute Uniquity, then, in fact, even this Uniquity cannot be asserted, for in absolute Uniquity the totality of consciousness cannot be contrasted with anything – that is why we say it is "non-dual."

But, for didactic reasons, let us stick to the "uniquity" of consciousness. Consciousness, both in general and as universality, can only be posited in the singular first person: as *my* consciousness. It is not, after all, the consciousness of a human being living within the limits of personality, since this human being itself can be grasped "within" (my own) consciousness – in my consciousness I can experience myself as a human being, as a being experiencing myself in a human way. If we were to assume that there is another consciousness outside of my own consciousness, it would not be intelligible – because it would not be experiential. For the uniquity of consciousness – which is identical with its universality – does not mean the consciousness of the individual in the mind, but the totality (for want of a better term) within which human consciousness arises. If the self-consciousness referred to were identified with the mind-consciousness of each human individual, then perhaps more consciousness could be assumed in relation to those who experience in a limited way. But this is not the case at all.

If we compare the position of non-dualism with other views, or even "philosophies," we can safely say that it is an extreme idealism. At the same time, it is also extreme realism, because the articulations of non-dualism are based solely on self-experience, free of any theoretical speculation. One of our fundamental theses, derived from sufficiently intense intuitive self-experience, is that objective reality cannot be grasped independently of the experiencing subject. If there is no experiencing subject, there are not and there cannot be objects of consciousness. It follows evidently that the experiencing subject is, in its ultimate essentiality, a creating, maintaining, and withdrawing subject. Objects of consciousness are just such: objects of consciousness. We can make this apparent tautology palpable if we say that objects are objects of the consciousness of the self – that is, of my universal subjectivity. The "independent" essentiality of the objects of consciousness, their independent existence, which is self-contained in themselves, cannot be assumed. The assumption of an objective reality existing independently of (my) consciousness is called naive realism, and this naive realism is the property of intellectually or even mentally blind people.

The false claim of an objective reality that is independent of consciousness comes from the human condition: as a human being, I have no perfect control over things, so things seem to be "of themselves," against my human will, following their own laws. Things appear, exist, cease to exist, without asking man's permission for their particular movements. In fact, things have an overwhelming superiority over man (especially modern man), giving the impression that man is utterly insignificant, that he has power only over his rational intellect, which he uses to investigate, follow, or use for his own benefit the laws of nature imposed upon him. If we consider the actual relation of man as man to the objective world, this is more or less the case, i.e., we can see what compels man to adopt an incorrect position, one that does not correspond to reality: his own insignificant power over things. But we cannot say that those things which have a superior power over me (as human) are independent of my own consciousness. For things ultimately follow from myself (as subject): they are objects of my consciousness. It must be emphasized once again in this connection: if I *am* not, there are no conscious objects, whether they are in my power or not.

That is, any world follows from myself as universal consciousness, as the universal subject of consciousness. Not from my human subjectivity, of course, but from my universal subjectivity. But my reduced and limited, human, personal subjectivity is nevertheless of paramount importance: it is only through it that one can enter into contact with universal consciousness, universal subjectivity. This latter statement implies a duality – the duality of personal and universal (i.e., divine) subjectivity. At the same time, it implies unity, i.e., non-duality: the degraded and the absolute subject cannot be different. My degraded, human and humanly experiencing subjectivity is the result of the will, the "play" of the absolute selfhood. Both are I myself, i.e., the two: one. Of course, this contradicts purely human logic, but perhaps even human logic allows the Absolute Will and Absolute Power to transcend all logic. That is to say, I can be both perfectly identical with myself and at the same time limited, while retaining my absolute being, and that in the spirit of perfect freedom. For perfect freedom implies that the absolute subject (which is nothing other than the Self in the first person singular) deprives itself of its freedom while remaining perfectly free. In this sense, we can say that the degraded, humanly experiencing subject and the absolute subject are one, not two. This is true at every moment when I construe and contemplate it with sufficient force, and it loses its truth (though it does not disappear completely) when one allows oneself to exist and act in a state of ordinarily being dispersed, dependent, and influenced.

The path to manifestation, dependence, and deprivation is a magical path, the result of a magical will. In the same way, the path to absolution is also magical. Here, the term *magic* should not be understood as sorcery, as any sort of witchcraft, but should be identified with the Sanskrit *māyā*, which means "existential magic" at the highest level. We must also emphasize the absolute will, both in the "unrolling" of the relative world of experience and in the recognition and restoration of the absolute position.

We must point out once again that it would be a great mistake to think that the doctrine of unity, of non-duality, can remain at the level of mere abstraction, or that it can be grasped by abstract speculation at all. The doctrine of non-duality, which is the metaphysical basis of Tradition and of all religion, cannot be conceived without higher aspirations and without the disciplines suggested by these higher aspirations. He who does not strive to transcend himself is not able to understand these doctrines. Tradition is inseparable from the aspiration to the Unconditioned, and inseparable from discipline – at all levels of human (and indeed cosmic) life. And the aspiration to the Unconditioned is inseparable from that which is the eternal and highest aspiration of human life: freedom and immortality.

There is no Tradition, then, without a claim to freedom and immortality, or, let us say, there is no Tradition without the *presence* of freedom and immortality. If one does not have the necessary degree of this claim (after all, one could say that everyone has it, but modern man lives it out in perverted and hopeless forms that are increasingly shackling), he will neither understand, nor accept, nor follow Tradition, beyond all forms and contingencies, in the spirit of a Unity that is supratemporal (and nonetheless temporal). At the centre of the discipline is freedom and immortality, no matter how indirectly or directly one may seek them. The notion and claim to freedom and immortality permeate every aspect and every level of a truly traditional life, from that of ascetics and kings to the activities of servants. There is no rational reason for all this: it is play and magic – both the limited existence and the need for and the path to liberation.

Absolute immortality implies absolute self-identity: it implies that I am entirely autonomous, simply because there is no "other," because everything is identical with my own consciousness and my own absolute subjectivity – that is, I am entirely myself. Absolute immortality (i.e., absolute freedom) is the active and possessed recognition that the world is in my consciousness, that it follows from me, and that the world is I am myself. For to be mortal is to identify my consciousness with something that is contingent, that is, to submit to contingency, and to see conditions – mistakenly – as subsisting in themselves, that is, to fail to recognize that conditions and contingency are determined for me *by myself*, beyond my person, in the sense of an absolute decision.

One of the greatest tragedies of modern man is that he has given up immortality as a possibility and even as a potentiality. Tradition is aware of both mortality and immortality, and holds the human being in a productive tension between these two poles, precisely through the discipline practiced for the sake and under the sign of immortality. This discipline is the dissolving of duality in the world of duality, that is, the transcending of the state of consciousness of duality – actively: volitionally, consciously, and freely. In other words, it means that the practitioner of the discipline – that is, of spiritual asceticism – takes possession of his own consciousness and thereby takes possession of his own being. If he takes full possession of his consciousness, he also takes full possession of all being, and this is only possible by transcending the ultimate duality, the duality of being and non-being. Again, however, it must be emphasized that consciousness is unique, and that it cannot be grasped in experience in any other way than as *my own* consciousness, as my consciousness of myself. The whole process, if the need to practice it arises in an effective way, can only be grasped by anyone in the first person singular, otherwise it degenerates into abstract philosophizing and thus distances one from the goal, which is also the beginning.

It is obvious from the above that the Absolute, which transcends being and non-being, cannot be conceived as an object. God is the absolute subject, the absolute possibility of my-self. God cannot be an object, because then he would be merely one entity among others, which is obviously absurd. The position of non-dualism on the supreme deity is therefore autotheism, which asserts the coincidence of my own essentiality and the essentiality of the Absolute beyond all duality, that is, that there is a single subject of being and consciousness, and that is my subjectivity.

Although it has been pointed out several times so far, it must now be emphasized again that the Self, my subject, cannot be confused with all that belongs to the sphere of personal reality: the body and the psychophysical organism, and all the "flow" that surrounds this organism as an external world and opposes it in a dual way. It is a common mistake, in fact, to conceive of non-dualism, the doctrine of the universality of consciousness and subject, as a kind of "superegoism," as if one wanted to absolutize corporeally determined individuality. This is a childish mistake, the result of the fears and attachments of immature minds. If one connects these thoughts with the teaching of the *upaniṣads* that Ātman is identical with Brahman, then one can immediately understand that this is not a deification of the limited man.

One common – but rather ill-considered – objection is based on the *anātma-vāda* of Buddhism, i.e., the teaching that things have no independent essentiality, no "being-in-themselves," and therefore one cannot consider any *ātman*. Things are interdependent, in a constant flow, and indeed the contingent world (*saṃsāra*) as a whole is itself this flow, a system of almost matrix-like interdependencies. Now, *things* really do not stand either in themselves or independently of consciousness – this conspicuousness forms the basis of all spiritual teachings. But this statement, which is first of all an experience and only then a construct of thought, must have (and indeed has) a basis of reference, which is absolute unconditionality, the immutable totality of consciousness, the subject which cannot be grasped in any relation of dependence. This is so also because Buddhism itself aspires to unconditionality, i.e., it is a Tradition which has at its core the realization of this unconditionality, of actively possessed non-duality, of absolute autodetermination, and which takes as its basis the conditionality, the eternal flow of things, of the whole manifested and unmanifested world (*saṃsāra*). Anyone who considers his own conscious life seriously can come to no other conclusion about *things* than that of Buddhism, and so it is not at all surprising that not only the Buddhist tradition claims this, but also all other traditions that emphasize spiritual realization.

The approach outlined above is, in a single world, called *solipsism*, regardless of the misunderstandings and even antipathy such a term might cause in some people. It should be clear from what has been said so far, however, that this is not the same as what academic philosophical texts interpret as solipsism. It does not therefore exhaust itself either in gnoseology (though it is also entirely true in gnoseology), in ethics, or in the methodology of thought and contemplation, since it does not identify subjectivity with a fully human, merely thinking subjectivity. What is at stake here is a monism (non-dualism) that extends to the whole of being and even beyond, which is not based on conclusions about existence and being, that is, on a passive and rigid view, but on a dynamic *contemplation* which includes the thinking human personality itself in the circle of contingencies and which looks at being – any category of existence – from the totality of consciousness, in a dynamic, living way. It is therefore not a mere theory, but also, so to speak, a test of intellectual courage. For there is only one subject, and it is identical with my own subjectivity. There is no other subject. Any other subject that may arise arises in my own consciousness, and is therefore not a subject but an object of consciousness. It is very easy to conceive this, yet almost all philosophers fail to conceive it, for fear of being existentially left alone. And this is precisely because they can only conceive of the singularity of the subject as human loneliness, which is simply not true.

Among the numerous and wide-ranging teachings of the leader of the Hungarian Traditionalist school, András László, who died in April 2024, solipsism is thought to be the most fundamental one. He himself considered it the most important, something without which Tradition would not recognize its ultimate metaphysical basis, the ultimate basis beyond all substance, without which all tradition would be mere convention, that is, the preservation of, attachment to, and nostalgia for customs of former times. Tradition is always an adaptation in time of that which is eternal, unchanging – that is, immortal and free. This doctrine is the basis and the goal of the search for truth. The aim is not nominal, rational, or philosophical, but the fulfillment of solipsism, the striving of consciousness to transcend the dualities of the at once real and illusory, and to actualise itself in the total possession, the total domination of power. András László said that solipsism is a doctrine that "cries out" for realization. We can only add, following Evola, that this teaching cannot be recognized or admitted except by one in whom the aspiration in this direction has reached a certain level of intensity. In other words, only those who do not "want to be merely good," but strive beyond good and evil to achieve perfect self-identity, self-fulfilment, which is the goal of *yoga* in its original sense. The goal cannot be abstract, so – to use András László's words again – the *ātman* cannot be understood as if it were an abstract object, but only as a self-as-myself (we have already discussed that its identification with the limited individual is also a fundamental mistake).

Let us read carefully the very concise definition below, given to us by András László as a personal teaching:

> There is no unconditional reality other than my innermost transcendental self. There is objective reality, but it is the objective reality of my self-consciousness; there is actional reality, but it is the actional reality of my self-consciousness; and there is subjective reality, but it is the subjective reality of my self-consciousness. There are objects and there are persons, but they are in and from my-self. I am only I-myself, and there is no other *ātmā* besides me, in me all the forms of the substantive verb are coincident.

András László represented this depth of contemplation in a completely autonomous way, which we deliberately do not call a "view." Nor can we say that he "formed," in the human sense of the word, the position of solipsism, since we have already indicated that this cannot be the result of a rational *sorites*. In common religious-historical terms, we can say that it is the articulation in words of an "intuitive insight," so it cannot in principle be said to be the result of inference or even of adoption. András László often emphasised his respect, even his love, for traditional authors, but he also stressed that he formulated his theses entirely independently, on the basis of his own essential consciousness. The writer of these lines can testify to this as well as to the fact that András László's explanations and clarifications place him among the greatest traditional authors of the 20th century. Because of the specific location of the Hungarian language, his teachings were limited to a small country and were largely oral (the author gave more than 3,000 lectures on metaphysical Traditionalism in his lifetime), but this has no real importance, because true teaching is eternal and leaves a trace in the subtle structure of consciousness even if it is not told to anyone. For everyone must realize that any true doctrine is an autonomously conceived doctrine. Even in the master-disciple relationship, where transmission and respect play an essential role, and rightly so, the task of the disciple is to find the doctrine in his own essentiality and to proceed on the spiritual path by the power of this evidence.

Solipsism also manifests itself temporally, since it is the magical, realizational basis of all higher traditions, even if it is not philosophically formulated or when the word "solipsism" is not even spoken. The word "solipsism" has not been uttered by various traditions, but they represent the *idea* of solipsism. As a philosophical term, solipsism is commonplace, and no doubt has thus given rise to many misunderstandings (even aversions). But if we understand it correctly (as we have tried to do in our writing), we can see in it a philosophical-idealist articulation of the aspiration to centrality, which, although it can be expressed rationally (as many traditions have done in other words), is absolutely in the sign of metaphysical centrality, subordinated to it, expressing it at all levels. And only when centrality is possessed intuitively can valid judgments be made about the periphery, about the world, about processes in the world, about man and nature and – by no means negligibly – then *the presence* of the metaphysical centre can be extended to the world, then the world can be imbued with light, even contemplated as light, and thus be in the spirit of Tradition.

Magical-metaphysical solipsism, as expounded by András László, is a radically non-dualistic view of consciousness (and thus of being). It points radically to the highest Goal of all possible aspirations, and states that the Goal is in the infinite, and at the same time is always present. For the present is the point which is symbolically "in contact" with the supratemporal and which, as a point, as a mathematical and symbolic point, includes the universe, that is, simultaneously all that is possible and all that is impossible in the sense of ordinary postulates. The limited human condition is an identification, one that inherently and immanently always implies a centre which, on the one hand, can only be grasped *hic et nunc*, and, on the other hand, is a representation of the metaphysical infinite. At the same time, self-identification as a human being – as a limited being – also implies a task, a task which can only be strictly the result of autonomous, volitional, and free determination, and therefore has nothing "obligatory" about it. The task is therefore to realize, through my self-experiential centre, the *suprastasis* which is the free subject of determination, i.e., the identifier. Once I have realized this, the contingent and the absolute coincide, and this coincides with the origin of all spiritual traditions.

In several traditions there is a motif of "hidden treasures," which means first of all that a master hides a key teaching in some physical form (scripture, object, medicine, ritual object) and at the same time determines who will find it in the future. This lineage is most stressed in Tibet, where the treasure is called a *terma* and the finder of the treasure is called a *tertön*. However, it is not only physical *terma*s, or *terma*s linked to a physical form, that can be placed, but also so-called psychic *terma*s (if we consider it more deeply, all *terma*s are essentially psychic – mental – in nature, because the *tertön* must understand the meaning they carry.) If a *terma* is of a mental nature, then the *tertön* "finds" it through an intuitive understanding, and passes this understanding on to his disciples. This circumstance alone constitutes a special mystery which leads its recipient to fundamental doctrines. For we must know that the hider of the *terma* is either an awakened person or a representative of the essence of awakening, so that the *terma* itself does not belong essentially to the circle of contingencies, but is a representative of unconditionality. The hider of the *terma*, the *terma* itself, as well as the *tertön* are at once representative of metaphysical awakening, and by extension, of the supratemporal. It is not difficult to see that there is *identity* in this chain, despite the differences in manifestation. The hider of the *terma*, the *terma* itself and the *tertön* are thus *one* beyond manifestation, although they have different faces in manifestation. What András László taught as solipsism is an essential doctrine, which is perennial in time and aeternal beyond time. The doctrine – and thus the Teacher himself – expresses a connection to the perennial-aeternal lineage in the sense of essential identity, where the person of the Teacher himself is subordinate to it, yet remains of the utmost importance.

Metaphysical tradition is based on spiritual realization, and the goal of this realization itself is awakening, absolute freedom, and immortality. All Order, all spiritual ascent, can only be real and appreciated in the light of this, converging towards it. Moreover, even happiness on earth, rightly understood, can only be established in its light. Every particular tradition converges towards this, and therefore every particular tradition is also a religion in the original sense of the word, otherwise it would not deserve the name of tradition. For this reason, the theoretical grounding of spiritual aims is decisive, because the definition of an aim cannot be a false doctrine, it cannot be based on any kind of error. If the orientation is wrong from the outset, the goal will certainly not be achieved, and however much the implementer may "err" in this respect, the result of his endeavor will be the opposite of the real goal. On the other hand, theory, orientation, can never be mere sophistry, but is already part of practice, since theory is the expression of a sensation of being, of a consciousness of being, and to this extent is itself a practical consequence. A correctly understood solipsism – i.e., what András László has explained and emphasized – cannot be a false doctrine, because it is fully verified at all levels of self-experience. I need do no more than absolutize what I have recognized at the beginning of the journey, so that the Truth must be present from the first moment in my experience and not be revealed "along the way." For as consciousness is non-dual, so is Truth.

It should be clear from the foregoing that any doctrine is only truly understood when the consideration of the doctrine is based not on "comparisons," but on our own autonomous judgement. This is especially true of traditional doctrines: we must therefore consider them by taking our own subjectivity as a basis and placing it in a hierarchy of consciousness on that basis. What is the basis of this hierarchy? The force with which the doctrine points to my own origin, to the situation in which I find myself, and to the most fundamental method of spiritual restoration. And the basis of this is what András László emphasised: being myself. The methods of spiritual realization must be sought in this light. If we have autonomy, we can enrich our insights with illustrations taken from particular traditions.

But something is not true because "someone else" said it — this is of utmost importance.

In the above lines, our intent was not to list and present one-by-one the doctrines of our teacher András László, but only to give a sense of the importance and weight of the thesis he considered the most important. We believe that the most appropriate way of expressing our respect for him is to understand and autonomously grasp what he taught and make it our own norm of life. András László's position on poetry was that a poem should record a momentary spiritual state of mind, and that this recording should open a path towards this spiritual state for the understanding reader. It is the same with the doctrine of solipsism: on the one hand, it records a vision, but this recording is not a solidification. Rather, it is the key to taking possession of this vision myself.

# THE IDEA OF TRADITION, ITS PRECEDENTS, AND SIGNS OF DECLINE

*Róbert Horváth*

### The Concepts of Tradition

Today's societies showcase many different notions of tradition, ranging from customs, folk traditions, and military tradition-keeping to the traditions of the world religions, and finally to Tradition (with a capital letter), which goes beyond religiosity. All of these are not just different traditions, but *different levels* of traditions. We will try to bring some order among the different concepts and meanings of tradition by distinguishing levels *T3*, *T2b*, *T2a*, and *T1*.

*T3* basically refers to customs, encompassing vast areas like the above-mentioned folk traditions or civil customs. René Guénon sharply contrasted customs with tradition.[407] This method may also have had something to do with the principle of "breaking habits" that from time to time played a prominent role in Sufism.[408] In any case, today we have no reason to think that certain customs have nothing to do with tradition, since they can involve fundamental and

---

[407] René Guénon, *Beavatás és spirituális megvalósítás*, trans. Tamás Bencze (Debrecen: Kvintesszencia Kiadó, 2006) 25-31. [René Guénon, *Initiation and Spiritual Realization*, trans. Henry D. Fohr (Hillsdale: Sophia Perennis, 2004), chapter 4: "Custom Versus Tradition"].

[408] Al-'Arabí ad-Darqáwí, *Az emlékezés rózsakertje: A lélekvezetés szúfí tudománya*, edited, introduction and notes by Ferenc Buji, trans. Ferenc Buji and István Medve (Budapest: Kairosz Kiadó, 2005), 351. [One hundred and seventy-fifth letter (*At-Tarjumana*)].

positive conservative aspects, such as the symbolic significance of ways of dressing.

T2, the next level of interpretation of tradition, refers to the religious traditions of mankind, also including the greatest spiritual traditions of humanity. To say "the greatest spiritual traditions of humanity" is not an exaggeration but an accurate designation, *even* in the scientific sense. It refers to the spiritual traditions emerging around the birth of – and unfolding within – the world religions existing in our day (Judaism, Brahmanism-Hinduism, Taoism and Confucianism, Zoroastrianism, Jainism, Buddhism, Christianity, Islam). We can add to these the philosophy of Western antiquity and Shamanism.[409] This will result in 8+2 world religions. Religions such as those of the Egyptian or Central and South American high cultures are, with all due respect, not included among world religions because they are no longer alive or are barely alive. Even though some great spiritual traditions were predominant for only a few hundred years (for example, the most-known exegetical period of Trika in India), their influence is still considerable and not only local. No post-modern or modern Western philosophy can dream of such a degree of permanence and fertilising effect, not to mention the several hundred years of history of the various literary traditions.

By *T2b* we mean general forms of traditions related to the world religions. András László made a distinction between confessional and religious religiosity. In applying this distinction, we make an exception for cases when *confessio* occasionally reached the superior level of religious traditions (*T2a*). The same can be said of devotionality, morality,

---

[409] On the former, see Huston Smith, "A nyugati filozófia mint nagy vallás," trans. Gábor Faragó, in *Tradíció: A Metafizikai Tradicionalitás Évkönyve* [Yearbook] (Debrecen, 2003), 155-172. [Huston Smith, "Western Philosophy as a Great Religion" in idem, *Essays on World Religion*, ed. M. Darrol Bryant (New York: Paragon House, 1992), 205-226]. On "Hyperborean Shamanism" beyond tribal shamanistic religions, see Frithjof Schuon, *Treasures of Buddhism* (Bangalore: Select Books, 1993), 177-178.

## The Idea of Tradition, Its Precedents, and Signs of Decline

dogmatics, or community rituals. In any case, *T2b* is the category under which we place the more popular religious traditions.

*T2a* includes not only devotional, moral, general theoretical, or ritualistic religious-spiritual traditions, but also, shall we say, metaphysical traditions featuring the most serious theological, dogmatical, liturgical, and symbological considerations, expositions, and practices. At this level of tradition, we can still rightfully speak of several different kinds of metaphysics: for example, Hindu, Tibetan, or Christian metaphysics (in the plural) – regardless of the otherwise not insignificant problem that the term metaphysics is understood differently by many; some consider it as a theoretical matter, others as purely ontology, excluding liturgical, symbological, or mythological considerations from its scope.

*T1* is the level of the ideal Tradition, with a capital 'T'. Here, metaphysics is essentially one and the same, beyond the plurality of ideas, where everything is wholly internal and related to the infinite, the inconceivable, the ultimate mystery. While at level *T2a* of the tradition, for example, in the case of the Christian sacred tradition, it is necessary to speak of temporal and external aspects, these no longer dominate at this level. At the same time, being tradition, it is engaging with the created, human, and historical world in a mysterious way. The Malays also made a distinction between Tradition in essence (*adat sebenar adat*) and tradition that has been handed down (*adat yang diadatkan* or *adat yang teradatkan*).[410]

According to Henry Corbin, the renowned scholar of Islam, tradition "is not a funeral procession," and in the words of Charles, Prince of Wales – now King Charles III – it

---

[410] Ferry Hidayat, "Hagyomány a perennializmus fényében. Első fejezet: Az örök Hagyomány," trans. Csaba Csík, *Magyar Hüperión: A jobboldali értelmiség folyóirata* X:2 (Budapest, Autumn-Winter 2022), 153. [Indonesian original: https://www.academia.edu/4031133/Adat_dalam_Sinaran_Perenialisme].

is none other than that which determines "what we 'can know' and what we 'can become'": Tradition – in one way or another, more or less clearly – is always "what enables us to turn towards God and reconnect with the divine."[411]

It is useful to understand the different circles and levels of tradition just categorised as organically interconnected. However, even if this method is theoretically correct, it runs into a number of problems. One of the foremost problems is that customary traditions do not lead to the highest, "essential," ideal and ultimate level of tradition. The folk tradition of pig slaughter, for example, rarely crosses over organically into religious traditions. Similarly, craft initiations are not the same as spiritual initiations in the stricter sense. Another problem is when there are attempts to turn customs that are only a few centuries old into an organic tradition. This is acceptable in the sphere of culture in its narrower sense, but not at the higher levels of tradition. For example, from a Roman Catholic point of view, Protestantism is not a tradition, as it contradicts the sacred tradition, and it also represents the "traditionalisation" of anti-traditional forces and phenomena. We will not go into this issue in detail here; suffice it to note that it is relatively often the case that anti-traditional factors also want to be integrated into the reality of tradition. Of course, it should be made clear that these cannot reach the level of *T1* or even *T2a*.

In spite of all these facts, many critics have not allowed for the discourse on Tradition (*T1*) to be considered valid. To criticise them only briefly in passing, we may say that, according to them, all things can have an underlying common concept, for example, behind every door there is "the door," except for tradition; according to them, there is

---

411 Charles, Prince of Wales, "Egy bevezetés," trans. István Umenhoffer, *Magyar Hüperión* X:2 (Budapest, Autumn-Winter 2022), 146. [English original: http://www.sacredweb.com/conference06/conference_introduction.html].

## The Idea of Tradition, Its Precedents, and Signs of Decline

no "Tradition," neither in an ideal nor an archetypal sense. T1 is a fantasy – according to them. Apart from the fact that most of these critics today stand for anti-mysticism and anti-intuition, they try to make a large population of university students believe that Tradition is a historical idea. They almost laugh out loud at the idea of "primordial tradition," as if Matgioi's and René Guénon's *Tradition primordiale* was the idea of a *historical* tradition from which all the great spiritual traditions of humanity have *historically* descended. Their clarity of vision is not very sharp with regard to the nature of ideas. Undoubtedly, there were and are temporal and spatial retro-projections with regard to the idea of Tradition in Guénon's works, and Béla Hamvas's grand "ancient, prehistoric humanity" is also one such, but the archaic has an essential meaning – beyond the temporal and spatial sense – of "primordial," and primordial means above all "of the first order," not merely ancient.[412] The idea of Tradition above religions is more complex than the "ancient" – it is still alive today. The same can be said of synonymous terms such as *philosophia perennis*, *religio perennis*, *sophia perennis*, integral tradition, or metaphysical tradition.

In short, the purpose of the Tradition with a capital 'T' (T1) is nothing less than man's radical striving for unity with the absolute (in theistic terms, with God), that is, the ultimate, the infinite, the inconceivable. This is not always achieved, neither in the past nor in the present, but it is common to all authentic religions and spiritual traditions, transcending their formal, temporal, and spatial specificities (sometimes capturing the end goal in a non-theistic way). *To aim at the absolute – that is Tradition. To represent this*

---

[412] Róbert Horváth, "A hagyomány ereje," *Magyar Hüperión* X:3 (Budapest, November 2013 - January 2014), 262. A great "Guénonian" philologist, Latinist, Catalanist, and Sanskritist, in one of his books, identified the primordial Tradition with the teachings of Śaṅkara and Ramaṇa Maharṣi, which is a very remarkable intuition, but certainly only one manifestation of it. See Bruno Hapel, *Râmana Maharshi et Shankara: La Tradition primordiale* (Paris: Guy Trédaniel Éditeur, 1991).

consistent pursuit in the world is traditionality,[413] which involves passing on effective tools and methods to support it. Problems of temporal origin, spatial relations, forms of teaching, their interactions and differences, variations in practical methods (T2) are secondary to Tradition, although interesting, important, and beautiful.

Today, there are different versions of traditionality, of the affirmation of tradition, of loyalty to tradition. In addition to traditional archery, there is, for example, Catholic traditionalism or universal traditionality (the latter meaning the affirmation of all authentic religious-spiritual traditions).

## Historical Background to the Idea of Tradition

Before one classifies as sectarian the adherents of *philosophia perennis*, *religio perennis*, *sophia perennis*, the integral-universal tradition, or the metaphysical tradition, one should reflect on the following facts.

In India, from about the 5th century to the 9th century (and later as well), several very different Tantric scriptures were written. The differences between them are almost as great as between the books of the *New Testament* and the *Old Testament*. However, Kashmiri exegetes between the 9th and 14th centuries accepted, affirmed, and analysed all of them, in several cases following simultaneously dualistic, dualistic-and-nondualistic, as well as non-dualistic *Tantras*. Likewise, there were "left-handed," "right-handed," and "mixed" spiritual directives (*ācāra*) or methods. The Hindu exegesis of

---

413 In the terminology applied by András László, the word "traditionality" is different from "traditionalism," just as in Guénon's case, "Tradition" is different from "traditionalism." We cannot judge exactly whether *traditionality* is entirely acceptable in English, but in any case, *traditionalitas* is far more than traditionalism, since it is neither merely human activity nor spiritual "representationalism," given that it does not exclude the condescension of God, divine grace, and all that is humanly unpredictable. This latter statement is not included in András László's key "agenda-setting" writing, "What is metaphysical traditionality?," *Őshagyomány* I:1 (Budapest, March 1991) 2-9.

## The Idea of Tradition, Its Precedents, and Signs of Decline

Somānanda, Utpaladeva, Abhinavagupta, Kṣemarāja, Jayaratha and others can be related to co-traditionality,[414] metaphysical traditionality, and the ideas of *philosophia perennis, religio perennis, sophia perennis,* and of an integral tradition.

Jayaratha's famous sentence from the 13th-century *Tantrālokavivekaḥ* ("Commentary on the Light on and of the Tantras"), a commentary on Abhinavagupta's *Tantrāloka* ("The Light on and of Tantra") written at the turn of the 10th and 11th centuries, reads: "Inside Kaula, outside Śaiva, Vedic in its worldly precepts" (*antaḥ kaulo bahiḥ śaivo lokācāre tu vaidikaḥ*).[415] The result is a synoptic view of very different religions and spiritual traditions as one, as beyond a religious inclusivism, an absorbing of all other religions and spiritual traditions. About 500 years later, the *Yonitantra* says similarly: "Inside Śākta, outside Śaiva, among men Vaiṣṇava, the Kaula wanders the Earth taking different forms."[416] The *Kaulopaniṣad*, which is difficult to chronologise, also confirms our theme: "Inside Śākta, outside Śaiva, in the world Vaiṣṇava, this is the rule."[417] The earlier *Kulārṇavatantra*, perhaps from before the 11th century, expresses the same: "As rivers flow directly or indirectly into the ocean, all teachings meet in the system of Kula. Just as the footprint of an elephant can encompass the footprint of every living being, so the Kula tradition

---

414 This is not an "intertraditional" relationship as Walter Heinrich called it, if we remember correctly, in his great book *Der Sonnenweg*, but rather an affirmation of different traditions beyond the geographical and historical links between them.

415 *The Tantrāloka of Abhinava Gupta, with Commentary by Rājānaka Jayaratha*, Vol. 3, ed. Paṇḍit Madhusudan Kaul Shāstrī, Kashmir Series of Texts and Studies 30 (Srinagar: Jammu and Kashmir Government, Research and Publication Department, 1921), ad *Tantrāloka* 4.24cd-25ab and 4.251ab. (Based on my Hungarian translation).

416 *The Yonitantra*, introduction and critical ed. J.A. Schoterman (New Delhi: Manohar Publications, 1980), 4.20. (Based on my Hungarian translation).

417 *Kaula and other Upanishads*, comm. Bhāskararāya, ed. Sîtârâma Shâstrî (Calcutta–London: Âgamânusandhâna Samiti–Luzac & Co., 1922 / Tantrik Texts 11), *Kaulopaniṣad* 9. (Based on my Hungarian translation).

encompasses all directions."⁴¹⁸ The Śaiva, Śākta, Kaula, Vaidika (Vedic) and Vaiṣṇava are very different lines of traditions. They are so different that they can be seen as separate traditions and religions. Their scriptures differ from each other not only as the books within the *Old Testament*, but also compared to the diversity of the *Old* and *New Testaments*. Nevertheless, the texts quoted above demonstrate the deep-rooted actuality of a unified view of the different religions, traditions, scriptures, and commentaries, which goes back a long time. Consequently, the idea of a metaphysical tradition encompassing different traditions and religions is not essentially new and without precedent – nor is it merely a matter of tolerance or ecumenism.

Some *Mahāpurāṇas* demonstrate a similar approach and orientation. For example, the *Kūrmapurāṇa*, as it is known today, developed between the 8th and 15th centuries, professes the unity of two distinct Hindu religions, the Vaiṣṇava and the Śaiva spiritual traditions: it considers Śiva and Viṣṇu as aspects of the same God.⁴¹⁹ Hence the Purāṇic name Harihara for Śiva, where Hari means Viṣṇu and Hara means Śiva. The God Śiva (Hara) is also none other than Viṣṇu (Hari). The respective iconography depicts Harihara in a way similar to the two-faced Western depictions of Janus.

The situation is similar in the case of the work *Sarvadarśanasiddhāntasaṁgrahaḥ* ("Summary of the realisation of all philosophical views") attributed to Ādi Śaṅkarācārya, which places not only Indo-Hindu but also Jain and Buddhist traditions in its hierarchy, according to the author's knowledge of them.⁴²⁰ In this case, it can no

---

418 *Kulārṇavatantra*, trans. Ram Kumar Rai, Tantra Granthamala 5 (Varanasi: Prachya Prakashan, 2010), 2.12-13. (Based on my Hungarian translation).

419 See *The Kūrmapurāṇam*, introduction and critical ed. C.R. Swaminathan (Delhi: Nag Publishers, 2002), I.9.

420 Sankara, *A védánta filozófiája és más bölcseleti rendszerek*, Hungarian translation with partial Sanskrit text, preface, commentary and notes by Ernő Fajd (Budapest: Farkas Lőrinc Imre Kiadó, 1996). The *saṁgraha*s of many other great Hindu teachers were written in the spirit of co-traditionality.

## The Idea of Tradition, Its Precedents, and Signs of Decline

longer be assumed that it was only a question of affirming unity within a single religion or line of tradition, namely Hinduism, about a thousand years ago.[421]

In the 19th century, a similar orientation developed within Tibetan Mahāyāna-Vajrayāna Buddhism as had previously developed among the great Śaiva-Śākta exegetes of Kashmir. The Rimé spiritual current saw and represented the practice of all four Tibetan Mahāyāna monastic orders as one. The meanings of the name *ris med* are: unprejudiced and impartial, all-encompassing, boundless, universal. A follower of this spiritual current is not required to follow all the different Tibetan traditions specifically, but they are required to recognise the validity of all the main teachings and practices.

The Dzogchen tradition, similarly to the aforementioned *Sarvadarśanasiddhāntasaṁgrahaḥ*, goes beyond the concept of unitarity within a specific religion in that it is as much concerned with the ancient Bon religion as with Tibetan Buddhism. Also similar is the position taken by a 19th-century Bengali saint, Rāmakṛṣṇa, who at different times in his life was equally a follower of Brahman, Kālī, Allāh, and Jesus Christ.[422] Only his adherents began to claim internationalist, liberal "interfaith dialogue," a "tolerance" that is certainly not saying enough in spiritual terms.[423] The case of another popular saint of India, Sāi Baba of Sirdī (c. 1838-1918),

---

421 It is not known whether Ādi Śaṅkarācārya or one of his successors wrote the latter work. It is probably a later *śaṅkarācārya*, but this does not change the fact that it is the same Advaita Vedānta spiritual lineage, and therefore also related to its root teacher.

422 See *Śrī Rāmakṛṣṇa evangéliuma*, trans. Mónika Tamás (Budapest: private publication, 2020). [Original English publication date: 1942].

423 Religious tolerance is too general and moral in its character to represent true universality. We are not talking about dialogue, but about a more profound and higher identification and experiencing, about reaching a transcendent, effective universality.

is similar: like the internationally much better known Kabīr, he was both Muslim and Hindu.[424]

Moreover, we also find similar antecedents of universal traditionality in the West. "The Rosicrucians are supposed to adopt the clothes of the countries to which they travel or where they take residence: in other words, they must choose an external way of appearance proper to the place and the environment in which they are supposed to act."[425] In essence, this was the same principle of Count Cagliostro in the 18th century. The first half of the quote shows that it was not just a way of opportunistic conformity: "I consciously participate in absolute existence, adapting my actions to the environment around me."[426] Earlier, in the 16th century, the Catholic Agostino Steuco (Eugubinus) applied the concept of *philosophia perennis* – later also used by Leibniz – which can be traced back to antecedents such as the works of Marsilio Ficino and Giovanni Pico della Mirandola.[427] Nicolaus Cusanus, in his *De pace fidei* ("On the Peace of Faith"), in 1453, took a keen interest in the Greek, Roman, Arab, Indian, Chaldean, Jewish, Scythian, Gallic, Persian, Syrian, Spanish, Turkish, Germanic, Tartar,

---

[424] Not to be confused with the miracle worker Sai Baba. See Arthur Osborne, *A csodálatos Szái Bábá. Egy modernkori szent élete és csodái*, trans. Borbála Kasza (s.l.: private publication, 2022). [Original English publication: 1957].

[425] Julius Evola, *A Grál misztériuma és a ghibellin birodalmi idea*, trans. András Bódvai (Debrecen: Kvintesszencia Kiadó, 2001), 201-202. [Julius Evola, *The Mystery of the Grail: Initiation and Magic in the Quest for the Spirit*, trans. Guido Stucco (Rochester: Inner Traditions, 1997), 161]. Perhaps there is no need to mention this, but nevertheless, by referring to the Rosicrucians, the author does not mean to imply that there is any connection with modern Rosicrucians.

[426] Alessandro di Cagliostro, "Vagyok, aki vagyok," trans. Borbála Soós, *Tradíció: A Metafizikai Tradicionalitás Évkönyve* [Yearbook] (Debrecen, 2000), 125. For the full context, see 125-127. [Cited by Marc Haven: *Le Maître Inconnu: Cagliostro. Étude historique et critique sur la haute magie* (Paris: Éditions Pythagore, 1932), 282-284].

[427] Charles B. Schmitt, "Perennial Philosophy: From Agostino Steuco to Leibniz," *Journal of the History of Ideas* XXVII:4 (Philadelphia, PA, October-December 1966), 506-507, 515-531.

## The Idea of Tradition, Its Precedents, and Signs of Decline

Armenian, Czech, and English notions and conceptions of God. The Cardinal's point of view, bearing a sincere interest, is sympathetic, informed, and integrative with respect to other traditions and "sages of nations."[428] In essence, he was already taking an inclusivist position, wanting to embrace everything as Catholic – as Juan Donoso Cortés[429] did 400 years later –, but his affirmation of different genuine spiritual traditions was clearer than it is nowadays.

It is not only through considering the works of particular authors or currents that we can see that Western and Eastern Christianity once respected and integrated the knowledge of many ancient authors, as well as elements of the traditions of Celtic, Germanic, Gallic, Nitrian Desert, or other indigenous peoples. In the case of the recognition of certain paraliturgical traditions, this is still church practice today. Even if over the course of history the Church has moved away from this attitude and became increasingly proselytising, in many manifestations of the Lord Jesus Christ we can see real signs of a universal orientation, not merely inclusivist or exclusivist. This universalism, or more precisely, universality, has nothing to do with internationalism, globalism, or today's irresponsible ecumenism, which is largely the result of a loss of identity.[430] It is more than

---

[428] Nicolaus Cusanus, *De pace fidei. A hit békéjéről. Latin és magyar nyelvű kiadás*, trans. Bálint Németh (Debrecen: Kvintesszencia Kiadó, 2016). [Latin text available online: https://cusanus-portal.de/content/werke.php?werk=15].

[429] Juan Donoso Cortés, "Esszé a katolicizmusról, a liberalizmusról és a szocializmusról fő alapelveik tekintetében. Két fejezet," trans. Edith Szepesi, *Magyar Hüperión* V:3 (Budapest, Autumn 2017) 319-320. [*Essay on Catholicism, Liberalism and Socialism, Considered in their Fundamental Principles*, Book I, Chapter 2. Original Spanish edition: 1851].

[430] At times, Western Traditionalist writers such as Ananda K. Coomaraswamy, Marco Pallis, and Frithjof Schuon have also used the term ecumenism in a positive sense, but this had nothing to do with the Parliament of the World's Religions or the later Second Vatican Council. The Hungarian Béla Hamvas has also been accused of internationalism because of his broad vision, but these are superficial "analogies."

just a dialogue between religions and different churches. There is an *oikumenē* in the spiritual sense beyond one's own religion, which essentially is *our universal nature and essence*. And can there be a better example of co-traditionality that has existed since the beginning than the *Holy Bible*, which binds together the scriptures of two *distinctly different* religions without any syncretism?[431]

We can also find the latter tendency in Islam. Jesus, although seen as only one of the prophets, and the Virgin Mary, although only as a saint, are included in the Muslim revelation, where we read, among other things: "So be steadfast in faith in all uprightness 'O Prophet' – the natural Way of Allah which He has instilled in 'all' people. Let there be no change in this creation of Allah. That is the Straight Way, but most people do not know." And further: "Indeed, We sent before you 'O Prophet' messengers, each to their own people, and they came to them with clear proofs."[432]

There are many parallels to be drawn from traditional Western and Eastern religions in relation to the idea of Tradition, but this is perhaps enough in response to the accusation that metaphysical traditionality, universal traditionality, perennialism, etc., is an entirely new idea and aspiration dating from the 20th century.

Tradition is not a syncretistic idea or one that would provide a synthesis from an outsider perspective. András László's word is synoptic (co-optive). He distinguished three degrees in this respect. The first is the *positional synopsis*,

---

[431] This question tracing back through history has, of course, nothing to do with the present-day perversion when many people take a particular pleasure in talking about Judeo-Christianity. These are two separate sets of traditions and religions, even if Christianity had the universality (and not just inclusiveness) to incorporate the holy books of Judaism into its own.

[432] *Holy Qur'ān* 30:30 and 30:47 [https://quran.com/30].

## The Idea of Tradition, Its Precedents, and Signs of Decline

which sees the validity of Tradition (i.e., not just of one's own religious tradition) in terms of a particularly highlighted tradition. The second one posits Tradition by keeping in mind the *totality* of traditions. The third one derives it from *the integral essence of* traditions.[433] Since all three are synopses, true seeing together and seeing as one, they are not just degrees. Without positionality, integrality is false, or at least superficial; real universality is not possible when positions are disregarded. At the same time, the aspiration of universal traditionality to be "fully Hindu, Buddhist, Muslim, Christian, Jain..." (András László) is rare. Usually, only the synopsis of one or two religions was achieved, and even that from a positional point of view: in the case of Henri Le Saux (Abhiṣiktānanda), Bede Griffith (Dayānanda) and others, from a Christian perspective on Hinduism; for Siddheśvarānanda, from a Hindu perspective on Carmelite mysticism; for the Japanese "Kyoto School," with respect to Christian mysticism and Western philosophy; for Hugo Enomiya-Lassale, from a Christian perspective on Zen Buddhism. Father Seraphim Rose became an Orthodox Christian through his knowledge of several religions, without denying or belittling them. Arthur Osborne, an early adherent of Guénon, became a follower of Ramaṇa Maharṣi's esoteric, *ātman*-centric teachings, but in editing Ramanasramam's journal, *The Mountain Path*, he always published essays on ancient Western, Christian, and Muslim subjects.

In recent decades, comparative theology has been remarkable, especially as practised by Francis Xavier Clooney, who affirmed the Vaiṣṇava tradition and certain forms of Kālī worship from a Catholic position. Also noteworthy is

---

[433] András László, "Különböző kézirattöredékekből," in Róbert Horváth and Tibor Murányi (eds.), *Láthatatlan rezgéseim tánca minden: A hetvenéves László András köszöntése* (Budapest: Aktémosyné, 2012), 49.

John R. Dupuche, an Australian Catholic priest, who has taken an interest in Hindu Tantrism and has translated from Sanskrit into English the 29th chapter of *Tantrāloka* and Jayaratha's commentary on it. Earlier, the Hungarian Béla Hamvas went beyond positional synopsis and – as in the case of several 20-century Traditionalist authors – it is virtually impossible that he meant another God, a different God, by Allāh, Śiva, Viṣṇu, the chief deities of antiquity, the One, the *brahman*, the *buddha*, the *dao, nirvāṇa, mahāśūnyatā* and other designated traditional notions (whether personal or impersonal).

Ernst Lothar Hoffmann (Anāgarikā Govinda lama) saw Theravāda, Mahāyāna, and Vajrayāna Buddhism as *degrees*, while affirming *all three*. We have long known similar all-affirming but hierarchical views, for example, of Christianity in relation to Judaism (including Jesus Christ's own way compared to that of John the Baptist), of Śaivism in general in relation to Vedic Brahmanism, of Hindu Kula and Trika in relation to the Vedicised Śaiva Siddhānta. These traditions have placed themselves higher, but not like Protestantism in Christianity. It is not about religious conflicts and wars, but about a *generally hierarchical and gradualist view of tradition*. This mainly concerned the ways and methods within each tradition, not the hierarchy of religions. For example, in Bon and Nyingma Buddhism, Dzogchen interpreted itself as a realisation of self above cause and effect (*atiyoga*), which transcends both Vajrayāna Buddhism and the highest *Tantras*.[434] It has placed at the centre a state (*rig pa*) from which the transcendental virtues (*prajñāpāramitā*) are also directly and spontaneously realised, because they are inherent in it. The situation is similar in

---

[434] Longchen Rabjam, *The practice of Dzogchen*, trans. Tulku Thondup, trans. and ed. Harold Talbott (Ithaca: Snow Lion Publications, 1989), 3-4; *Bonpo Dzogchen teachings according to Lopon Tenzin Namdak*, trans. and ed. John Myrdhin Reynolds (Kathmandu: Vajra Publications, 2006), 9-10, 15-19, 22-24.

the Advaita Vedānta, Kula, and Trika traditions.[435] The arguments of these traditions all point towards *T1*.

In any case, the latter hierarchisations justify talking about different levels and pinnacles of tradition – not in the modern but in the traditional sense. In the Christian tradition, for example, this is the case of apophatic theology, which, according to several church fathers, goes beyond – though does not exclude – the more commonly known cataphatic theology and its practical approaches. Advaita Vedānta, Trika, and Dzogchen also claim to be the highest path, *but they practice the methods of the lower paths as well.* Dzogchen masters were happy to do the lower preparation and Tantric purification practices for the rest of their lives. The masters of *Rāja Yoga* have voluntarily observed and subjected themselves to in-depth consideration the two lowest Yogic degrees: the prohibitions (*yama*) and the precepts (*niyama*). This was the case for all these traditions with respect to morality and collective rites.

## Some Signs of the Decline of Traditionalism

In a certain sense, René Guénon did nothing more than try to bring to light all that can be considered as of the highest order in the traditional religions. To emphasise this, he distinguished between religiosity and metaphysics, religion and Tradition. However, he did not separate them definitively in the form of some kind of extreme dualism.[436] True, some

---

435 On the superiority of the Advaita Vedānta, see Sankara, *A védánta filozófiája és más bölcseleti rendszerek*, 104, 119. On the superiority of the Kula and the Trika, Abhinavagupta, *Tantrāloka* 13.300b-302. [https://gretil.sub.uni-goettingen.de/gretil/corpustei/transformations/html/sa_abhinavagupta-tantrAloka.htm]. On the superiority of the Trika, see Abhinavagupta, *Parā-trīśikā-Vivaraṇa: The Secret of Tantrick Mysticism*, trans. Jaideva Singh, Sanskrit corr. Swami Lakshmanjee, ed. Bettina Bäumer (Delhi: Motilal Banarsidass Publishers Private Limited, 2014), 236, 158 (introduction to verse 19 of the *Parātrīśikā*).

436 For example, he acknowledged the need for traditional exoterism and rituals. See René Guénon, *Initiation and Spiritual Realization*, chapters 7 and 9. Many other passages could be quoted in this connection.

of his distinctions – for example between mysticism and metaphysics, initiation and Christianity, or salvation and Liberation – were too markedly divisive, but such could have been due to the lack of information and sources about Christianity at the time, and to his own individual situation (Islam, Egypt).[437] Guénon nevertheless made use of the rhetorical and pedagogical possibilities offered by antagonisms (a traditional method), although he was not a dualist. From a distinctly spiritual-metaphysical point of view, the latter can be easily ascertained by a close reading of his works, and by paying attention not only to his criticisms of the modern world, but also to his spiritual assertions and teachings.

Guénon thus hierarchised the levels within religion, putting the emphasis on their highest elements pointing towards *T1*.[438] All typifications and dualities on his part were intended to serve this purpose. When he did not speak specifically of the primordial Tradition, he usually meant *T2a* as tradition. In achieving the goal of elevating *T1*, *he mainly emphasised metaphysics, esoterism, primordial state and Tradition, initiation, spiritual-metaphysical realisation, and the role of symbols and centers of fundamental importance.*

---

437 Here we can mention other points, such as his underappreciation of magic, philosophy, or religious studies. However, we would like to draw the reader's attention to the fact that the way Guénon understood and explained these concepts is logically consistent and fully coherent. To recognise this, we need to put aside our own value judgements, attractions, and repulsions in relation to these categories. However, his categorisations are not perfect (like any categorisations in general). Where Guénon's conceptual classifications do not hold their own is mostly in the history and phenomenology of religion. – When we once asked András László if he had any reservations about the work of Guénon and Evola, he replied that he had only one: their tendency to typify. He knew, of course, that classifications and typifications are inevitable at the beginning, during the learning phase, and that refining categories is an important part of the recipient's task and intellectual journey. However, in order to do this, it is essential to set them up and understand them precisely.

438 Cf. "In our understanding – and in line with our approach – tradition always means metaphysical tradition, and metaphysics always means traditional metaphysics." András László, "What is metaphysical traditionality?", 2-3.

He used the term *esōteria*, of course, not in the modern sense, but etymologically: the Greek word means "more internal." To deny traditional esoterism would be to claim that religion has only levels directed to the masses, without inner planes or deeper meanings, i.e., no core, just the skin. The affirmation of traditional esoterism can be derived not only from a false elitism, but from a multitude of facts of religious history, religious philosophy, and religious phenomenology (while intending to preserve the deepest-highest layers of religions). If we deny it, we hold that religions do not have deeper and higher levels, and that all religions are – moreover, *ab ovo* – only such as the majority practice them today.

Guénon's concept of initiation is fundamentally correct, true in terms of the structure of all its variants, and, given the limitations of the period in which he formulated it (c. 1932-1950), also brilliant. Whatever is problematic – apart from readers' interpretations – is due to a similar reason as in the case of his understanding of mysticism: many texts and information that are known today were not available then. For example, he was not familiar with Tibetan and some Hindu forms of initiation. As a consequence, he overrepresents the aspect of initiation as a single event without sufficiently emphasising its processual nature (although he does have this in mind in the idea of the transition from virtual to effective initiation). The Tibetans had many masters and received many initiations – confrontations and empowerments. This was also essentially the situation in the ancient West. Guénon was also not well acquainted with the concept of initiation in Christianity, which, after the initial rite, is a process, continuing in the Christian sacraments and their associated contemplations, such as the androgynous sacrament of marriage, ritual penance, the recurrent Eucharist and, in Eastern Christianity, the almost continual Jesus Prayer. It should be noted, however, that he was preoccupied with the questions around Christian initiation towards the end of his life in Cairo. He inspired the Muslim Michel Vâlsan to do research on the subject and inform him of his findings.[439]

As far as metaphysics is concerned, Guénon has provided an essentially complete and impeccable doctrine in this respect, as much as can be expounded at all. He was the greatest Western metaphysician of the 20th century, who should have been, and must be, acknowledged in terms of philosophical metaphysics as well. Despite his rational explanations, he maintained that metaphysics is a mystery, and a great mystery at that. He did not reduce it to a theory, to a mere abstraction, a sort of theoretical style. Nor has he degraded it to an ontology, a theory of being and existence, as if it were simply that, or merely the apex of the hierarchies of existence. He posited it as something above existence and ontology, which demands a "leap" to break away from and surpass the level of existential states and ontology as a whole, and to progress towards unconditionality, towards the unconditional. Some of his expressions like Non-Being, Metaphysical Zero, or Universal Possibility, apart from *not* signifying nothingness and annihilation, are not definitively divorced from human existence, ontology, or traditional cosmologies, into which, according to him – at key points such as the winter solstice – metaphysics is seen to be projected, just as into the essence of certain central or axial traditional symbols.

---

[439] Michel Vâlsan, "Keresztény beavatás: Válasz Marco Pallisnak," trans. Endre Horváth, *Magyar Hüperión* V:4 (Budapest, Winter 2017), 438-460. ["L'Initiation chrétienne. Réponse à M. Marco Pallis," *Études traditionnelles* 389-390 (Paris, May-June and July-August 1965), 148-184]. See idem, "La question de l'Initiation chrétienne. Mise au point," *Études traditionnelles* 406-408 (March-August 1968); "Études et Documents d'Hésychasme" in ibid; idem, "À propos de l'Hésychasme," *Études traditionnelles* 411 (January-February 1969). We are grateful to Mr. Claudio Mutti for providing us with copies of these studies at the time. – Later, Jean Hani, Jean Borella, Wolfgang Smith, and James S. Cutsinger clarified (better than Vâlsan) the questions of the relationship between esoterism, initiation, and the Christian tradition.

We would now like to highlight three circles of his followers who have deviated from the mission of highlighting *T1* and moved too far downstream from *T1*.

Frithjof Schuon emerged around 1933 around the journal *Le Voile d'Isis* – later *Études traditionnelles*[440] – and can be said to have been the first to recognise that what Guénon taught should be more strongly and forcefully represented on the strength of its indisputable truth. Personally, and individually, Schuon gradually slipped into a kind of "representationalism," but the contemplative basis of his writings and later books, his less typifying and rationalising style than Guénon's, and his more artistic character, allowed him to clarify certain details, in addition to raising new themes. In this way, he made clearer the links between *T1* and *T2a*, the practical connections between esoterism and exoterism, the significance of Christianity, and more. András László – who did not like him very much – said that Schuon's greatest merit was that he never played one tradition or religion off against another, never argued one against the other, and that he brought religions such as Shinto or North American Indian beliefs (which Guénon had only just mentioned) into the sphere of investigation and reflection.

Those who, until Schuon's emergence, thought in terms of esoterism or metaphysics as a goal, largely imagined that exoterism was exclusively opposed to esoterism, that there was a crucial gap between religion and Tradition, and that we should seek separate esoteric directions to achieve the end goal. Schuon has made it more or less clear that these two are not entirely separate realms, that religious dogmas, teachings, formulas, and practices can be experienced esoterically,

---

[440] Jean Reyor, *Emlékeim René Guénonról és az Études traditionnelles-ről* (Pécs: Varázsló Macska Kiadó, 2023), 90. [In French: http://dossierschuonguenonislam.blogspirit.com/files/Dossier%20confidentiel%20inedit.pdf]. Despite its value as a historical source, this document should be treated with reservations, for example because it is explicitly hostile to Schuon, whose books it does not even examine.

and that the depth of their experience is what constitutes esotericism in religions, nothing else. In this respect, not only the *mantras*, but also canonised prayers such as the Lord's Prayer can be experienced both exoterically and esoterically.

Marco Pallis, who became a follower of Schuon despite his advanced age, was also right to speak of an "eso-exoteric structure" in the Christian tradition.[441] The same is true for Titus Burckhardt, Seyyed Hossein Nasr, and others who have stressed the importance of religious practice alongside esoterism. However, there is a serious problem here, to which they seem not to have paid sufficient attention: the difference between *T2b* and *T2a*. Indeed, emphasising the direct transition between *T2* and *T1* may harm the primacy of *T1* if *T2* is dominated by *T2b*. This happened several times throughout the history of Traditionalism in the 20th century. Many Traditionalists came to see religious conversion as initiation, whereas Guénon was not talking about religiosity, but initiation. There may be a connection between regular religious conversion and initiation, but the two are not the same, neither categorically nor in practice. And this is precisely where the story of Western Traditionalism, which culminated after Guénon's death, began, with the focus shifting towards the lower levels of tradition and religiosity.

René Guénon abhorred religious sentimentalism. This, he believed, was one of the main reasons for the separation of religion from deeper Tradition, with the later consequence of the intellectual decline of religion. Although he acknowledged and even demanded *devotion*, alongside and in the midst of all intellectual activity, he considered sentimentality as the main cause of the degeneration of religions, as well as the substitution of emotions and externals for cognition and understanding. Yet this is what usually happens: no matter

---

[441] Marco Pallis, "A Templom függönye: Tanulmány a keresztény iniciációról," trans. László Virág, *Pannon Front* 34 (Budapest, August 2001), 14. [Marco Pallis, "The Veil of the Temple: A Study of Christian Initiation," *Tomorrow* 12:2 (Spring 1964), also published at http://studiesincomparativereligion.com/public/articles/The_Veil_of_the_Temple-by_Marco_Pallis.aspx]

how much one tries to emphasise the differences between them, *T2b* and *T2a* are so intertwined that there is hardly any (valid, valuable) mention of pure *T1*. It is true that without faith there is no knowledge, but if faith does not lead to effective knowledge, it easily becomes sentimentalism. The level of *T1* is then already inaccessible. The language and way of thinking of Schuon's books – while recognising their essential contemplative value and artistic character – is related to this problem. Schuon and his followers have sometimes degraded the idea of Tradition, of *T1* to *T2*.

Martin Lings writes:

> If it can be said that Schuon's work is summed up in the title of his book *Esoterism as Principle and As Way*, the same could not be said of Guénon, because he does not expound esoterism as way. Method is not one of his themes, nor was it his function to be instructive about the spiritual life in general. Nonetheless, it would be possible to sum up the main part of his work in the words 'no esoterism without both principle and way', for although he did not write *about* the way, he always wrote *with a view to* the way.[442]

Now, Lings, with all due respect, was not right that Guénon did not explain "esoterism as a way" or give guidance on spiritual life in general. For him, the way was precisely the *practical and ongoing focus on* the ultimate metaphysical principle or metaprinciple, and he taught this as a primary *method*.[443] Guénon was perfectly aware that religious methods, techniques, and tools are no longer purely in the spirit of *T1* and that they easily – in fact, too often – end up drowned in *T2b*.

Would prayer, for example, which Schuon taught as a method, really always be so pure, esoteric, and metaphysical?

---

442 Martin Lings, "The Tenth Man, by Robin Waterfield," *Avaloka: A Journal of Traditional Religion and Culture* II:2 (1988), 28-29.

443 See, for example, what he said about "concentration" in his lecture "A keleti metafizika" in René Guénon, *Metafizikai írások I*, trans. Pál Darabos (Budapest: Farkas Lőrinc Imre Kiadó, 1993), 16. [René Guénon, "Eastern Metaphysics," in *Studies in Hinduism*, trans. Henry D. Fohr (Gent, NY: Sophia Perennis, 2001), 94].

We do not deny that it can be effectively esoteric, but the path is not yet the Principle and the method is not the same as reaching the destination, just as *T2b* is not *T1*. Although *T2b*, together with *T2a*, can help one reach one's goal, it is not the goal (just as *T1* is only a method to reach the goal). Actually, Schuon did not do a good job of hierarchising the spiritual-metaphysical methods of realisation, which according to Trika are related to the human point of view (*āṇavopāya*), to the aspect and realities of *śakti* (*śāktopāya*), and specifically to the perspective, reality, and essence of eternity, the Lord God (*śāmbhavopāya*). Of course, we are not demanding of Schuon a doctrinal knowledge of the Trika tradition; we are merely saying that he associated human methods with the ultimate methods as well as Śaktic methods (at a rather low level of interpretation of *śakti*).

In Professor Nasr's case, too, there is a lack of the aspects of *śāmbhavopāya*. For example, in an interview he said: Guénon "never practised" Hinduism.[444] Beyond the question of how the Professor knows this with such certainty, the problem is more serious. What is practice in a specifically spiritual-metaphysical sense? There is formal practice on the one hand and informal practice on the other. The importance attached to the latter cannot be denied in the case of Guénon, since the idea of metaphysical realisation that he puts forward is largely one of informal practice, of pure cognition and knowledge. *T2* as a whole requires the fulfilment of a set of formal conditions that one should not shy away from, but *T1* implies unconditionality, the surpassing of conditions, and is, therefore, not a function of religious practice. A typical task of metaphysical realisation is to be free from conditions, and to keep it within reach and sustain it even in circumstances where one has no way to perform rituals or say formal prayers. In short, this can be ensured

---

444 Jay Kinney, "Az iszlám, a hagyomány és a Nyugat," trans. Tibor Imre Baranyi, *Pannon Front* IV:3 (Budapest, June 1998), 28. [Jay Kinney, "Islam, Tradition, and the West: A *Gnosis* Interview with Seyyed Hossein Nasr," *Gnosis Magazine* (California, Autumn 1995), 54].

by the recognition of the importance of unconditionality, by practising independently of conditions, and by following the *metaphysical way of realisation*. Every time we fall asleep, at night, especially in deep sleep, we can no longer continue our religious practices, we cannot say our prayers, yet we can have full certainty of metaphysical reality if we make the right preparations, establishing its unconditionality during waking states. So religious practices are – in part – indeed separate from metaphysical realisation. Anyone who does not think so is narrowing down the possibilities for realisation.

We are now apparently taking an excursion. In the early 2000s, we had a strange experience: on an exclusive Traditionalist mailing list of *religioperennis.org*, Tamás Bencze translated the beginning of one of our writings ("On the problems of the international reception of Julius Evola"), in which Julius Evola was mentioned alongside René Guénon and Frithjof Schuon. A well-known supporter of Schuon replied that this was the first time he had seen Evola's name written alongside such names. The story is quite typical of what is at stake here: for some, traditionality ceases to exist if religiosity is not dominant. But this should not be the case. As we shall see, Guénon himself has proved this.

In 1925-1926, Evola and Guénon had a very heated debate in the pages of *L'Idealismo realistico*,[445] which Evola continued to reel off in *Krur* (1929) and much later, unfortunately, in *Il cammino del Cinabro* (1972), but in 1938 he reconciled and wrote a positive review of Guénon's *L'Homme et son devenir selon le Vêdânta* (*Man and His Becoming According to the Vedānta*).[446] Between 1934 and 1940, he involved

---

445 Reprinted in Julius Evola, *L'Idealismo Realistico: 1924-1928*, ed. Gian Franco Lami (Todi: Antonio Pellicani Editore, 1997, 87-113). [In English see https://www.scribd.com/document/618358390/Evola-A-Controversy-About-the-Vedanta]. Previous edition: Julius Evola and René Guénon, *Polemica sulla metafisica indiana*, Quaderni del Basilisco (Genova: Il Basilisco, 1987). This edition is not recommended because of the unfair preface.

446 Reprinted in Julius Evola, *Esplorazioni e disamine. Gli scritti di "Bibliografia fascista,"* vol. I, ed. Claudio Mutti, Collana "Sophia" (Parma: Edizioni all'Insegna del Veltro, 1994), 163-171.

Guénon in the "Diorama filosofico" column of the journal *Regime fascista*, where 24 of his writings were published, presumably translated by Evola.[447] The later part of their correspondence is even more interesting, because despite all their disagreements, Guénon clearly liked Evola.[448] This also covered things that other 20th-century Traditionalist writers criticised Evola for overemphasising: royalty, temporal power, Western traditions. Of course, Coomaraswamy, Burckhardt, Nasr, and even Schuon wrote positive things about Evola's work,[449] but Guénon valued Evola more than them. What could be the reason for this?

While acknowledging the possibility of error, we think that, beyond the human and collaborative relationship between them, it was above all Evola's esoterism that Guénon found valuable: an esoterism that, although linked to religions (Hermetism, the mystery religions of Rome, Buddhism,

---

447 René Guénon, *Precisazioni necessarie: I saggi di Diorama*, Il Cavallo alato (Padova: Edizioni di Ar, 1988). On Guénon's interest in the Right, see also the above-cited Jean Reyor, *Emlékeim René Guénonról és az Études traditionnelles-ről*, 91-92.

448 René Guénon, *Lettere a Julius Evola, 1930-1950*, introduction, trans., and notes Renato Del Ponte (S.l.: Edizioni Arktos, 2005).

449 In his 1942 work, the elder Coomaraswamy condemns Evola for reversing the traditional hierarchy of high priest and king and placing the Regnum above the Sacerdotium, while at the same time praising the chapter on "Man and Woman" in *Rivolta contro il mondo moderno*, translated into English by his wife. See Ananda K. Coomaraswamy, *Spiritual Authority and Temporal Power in the Indian Theory of Goverment*, ed. Keshavram Iengar and Rama P. Coomaraswamy (New Delhi – Bombay – Calcutta – Madras: Indira Gandhi National Centre for Arts, 1993), 1 and 39-49. In 1962, Burckhardt criticised Evola for his positive image of machines and modern architecture in *Cavalcare la tigre*, but often mentions his "masterful criticism," "acuity," "pertinent responses," and "overall correctness." See Titus Burkhardt, "Tigrislovaglás," trans. Norbert Németh, *Tradíció: A Metafizikai Tradicionalitás Évkönyve* [Yearbook] (Debrecen, 1999), 175-176. [Titus Burckhardt, "Riding the Tiger," in *Mirror of the Intellect* (Cambridge: Quinta Essentia, 1987), 68-69]. In 1967, Schuon criticised Evola for putting the kṣatriyas above the brāhmaṇas and for considering the spiritual role of the West more important than that of the East, and that he "chooses Mussolini" [sic!]. Frithjof Schuon, "A Face of Eternal Wisdom [three interviews with Schuon by Jean Biès]," trans. Patrick Laude, *Sophia: The Journal of Traditional Studies* IV:2 (1998), 11. In a German-language letter written in Pully in 1979, he describes Evola as a "philosopher of culture" [sic!] (alongside Leopold Ziegler), but adds

Hindu Tantrism), is not bound to religious concepts, religious expressions, methods, techniques, and tools. Evola's conception was in some respects closer to Guénon's idea of *T1* than the complex *T2* of Schuon and his followers, of whom the uncomprehending and ungrateful posterity, of course, "found out" that he was not really religious.[450]

How did Guénon put it?

> Words, symbolic signs, rites, or preparatory methods of various kinds have no other raison d'être or function; as we have already said, they are supports and nothing else. [...] At a certain stage all multiplicity disappears, but at that stage, the individual and contingent means will have played their part. This part, which is unnecessary to enlarge upon, is compared in certain Hindu writings to a horse that helps a man to reach the end of his journey more quickly and easily, but without which he could still reach it. Rites and various methods point the way to metaphysical realisation, but one could nevertheless set them aside, and by unswervingly setting the mind and all powers of the being on the aim of this realisation, could finally attain the supreme goal.[451]

---

that he "also wrote many correct things." See Frithjof Schuon, "Levél Hamvas Béláról," trans. Tibor Palkovics, *Magyar Szemle* XXXIII: 5-6 (Budapest, May-June 2024), 108. In his 1981 Gifford Lecture, Nasr counts Evola among the traditional authors, and in the interview cited above, he speaks of his remarkable knowledge in relation to the Hermetic tradition, and calls *La dottrina del Risveglio* "a very important work." See Seyyed Hossein Nasr, "A szent újrafelfedezése: a tradíció újraélesztése," trans. Tibor Imre Baranyi, *Tradíció: A Metafizikai Tradicionalitás Évkönyve* [Yearbook] (Debrecen, 2000), 37. [Seyyed Hossein Nasr, *Knowledge and the Sacred* (New York: State University of New York Press, 1989), 98]; and Jay Kinney, "Islam, Tradition, and the West," 54. These accolades are unknown to most American Perennialists today (perhaps since Rama P. Coomaraswamy's harsh critique of Evola), although now they have his books available in English for reading.

450 Mark Koslow's Account of the Schuon Cult. Written September 1991 for cult members to help them get out, typed by Rama Coomaraswamy [https://archive.org/details/KoslowMemoireENG_201806/page/n3/mode/2up?view=theater]. We have to say the same about this writing as we said about Jean Reyor/Marcel Clavelle in note 440. In any case, the main sources for questions of spiritual history are written works, not personal information. Awareness of worldly facts often serves no other purpose than to learn nothing from those about whom such facts come to our knowledge.

451 Guénon, "A keleti metafizika," 15, 17. [Guénon, "Eastern Metaphysics," 93, 94-95].

We do not think that Schuon, Burckhardt, Lings, Nasr and the second generation of 20th-century traditional authors did not know all this, only that they moved too much away from *T1* towards *T2*, and within that, towards *T2b*. Meanwhile, as we said, religious people not only did not appreciate but have criticised and continue to criticise their activities, so the whole thing did not make much sense other than what we said above. In other words, the appeal to religiosity does not make much sense because purely religious, "dogmatic" people can easily "find out" that you are not "really religious" – as happened in the case of Frithjof Schuon.

The next group of Guénon's supporters are even more obviously partakers in the decline of the idea of Tradition. This can be more succinctly described than the previously discussed degree of descent, which, in a sense, is its counterpart. We are talking about Traditionalists – in several cases "Evolians" – for whom Tradition is exclusively supra-religious.

Let's start with what we have already mentioned: it is valid to draw attention to the highest levels of reality in traditional religions. However, imposing a strict separation is a typification that is far from perfect, both historically and practically. Any higher levels of pairs of opposites – religion and metaphysics, religion and Tradition, exoterism and esoterism – are easily left hanging in the air without concrete, religious-philosophical affirmations and, above all, methods of realisation. It is, however, unfair that while we single out the higher elements, aspirations, and levels of reality in religions, we ignore the womb in which we found them, in which they exist and live. Spiritual-metaphysical traditions were not only enveloped by and existed above religions, but also unfolded within them.

Supra-religiosity as such, even if it exists, is mostly theoretical, intellectual, and mental. Moreover, it can easily be associated with an excess of pride, self-confidence, and even haughtiness. Worst of all, in practical terms it is a "roadless

## The Idea of Tradition, Its Precedents, and Signs of Decline

path," or even a false road. It often leads to writings and lectures that are slipshod, merely responding to the era, reflective, having an individual bias or repeating others; all in all, weak in *logos*. Tradition itself becomes a concept, barely a thing, insomuch that it cannot be followed, cannot be walked on. We need methods, tools, techniques to get to and live in the reality of the ideal. And these, if not to be found in sufficient measure in mere religiosity, can be drawn from the well-rounded, whole, beautiful world of religion. Father Gellért, one of the foremost contemporary Hungarian exponents of the old Roman Catholic liturgy, said that "real progress can never come from *violent ruptures and the imposition of the ideas of a small elite on the majority*."[452] This is precisely why we talk about *tradition* – also in the case of primordial Tradition. Without tradition, there is nothing spiritual in the world. Modern man needs the blessings of the lower degrees of tradition, too.

It is certainly not the case that religion and tradition are always superior, as if religiosity always followed its own innermost traditions. Religion can also quite frequently be a means to make the Absolute unattainable. Yet traditional religions carry the most intense sphere of intensification and the most effective set of instruments in terms of what can lead to the Absolute. Traditionalist separations of religion from Tradition are not unjustified, but an excessive separation is indefensible. In this way, one would also put at risk the possibility of realising the ultimate and real purpose of Tradition, by undermining it with a purely logical superiority (perhaps without even noticing).

For example, from a Catholic perspective, the creed "seated at the right hand of God the Father Almighty" does not exclude *complete* unity between Father and Son. Confession

---

[452] Magyar Hüperión, "'Ez a liturgia valójában átimádkozott katolikus dogmatika:' Interjú Kovács Ervin Gellért atyával," *Magyar Hüperión* V:3 (Budapest, Autumn 2017) 335, emphasis added.

of faith (*confessio*) is sometimes a *de facto* reconnection (*religio*). To take a personal place among the saints and the saved, in the heavenly sphere of existence, does not necessarily contradict the idea of Liberation – as Guénon wrote – as truly transcending individuality. The doctrine of Buddhist *loka*s, where even the supreme worlds differ from the ultimate state, is an imprecise analogy in the sense just given. From the incarnation of Christ, Christianity ascribes to the person a dignity that can only be perceived and represented iconographically in an imperfect cosmological form, yet still does not exclude the ultimate identity, the absolute possibility of the human person in relation to God. At its best, Christianity is both a dualistic *and* non-dualistic tradition. Although it consistently distinguishes between man and God, emphasising the importance of Creation and individuality, it also acknowledges the possibility of the absolute in God, since its concept of personhood is rooted in the likeness to the divine Persons of God.

Finally, the third circle or tendency that we would like to mention in the context of the decline of the idea of Tradition is the case of political Traditionalists. In fact, this is not just about politics, but about the reduction of metaphysical realisation to the individual-existential and communal-social level. Tradition is not the "resolution" of one's destiny, as Hamvas thought. For Guénon, realisation was *metaphysical* realisation, and in the cases mentioned above it is not. Of course, we are not in the least suggesting that metaphysical realisation has no existential, social, and political implications. But these are areas of application of traditional knowledge, which are bound by higher rules, and ultimately cannot be best achieved without us being *in a state of spiritual-metaphysical principality*, connected to God. Otherwise we cannot talk about traditional *applications*.

## The Idea of Tradition, Its Precedents, and Signs of Decline

We do not agree with Anglo-American perennialism's flight from or avoidance of political positions,[453] nor can we agree with the civic orientation and conformism of Western European Traditionalism, but neither do we agree with the sheer activism and predominantly collective, political thinking of Central and Eastern Europe. All these are signs of the decline of the idea of Tradition, now with a focus on T3.

## A Praise of Traditionalism

It is important to note that, despite the criticisms stated in the previous section, we consider Traditionalism to be the most significant and important intellectual current of our time. Representatives of Traditionalism in this sense may be traditional authors, either in some respects only or, less often, in terms of their entire literary oeuvres. For us, the emergence of the idea of Tradition, as in universal traditionality and metaphysical tradition, is the greatest event of the 20th century and of our time (also in the sense of Heidegger's *Ereignis*) and a true *katechon*. Thanks to a geopolitical opening and the resulting unveiling of possibilities to attain knowledge through various religions, this idea *does not lead to an external, earthly possibility of universality*, but instead, to a true, inner, transcendent universality: universal Self-experience.

---

[453] For a brief summary of the political orientations of 20th-century traditional authors, see Róbert Horváth, "A Critique of Mark Sedgwick's *Against the Modern World: Traditionalism and the Secret Intellectual History of the Twentieth Century*," *Studies in Comparative Religion* (web edition, 2009), notes 13-14 [https://www.academia.edu/2911028/Mark_Sedgwick_Against_the_Modern_World_Traditionalism_and_the_Secret_Intellectual_History]. We can also add the case of Vasile Lovinescu (French pen name Géticus), who as a Muslim was also a supporter of Ion Antonescu in Romania (similarly to how Martin Lings appreciated Francisco Franco). Earlier, in 1935, in the famous journal *Vremea*, he wrote: "like all those who place themselves in the perspective of the Infinite, René Guénon is a complete man, because he embraces all the possibilities of being which originate in and are contained in the Infinite; in other words, he is not only a contemplator but also a warrior." Vasile Lovinescu, "Hét politikai vonatkozású írás," trans. László Nagy, *Magyar Hüperión* XII:1 (Budapest, Spring-Summer 2024), 112.

## The Idea of Tradition, Its Precedents, and Signs of Decline

Having read the works of the first and second generation of Traditionalists of the present era (Coomaraswamy, Pallis, Guénon, Evola, then Schuon, Burckhardt, Lings, Nasr, and so on), we have also familiarised ourselves with the works of later Traditionalists – as far as we have had the opportunity and the ability to do so.[454] We also studied articles in journals such as *Études traditionnelles* (France), *Vers la Tradition* (France), *Connaissance des religions* (France), *Imperium* (Italy), *Vie della Tradizione* (Italy), *Studies in Comparative Religions* (UK), *Rivista di studi tradizionali* (Italy), *Arthos* (Italy), *Politica Hermetica* (France), *L'Age d'Or* (France), *Totalité* (France), *Orion* (Italy), *Kalki* (France), *Rebis* (France), *Heliodromos* (Italy), *Symbolos* (Spain), *Règle d'Abraham* (France), *Avaloka* (UK), *Temenos Academy Review* (UK), *Caminos* (Mexico), *Sacro e Profano* (Italy), *Axis Mundi* (Spain), *Mily Angel'* (Russia), *Sophia* (US), *Sacred Web* (Canada), *Traditsiia* (Russia), *Warha* (Russia), *Tyr* (US), *Contro Corrente* (Italy), *Letra y Espíritu* (Spain), *Convivium* (Italy), *Őshagyomány* (Hungary), *Arkhé* (Hungary), *Tradíció Yearbook* (Hungary), *Axis Polaris* (Hungary), *Elementy* (Russia), *Origini* (Italy), *Letterature-Tradizione* (Italy), *Északi Korona* (Hungary), *Sacrum Imperium* (Hungary), *Reakcjonista* (Poland), *Magyar Hüperión* (Hungary), *Hasta* (Hungary), *Ars Naturæ* (Hungary), *Duo Gladii* (Hungary), *Layakriyā* (Hungary), and the present *Passages* (international). Getting to know the writings of these periodicals is a great experience, especially if one reads them in order of publication and in continuity. This list is just as incomplete as the list of writers in our previous article "Regarding the Term 'Traditional Authors'" in the present forum.

With such an extent and intensity, Traditionalism also serves as an education in reading, comprehension, and thinking. Such a language and education cannot be

---

[454] For a non-partisan list, see the previous issue of this journal, *Passages: Studies in Traditionalism and Traditions*, vol. I (PRAV Publishing, 2023), 64-66.

provided by postmodern philosophical and political canons, courses and texts, despite the abundance of their forums, topics, and information. By actively reading the writings of Traditionalists – and even more so, of Traditionalist authors of the present era – one learns to understand difficult texts, without the need to study postmodern philosophical or even politological writings, which, moreover, would influence one towards today's conformist values and views. And after a while, years later, after having understood the most difficult Traditionalist texts in their continuity and in all their detailed aspects, one will also understand postmodern texts, and will clearly see the limits of their aspects and the mechanisms of their influencing power (including fiction and other aesthetic, artistic writings). This is why we have called Traditionalism the most significant, most important intellectual-spiritual current of our time – even if Traditionalism is often not only not Tradition, but also not *traditionality*.

Finally, we must add that the latter results in textual understanding and the study of *Weltanschauungen* are far from matching all that the scriptures and their traditional commentaries offer. Not even a thorough knowledge of the works of authors who were so explicitly metaphysical – and how serious and important they were! – like Leo Schaya or John Levy.[455] There is no substitute for reading the antique authors, holy scriptures, and their traditional commentaries –

---

[455] We mention these two authors because in their case, *T2b* was not predominant over *T2a*, as they were metaphysical writers indeed. We are not referring here to the famous book on Kabbalah by Schaya, who was, to our knowledge, the last editor of *Études traditionnelles*, but to the following: Leo Schaya, *Az egység szúfí tanítása*, trans. Anna Isztrayné Bíró, Libri religionis 1 (Budapest: Arcticus Kiadó, 2001); idem, *Szellemi születés*, trans. Anna Isztrayné Bíró (Budapest: Napkút Kiadó, 2016). [Leo Schaya, *La doctrine soufique de l'unité*, Initiation à l'Islam (Paris: A.-Maisonneuve, 1962); idem, *Naissance à l'esprit*, Collection "Mystiques et religions" (Paris: Dervy-Livres, 1987]. John Levy, who bought for Guénon his house in Cairo, was a renowned collector of traditional music. We are referring here to this book: John Levy, *The Nature of Man according to the Vedanta* (London: Routledge & Kegan Paul, 1956).

not even Whitall Perry's brilliant compendium,[456] although it can be of help, along with a number of serious scholarly research and study materials. The sacred texts and their traditional exegeses convey not only the atmosphere but the spirit of the Tradition with an abundance, depth, spiritual influence, and level of impact like nothing else. Moreover, they can lead one further towards one's own spiritual-metaphysical experience and reality.

*Translated by Gábor Faragó*

---

[456] Whitall N. Perry (ed.), *A Treasury of Traditional Wisdom*, The Wisdom Foundation Series (Louisville, KY: Fons Vitae, 2000), 1144 pages.

# ABOUT THE AUTHORS

**Askr Svarte (Evgeny Nechkasov)** is a Traditionalist philosopher and pagan of the Germanic-Scandinavian tradition. He is the founding editor of the journal *Alföðr* (previously *Warha*) and the author of numerous works published in Russian and English, such as *Polemos: The Dawn of Pagan Traditionalism* (PRAV Publishing, 2020), *Polemos II: Pagan Perspectives* (PRAV Publishing, 2021), *Gods in the Abyss: Essays on Heidegger, the Germanic Logos, and the Germanic Myth* (Arktos, 2020), *Tradition and Future Shock: Visions of a Future that Isn't Ours* (PRAV Publishing, 2023), *What the Gods Have Left: The Askr Svarte Notebooks* (PRAV Publishing, 2024), and *Towards Another Myth: A Tale of Heidegger and Traditionalism* (PRAV Publishing, 2024). He lives in Novosibirsk, Russia.

**Alexander Dugin** is a Russian philosopher, geopolitician, and the founding leader of the International Eurasian Movement. He serves as the director of the Ivan Ilyin Higher School of Politics at the Russian State University for the Humanities. In the late Soviet Union, Dugin was a member of the underground Yuzhinsky Circle which introduced Traditionalist thought to Russia and translated and published the first Russian editions of René Guénon and Julius Evola. Formerly the head of the Department of Sociology of International Relations at Moscow State University, where he founded the Center for Conservative Studies, in 2011 Dugin oversaw the organization of the international Traditionalist conference "Against the Post-Modern World: Actual Problems of Traditionalism" and the journal *Traditsiia*. The author of more than 60 books translated into a dozen languages, Dugin's most recent book in English is *Politica Aeterna: Political Platonism and the Dark Enlightenment* (Arktos, 2024).

*About the Authors*

**Maxim Medovarov** (b. 1987), Ph.D, is a Russian historian, philosopher, and Associate Professor at Lobachevsky State University of Nizhny Novgorod. He serves on the editorial board of the *Solovyov Studies* journal, is the author of two books and approximately 300 research articles, and has translated and edited nearly 50 titles, including three volumes by Oswald Spengler and Antanas Maceina. His foremost research interests include Neoplatonism, Romanticism, Christian theology, and Integral Traditionalism.

**Andrea Scarabelli** has collaborated with the University of Milan's Chair of the History of Philosophy I and the Roman School of Political Philosophy. He is a deputy secretary of the Julius Evola Foundation and the head of the Philosophy division of the Italian branch of the Research and Study Group for European Civilization (GRECE). He directed the column *"Mattini dei maghi"* in the magazine *Storia in Rete*, manages the blog *Attuali e Inattuali* (*ilGiornale.it*), and has translated and edited around 80 books. At the publishing house Edizioni Bietti, he directs the magazine *Antarès* and the *l'Archeometro* and *Minima Letteraria* book series. His essays have appeared in various newspapers and collective volumes. His most recent book, *Vita avventurosa di Julius Evola* (Edizioni Bietti, 2024), the first ever biography of Julius Evola, is forthcoming in English.

**Tamás Bencze** (b. 1965) teaches translation theory, English, and Hungarian at the University of Debrecen in his hometown in Hungary. He studies Eastern and Western forms of Tradition and metaphysics. He has published a number of essays on, and translations of, Traditional authors in Hungarian Traditional periodicals. He has translated two of René Guénon's books into Hungarian.

**Sebastiano Fusco** is a professional journalist, translator, and editor. Having been the editor of several popular science periodicals, in 2000 he founded the publishing company Mondo Ignoto, dedicated to archaeology, cinema, and science fiction. He has served as the editorial director, alongside Gianfranco de Turris, of Edizioni Fanucci, as the director of a regional television network, and as an editorial consultant and translator for various publishing houses. Since 1970, he has produced a number of books under his own name as well as pseudonyms (among them "Jorg Sabellicus") with various publishing houses, including Mondadori, Edizioni Mediterranee, Bietti, Solfanelli, and others on science, magical traditions, alchemy, esotericism, and fantasy fiction. He has translated and edited the collected works of authors such as H.P. Lovecraft (of whom he has written a biography), Robert E. Howard, Arthur Conan Doyle, Gilbert K. Chesterton, Philip K. Dick, and many others. In the magical, esoteric, and Traditionalist field, he has written numerous essays and worked on critical editions of classical texts, in particular translations and commentaries on the "Solomonic" grimoires, the *Sepher Yetzirah*, and the *Chaldean Oracles*. His most recent works include a critical edition of Julius Evola's edition of Cesare della Riviera's *Il mondo magico de gli heroi* [1605] (Edizioni Mediterranee, 2022).

**Nuccio D'Anna** is a scholar of sacred symbolism, spiritual doctrines, and the history of religions. He has written around 30 books and several hundred scholarly articles. He is a member of the Italian Society for the History of Religions (SISR), and for 10 years he directed *ATRIUM*, an international journal for the history of religions. He collaborates with various Italian, European, and Indian journals engaged in the study of religious phenomena. His most recent books are *I Sabei di Harrān e la scuola di Atene* (2022), *Wolfram von Eschenbach e i Custodi del Graal* (2022), and *I cicli cosmici. Le dottrine indiane sui ritmi del tempo* (2024).

## About the Authors

**Giovanni Sessa** is a secretary of the Julius Evola Foundation. He has edited dozens of books and his writings have appeared in newspapers, journals, collective volumes, and conference proceedings. His recent books include *Julius Evola e l'utopia della Tradizione* (2019), *L'eco della Germania segreta. "Si fa di nuovo primavera"* (2021), *Azzurre lontananze. Tradizione on the road* (2022), and *Icone del possibile. Giardino, bosco, montagna* (2023).

**Adolfo Morganti** was Co-Founder and Director of *I Quaderni di Avallon*, a journal for the study of religious anthropology. Since 1989, he has been Professor of Pedagogy and the Psychology of Religion at the A. Marvelli Higher Institute of Religious Studies (ISSR) of Romania. In 1996, he co-founded the International Cultural Association *Identità Europea*, chaired by Prof. Franco Cardini, and subsequently served as the association's National Coordinator and Third President. From 2001 to 2017 he served as the Republic of Romania's Honorary Consul to the Republic of San Marino. In 2016, he was appointed Coordinator of the "Interreligious Dialogue and International Relations" course organized by the ISSR in collaboration with the University of San Marino's Graduate School of Historical Studies, where he currently teaches the History of Religions. He is a practitioner and teacher of traditional Japanese martial arts and a knight of the the Equestrian Order of the Holy Sepulchre of Jerusalem, the Constantinian Order of Saint George in Madrid, and the Order of Vitéz in Budapest. His most recent books include *Bushidō e Cristianesimo. Maestri e Sapienti fra due mondi (XVI-XXI secolo)* (Il Cerchio, 2021) and *Carlo I, un Imperatore per l'Europa. La Massoneria europea contro l'Impero Asburgico* (Il Cerchio, 2022), co-authored with Mauro Faverzani.

## About the Authors

**Veleslav Cherkasov** is a leading figure of the Slavic pagan movement in Russia and the author of dozens of books and lectures on Russian Native Faith and the Left-Hand Path. He is a member of the Slavic department of the Petrovskaya Academy of Sciences and Arts.

**Maxim Makovchik** (b. 1987) is a philosopher, translator, teacher of Sanskrit, and researcher of tradition. He holds a Master's in Philosophy from the Saints Methodius and Cyrill Institute of Theology at Belarusian State University. He is the lead translator and editor of the "René Guénon Minsk Corpus," a project dedicated to producing new Russian editions of Guénon's writings.

**Alisa Zagryadskaya** is a philosopher and doctoral candidate at Saint Petersburg State University. Specializing in aesthetics and the philosophy of culture, she is the author of numerous articles on the historical transformations of Western European aesthetics, particularly pertaining to the Renaissance. Her research interests include the interpretation of corporeality, the irrational sides of culture, the sacred and de-sacralization, and metaphysical ruptures in the history of thought.

**Dmitry Moiseev** holds a PhD in Philosophy from the National Research University – Higher School of Economics (HSE University) in Moscow, where he is a senior lecturer. He is a member of the Russian Philosophical Society and the Russian Society for the History and Philosophy of Science. His recent publications in English include the Introduction in the new English edition of Julius Evola's *Pagan Imperialism* (Arktos, 2024) and the monograph *The Philosophy of Italian Fascism: Formation and Evolution* (Arktos, 2024).

*About the Authors*

**László Virág** (b. 1969) is a philosopher, poet, writer, and translator. He is a founding speaker at the Last Exit Community Centre in Budapest. He has edited the Hungarian editions of several books by Julius Evola and is the founding editor-in-chief of *Hasta*, a journal dealing with central issues of traditional metaphysics, symbolism, and spiritual realisation. His main field of interest is the symbolism and spiritual practice of alchemy. As a graduate biologist, he is a critic of evolutionism, progressivism, and Darwinism.

**Róbert Horváth** (b. 1971) is a philosopher, scholar of religious studies, book and journal editor. He is one of the best known personalities of today's Hungarian "Traditional School." His main research areas are Śaivism, comparative theology, and environmental philosophy. He is a leading lecturer at the Last Exit Community Centre in Budapest.

www.ingramcontent.com/pod-product-compliance
Lightning Source LLC
Chambersburg PA
CBHW070045080526
44586CB00013B/923